745 DUR

D1436746

O·RNAME·NT

A survey of decoration since 1830,
with 729 illustrations

STUART DURANT

ORNAMENT·

*A survey of decoration since 1830,
with 729 illustrations*

STUART DURANT

Macdonald

For Miriam, Owen and Galia

A **Macdonald** BOOK

Copyright © 1986 Stuart Durant

First published in Great Britain in 1986
by Macdonald & Co (Publishers) Ltd
London & Sydney

A member of BPCC plc

British Library Cataloguing in Publication Data
Durant, Stuart
   Ornament: 1830–1980.
    1. Decorative arts—History—19th century
    2. Decorative arts—History—20th century
   I. Title
   745'.09   NK775

   ISBN 0–356–10581–4

This book was designed and produced by
John Calmann and King Ltd, London
Designer: Richard Johnson

Typeset by Fakenham Photosetting Ltd, Norfolk
Printed in Singapore by Toppan Ltd

Macdonald & Co (Publishers) Ltd
Greater London House
Hampstead Road
London NW1 7QX

Frontispiece: Fabric design by Verena Kiefer

Contents

Preface

When the art of ornamentation was at its zenith, during the nineteenth century, ornament was described as 'a natural want'. Not so long ago, every self-respecting architect or designer needed to have a thorough understanding of the grammar of ornament, as well as to know how to employ the historic styles. Even civil engineers were expected to have a working knowledge of ornament. It was seldom questioned whether or not a surface, or a piece of furniture, or a building, should be decorated. What was at issue was whether ornament was appropriate for a particular situation, whether it was elegant, or whether it was scholarly. Ornament was often the subject of lively critical debate. A great number of books were published on the subject. Ornamentation, remember, could transform a humdrum design into a work of art.

During the ascendancy of the Modern Movement the fortunes of ornament declined. It was despised and ridiculed. H. S. Goodhart-Rendel, the architect, who regarded the pronouncements of his Modernist contemporaries with a wry detachment, commented on the situation. 'A fondness for ornament,' he wrote in 1935, 'is no more readily acknowledged by refined persons than would be a fondness for gin,' while 'the natural appetite of the unrefined for pretty patterns' needed 'drastic methods' if it was to be cured. The physicians of the Modern Movement never did succeed in curing this particular malady. The austerity of the style did not render it psychologically satisfying to the masses. Herbert Read once described ornament as a 'psychological' necessity. He may well have been correct. It is not my intention, however, to examine the psychology of ornament. Besides, E. H. Gombrich has already considered this subject in his admirable *The Sense of Order. A study in the psychology of decorative art*, 1979. I am concerned primarily with the practice of decoration.

The word 'ornament' has a mildly archaic ring to it. But, just as decoration itself is returning to favour, so, too, is the word 'ornament'. The fact is that I could have as well called this book *Decoration*, or *Decoration and Pattern*.

Dictionaries will not help us greatly if we try to discriminate between 'ornament' and 'decoration'. In both cases we are merely fobbed off with synonyms, like 'adornment' and 'embellishment'. Even in the best dictionaries, neither ornament nor decoration, nor yet pattern, are adequately defined. Fortunately, we recognize these phenomena easily enough when we encounter them, even if we are uncertain about how to differentiate between them. They are best demonstrated by visual example. Of the three terms 'ornament' was the most widely used in the last century. It also has the advantage of being common to the major European languages. I have to confess, however, that like many of my predecessors, I have alternated between 'ornament' and 'decoration'.

Each of the twelve chapters in this book deals with a broad theme. I say 'theme' because it is not my aim to provide a classificatory system, or a taxonomy, for ornament (taxonomies are, in any case, especially vulnerable to the ravages of time). Furthermore, categories or species of ornament merge, or coalesce, one with another. For example, motifs based upon natural forms are to be found in almost all kinds of ornament. The same could be said of geometrical construction. Nature and Geometry are, because of their importance, given particular prominence. This is especially true of Nature. At the level of the unconscious, the themes of Nature and Geometry suggest the preoccupations of so many people during the last century and our own: concern for the welfare of our planet and the belief in the mechanized millennium. I trust, however, that each of my themes will convey to the reader the richness and variety of ornament which has been created during the last hundred and fifty years. I trust, too, that the capacity of ornament to express different ideologies—aesthetic, moral, as in the work of William Morris and other followers of the Arts and Crafts movement, or even political, as in the post-Revolutionary Russian designs incorporating tractors as symbols of progress—will be observed.

Ornament is now in the process of being 'rediscovered' as a visual language. I hope that this book will assist in this process.

I should like to give my warmest thanks to the following individuals who have helped me during my researches:

Finch Allibone, formerly of the RIBA Drawings Collection;
Hans Brill, Librarian of the Royal College of Art;
Margot Coatts;
Diana Davies;
N. S. Doniach;
J. H. Hopkins, Librarian of the Society of Antiquaries;
Philip Hughes;
Tim Imrie;
Elisabeth Ingles;
Christine Kapiteijn;
Dr Peter Lloyd Jones, Head of the School of Design, Kingston Polytechnic;
Eduardo Paolozzi;
Susan St Clair;
Messrs Sims, Reed and Fogg, booksellers, Jermyn Street, London SW1;
Sue Smith, formerly Librarian of the Royal College of Art Colour Library;
Gillian Varley, Campus Librarian, Knights Park, Kingston Polytechnic;
Sue Wagstaff;
Christine Woods, Archivist of Arthur Sanderson & Sons Ltd.

I should also like to thank the staff of the Print Room and the Library of the Victoria and Albert Museum who offered me advice and assistance on many occasions.

Stuart Durant
Richmond
April 1986

Sources of Photographs

The author and John Calmann and King Ltd would like to thank the following for supplying photographs:

The Architectural Review: 11.5, 11.11, 11.20, 11.47;
Archives d'Architecture Moderne, Brussels: 11.2, 11.3;
The Arts Council of Great Britain: 3.59, 3.60, 7.24, 10.12, 10.13, 10.14, 10.24, 1025;
Terence Conran: 12.16, 12.17, 12.23;
The Crafts Council: 10.8, 10.9, 10.10;
Lucienne Day: 12.4, 12.6, 12.12, 12.15;
Antoinette de Boer: 12.43, 12.44;
Margaret Hildebrand: 12.13;
Valerie Jaudon: 3.62;
Verena Kiefer: Frontispiece;
Kenneth Martin: 3.59;
François Morellet: 3.56, 3.57;
Eduardo Paolozzi: 12.18, 12.45;
Centre Pompidou, Paris: 11.8;
Bernd Rau: 12.8, 12.25, 12.26;
Zandra Rhodes: 12.41, 12.42;
RIBA, Drawings Collection: 6.9, 9.19, 9.21;
Royal College of Art: 3.3;
Sanderson & Sons: 12.1, 12.3, 12.5, 12.7, 12.19–21, 12.23, 12.27–33, 12.36–9;
Allan Smith: 3.53;
Victoria and Albert Museum: 7.22, 7.25, 7.27, 9.5–9, 10.1, 10.26, 10.27, 10.32, 10.45–8, 11.18–41, 11.51–5, 11.57, 11.58, 12.22, 12.24, 12.34, 12.35

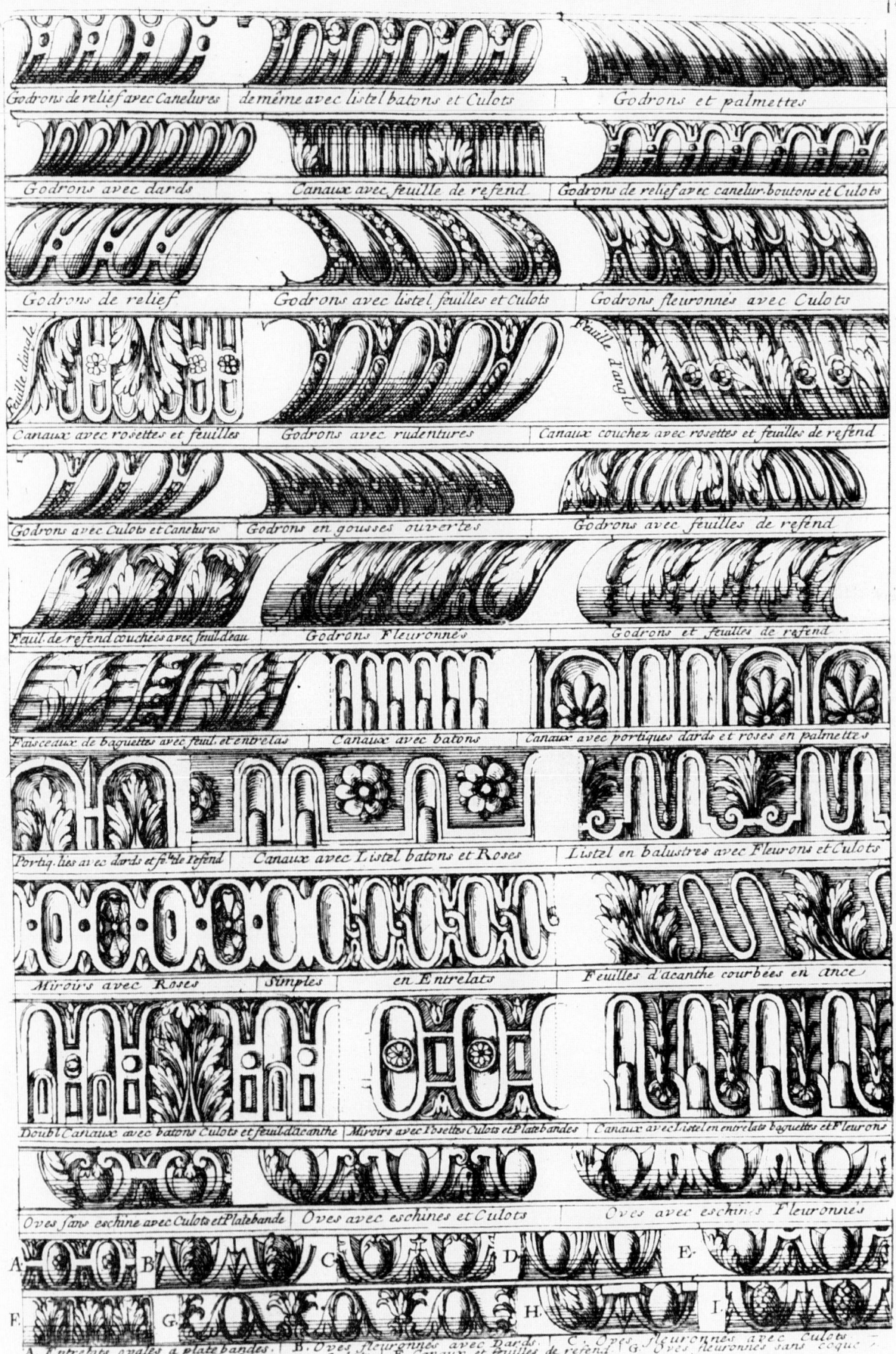

Godrons de relief avec Canelures — de même avec listel batons et Culots — Godrons et palmettes

Godrons avec dards — Canaux avec feuille de refend — Godrons de relief avec canelur. boutons et Culots

Godrons de relief — Godrons avec listel, feuilles et Culots — Godrons fleuronnés avec Culots

Feuille d'angle — Canaux avec rosettes et feuilles — Godrons avec rudentures — Canaux couchez avec rosettes et feuilles de refend — Feuille d'angle

Godrons avec Culots et Canelures — Godrons en gousses ouvertes — Godrons avec feuilles de refend

Feuil. de refend couchées avec feuil. d'eau — Godrons Fleuronnés — Godrons et feuilles de refend

Faisceaux de baguettes avec feuil. et entrelas — Canaux avec batons — Canaux avec portiques dards et roses en palmettes

Portiq. liés avec dards et feuille refend — Canaux avec Listel batons et Roses — Listel en balustres avec Fleurons et Culots

Miroirs avec Roses — Simples — en Entrelats — Feuilles d'acanthe courbées en ance

Doubl. Canaux avec batons Culots et feuil. d'acanthe — Miroirs avec rosettes Culots et Platebandes — Canaux avec Listel en entrelats baguettes et Fleurons

Oves sans eschine avec Culots et Platebande — Oves avec eschines et Culots — Oves avec eschines Fleuronnés

A. Entrelats ovales a platebandes. B. Oves fleuronnés avec Dards. C. Oves Fleuronnés avec Culots. D. Oves avec fleurures. E. Oves avec Culots. F. Canaux et feuilles de refend. G. Oves fleuronnés sans coque. H. Oves simples avec dards et Listel. I. Oves en Pomme de Pin.

CHAPTER ONE

Encyclopedias of Ornament

One of the consequences of the Industrial Revolution was an unprecedented increase in the demand for ornamented goods. Ornament, which had always been associated with luxury and laboriousness, enhanced status and with the rise in the general level of prosperity was no longer the prerogative of the very rich. Furthermore, improvements in production and the invention of new techniques and new machinery opened up possibilities for the mass-manufacture of a whole range of ornamented goods—including textiles, wallpapers, carpets, bookbindings, decorated china and glass, cast-iron ware, furniture and furnishings. The need on the part of manufacturers, architects and pattern-makers for a comprehensive encyclopedia of ornament showing a variety of styles was becoming pressing. In 1836, George Morant of London's New Bond Street firm of house decorators, Morant & Son, when giving evidence before the Parliamentary Select Committee formed to 'enquire into the best means of extending knowledge of the Arts and of the Principles of Design', was able to cite only three current published collections of ornament.

The first modern encyclopedia, Ephraim Chambers' *Cyclopedia*, published in two volumes in 1727, gives little space to the arts, and still less to ornament. Denis Diderot and Jean le Rond d'Alembert's renowned *Encyclopédie* began life in 1751 as a translation of Chambers' work, but grew into one of the most ambitious of all eighteenth-century publishing ventures in France or anywhere else. In all, thirty-five volumes were published over a period of some twenty years. Diderot was a meticulous observer of manufacturing and craft processes and the plates in the *Encyclopédie* constitute by far the best illustrated records of eighteenth-century techniques. But Diderot treats ornament only incidentally.

The earliest major collection of ornament to be published was Jombert's *Repertoire des Artistes, ou recueil de compositions d'architecture et d'ornemens antiques et modernes* ('Artists' Repertory, or a selection of architectural compositions and antique and modern ornament') (Paris, 1765). Charles-Antoine Jombert (1712–84) was a publisher who had already successfully produced *Oeuvres d'Architecture de Jean le Pautre* (1751), *Cours d'Architecture* (1760) and *L'Architecture Moderne* (1764), besides many other admirable works. *Repertoire des Artistes* consists of fifty-six suites of engraved ornament which include some pictorial plates intended as suggestions for designers and craftsmen. The earliest plates are of arabesques and grotesques (see Plate 1.2) by the architect Jacques Androuet Du Cerceau (1510–84), who was his own engraver. A suite of Raphael's decorative designs is also included, but the plates were engraved in the seventeenth century. Among other important designers listed are Jean Berain (1640–1711), Alexandre Le Blond (1679–1719), Jean Marot (1619–79) and Pierre le Pautre (c. 1648–1716). In total there were 688 plates, illustrating all manner of ornament and design.[1]

Can Jombert's impressive work properly be described as 'an encyclopedia of ornament'? Certainly the idea of publishing a collection of long-outmoded suites of ornament as historical documents may well have suggested itself to Jombert after he had observed the success of the

1.1 *Opposite* ANONYMOUS: **Seven-page suite of ornaments and mouldings.** Late seventeenth century. Jombert, *Repertoire des Artistes*, 1765.

This illustration showing the antique and modern styles is taken from a small work which would have been used principally by craftsmen.

Encyclopédie. In addition, Jombert gave *Repertoire des Artistes* some of the trappings of an encyclopedia by supplying short and sometimes critical biographies of his artists.

The social and cultural changes affecting Europe in the early nineteenth century also resulted in an upsurge of interest in interior decoration and furnishings. One of the most important publications in this field was the *Recueil de Décorations Intérieures* (1801) by Charles Percier (1764–1838) and Pierre François Léonard Fontaine (1762–1838).[2] This showed a variety of interiors with details of their ornament and furnishings, but sounded a warning note about the dangers of cheap imitation. Dominique Vivant, Baron Denant (1754–1825), in his *Voyage dans la Basse et Haute Egypte* (1802) reflected the new interest in Egyptian taste and furniture, and influenced the English connoisseur and furniture designer Thomas Hope (1769–1831), whose *Household Furniture and Decoration* appeared in 1807. Although not strictly encyclopedias all these works had considerable impact on design, and introduced their readers to a wide range of ornament and furnishings.

The serendipitous discovery of lithography by Aloys Senefelder (1771–1834) in 1798 heralded a new era in the publication of collections of ornament.[3] Henceforward ornament could be printed in colour at comparatively little expense. Previously colour in books had been possible only by the costly process of colouring by hand.

The first collection of ornament to be printed in colour by lithography was Zahn's *Die schönsten Ornamente und merkwürdigsten Gemälde aus Pompeii, Herkulanum, und Stabiae* ('The finest ornaments and most remarkable paintings of Pompeii, Herculaneum and Stabiae') which was issued in parts from 1829. Better known was Zahn's *Ornamente aller Klassischen Kunstepochen* ('Ornaments of all classic art epochs') (1831–43)—a work admired by the London decorator Morant. Johann Karl Wilhelm Zahn (1800–71), architect and archaeologist, was born in Rodenburg, near Hanover, and educated at the Academy at Kassel. He studied for two years in Paris and completed his artistic education in Italy. According to Morant, Zahn's *Ornamente aller Klassischen Kunstepochen* was commissioned by the Austrian government to educate the public in matters of taste applying to interior decoration. Zahn illustrates Pompeian wall decorations, mummy cases, antique vases and decorations by Giulio Romano, Raphael's chief pupil, for the Palazzo del Te at Mantua. Zahn's selection of designs was somewhat narrow and idiosyncratic—by later standards at least. But his book was, nevertheless, the authentic precursor of the brilliant chromolithographic ornamental encyclopedias of Owen Jones and Racinet.

Two other early German encyclopedias of ornament were Peter Beuth's *Forbilder für Fabrikanten und Handwerker* ('Examples for manufacturers and craftsmen') of 1830 and C. E. von Bötticher's *Ornamenten-Buch* ('Ornament Book') of 1834 (Plate 1.3). The architect Karl Friedrich Schinkel (1781–1841) was largely responsible for the earlier part of Beuth's work, which deals mainly with designs for architecture and interiors, and was the earliest government-commissioned collection of designs for industry.

In France, Charles-Ernest Clerget's *Mélanges d'Ornemens* ('Selection of Ornaments') (1838) was followed by the first collection of ornament to bear the title 'encyclopedia'—Clerget and Martel's *Encyclopédie Universelle d'Ornements Antiques* (1840?). This contains examples of Greek, Roman, Egyptian, Islamic, Indian, Chinese, Japanese and medieval and Renaissance decoration. Clerget (b. 1812) himself was a versatile designer and must have been aware of the needs of industry for he was for a time deputy librarian at the Union Centrale des Beaux-Arts appliquées à l'Industrie in Paris. He also designed porcelain for the Sèvres factory and tapestry for the Gobelins factory.

1.2 JACQUES ANDROUET DU CERCEAU: **Grotesque design.** Jombert, *Repertoire des Artistes*, 1765.

Jombert's extensive collection was effectively the earliest encyclopedia of ornament. Du Cerceau was greatly influenced by Italian ideas and has an important place in the early history of Renaissance architecture in France. He liked working on a small scale and published many prints of ornament as well as designs of furniture and grotesques. This design first appeared in *Les Petits Grotesques*, 1550.

George Phillips' *Rudiments of Curvilinear Design* (1838–40) has a selection of fine engraved plates of original designs (Plates 1.14–18) in an astonishing variety of styles—often highly accomplished pastiches in fact—but his work cannot be described as an encyclopedia. Henry Shaw's *Encyclopedia of Ornament*, on the other hand, is properly so-called. It is a wide-ranging work and its fifty-nine plates—coloured woodblocks, hand-coloured line engravings, aquatints and a zincograph—reflect Shaw's antiquarian and architectural interests (see Plate 1.6).

William Bell Scott (1811–1900), an engraver and book-illustrator and a minor member of the Pre-Raphaelite circle, published *The Ornamentist, or Artizan's Manual in the various branches of ornamental art*, which was completed in 1845. Scott took his examples of ornament from published works not ordinarily accessible to the average craftsman.

One of the most ambitious and handsomely printed of all the early chromolithographic books on ornament was *Specimens of Ornamental Art selected from the best models of the Classical epochs* by Ludwig Gruner (1801–82), art adviser to Albert, the Prince Consort. It was commissioned by the authorities of the Government School of Design which had been set up at Somerset House, London, in 1837. Gruner was asked to supply a selection of examples of historical designs which could be studied and copied by students of ornamental design. He chose a wide variety of illustrations, including samples of Pompeian, Roman (see Plate 1.8), medieval and Cinquecento work. Despite the book's splendour, the teachers at Somerset House were critical of Gruner's selection of ornament—particularly of his Pompeian examples (Plate 1.15), which were associated with the supposed degenerate morality of Pompeii.

In 1851, the architect Charles James Richardson (1806–71), a pupil of Sir John Soane, published, on his own account, *Studies of Ornamental Design* (Plates 1.13, 14). This was very evidently intended to compete with Gruner's *Specimens of Ornamental Art*: Richardson began work on the book in 1847, at almost exactly the same time as Gruner. Richardson was a fine and sensitive draughtsman who had successfully published, again at his own expense, the first study of Elizabethan and Jacobean architecture—*Architectural Remains of the Reigns of Elizabeth and James I* (1838). Richardson taught for several years at the Government School of Design and his selection of ornament—which includes some Oriental designs—reflects current official attitudes more accurately than that of Gruner, who was mistrusted as a foreigner.

The Great Exhibition of 1851 in London demonstrated the need—now more urgent than ever—for the rigorous study of ornament. Most of the ornamented goods seen at the exhibition were ugly. The decoration of textiles, carpets, wallpapers, ceramics, cast-iron and furniture, was generally either crudely historicist or meretriciously naturalistic—frequently both. But the gorgeous fabrics exhibited by the East India Company made a great impression on those who were interested in the reform of design.

Indian ornament was studied, very much in a scientific spirit, by such authorities as Owen Jones (1809–74) and Richard Redgrave (1804–88). Jones' views on the merits of Indian design appeared for the first time in the *Catalogue of the Museum of Manufactures* (1852). This museum, the ancestor of the Victoria and Albert Museum, had been set up at Marlborough House specifically to display the ornamental productions officially purchased at the Great Exhibition. It was intended to educate the public at large, as well as students of design. In his *Supplementary Report on Design* (1852), Redgrave expressed an enthusiasm for Indian decoration which echoed that of Jones. Henceforward encyclopedias of ornament were to devote considerable space to Oriental design. Who can measure the true impact upon the West of such exposure?

1.3 C. E. VON BÖTTICHER: **Decorations** from *Ornamenten-Buch zum praktischen Gebrauche für Architektur*, 1834–44.

Lithography—and chromolithography in particular—were especially well suited for books of ornament. With Wilhelm Zahn, Bötticher was one of the earliest authorities to exploit this process. The boldness and simplicity of these two designs are worth commenting on, for they appear to foreshadow later developments.

John Leighton (1822–1912), an accomplished designer in many media, in his *Suggestions in Design, including compositions in all styles* (1853), also included designs based upon Oriental models. But like Phillips' *Rudiments of Curvilinear Design*, the work is an eclectic pattern-book rather than an encyclopedia. It was re-issued in a much revised edition in 1880, where the original work was claimed to be the first of its kind 'in which all styles of ornament were displayed ... Indian art was then only beginning to be appreciated and the art-value of Japanese work was still unknown'.

Wornum's *Analysis of Ornament* (1855), the earliest standard history of ornament to be published, ran into numerous editions and was known to generations of British art students. Ralph Nicholson Wornum (1812–77) was Keeper of the National Gallery, London, and the author of a popular history of painting. His *Analysis of Ornament*, which was based on a series of lectures he had given at the School of Design in the late 1840s, deals with Egyptian, Greek, Roman, Byzantine, Saracenic and Gothic styles of ornament, and three 'modern' styles—Renaissance, Cinquecento and Louis Quatorze. He ignores—with the exception of 'Saracenic'—the Oriental styles. The book, intended as no more than a student's handbook, is distinguished by the excellent bibliographies which follow each chapter. It is evident from these bibliographies that, although a good deal had been published on historic monuments, no serious analyses of the characteristics of individual styles of ornament had yet been undertaken.

By far the most important book on ornament to be published in these years was, of course, Owen Jones' beautiful *Grammar of Ornament* (1856), one of the great achievements of nineteenth-century colour printing and, more significantly, the earliest work to adopt an analytical approach to the study of ornamental art. An architect, designer and antiquarian, Jones stressed the importance of a rigorous study of worldwide decorative traditions and sought to devise an ornamental language appropriate to the new industrial age.

The *Grammar of Ornament* (see Plate 1.16) owed its origin to the museum created by the Crystal Palace Company. After the closing of the Great Exhibition on 15 October 1851, the Crystal Palace Company was formed for the purposes of finding a new use for Paxton's building. The great structure was moved from Hyde Park and re-erected at Sydenham, South London. After suitable modifications the palace was transformed into a novel architectural museum containing a series of architectural 'courts', together with a portrait gallery of eminent people, a photographic gallery and an ethnological gallery. The architectural courts epitomized, admittedly in coloured plaster, the major historical styles. Among the styles represented were the Egyptian, the Byzantine and Romanesque, the Greek and Roman, the Medieval, the Renaissance and the Elizabethan. There was also a 'Ninevah' Court and an Alhambra Court.

Owen Jones was responsible for the Greek and Roman Courts, the Alhambra Court and, with the sculptor Joseph Bonomi (1789–1878), for the Egyptian Court—the largest and, with its colossal figures, the most dramatic of all. An immense amount of scholarly labour went into establishing the essential characteristics of the styles in the courts and Jones conceived the idea of publishing his researches, and those of his collaborators.[4]

The range of subject-matter in the *Grammar of Ornament* is far wider than that in any earlier encyclopedia of ornament. Besides all the styles considered by Wornum, Jones examines Celtic, Arabian, Turkish, Persian, Indian, 'Hindao' (pre-Islamic Indian) and Chinese ornament. Almost a third of his plates illustrate Oriental ornament. Jones also recognized—earlier than anyone else—the qualities of primitive design and devoted the first three plates to the ornament of 'Savage Tribes'—Polynesians and Melanesians.

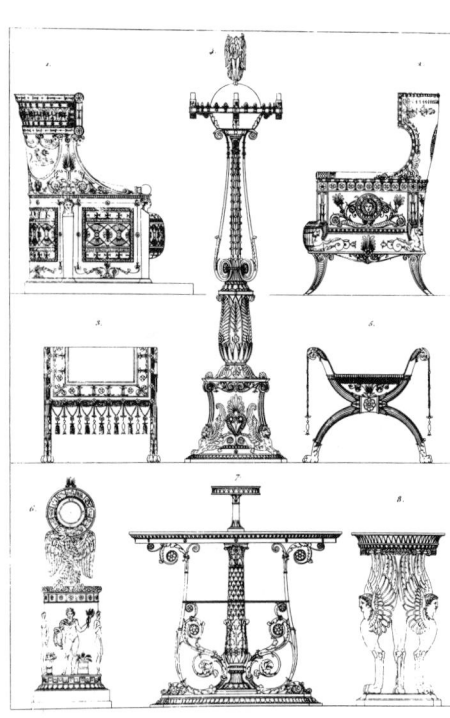

1.4 Charles Percier and Pierre François Léonard Fontaine: **Fauteuils, a candelabrum, a stool, small tables and a clock.** From *Recueil de Décorations Intérieures*, 1812.

Percier and Fontaine spent several years in Rome studying ancient and modern architecture, and their decorative work reflects this. Their book was influential throughout Europe—a second edition was published in 1827 and an Italian edition as late as 1843.

Their ornament is examined and found to conform to universal principles.

As well as being an incomparable visual source-book, the *Grammar of Ornament* is important for its theoretical content. Jones sought to establish aesthetic principles which were based upon carefully recorded observations. He had studied the way in which ornament is comprehended by the eye and observed how order was preferred to randomness. He had also made a detailed study of colour and was well read in contemporary colour theory.

Jones set out his findings as thirty-seven 'Propositions' of which, incidentally, twenty-one are concerned solely with colour. Here is a sampling:

Proposition 1
The Decorative Arts arise from, and should properly be attendant upon architecture.

Proposition 5
Construction should be decorated. Decoration should never be purposely constructed.

Proposition 8
All ornament should be based upon a geometrical construction.

Proposition 11
In surface decoration all lines should flow out of a parent stem. Every ornament, however distant, should be traced to its branch and root.

Jones was sanguinely optimistic about his times. He had no fear of science or the machine. His Propositions—though rigid and inhibiting by our standards—represent a valiant attempt to formulate a rational aesthetic for the coming industrial age.

The aesthetic problems posed by industrialization prompted the German architect and theorist Gottfried Semper (1803–79), to publish *Der Stil* ('Style') between 1860 and 1863 (see Plate 1.17). This deals with the applied arts and architecture. Together with the great Neo-classicist Karl Friedrich Schinkel, Semper was a dominant influence in nineteenth-century architecture. *Der Stil* is not an encyclopedia in the manner of the *Grammar of Ornament*, but it is evident that Semper, who lived in England in the early 1850s and moved in the Owen Jones circle, was strongly influenced by Jones' universalist views on design. Like Jones, Semper saw vitality in non-Western decorative traditions. And, like Jones, he sought to discover guiding principles through the study of both primitive and sophisticated traditions. Alois Riegl (1858–1900) quoted both Semper and Jones in the first of his books to concern itself with decoration, *Altorientalische Teppiche* ('Oriental Carpets') of 1891, but it was his next book, *Stilfragen*, published in 1893, which was to have the greatest impact. E. H. Gombrich in *The Sense of Order* called it 'perhaps the one great book ever written about ornament'.[5] As a work of scholarship it has yet to be surpassed, but its concentration on one motif—the palmette—places it outside the context of encyclopedias.

The *Grammar of Ornament*, which appeared in French and German editions, was the inspiration for several other ambitious encyclopedias of ornament. The finest of these was *L'Ornement Polychrome* (see Plate 1.18), which was compiled by Albert Charles Auguste Racinet in 1869 and bears a close resemblance to Jones' work in format. But Racinet was careful to see that he did not duplicate Jones' material. In 1889, in Germany, H. Dolmetsch published *Ornamentenschatz* ('A treasury of ornament'), which also resembles the *Grammar of Ornament*. The last true descendant of the *Grammar of Ornament* was H. Bossert's *Das Ornamentwerk* (1924), which came out simultaneously in English as *Ornament in Applied Art*. Bossert's work is particularly rich in examples of primitive and peasant-European work.

1.5 CHARLES PERCIER AND PIERRE FRANÇOIS LÉONARD FONTAINE: **Design for Napoleon's throne at the Tuileries.** From *Recueil de Décorations Intérieures*, 1812.

Percier and Fontaine were Napoleon's principal architects. They were especially skilled in adapting the Roman decorative style which, with its imperial associations, was thought particularly appropriate for Napoleon's court.

Inexpensive encyclopedias of ornament printed in black and white abounded in the late nineteenth and early twentieth centuries. Some of the most useful are F. Edward Hulme, *Principles of Ornamental Art* (1875) (see Plate 1.19) and *The Birth and Development of Ornament* (1893); James Ward, *Historic Ornament* (1897); R. Glazier, *A Manual of Historic Ornament* (1899) (see Plate 1.20); A. Speltz, *The Styles of Ornament* (English edition 1910); A. D. F. Hamlin, *A History of Ornament* (1916), but these titles are only a representative selection.

The encyclopedia of ornament helped to make ornament a respectable and even academic study. Works like those listed above were widely used by students of architecture, the applied arts and even painting. But the encyclopedia sometimes led to the mindless copying of historical examples which had been chosen, all too often, not for aesthetic considerations, but because of historical associations real or imagined. Nevertheless, the encyclopedias of ornament remain as impressive records of the time when interest in ornament was at its apogee.

1.6 *Below* HENRY SHAW: **Capitals and entablature of marble from the façade of the Certosa di Pavia.** *The Encyclopaedia of Ornament*, 1842.

Shaw was trained as an architectural draughtsman. He became one of the leading antiquarians of his day. The richly decorated Carthusian monastery known as the Certosa di Pavia was begun in 1396 as a mausoleum for the Visconti dynasty and illustrates the transition between the late Gothic style and the Renaissance.

1.7 *Left* LOUIS ROUPERT: **Title-page of a suite of designs.** Jombert, *Repertoire des Artistes*, 1765.

Roupert, a leading jeweller, was a native of Metz.

.8 *Left* LUDWIG GRUNER: **Part of ancient pilaster in the Villa Medici at Rome.** *Specimens of Ornamental Art*, 1850.

Gruner's illustrations were intended to serve as models for trainee designers to copy. He was severely criticized by 'reformers' like Richard Redgrave for his selection of examples.

.9 OWEN JONES: **Egyptian ornament.** Original watercolour and pencil illustration for *The Grammar of Ornament*, 1856. The Print Room, Victoria and Albert Museum, London.

.10 WILHELM ZAHN: **Decorations from the Ducal Palace, Mantua.** *Oramenteller klassischen Kunstepochen*, 1831–3.

These decorations were attributed to Giulio Romano (1499?–1546), one of the earliest exponents of Mannerism, and Raphael's assistant and pupil.

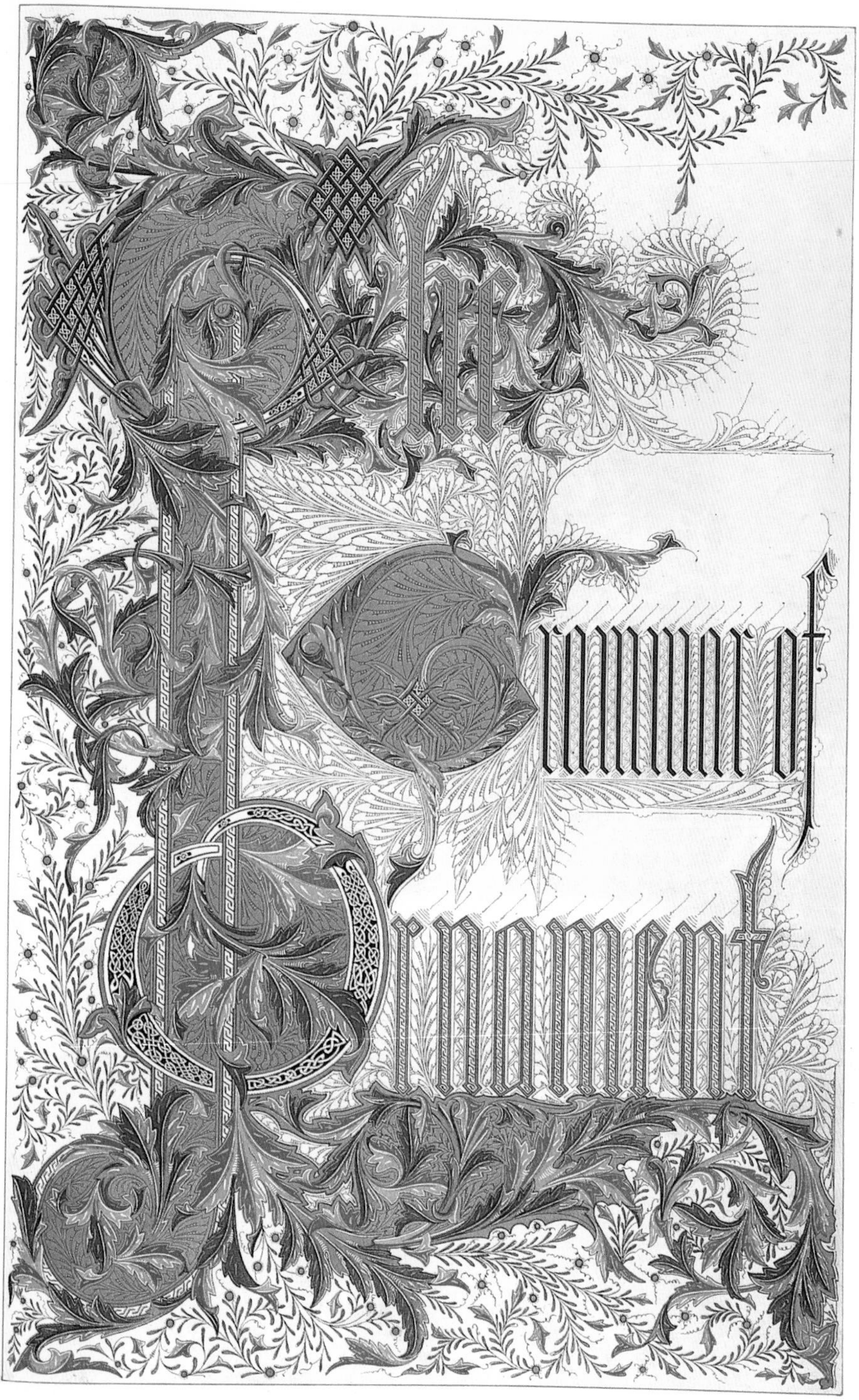

1.11 Owen Jones: **Decorated chromolithographic title-page.** *The Grammar of Ornament*, 1856.

A number of Jones' early 'illuminated' gift books were decorated in a similar medieval manuscript style.

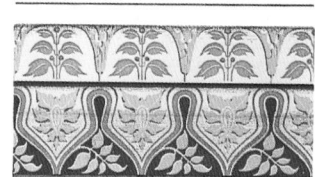

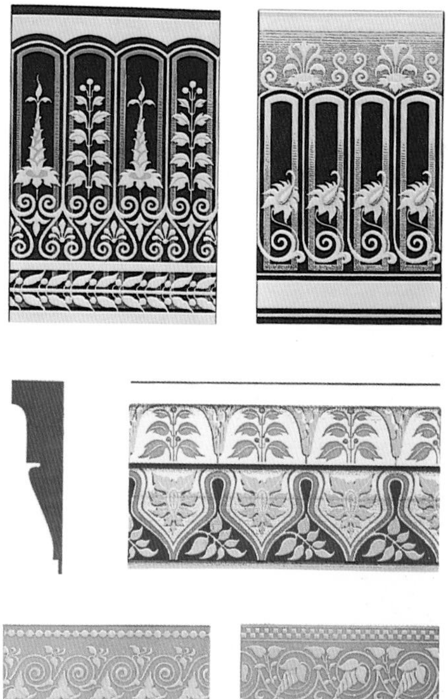

1.12 C. Boetticher: **Borders.** *Ornamenten-Buch*, 1856.

2.1 OWEN JONES: **Design for a wallpaper or textile.** Dated July 1860. The Print Room, Victoria and Albert Museum, London.

2.2 MESSRS. TOWNSEND & PARKER, London. **Wallpaper decorations.** Matthew Digby Wyatt, *The Industrial Arts of the Nineteenth Century at the Great Exhibition, MDCCCLI*, 1851–3.

Contemporary British authorities condemned such representations of floral forms for being too naturalistic or 'imitative'.

19

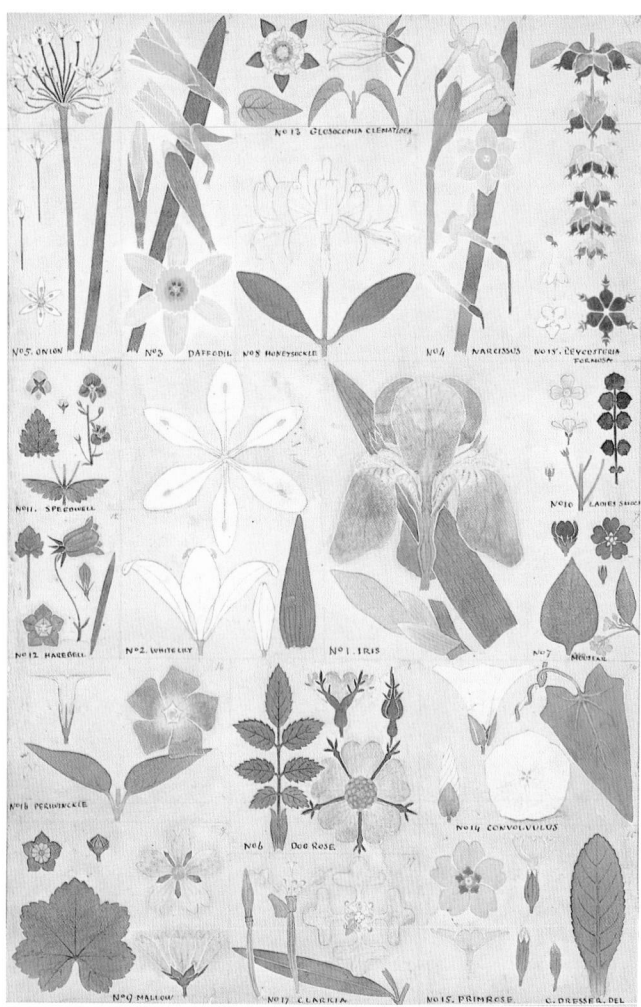

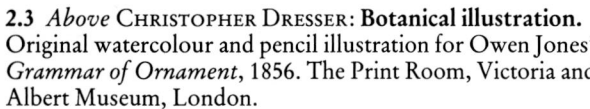

2.3 *Above* CHRISTOPHER DRESSER: **Botanical illustration.** Original watercolour and pencil illustration for Owen Jones' *Grammar of Ornament*, 1856. The Print Room, Victoria and Albert Museum, London.

2.4 *Above right* HECTOR GUIMARD: **Decorations for Castel Béranger**, *14 rue la Fontaine, Paris, 16e.* (1894–8). *Le Castel Béranger*, 1898.

The decoration is based on the movement of water.

2.5 ERNST HAECKEL: **Ascidiae.** *Kunstformen der Natur*, 1899– 1904.

1.14 *Right* THOMAS STOTHARD: **Decorative figures in silver.** C. J. Richardson, *Studies of Ornamental Design*, 1851.

Richardson had a particular penchant for Elizabethan work, despite the fact that it was considered somewhat uncouth by his colleagues at the Government School of Design.

1.13 *Below* C. J. RICHARDSON: **Appliqué embroidery from the Electoral Chair of Saxony,** *c.* 1620. *Studies of Ornamental Design*, 1851.

Richardson's collection is less extensive than Gruner's, but found more official favour. This design is from the collection of Thomas Baylis of Kensington, London.

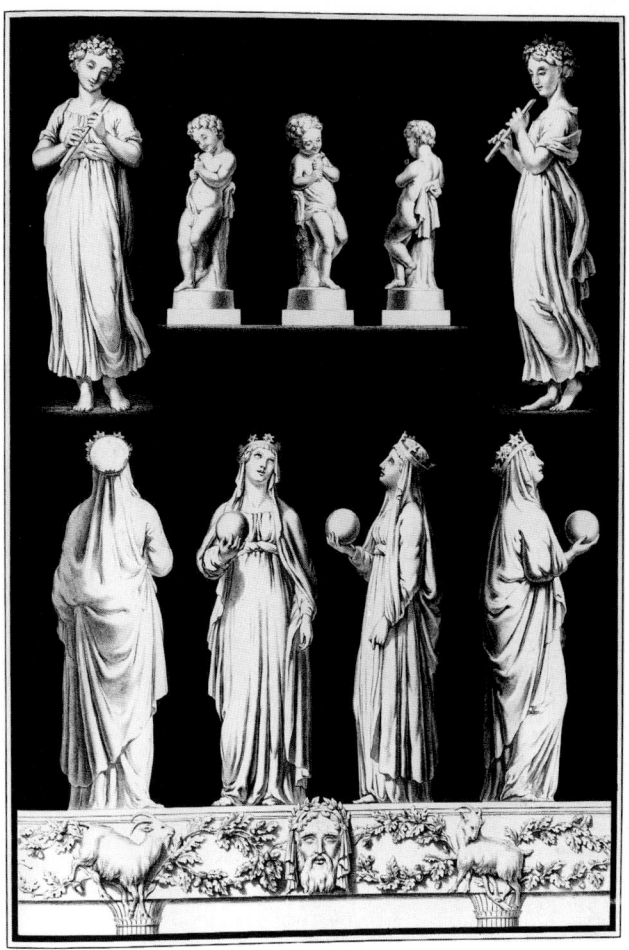

1.15 *Right* LUDWIG GRUNER: **Portion of a painted wall in the House of the Second Fountain.** *Specimens of Ornamental Art*, 1850.

THE

GRAMMAR OF ORNAMENT

BY

OWEN JONES.

ILLUSTRATED BY EXAMPLES
FROM VARIOUS STYLES OF ORNAMENT.

ONE HUNDRED FOLIO PLATES,

DRAWN ON STONE BY
F. BEDFORD,

AND PRINTED IN COLOURS BY
DAY AND SON.

LONDON:
PUBLISHED BY DAY AND SON, LITHOGRAPHERS TO THE QUEEN,
GATE STREET, LINCOLN'S INN FIELDS.
MDCCCLVI.

DER STIL

IN DEN

TECHNISCHEN UND TEKTONISCHEN KÜNSTEN

ODER

PRAKTISCHE AESTHETIK.

EIN HANDBUCH FÜR TECHNIKER, KÜNSTLER UND KUNSTFREUNDE

VON

PROFESSOR DR. GOTTFRIED SEMPER,
K. K. OBERBAURATH UND MITGLIED DES BAUCOMITE FÜR DIE MUSEEN UND DAS NEUE HOFSCHAUSPIELHAUS IN WIEN.

ERSTER BAND.

TEXTILE KUNST.

ZWEITE, DURCHGESEHENE AUFLAGE.

MÜNCHEN.
FRIEDR. BRUCKMANN'S VERLAG.
1878.

1.16 *Left* OWEN JONES: **Title-page of** *The Grammar of Ornament*, 1856.

Incredibly, this large folio volume was produced within a year. Jones had many collaborators in its production, including Christopher Dresser and J. B. Waring and Matthew Digby Wyatt. The idea of producing such a work came after the popular success of the Crystal Palace architectural museum and in a sense *The Grammar of Ornament* can be described as a 'portable Crystal Palace'. It was ecstatically reviewed on its publication.

L'ORNEMENT
POLYCHROME

CENT PLANCHES EN COULEURS
OR ET ARGENT
CONTENANT ENVIRON 2,000 MOTIFS DE TOUS LES STYLES
ART ANCIEN ET ASIATIQUE
MOYEN AGE
RENAISSANCE, XVIIe ET XVIIIe SIÈCLE

RECUEIL HISTORIQUE ET PRATIQUE
PUBLIE SOUS LA DIRECTION
DE M. A. RACINET
AVEC DES DESIGNATIONS DE MOTIFS SUR LE LA RENAISSANCE, DES ARTS SOMPTUAIRES, DE LA CERAMIQUE SUPERBEMENT, ETC.
AVEC DES NOTICES EXPLICATIVES
ET UNE INTRODUCTION GENERALE

PARIS
LIBRAIRIE DE FIRMIN DIDOT FRERES, FILS ET Cie
IMPRIMEURS DE L'INSTITUT
RUE JACOB, No 56

1.18 *Above* ALBERT CHARLES AUGUSTE RACINET: **Title page of** *L'Ornement Polychrome*, 1869.

Racinet's work was clearly modelled on Jones' *Grammar of Ornament*, but actually surpassed it in the splendour of its chromolithographic plates. *L'Ornement Polychrome* was the most extensive published compendium of decoration and was so successful that a second volume was published in 1883.

1.17 *Left* GOTTFRIED SEMPER: **Title-page of** *Der Stil in den Tektonischen Kunsten*, 1860–3, 1878 edition.

This was published when the crisis of industrialization was beginning to preoccupy German architects and designers. For a short time Semper was Professor of Metal Work at the Department of Practical Art, Marlborough House, London, under Henry Cole and Richard Redgrave.

1.19 *Above* F. Edward Hulme: **A page from his** *Principles of Ornamental Art,* 1875.

Hulme, one of the best-known late nineteenth-century 'art botanists', was a tireless collector of motifs and published several excellent ornament books. Two only, however, can be described as 'encyclopedias'—*The Principles of Ornamental Art* and *The Birth and Development of Ornament* (1893).

1.20 *Right* Richard Glazier: **A page from his** *A Manual of Historic Ornament,* 1899.

Glazier's inexpensive encyclopedia of ornament was among the best of its kind and was very widely used by design students. It was more concerned with archaeology than Lewis F. Day's small manuals of ornament.

CHAPTER TWO
Nature and Ornament

The idea of nature as the noblest source of inspiration to the imagination is of very considerable antiquity. Plato had declared: 'God devised the gift of sight for us that we might observe the movements which have been described by reason in the heavens, and apply them to the motions of our minds.' Over a period of two millennia, thinkers as diverse as Longinus, Philostratus, Plotinus, Addison, Baumgarten, Kant, Wordsworth and Coleridge had stressed the sublimity of nature. The medieval dependence upon nature as a source-book can be confirmed by the most cursory glance at a Gothic cathedral or an illuminated manuscript.[1] Vasari, in 1550, claimed that the first model for the artist was 'the beautiful fabric of the world'. Jean-Jacques Rousseau, in 1762, began *Émile* with the words: 'Everything which emanates from the hand of the Author of All Things is good.'

During the nineteenth century, as never before, nature was viewed as an inexhaustible fountainhead, providing an endless supply of decorative motifs. In part the fascination with nature stemmed from a belief in God as the Supreme Designer. Intricate natural forms confirmed the existence of a beneficent creator who had made the world for the benefit and delight of humanity. Thus taught William Paley (1743–1805), whose *Natural Theology: or evidence of the attributes of the Deity collected from the appearances of nature* (1802) was into its twentieth edition by 1820. Such views became part of the general consciousness. By the end of the century, however, there was a fundamental shift: scientific materialism had become the dominant intellectual mode, attaining its apotheosis in Darwinism. It spoke not of a kindly God, but of blind forces and mechanical necessity. Nature was now no longer to be revered—but dissected and exploited.

By the 1830s, as we have seen, industrialization had brought in its wake an ever-increasing demand for decoration. This intensified the search for new motifs. George Phillips' *Rudiments of Curvilinear Design* anticipates the preoccupations of later theorists. The range of styles in which he designed was far wider than one would expect at the end of the 1830s—he even included one engraving of a decorative composition in the Japanese style. More significantly, he suggested insects, the feathers of birds and even sea-urchins as sources of inspiration for the ornamental designer. However, although Phillips clearly understood the value of nature as a source-book, he suggested no systematic way in which nature could be transformed into ornament.

The Scottish painter William Dyce (1806–64) was one of the first teachers to place such faith in botanical nature as a source of inspiration. In his youth, Dyce was intended for a career in the church or medicine but, despite his father's opposition, he determined to take up painting. He studied in London and Rome, where he came under German Nazarene influence, evident in the unbending severity of his painting style. On his return to Edinburgh he became associated with several members of the Board of Trustees for Manufactures who regularly consulted him on how design could be applied to industry. Dyce's ideas soon came to the attention of the council of the Government School of Design at Somerset House, London. Dyce was asked to make a report on the organization and teaching methods of similar institutions which had been set up in France and Germany. He returned in

2.6 CHRISTOPHER DRESSER: A design exemplifying 'power'. *The Technical Educator*, 1870–3, also in *Principles of Design*, 1873.

Dresser describes this as an original sketch in which he had tried to embody 'power, energy, force or vigour as a dominant idea'. He made use of 'such lines as we see in the bursting buds in Spring . . . certain bones of birds which are associated with the organs of flight, and which give us an impression of great power, as well as those which we observe in the powerful propelling fins of certain species of fish'. His amalgam of natural forms was unexpected in the early 1870s and seems to foreshadow the attempts to 'distil' the essence of nature of later designers.

1838 and his officially published report led to the reorganization of the School.

His *Drawing Book of the Government School of Design* (1842–3) is probably the earliest, certainly the most complete, record of a basic course in industrial design. A series of graduated exercises in simple geometry is the starting point (see also Chapter Three). Dyce next set his students to draw the 'outlines' of ornament. These outlines—which came to be nicknamed 'Dyce's outlines'—are no more than the skeletons of Classical or Neo-classical ornaments. Having mastered these outlines, the pupil could clothe them with foliage to create new ornament. The process must have involved a rudimentary study of botanical drawing. Writing in Henry Cole's *Journal of Design* in 1849—the first year of its publication—Dyce described ornamental design as 'a kind of practical science which investigates the phenomena of nature for the purposes of applying natural principles and results to some new end'. Dyce's method of teaching ornament was used for several generations.

Dyce was by no means the only important authority on decoration in the 1840s to advocate the study of nature. A. W. Pugin, the architect, able publicist that he was, brought together two topical themes—the revival of medieval practice and the celebration of nature—in *Floriated Ornament* (1849). It contains well over a hundred formal and geometrical arrangements of flowers. The boldness and clarity of these designs are most pleasing. In their somewhat mechanical perfection one can detect the influence of the new 'conventional' design (Plate 2.25).

'To conventionalize' corresponds exactly with our term 'to stylize'. 'Conventional' ornament is invariably based upon plant forms. Owen Jones was its principal champion. In a lecture at the Royal Society of Arts in April 1852—'An Attempt to Define the Principles which should regulate the Employment of Colour in the Decorative Arts'—he put forward the doctrine of conventionalism: 'Flowers or other natural objects should not be used as ornament, but conventional representations founded upon them, sufficiently suggestive to convey the intended image to the mind without destroying the unity of the object they are employed to decorate.' Does one detect here a primitive understanding of Gestalt perception?

Jones believed that the art of the painter and the art of the ornamentalist were distinct. The ornamentalist should never make use of the illusionistic devices of the painter. Ornament—if flat—should proclaim itself to be flat. Naturalism, though not nature, was to be studiously avoided. Jones had been an early student of Islamic design and was obviously influenced by its love of abstraction.

Pugin's views on conventionalism were not altogether unlike Jones'. His *Glossary of Ecclesiastical Ornament* (1844), containing many brilliantly coloured paraphrases of medieval decoration, helped to popularize conventional design. In *The True Principles of Pointed or Christian Architecture* (1841), he stressed the importance of decorative design 'without shadow'. This preoccupation with flatness bears a close relation to the contemporary enthusiasm for conventionalism.

John Ruskin (1819–1900) shrank away in horror from the thought of conventionalizing nature. Nature was too holy to be subjected to such barbaric treatment. Absolute symmetry, regularity and uniformity—the essential characteristics of conventional design—represented not so much nature which had been idealized, but nature which had been treated like a machine. He delivered his most virulent attack on conventional design in an evening lecture at the South Kensington Museum, London, in 1858. Uncomfortably titled 'The Deteriorative Power of Conventional Art over Nations', it was published in Ruskin's *Two Paths* in 1859. In it, he singled out Indian design for attack, criticizing it for being opposed to 'all facts and forms

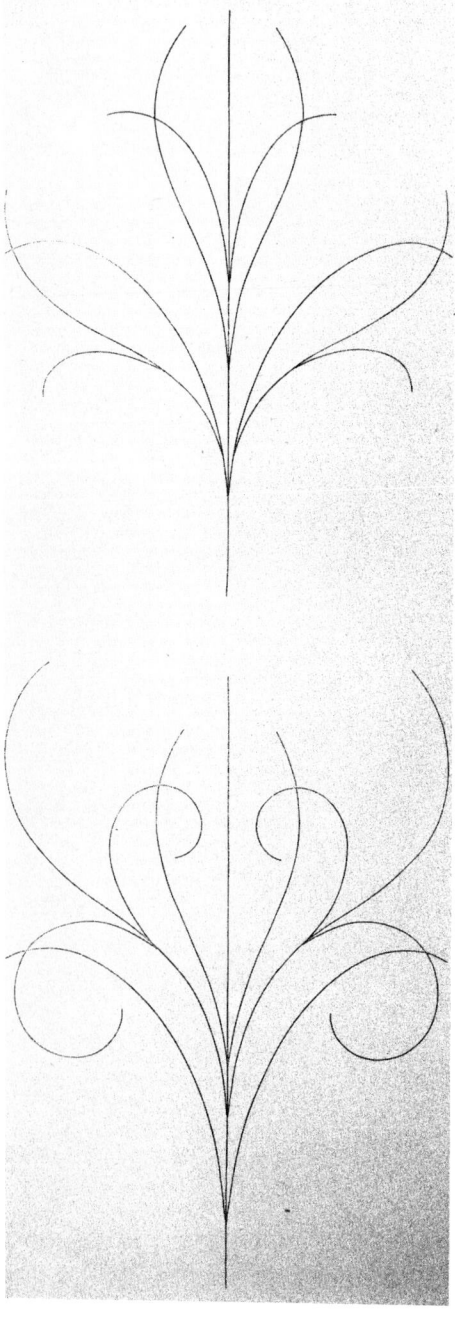

of nature ... it will not draw a flower, but only a spiral or a zig-zag'. Influenced by the recent Indian Mutiny which had horrified his country, Ruskin saw Indian art as the outpouring of the imagination of a people capable of great cruelty. His stern moral censures of conventionalism—for all their naïvety—impressed later Arts and Crafts workers. Their treatment of nature is always reverential and never mechanical. And his championship of the Pre-Raphaelite painters was to a great extent due to their reverence in the presence of nature. Sir John Millais's *Ophelia* of 1852, for example, represents river-bank flora in almost obsessive detail.

In 1852, the botanist Dr John Lindley (1799–1866) was asked to give three lectures to the students of ornamental design at the Department of Practical Art at Marlborough House in London. For the first time an eminent scientist had been called upon to discuss the application of science—botanical science in this case—to design. Dyce's talk of design as 'a kind of practical science' had been heeded. Lindley's lectures were published under the title of *The Symmetry of Vegetation* (1854). They reveal, incidentally, that he was familiar with Jones' teachings on conventional design.

At about the same time, Professor Edward Forbes (1815–54), another distinguished scientist, lectured at Marlborough House on 'The Variety and Symmetry of Animal Forms and The Symmetry of Radiated Animals'. 'Symmetry' in the context of these lectures not only related to the general proportion or balance but also to the order and regularity—the bi-lateral or the multi-lateral symmetry—of natural forms. Such conceptions have an obvious value to the designer of conventional ornament. There also lurks in them the idea of the designer-God. Forbes, it has been said, 'looked on the world not as a mechanism, but as a visible manifestation of the ideas of God'.

The designer and writer Christopher Dresser (1834–1904), the most successful of the Marlborough House students, had a lifelong enthusiasm for the application of science to design. In *The Art of Decorative Design* (1862) he likened art and science to 'two angelic figures'. A gifted child, Dresser began studying at the School of Design in 1847, when he was thirteen. In 1849 he must have attended two lectures by the painter Richard Redgrave, who spoke on 'The Importance of the Study of Botany to the Ornamentist' (these were reproduced in Cole's *Journal of Design*). Redgrave, though by no means an original thinker, was to play an important part in co-ordinating official Department of Science and Art theory. He told students not to take up time-consuming scientific botany, but to learn enough about plants to be able to represent them accurately. Dresser became an accomplished botanical draughtsman, and his painstaking study of the external forms of plants led him to ponder on the common factors that linked the different species of plants and the relationships of their various organs. He was interested in the structure of the plant—not its physiology. His speculations straddle the frontier between science and art, and were treated with respect in scientific circles. In 1860 the University of Jena, which had the strongest botanical faculty in Europe, awarded him a doctorate 'in absentia' for his work. Although it is not as a botanist that Dresser is remembered, he can properly be described as the earliest 'art-botanist'.

Dresser's first appearance as an art-botanist was in Owen Jones' *Grammar of Ornament*, to which he contributed a coloured lithographic plate showing 'the geometrical arrangement of flowers'. Dresser published three books on botany, *The Rudiments of Botany* (1859), *Unity in Variety* (1859) and *Popular Manual of Botany* (1860). The first two were intended for art-students. They are, with the exception of Lindley's *Symmetry of Vegetation*, the earliest published works on art-botany.

One of the best known of later art-botanists was F. Edward Hulme. He established his reputation with *A Series of Sketches from Nature of Plant Form*

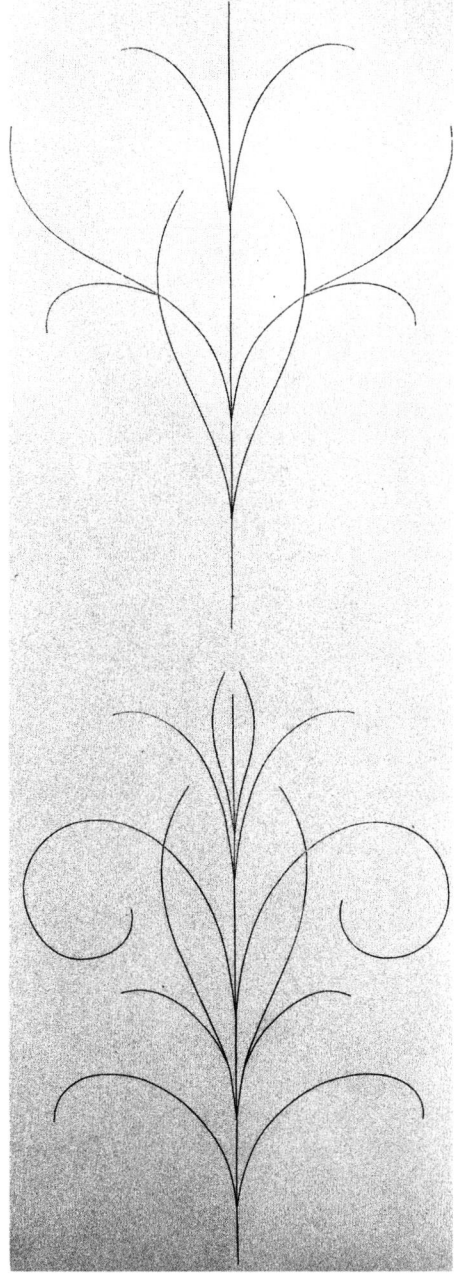

2.7 and **2.8** WILLIAM DYCE: **Dyce's outlines.**
The Drawing Book of the Government School of Design, 1842–3.

After his students had mastered simple geometry, Dyce set them to draw these skeletons of ornament—innumerable variations could be produced. The next stage was to clad the 'outlines' with foliage.

27

2.9 RICHARD REDGRAVE: **Sketch of a plant, the Sonchus (or sow-thistle) pictorially drawn as it grows.** *Manual of Design*, 1876.

Redgrave's *Manual* describes the teaching methods he had evolved in the 1850s.

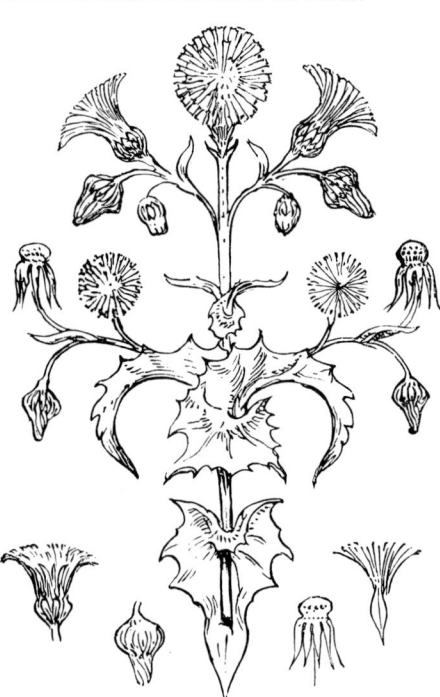

2.10 RICHARD REDGRAVE: **Sow-thistle arranged geometrically.** *Manual of Design*, 1876.

'The plant is displayed and flattened, whilst the form of the buds, the open blossoms, the seed vessels and the leaves are examined as new motives for ornament . . . Many figures would be wanted to show all that could be obtained from this single plant.'

(1868). In 1872, he made an appearance in a work which yet again affirmed the intensity of the enthusiasm for nature as a source-book: *Art Studies from Nature, as applied to design*. This work contains Hulme on 'The Adaptability of our Native Plants to the Purposes of Ornamental Art'; S. J. Mackie on 'Seaweeds as Objects of Design'; James Glaisher on 'The Crystals of Snow as applied to the Purposes of Design'; and Robert Hunt on 'The Symmetrical and Ornamental Forms of Organic Remains'. These chapters had all appeared earlier in *Art Journal*, the only art magazine of the day in Britain.

Among other important British art-botanists were George Haité, A. E. V. Lilley and W. Midgley, authors of the standard work of the late 1890s, *A Book of Studies in Plant Form* (1898), and Miss J. Foord, who drew exquisitely in a rather Japanese manner (Plate 2.88). James Kellaway Colling's *Art Foliage* (1865), a study of neo-Gothic carved ornament, bears a fairly close relationship to art-botany. Frank Furness (1839–1912), the Philadelphia Gothic Revivalist, also designed botanical ornament for his buildings very much in the Colling manner.

Eugène-Emanuel Viollet-le-Duc (1814–79)—theorist, historian and restorer—designed a great deal of plant-based ornament for the redecoration of the interior of Notre-Dame, Paris. His schemes for the side chapels were published in a handsome folio volume, *Peintures Murales des Chapelles de Notre-Dame de Paris* (1870). The sinuous and brilliantly coloured plant forms seem, at first sight, to have been inspired by medieval manuscript decoration. But there is in the Notre-Dame decorations evidence of a more than common sympathy for the essential vitality of organic form—and this despite Viollet-le-Duc's insistence upon geometrical perfection in the organization of his ornament. The same sympathy can be seen in his ecclesiastical metalwork in which organic form is treated in the more or less abstract way that has come to be associated with such later designers as Hector Guimard.

Like Ruskin, Viollet-le-Duc had the greatest faith in the training of the eye. His attitude towards nature is that of scientific, confident, nineteenth-century man. His rational, unworried thinking was to be echoed in the work of such later exploiters of nature as M. P. Verneuil and Eugène Grasset (see Plates 2.108–9 and 102–5).

Any discussion of the nineteenth-century exploitation of nature for decorative ends must take into account the ideas of Ernst Haeckel (1834–1919) of Jena. He is probably best known for his work on Radiolaria—unicellular marine organisms—first published in 1862. He was one of Darwin's earliest champions and was responsible, so Darwin came to believe, for the wide acceptance of his ideas in German-speaking countries. Haeckel was fascinated with the idea of the cell and posited a theory that all living cells possessed, if not a soul, at least a will. Such thinking certainly constituted an attempt to compensate for the loss of the reassuring notion of a God well-disposed towards man. Haeckel's exquisite drawings for the study of Radiolaria became known in artistic circles in the 1890s. With *Art Forms of Nature*[2] Haeckel brought his drawings to a non-scientific audience, and extended the range of his illustrations to include jelly-fish, water-plants and even land animals. Such German designers as August Endell and Hermann Obrist were the inheritors of Haeckel's peculiarly nineteenth-century brand of pantheism.

The architect René Binet (1866–1911), who designed the Porte Monumentale of the Paris Universal Exhibition of 1900, acknowledged his indebtedness to Haeckel in his published portfolio *Esquisses Decoratives* ('Decorative Sketches') of 1903. Here Binet demonstrated how Haeckel's illustrations could provide inspiration to the designer of electric light-fittings, jewellery, moulded and flat decoration or even brick structures (see Plate 2.91). However, Binet interpreted nature too literally. Despite his remarkable virtuosity as a draughtsman there is a certain monotony and lack of invention in his work.

Binet can be seen as being in many respects the typical French Art Nouveau designer, although historians have not ranked him highly. Art Nouveau, together with its German and Italian equivalents Jugendstil and Stile Liberty, was a decorative style founded upon the study of natural forms. Authorities like Stefan Tschudi Madsen and Robert Schmutzler have sought to identify as well as to explain historically the Art Nouveau movement.[3] However, the style is essentially a mannered version of the botanically based decorative style of the 1860s and 1870s. For this reason it has not been treated here as a separate ornamental style, although work by many of the designers popularly associated with Art Nouveau is illustrated. Among these are Binet, Dufrene, Endell, Grasset, Guimard, Lalique, Koloman Moser, Mucha, Obrist and Van de Velde (see Plates 2.54, 69, 70, 72–3, 81, 86, 90, 100, 102–7).

The American architect Louis Sullivan (1856–1924) was among the most fluent designers of ornament to have sought inspiration in nature. His carved and cast ornament decorates some of Chicago's earliest tall commercial buildings. Sullivan's reputation as one of the founding fathers of Modernism is secure. His famous pronouncement, 'Form follows Function', is incised upon his monument, and kept his memory fresh among the rising generation of American architects in the 1930s. It is thus somewhat ironic that Sullivan's last publication, *A System of Architectural Ornament, according with a philosophy of man's powers* (1924), should have been one of the most complete accounts of an individual method of designing ornament. He was a dying man when he prepared the drawings for his book, but there is not the slightest hint that his powers were diminishing (see Plate 2.117).

Sullivan's 'philosophy of man's powers' seems to owe more than a little to Goethe. Sullivan saw the process of the seed becoming the plant as an allegory of the creative process. In 1787 Goethe had declared that if he could discover the *Urpflanze*—the Primal Plant and the ancestor of all plants—he would himself be able to invent plants endlessly according with the laws of nature. It is unlikely that Sullivan knew anything directly of Goethe, but he may well have half-remembered a saying of Dresser's—itself reminiscent of Goethe—which had appeared in *The Art of Decorative Design* (1862): 'The designer's mind must be like the vital force of the plant, ever developing itself into forms of beauty.' Such ideas, whatever their precise origins, had become part of the intellectual subconscious of the nineteenth century.

Whether allegiance was owed to God or to scientific truth, the nineteenth century willingly accepted nature as the supreme model for its creations. The tensions induced by the incursions of materialist philosophy and the decline of faith brought poignancy to its attempts to understand nature. But out of the tensions came a vivid energy. This was as true of the lesser art of ornament as it was of writing or painting. Nature still serves us as a source-book, but our passion has diminished. Twentieth-century ornament derived from nature is often ingenious or diverting, but it rarely moves us.

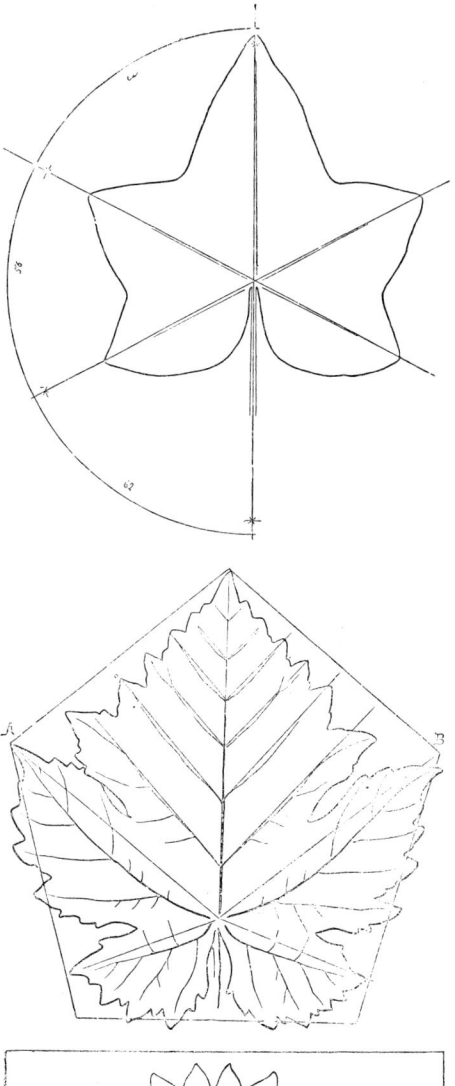

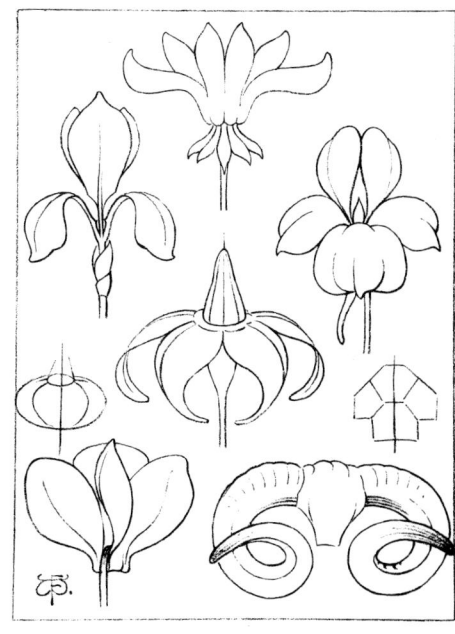

2.11 Eugène-Emanuel Viollet-le-duc: **An ivy leaf, with the angles of the veins.** *Histoire d'un Dessinateur*, n.d. (1879).

In this popular educational book, Viollet-le-Duc tells the story of how Jean, the son of a gardener, is taught the rudiments of drawing. One of the first things Jean learns is 'how geometry can be applied to many things', in this case botany.

2.12 Eugène-Emanuel Viollet-le-duc: **Vine-leaf enclosed within a regular pentagon.** *Histoire d'un Dessinateur*, n.d. (1879).

2.13 Anonymous: **Outlines of flowers with ram's horns.** *The Practical Teacher's Art Monthly*, Vol. IV, 1901–2.

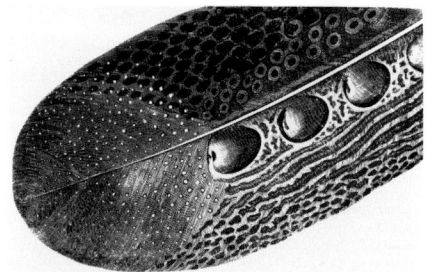

2.14 *Left* GEORGE PHILLIPS: **Hints for a composition.** *Rudiments of Curvilinear Design* (1838–40).

Phillips' book is something of a curiosity. It was 'intended to show the practicability of treating the several styles in a new . . . and efficient manner, adapted to the habits and wants of our own times'.

2.15 *Above* GEORGE PHILLIPS: **Pinion feather of the wing of the Argus pheasant.** *Rudiments of Curvilinear Design* (1838–40).

Phillips leafed through the sourcebook of nature more thoroughly than his contemporaries in his search for inspiration.

2.16 *Below* GEORGE PHILLIPS: **'Spiniferous sea-egg' and the patterns derived from it.** *Rudiments of Curvilinear Design* (1838–40).

Phillips' attempts to understand the phenomena of pattern may appear clumsy now—but he was a pioneer.

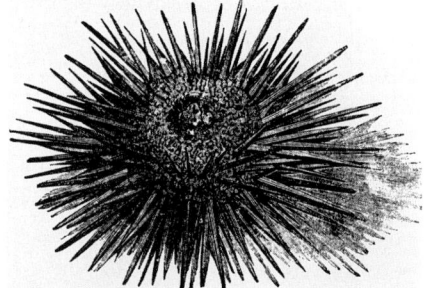

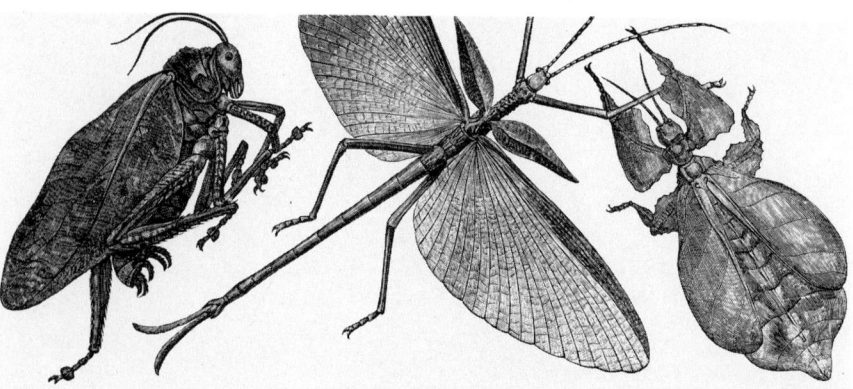

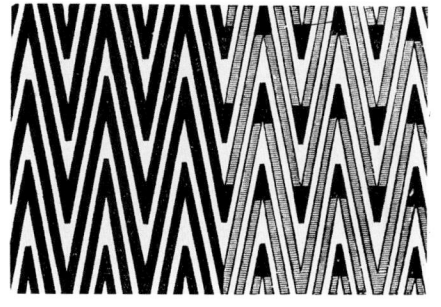

2.17 GEORGE PHILLIPS: **Insects suggested as sources of design.** *Rudiments of Curvilinear Design* (1838–40).

Phillips' advocacy of insects as sources of inspiration anticipates early twentieth-century French and Austrian authorities.

2.18 *Left* George Phillips: **Tailpiece.**
Rudiments of Curvilinear Design (1838–40).

This composition has a neo-classical feel
about it. The illuminating sun and its rays
hint at the work of such German painters
as Phillip Otto Runge and Caspar David
Friedrich.

2.19 *Above* I. Page: **Designs for moulding or carving.** *Guide
for Drawing the Acanthus*, 1840.

Page's book was in print until the 1880s. Although the ornament
he designed was unimaginative, his method of teaching was
sound enough. The book was evidently intended for artisans.

2.20 *Right* I. Page: **Part-wrapper.** *Guide for Drawing the
Acanthus*, 1840.

Although popular books on watercolour painting were by no
means uncommon by 1840, this appears to be the earliest
popular work on ornament. Page taught ornament and design at
the Society For Promoting Practical Design, London, which had
been founded by the reforming M.P., William Ewart.

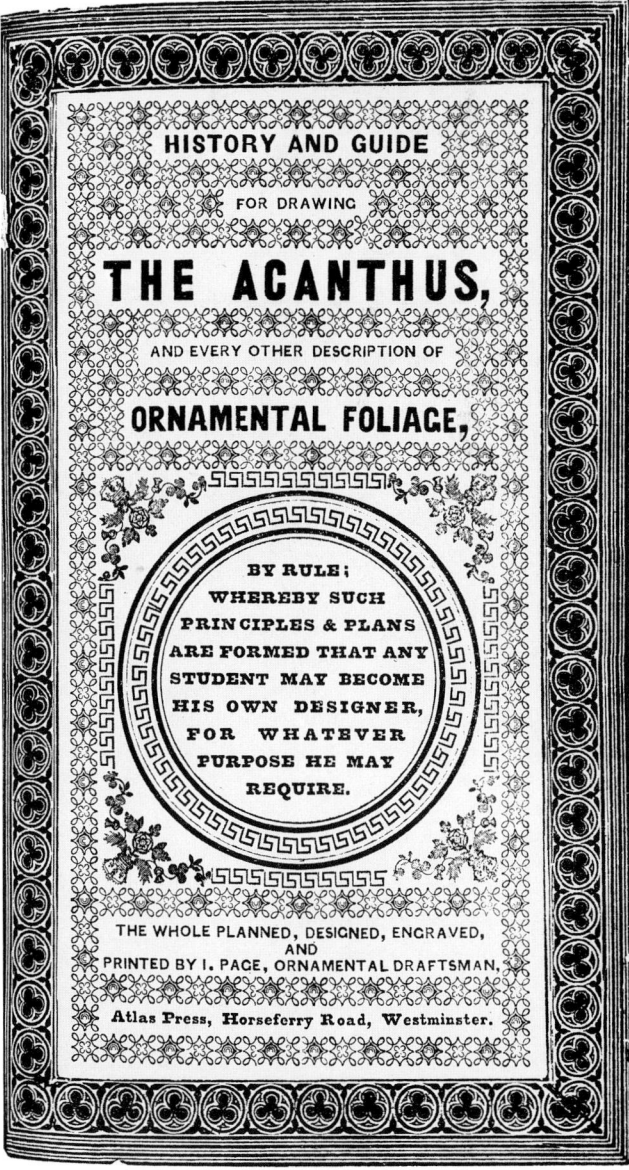

HISTORY AND GUIDE

FOR DRAWING

THE ACANTHUS,

AND EVERY OTHER DESCRIPTION OF

ORNAMENTAL FOLIAGE,

BY RULE;
WHEREBY SUCH
PRINCIPLES & PLANS
ARE FORMED THAT ANY
STUDENT MAY BECOME
HIS OWN DESIGNER,
FOR WHATEVER
PURPOSE HE MAY
REQUIRE.

THE WHOLE PLANNED, DESIGNED, ENGRAVED,
AND
PRINTED BY I. PAGE, ORNAMENTAL DRAFTSMAN,

Atlas Press, Horseferry Road, Westminster.

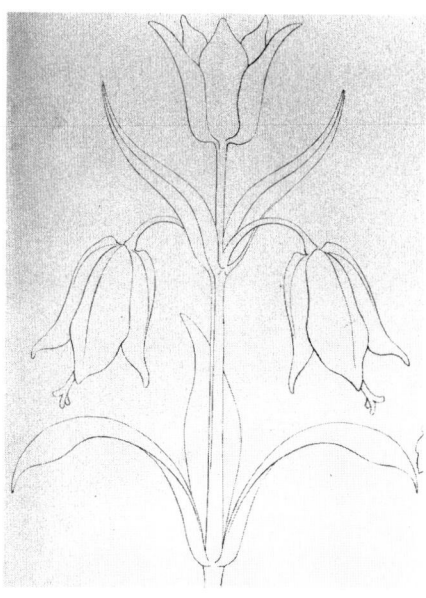

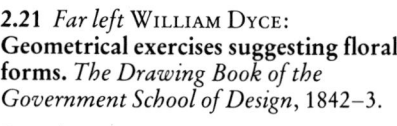

2.21 *Far left* WILLIAM DYCE: **Geometrical exercises suggesting floral forms.** *The Drawing Book of the Government School of Design*, 1842–3.

Dyce became Director of the Government School of Design in 1838. His method of teaching ornament by graduated exercises is preserved in his Drawing Book.

2.22 *Top centre* WILLIAM DYCE: **'Dyce's outlines' clad with foliage.** *The Drawing Book of the Government School of Design*, 1842–3.

Simple foliage was superimposed on the skeletons— or 'outlines'. Dyce's teaching ushered in an era of botanically based ornament.

2.23 *Top* WILLIAM DYCE: **Simple botanical drawings.** *The Drawing Book of the Government School of Design*, 1842–3.

When Dyce's students had mastered the 'outlines' they learned how to produce simple, precise drawings of plants from nature.

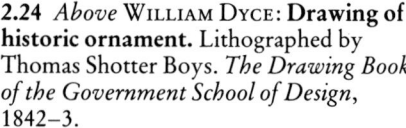

2.24 *Above* WILLIAM DYCE: **Drawing of historic ornament.** Lithographed by Thomas Shotter Boys. *The Drawing Book of the Government School of Design*, 1842–3.

Although Dyce emphasized the importance of the study of nature and geometry he also insisted that his students should be able to draw from historical models. Students would be set to copy this very drawing.

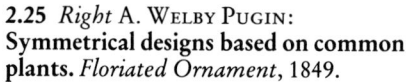

2.25 *Right* A. WELBY PUGIN: **Symmetrical designs based on common plants.** *Floriated Ornament*, 1849.

This was one of the most influential of mid-nineteenth-century pattern books. Pugin justifies his new-found interest in nature by citing the example of medieval craftsmen, but in fact he took his models from a sixteenth-century German herbal.

2.27 *Right* MESSRS WEBB & SONS, SPITALFIELDS, MANUFACTURERS: **Table-cloth for Messrs Dewar and Co. of London.** *The Art-Journal Illustrated Catalogue. The Industry of All Nations, 1851,* 1851.

Naturalism of the kind represented by this design was extremely well represented at the Great Exhibition of 1851.

2.26 *Below* E. T. PARRIS, DESIGNER: **Carpet manufactured by Turbeville Smith and Co.** *The Art-Journal Illustrated Catalogue, The Industry of All Nations, 1851,* 1851.

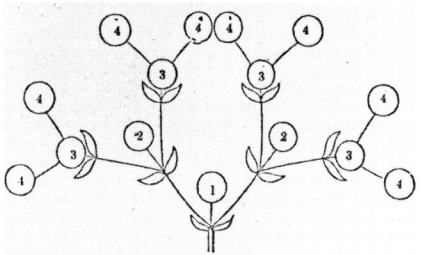

2.28 *Above* JOHN LINDLEY: **Arrangement of blossoms in Laurustinus.** *The Symmetry of Vegetation,* 1852.

John Lindley was the first professional botanist of major standing to become interested in the application of scientific botany to design. An English School of 'art botany' was soon to develop.

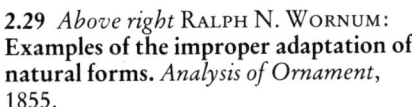

2.29 *Above right* RALPH N. WORNUM: **Examples of the improper adaptation of natural forms.** *Analysis of Ornament,* 1855.

Wornum objected to the illogicality and dishonesty of representing a flame coming from a flower in a gas-jet, 'a basket on an animal's head to hold a liquid' and a 'bell made of leaves'.

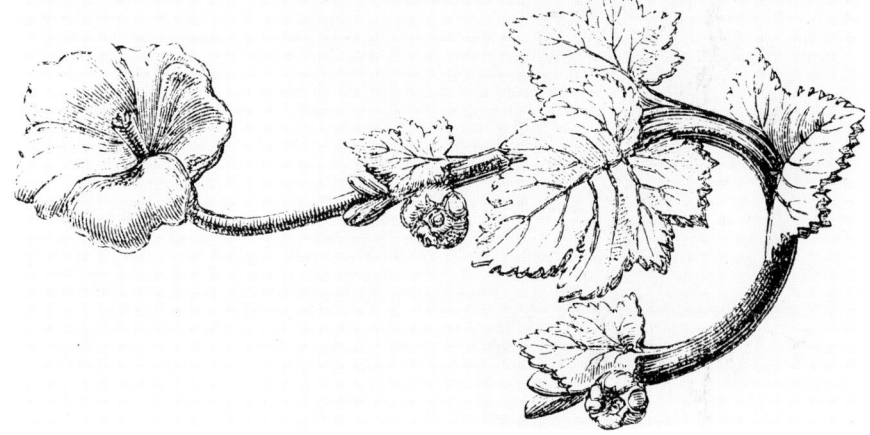

2.30 *Right* GAETANO FERRI: **'On the education of the eye'—leaf drawing.** *Corso Elementare di Ornato,* 1854.

Ferri devotes an appendix in his book to 'botanica artistica e della simbolica', a comparatively early treatment of the theme of art-botany.

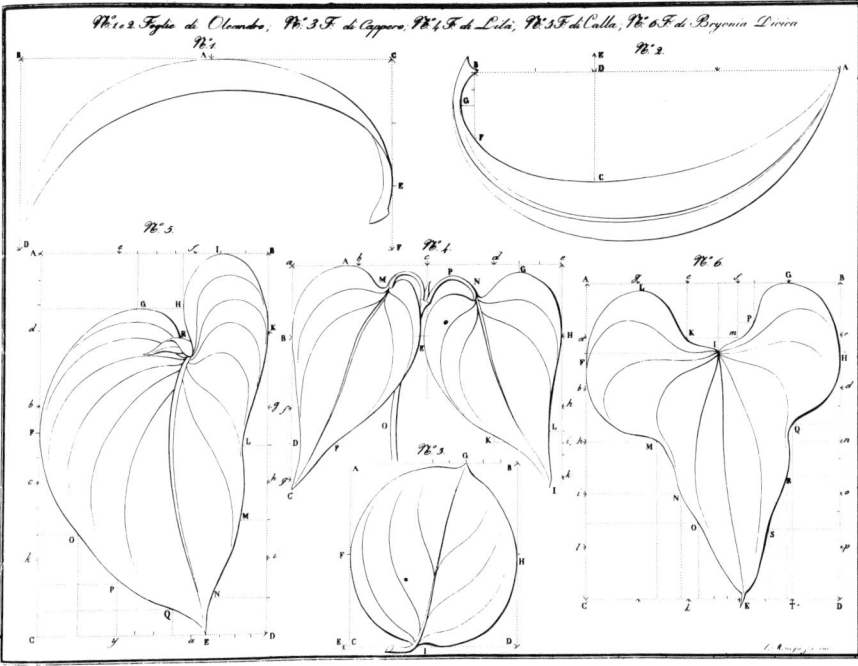

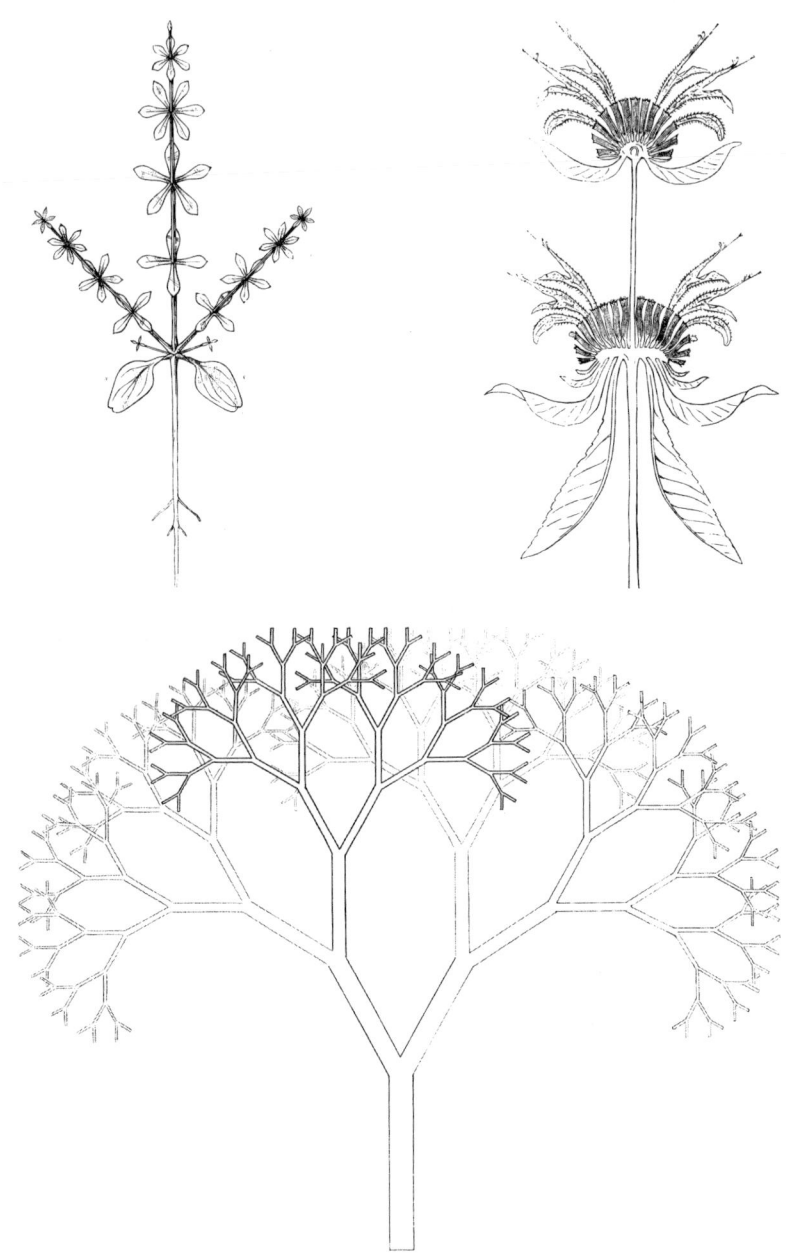

2.31 *Far left* CHRISTOPHER DRESSER: **Young plant of the Goosegrass or Cleavers family (*Galium aparine*).** *The Rudiments of Botany*, 1859.

As a student Dresser became an able botanical draughtsman. The arrangement of the plant in this illustration is based upon the 'outlines' advocated by Dyce.

2.32 *Left* CHRISTOPHER DRESSER: **A vertical slice from the upper portion of a plant of *Monarda fistulosa*.** *The Rudiments of Botany*, 1859.

There can be no doubt from this formal and symmetrical arrangement of the section of a plant that Dresser was suggesting new sources of inspiration to the designer of ornament.

2.33 *Centre left* JOHN RUSKIN: **Sketch by a clerk of the works.** *Modern Painters*, Vol. V, 1843–60.

Although credited to a clerk of works, the drawing is by Ruskin and shows the growth system of a tree. It is probably borrowed from Dresser.

2.34 RICHARD REDGRAVE: **A printed *barège*.** *Manual of Design*, 1876.

Barège was a light dress fabric first made in the village of Barèges in the Hautes-Pyrénées. It became popular in the 1850s.

2.35 RICHARD REDGRAVE: **Light woollen fabric.** *Manual of Design*, 1876.

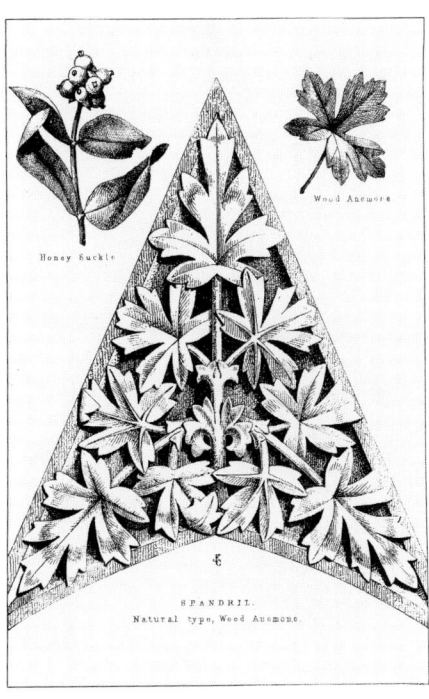

2.36 *Top* J. K. COLLING: **Carved vesica shape, with decoration based upon the ground ivy.** *Art Foliage*, 1865.

Colling held the view that 'in any new and distinct style of Architecture ... foliated decoration must hold an important part'.

2.37 *Above* J. K. COLLING: **Carved spandrel, with decoration based upon the wood anemone.** *Art Foliage*, 1865.

Colling's influence has been underestimated by historians. Thomas Hardy, while articled to the Weymouth architect G. R. Crickmay, drew many sketches of ornament in the Colling manner in his notebook, as did the Philadelphia architect Frank Furness.

2.38 BRUCE J. TALBERT: **Design in watercolour and pencil with butterflies.** Probably mid-1870s. The Print Room, Victoria and Albert Museum, London.

Talbert was an architect who became one of the most successful commercial designers of his generation. Once an exponent of the Gothic, Talbert later recanted and embraced the Queen Anne Style.

2.39 *Right* CHRISTOPHER DRESSER: **Motif to be used in diagonal repeat.** *Studies in Design*, n.d. (1874–6).

In this curious design Dresser attempts to capture the essence of nature without making precise reference to either plant or animal forms. The central design, however, is based on the bones of birds.

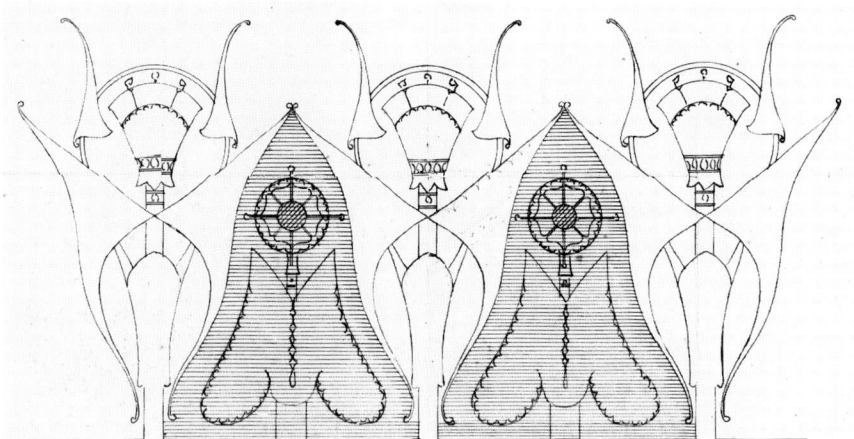

2.40 *Above* LOUIS SULLIVAN: **Design for fresco border**, dated 1 April 1875. The Avery Architectural Library.

An early example of Sullivan's ornament. Although Sullivan studied briefly at the École des Beaux-Arts in Paris in 1874–75 this design appears to relate more closely to the work of Frank Furness, the Philadelphia Gothic Revival architect, for whom Sullivan worked in 1873. Sullivan had rejected the rigid conventionalized ornament of the British school by the 1880s and developed his own highly personal approach to designing foliated ornament.

2.41 *Right* LOUIS SULLIVAN: **Detail of newel post.** The Auditorium Building, Chicago, Illinois, 1888–9. The Avery Architectural Library.

Sullivan was a keen student of botany and his mature ornament is invariably naturalistic. This illustration although designed by Sullivan was drawn by an assistant.

2.42 ALPHONSE MARIE MUCHA: **Alphabet.** *Documents Décoratifs*, 1902.

2.43 PETER BEHRENS: **Design for wallpaper.** *Dekorative Kunst*, Vol. III, 1900.

A stylized representation of a peacock's feathers.

2.44 *Far left* J. Foord: **Tulip.** Dated 1899. *Decorative Flower Studies*, 1901.

2.45 *Centre left* Lindsay P. Butterfield: **Design for a woven textile.** Watercolour, *c.* 1905. The Print Room, Victoria and Albert Museum, London.

2.46 *Above* M. P. Verneuil: **Decorative composition with praying mantis.** *Art et Décoration*, Vol. 15, 1904.

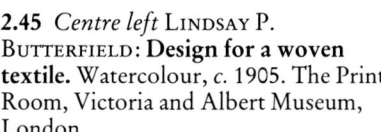

2.47 Walter Crane: **'The Meadow' wallpaper, with 'The May Tree' frieze.** Manufactured by Jeffrey & Co., *c.* 1905. Walter Shaw Sparrow, ed., *The Modern Home*, n.d. (*c.* 1905).

2.48 MARGERY TOMLIN: **Design for block-printed silk.** *The Studio*, Vol. 91, 1926.

2.49 F. GILLAR: **Decorative composition.** *Das Interieur*, Vol. XII, 1911.

By a pupil of Josef Hoffmann at the Kunstgewerbeschule, Vienna.

2.50 E. A. SÉGUY: **Decorative composition based upon crystal structures.** *Prismes*, n.d. (after 1931).

2.51 *Right* F. EDWARD HULME: **Designs for carving based on common species of plant.** *Plants, their Natural Growth and Ornamental Treatment,* 1874.

Hulme drew plants effectively and with authority, but there is a certain monotony in his work. His style remained rooted in the 1860s when he had studied art-botany—almost certainly under Dresser—at the South Kensington School of Art, London.

2.52 *Below* F. EDWARD HULME: **Conventional decoration based on familiar plants.** *The Building News,* 10 December 1875.

Redgrave had encouraged his students to base their conventional ornament on the plants of the locality. This was probably based on medieval practice. Illustrations of exotic plants were readily available throughout the nineteenth century—the desire to represent native plants has an element of nationalism in it.

2.53 *Below right* F. EDWARD HULME: **Conventional decoration based upon plant forms.** *The Building News,* 12 November 1875.

The composition is essentially geometric—bold, ingenious, but somewhat schoolmasterly.

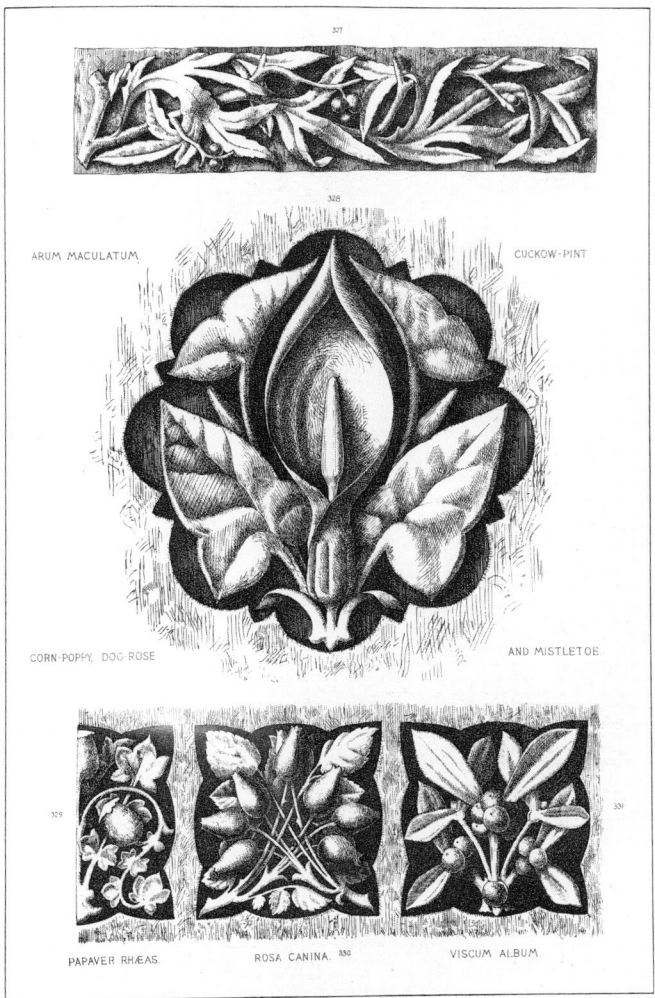

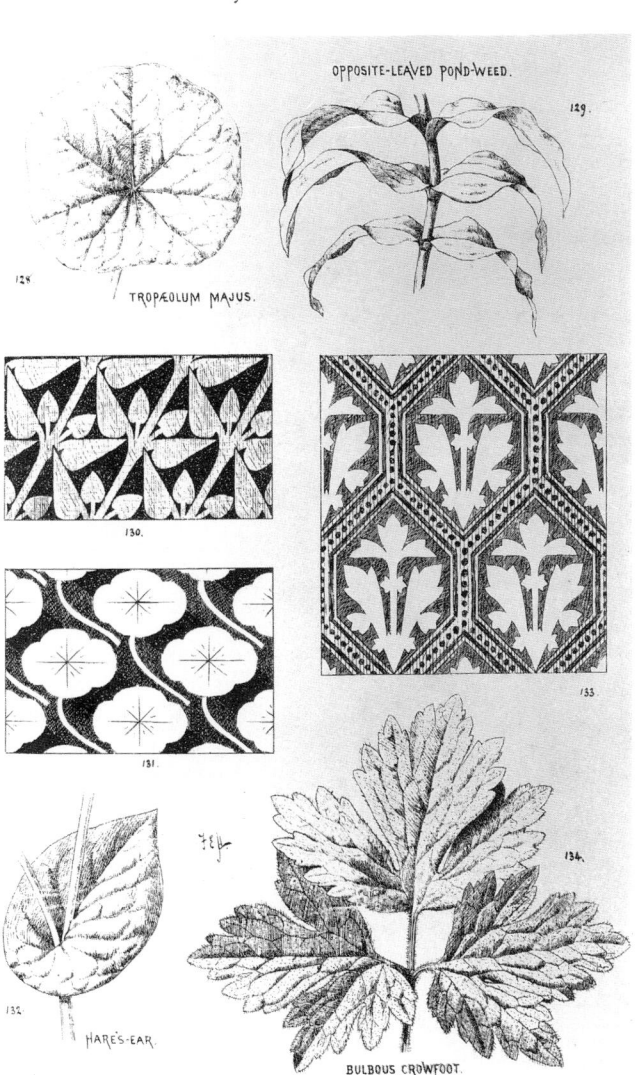

2.55 *Left* JOHN RUSKIN: **Study with the lead and single tint. Leaf of Herb-Robert.** *The Laws of Fesole*, 1906.

Ruskin's drawing of the leaf celebrates the fact that it cannot be reduced to a regular geometric shape. He complained of 'the construction of entirely symmetrical or balanced forms for exercises in ornamental design—whereas every beautiful form in this world is varied in the minutiae of the balanced sides'.

2.54 *Above* EUGÈNE GRASSET: **Design for end-paper.** *The Studio*, Vol. IV, 1894.

Grasset's treatment of plant forms in this design is somewhat reminiscent of the conventionalized decoration of Christopher Dresser or F. Edward Hulme which dates from the 1860s and 1870s.

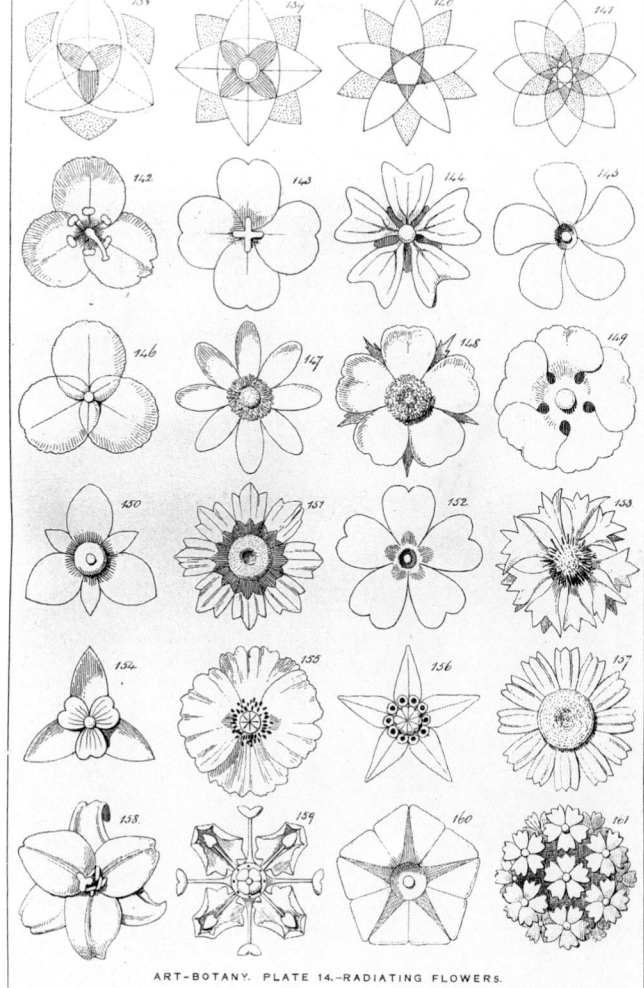

2.56 *Right* ANONYMOUS: **Art-botany—radiating flowers.** *The Furniture Gazette*, 11 August 1877.

The designs in the top row are evidently intended as suggestions for inlay-work. Their stiff formality is reminiscent of Dresser's published illustrations of the 1850s.

2.57 *Above* WALTER J. PEARCE: **Design for a tapestry curtain.** *Decoration*, September 1882.

A reaction against the rigid conventionalism of the 1850s and 1860s came in the 1870s, triggered by the discovery of Japanese design and the arrival of the happily eclectic Queen Anne Style. In addition, the tide of the Gothic Revival was ebbing. This was the period of the Aesthetic Movement.

2.58 *Top right* OWEN W. DAVIS: **'Rydal' wallpaper designed for Messrs Woollams & Co.** *Decoration*, September 1886.

Davis was an able designer in many styles. Born in 1838, the same year as Bruce Talbert, and trained by J. R. Colling, he came from the generation which rejected medievalism. In this design he skilfully minimizes, if not conceals, the repeats. Morris and Lewis F. Day were masters of this technique.

2.59 *Right* HENRY W. BATLEY: **Tapestry design.** *Decoration*, September 1886.

During the 1880s Batley became very well known as a designer—particularly of furniture and interiors. The Victoria and Albert Museum, London, possesses a piano designed by him in 1878 which abounds with carved motifs taken from Japanese pattern-books. In this tapestry design Batley has cast aside conventionalism and embraced a highly organized naturalism that savours a little of William Morris.

2.60 *Above* GEORGE HAITÉ: **Asparagus** (dated 1883). *Plant Studies for Artists, Designers and Art Students*, 1886.

Haité was a successful and prolific designer. The elegant disposition of his plant drawings suggests an acquaintance with Japanese black-and-white wood-block prints. Books containing such prints had been readily available in London since the 1870s.

2.61 *Above right* CHRISTOPHER DRESSER: **Decorative composition 'intended to give the idea of evening'.** *Modern Ornamentation*, 1886.

Dresser sometimes tried to outdo the pictorial artist in his decorative compositions. His notebook contains many such compositions—some inspired by well-known poems. Two particularly fine compositions evoking evening and night can be seen in *The Art of Decorative Design* (London 1862). In this composition Dresser organizes decorative elements in a way which harks back to the era of Dyce—some forty years earlier.

2.62 *Right* LEWIS F. DAY: **Scale patterns and derivatives.** *The Planning of Ornament*, 1887.

Day published a number of the standard late Victorian works on decorative design. He was eclectic in his approach and had an encyclopedic knowledge of pattern-making. A keen student of nature, he was also an accomplished botanical draughtsman.

2.63 *Far left* HUGH STANNUS: **Design of foliage, with faults enumerated. 2.64** *Left* **Design of foliage, with faults corrected.** *The Decorative Treatment of Natural Foliage*, 1891.

These two plates were used to illustrate a series of lectures delivered before the Society for the Encouragement of Arts Manufactures and Commerce. Although Stannus could have had no knowledge of Gestalt theory, he seems to have had an intuitive, or empirical, understanding of its principles. The 'corrected' design is in fact less confused than the 'uncorrected' version.

2.65 GEORGE ASHDOWN AUDSLEY and MAURICE ASHDOWN AUDSLEY: **Crestings . . . in conventional floral style.** *The Practical Decorator and Ornamentist*, 1892.

The upper of the two friezes appears to have been 'borrowed' from an early illustration of Dresser's and Dresser himself was not above borrowing designs. The Audsley brothers were prominent Liverpool architects.

2.66 *Above left* THE SILVER STUDIO: **Preliminary drawing of the Fuchsia.** *The Studio*, Vol. III, 1894.

Arthur Silver (1853–96) had been told that designs based on the fuchsia were considered unsaleable. He could see no reason why and set his studio the task of producing such designs.

2.67 *Above* JOHN ILLINGWORTH KAY: **Design based on the Fuchsia.** *The Studio*, Vol. III, 1894.

This design, possibly produced as a wallpaper, has something of the swirling, undulating quality which is associated with Art Nouveau. It was in fact influenced by Japanese colour prints, which made bold use of curves for decorative effect, and also by the popular rediscovery of the engravings of William Blake, who was fascinated by sinuous plant-like forms. John Illingworth Kay (1870–1950) was a member of the Silver Studio.

2.68 *Left* THE SILVER STUDIO: **Design based on the Fuchsia.** *The Studio*, Vol. III, 1894.

This treatment of the fuchsia, though ingenious, seems mannered and clumsy when compared with the design by Kay (Plate 2.67).

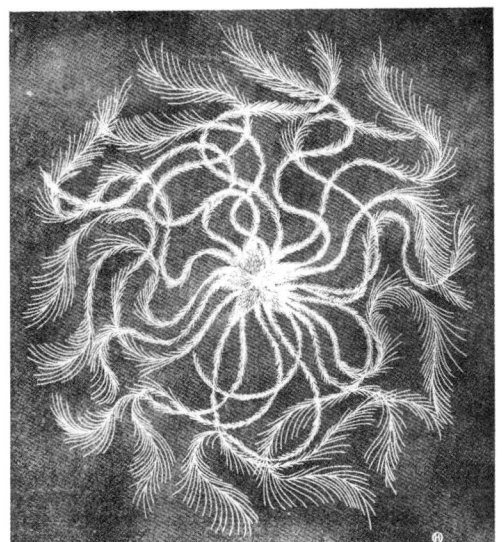

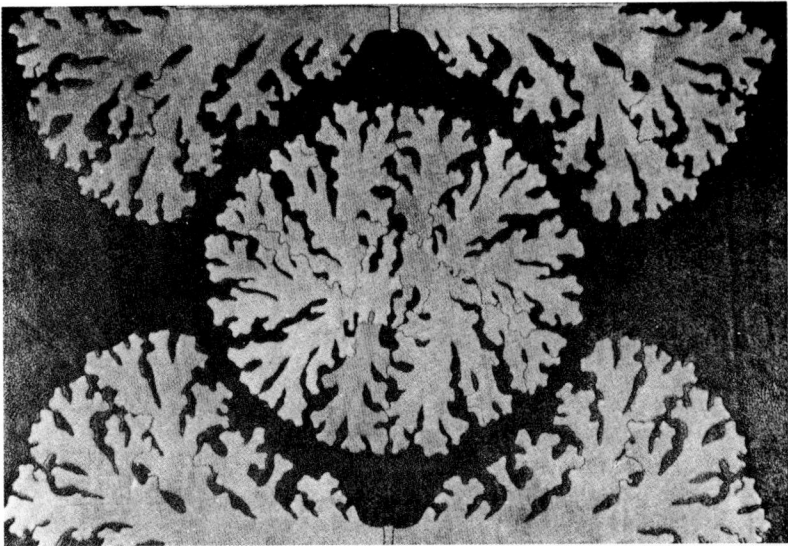

2.69 *Above* HERMANN OBRIST: **Embroidered table-cloth. Design based upon a sea creature.** Executed by Berthe Ruchet. *The Studio*, Vol. IX, 1896.

Obrist was one of the most influential of Jugendstil designers. In addition to a highly developed decorative sense he was able to create original plastic form. He had an especial ability to capture the essence of living organisms and was able to 'invent' living forms which accorded with nature's laws. He founded his embroidery workshop in Florence in 1892; he moved it to Munich in 1894.

2.70 *Above right* HERMANN OBRIST: **Appliqué work.** Executed by Berthe Ruchet. *The Studio*, Vol. IX, 1896.

2.71 *Right* M. P. VERNEUIL: **Book-cover.** *L'Animal dans la Décoration*, 1898.

Verneuil responded to the interests of his day—he was not an initiator of ideas in the sense that Obrist and Guimard were. This design suggests a passing acquaintance with the work of Walter Crane.

2.72 *Left* HENRY VAN DE VELDE: **Stencil frieze.** *Dekorative Kunst*, Vol. I, 1898.

Van de Velde's ornament depicts no natural forms—rather it represents the characteristic manner in which nature expands and contracts. Van de Velde claimed he was guided by three rules in the design of ornament: 'Complementary contrasts; repulsion and attraction; and the desire to give negative forms the same degree of significance as the positive forms.'

2.73 *Below left* HENRY VAN DE VELDE: **Advertisement for Van de Velde's atelier.** *Dekorative Kunst*, Vol. I, 1898.

Van de Velde's early decorations suggest the contained energy of living organisms.

2.74 *Below* HENRY VAN DE VELDE: **Invitation card for a Brussels firm.** *Dekorative Kunst*, Vol. I, 1898.

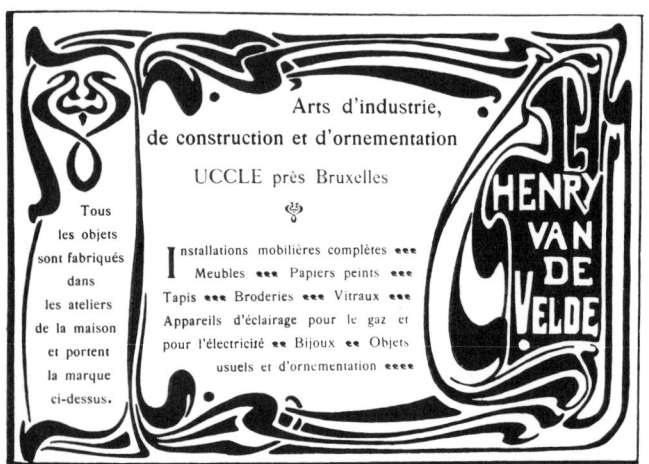

2.75 *Left* JOHAN THORN-PRIKKER: **Design for book-binding.** *Dekorative Kunst*, Vol. I, 1898.

This design consists of a crane surrounded by foliage, put into a mirrored repeat. Like Van de Velde, Thorn-Prikker skilfully opposed figure and ground. He was to become one of the greatest of twentieth-century stained-glass artists. His later windows are often expressionistic, although he also designed in a Mondrian-like idiom.

2.76 L'Atelier de Glatigny: **Bands of decoration, based upon microscope studies.** *Art et Décoration*, Vol. IV, 1898.

The microscope was an essential tool in the search for new organic form. One of the fundamental principles of the Glatigny studio was that its workers should remain anonymous.

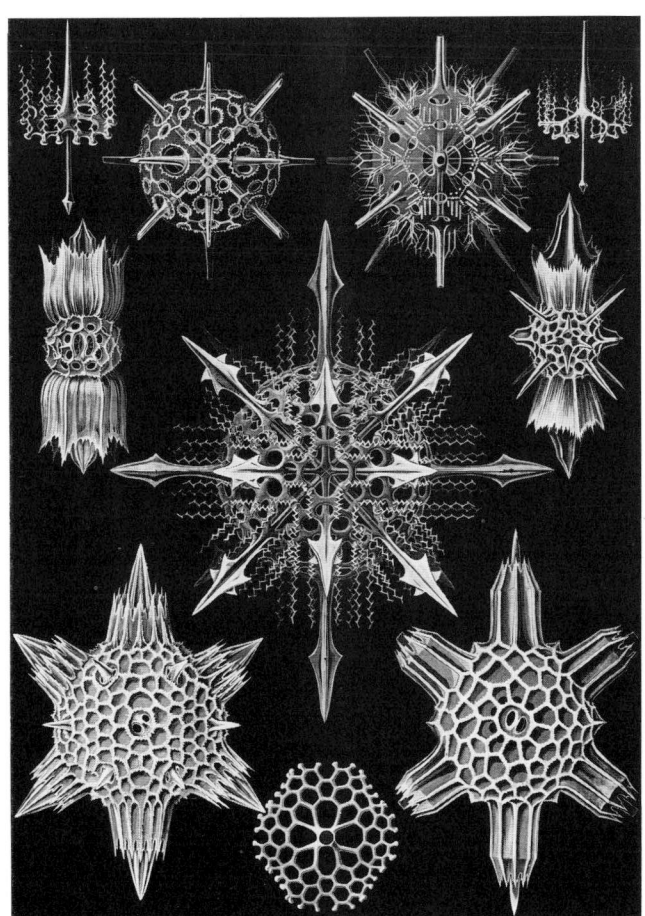

2.77 *Above* Ernst Haeckel: **Peridinea.** *Kunstformen der Natur*, 1899–1904.

Haeckel was the foremost marine biologist of the nineteenth century. He began his study of radiolaria—minute unicellular undersea organisms—in the winter of 1859–60. Ehrenberg, the Berlin microscopist, was their true discoverer, but Haeckel recognized their beauty and potential applicability to design. His drawings of them were made with the aid of a microscope.

2.78 *Left* Ernst Haeckel: **Acanthophracta.** *Kunstformen der Natur*, 1899–1904.

Radiolaria were for Haeckel a link between the organic and inorganic worlds because of their crystal-like development. He developed his own brand of monism which denied the irreconcilability of mind and matter. This nineteenth-century form of pantheism was widely admired. His drawings carry the message of his philosophy.

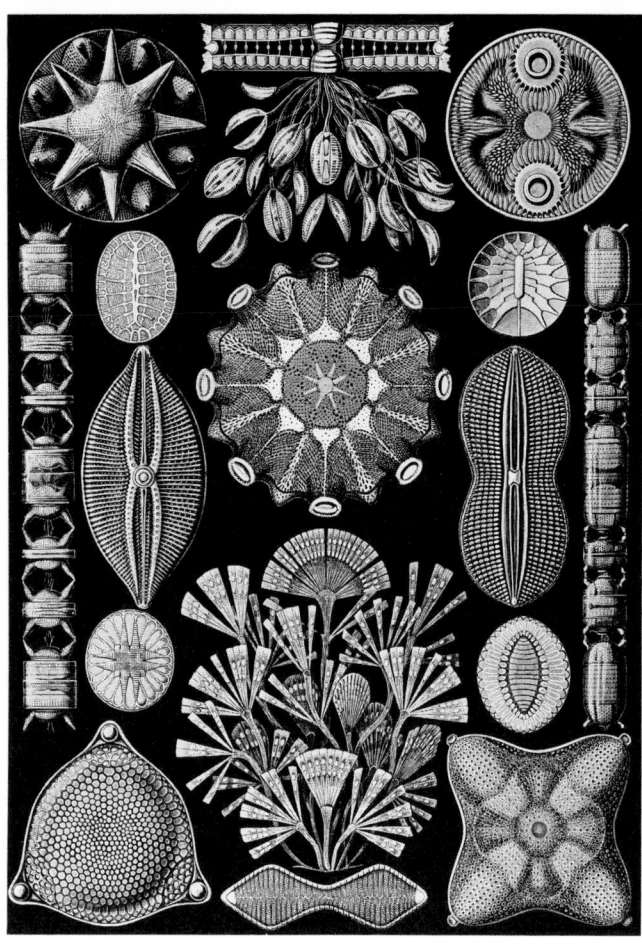

2.79 *Above* ERNST HAECKEL: **Diatomea.** *Kunstformen der Natur*, 1899–1904.

2.80 *Right* ERNST HAECKEL: **Thalamophora.** *Kunstformen der Natur*, 1899–1904.

Haeckel possessed an uncommon aesthetic sensibility. Despite the considerable demands of his scientific life he was a keen painter—a book of reproductions of his landscape paintings was published in 1905.

2.83 *Below* R. Grimm: **Book decoration.** *Dekorative Kunst*, Vol. II, 1899.

A good example of Jugendstil decoration.

2.81 *Top* Koloman Moser: **Repeat pattern.** *Dekorative Kunst*, Vol. II, 1899.

Like Van de Velde, Moser used shapes which symbolize natural forms, and showed considerable skill in opposing figure and ground.

2.82 *Above* Tony Selmersheim: **Ceramic tiles.** *Art et Decoration*, Vol. XII, 1902.

Selmersheim's fanciful plants—despite their graceful art nouveau curves—have much in common with the decorations found in medieval manuscripts or perhaps with Viollet-le-Duc's elegant paraphrases of medieval ornamental foliage.

2.84 *Above* Georges Lemmen: **Decorative designs.** *Dekorative Kunst*, Vol. III, 1900.

Lemmen modifies a single stylized leaf-motif and skilfully rearranges it to produce six designs. Dresser had advocated similar exercises in *The Art of Decorative Design* (London 1862).

2.85 *Left* GEORGES LEMMEN: **Wallpaper.** *Dekorative Kunst*, Vol. II, 1899.

Like Van de Velde, his fellow Belgian, Lemmen made particularly skilful use of simple motifs derived from natural forms.

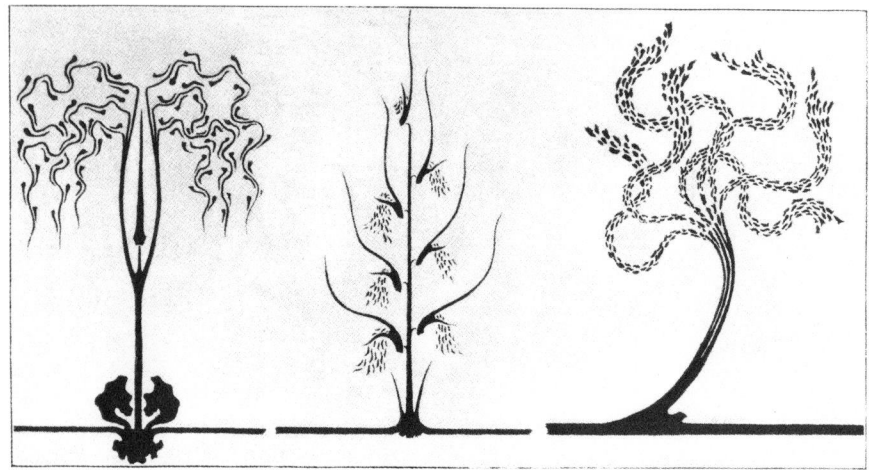

2.86 *Above* AUGUST ENDELL: **Stencil motifs for friezes.** *Dekorative Kunst*, Vol. III, 1900.

Endell's principal influence was Obrist—he lived for several years in Munich and was a member of the Obrist circle. Here he uses Obrist's 'whiplash' line to suggest movement and hence life.

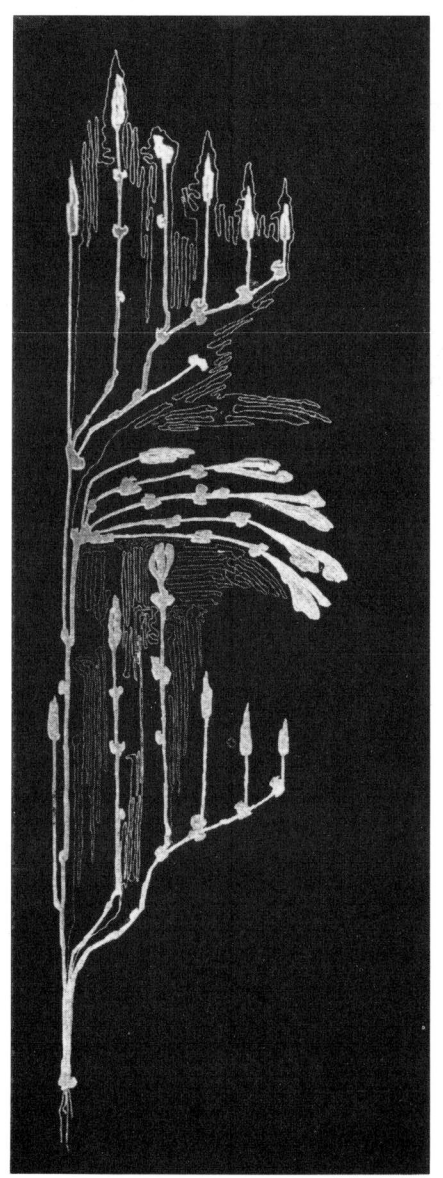

2.87 *Right* MARGARETHE VON BRAUCHITSCH: **An embroidered portière.** *Dekorative Kunst*, Vol. III, 1900.

The influence of Obrist's embroidery design is very evident here.

2.88 *Above* J. FOORD: **'Solomon's seal'.** *The Studio*, Vol. XXIII, 1901.

Miss Foord's plant studies provided inspiration for decorative designers. Her clear, precise drawings are among the most pleasing to have come from the hand of any art-botanist. Her indebtedness to the Japanese wood-block print is very evident.

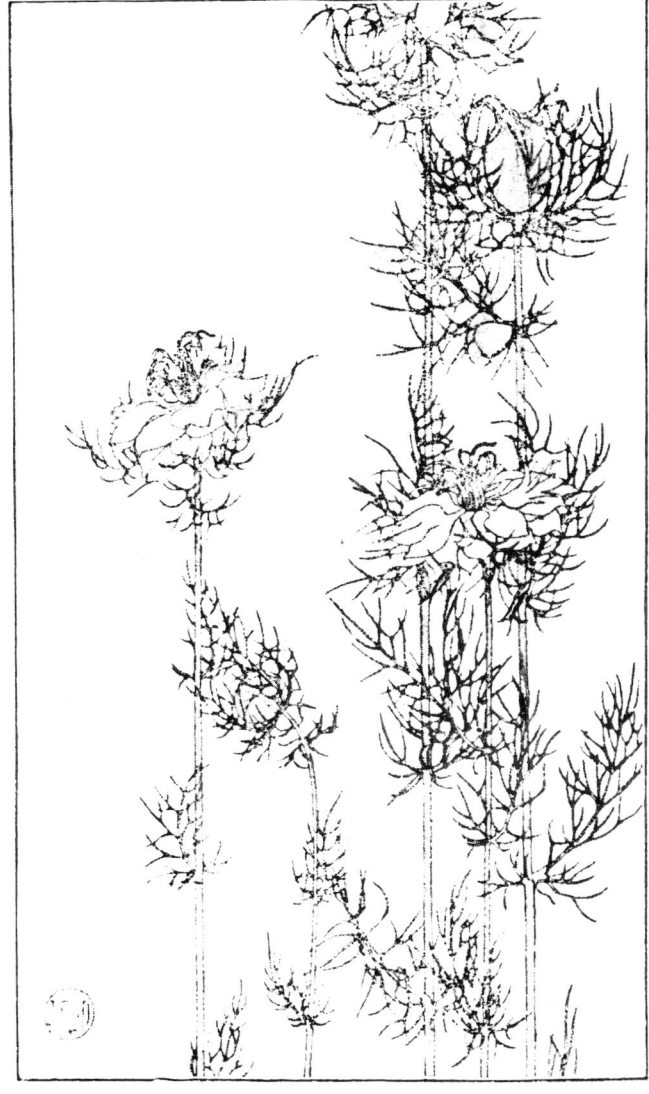

2.89 *Right* J. FOORD: **'Love-in-a-mist'.** *The Studio*, Vol. XXIII, 1901.

2.91 *Right* RENÉ BINET: **Designs for electric-lighting pendants.** *Esquisses Decoratives*, 1903.

An architect, Binet is best remembered for his Magasins du Printemps (1891–5), in Paris, and for his ornate and capricious entrance to the Paris Universal Exhibition of 1900. The design for the top light-fitting is based on one of Haeckel's published drawings of radiolaria.

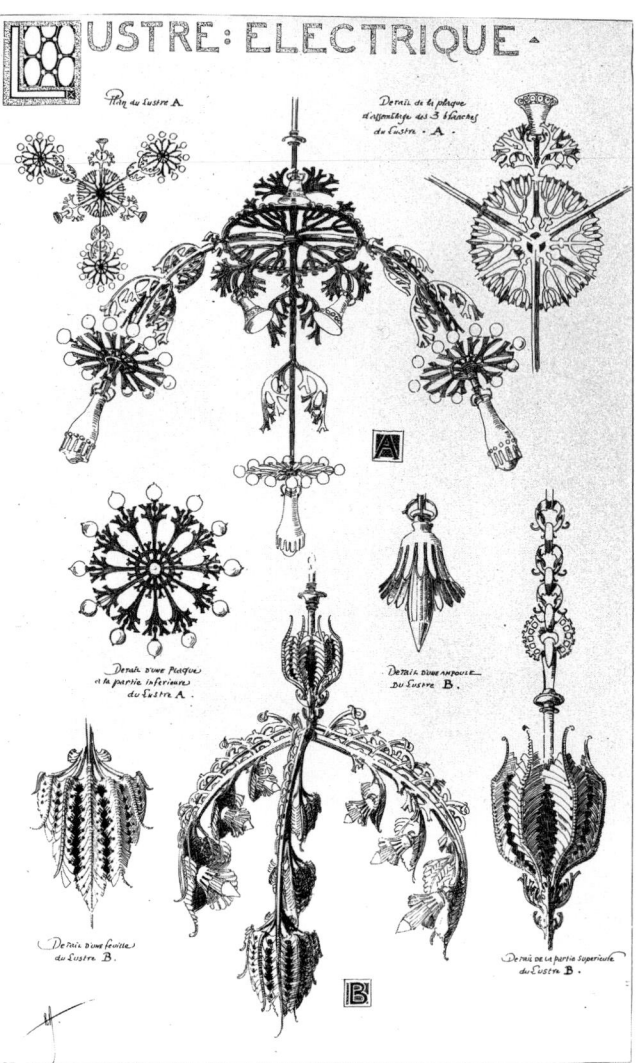

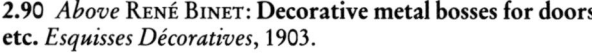

2.90 *Above* RENÉ BINET: **Decorative metal bosses for doors etc.** *Esquisses Décoratives*, 1903.

Binet's delight in the 'architecture' of organic forms derives from the powerful Ecole des Beaux Arts tradition in which he had grown up.

2.92 *Right* A. BAYER: **Plant study and its adaptation to wood-carving.** From a booklet published by Oesterreich K. K. Ministerium für Kultur und Unterricht, for the World Exhibition, St Louis, 1904.

Bayer was a student at the Salzburg Craft School. The adaptation of natural forms for ornamental use was a standard part of the curriculum.

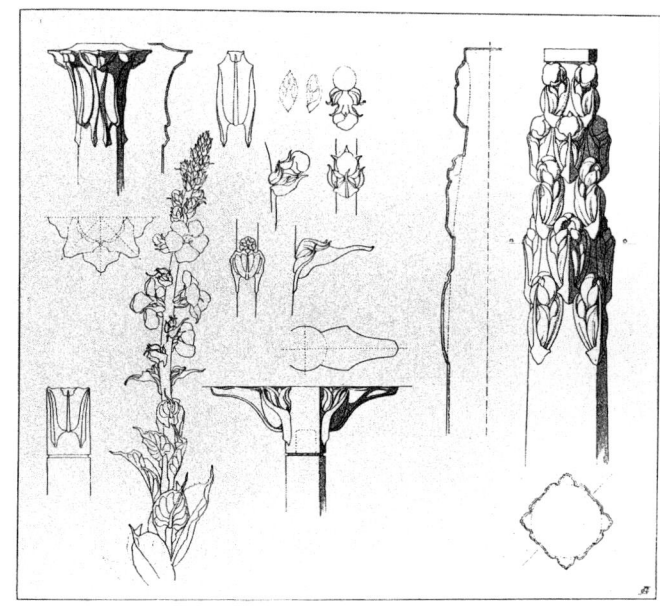

2.93 *Right* R. STREIT: **Natural forms applied to end-papers.** *The Studio*, Vol. XXXIV, 1905.

Streit was a student at the Gablonz Craft School in Czechoslovakia.

2.94 *Below right* HABERT DYS: **Study of cockchafer beetle (Hananeton).** *Art et Décoration*, Vol. XV, 1904.

During the early 1900s *Art et Décoration* published many articles on how decoration could be based on living forms.

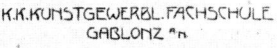

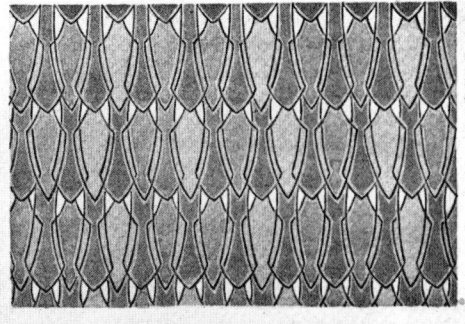
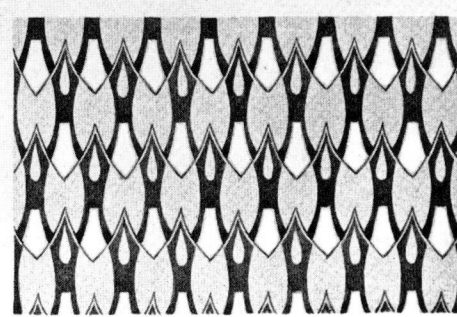

2.95 *Below* A. BAYER: **Plant studies.** From a booklet published by the Oesterreich K. K. Ministerium für Kultur und Unterricht, for the World Exhibition, St Louis, 1904.

Botanical drawing formed a very important part of the curriculum in Austrian design education early in the century.

2.96 *Below right* E. FROMEL: **Design for a damask tablecloth.** *The Studio*, Vol. XXXIX, 1907.

Fromel was a pupil of Professor Oscar Beyer, Director of the Kunstgewerbeschule in Vienna.

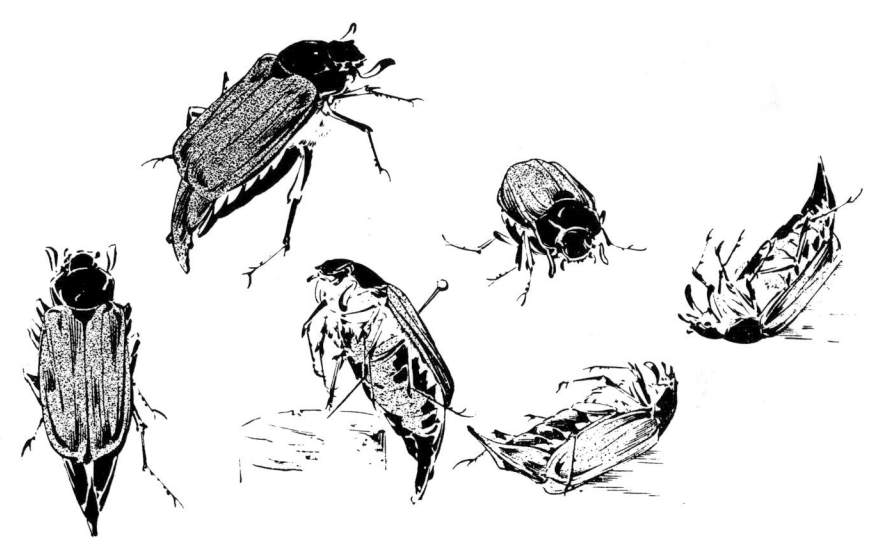
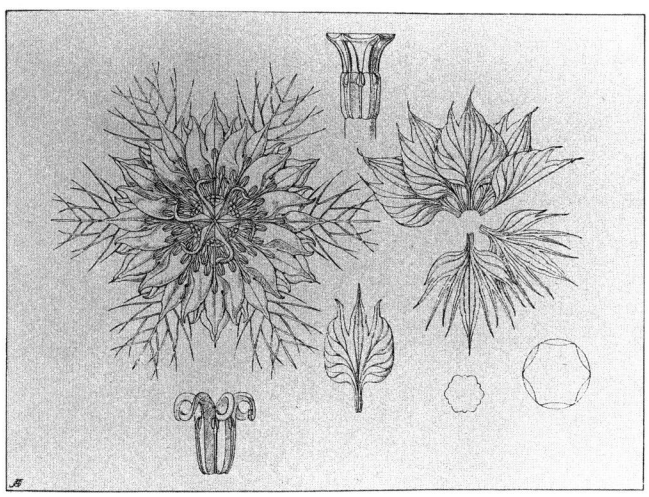

2.97 *Above* HABERT DYS: **Repeat pattern based upon the cockchafer.** *Art et Décoration*, Vol. XV, 1904.

Christopher Dresser also used beetles in some of his designs.

2.98 *Right* MUCHA: **Decorative panel.** *Art et Décoration*, Vol. XXVIII, 1910.

Mucha is, of course, best known for his posters, most of which illustrate splendid young women. In his graphic work he made great use of ornament. His abstracted natural forms are in the manner of Van de Velde or Georges Lemmen, but Mucha's work is less restrained and almost Rococo in its profuseness. This is an untypically modest design.

2.99 *Above* HENRI SAUVAGE: **Headpiece.** *Art et Décoration*, Vol. V, 1899.

During the 1920s Sauvage was among the most successful Parisian architects. He designed the 1926 extension of Les Grands Magasins de la Samaritaine (in collaboration with Frantz Jourdain). He was also an accomplished designer of decoration based upon natural forms.

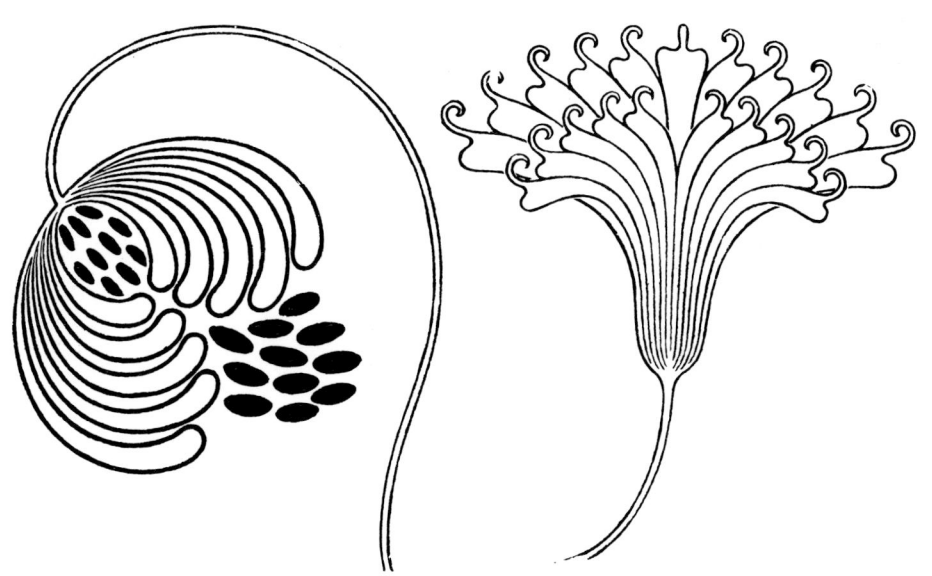 

2.100, 2.101, 2.102, 2.103 *Above and right* EUGÈNE GRASSET: **Four illustrations** taken from his *Méthode de Composition Ornamentale*, 1905. *Art et Décoration*, Vol. XVII, 1905.

Grasset ran a three-year course in decorative design at Montparnasse—his book describes his teaching method in great detail. Like Van de Velde and Obrist, or Dresser much earlier, Grasset attempted to convey the energy of growth in his designs.

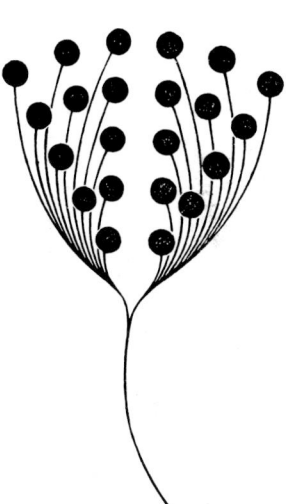

2.104 *Below* MAURICE DUFRÊNE: **Pattern based on the chameleon.** *Art et Décoration*, Vol. XX, 1906.

Art et Décoration published several articles on decoration based on insects, fishes, birds and reptiles. Dufrêne later became prominent as an exponent of Art Déco.

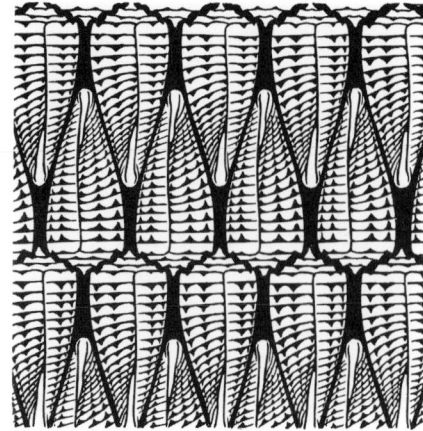

2.106 *Above* M. P. Verneuil: **Patterns based upon sea-shells.** *Art et Décoration*, Vol. XXVII, 1910.

Verneuil produced a number of designs based on the theme of the sea.

2.105 *Left* René Lalique: **Design for scarf.** *Art et Décoration*, Vol. XXI, 1907.

The apparent naturalism of this drawing conceals its sophisticated decorative organization.

2.107 *Below far left* M. P. Verneuil: **Decorative composition based on the squid.** *Art et Décoration*, Vol. XXVII, 1910.

2.108 *Below left* M. P. Verneuil: **Frieze based on the salamander.** *Art et Décoration*, Vol. XXVII, 1910.

2.109 *Below* T. S. Stephenson: **Design based upon the cuttlefish.** *Seashore Life and Pattern*, 1944.

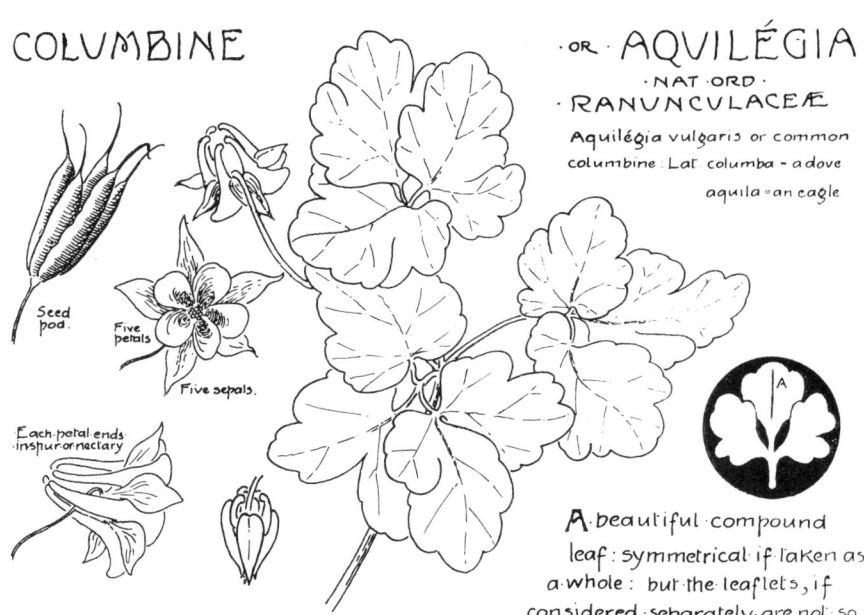

COLUMBINE ·OR· AQUILÉGIA
·NAT·ORD·
·RANVNCVLACEÆ·

Aquilégia vulgaris or common
columbine: Lat· columba – a dove
aquila =an eagle

Seed pod.

Five petals

Five sepals.

Each petal ends in spur or nectary

A· beautiful ·compound·
leaf: symmetrical ·if· taken ·as·
a·whole : but· the ·leaflets, if
considered ·separately· are not ·so·
except· the · central· one. A ·continuing· the· line· of· the· midrib, from·the· leaf· stalk·
Pull· off· the· lateral· leaflet· of· any· compound· leaf. It· will· not· seem· perfect· as·
a· separate· leaf· but· as· a· part· of· one· larger· leaf. Below· are· exercises & examples·
of· background· and· mass· brushwork : forming· three· borders· or· an· all-over·diaper-
ing· pattern· i·e· the· covering· of· a· space· with· the· same· ornamental· unit· closely· repeated.

2.110 *Above* EMANUEL JOSEF MARGOLD: **Vignette.** *Das Interieur*, Vol. XI, 1910.

Margold, an architect and interior designer, was trained under Josef Hoffmann. His treatment of floral decoration is very like Hoffmann's—simple, elegant, but perfunctory.

MODERNE
BLUMEN-ORNAMENTIK.

2.111 *Top* HERBERT WELLER: **Repeat designs based upon the Columbine.** *Nature and Design*, n.d. (*c.* 1895).

This design is founded upon accurate plain drawings. The method of designing in this fashion has been taught in Britain since the 1850s.

2.112 *Above* CHRISTIAN STOLL: **Title-page of** *Moderne Blumen—Ornamentik,* n.d. (*c.* 1900).

This work was one of many collections of floral ornament published at the turn of the century. M. P. Verneuil's *Étude de la Plante* was probably the most comprehensive study of the subject.

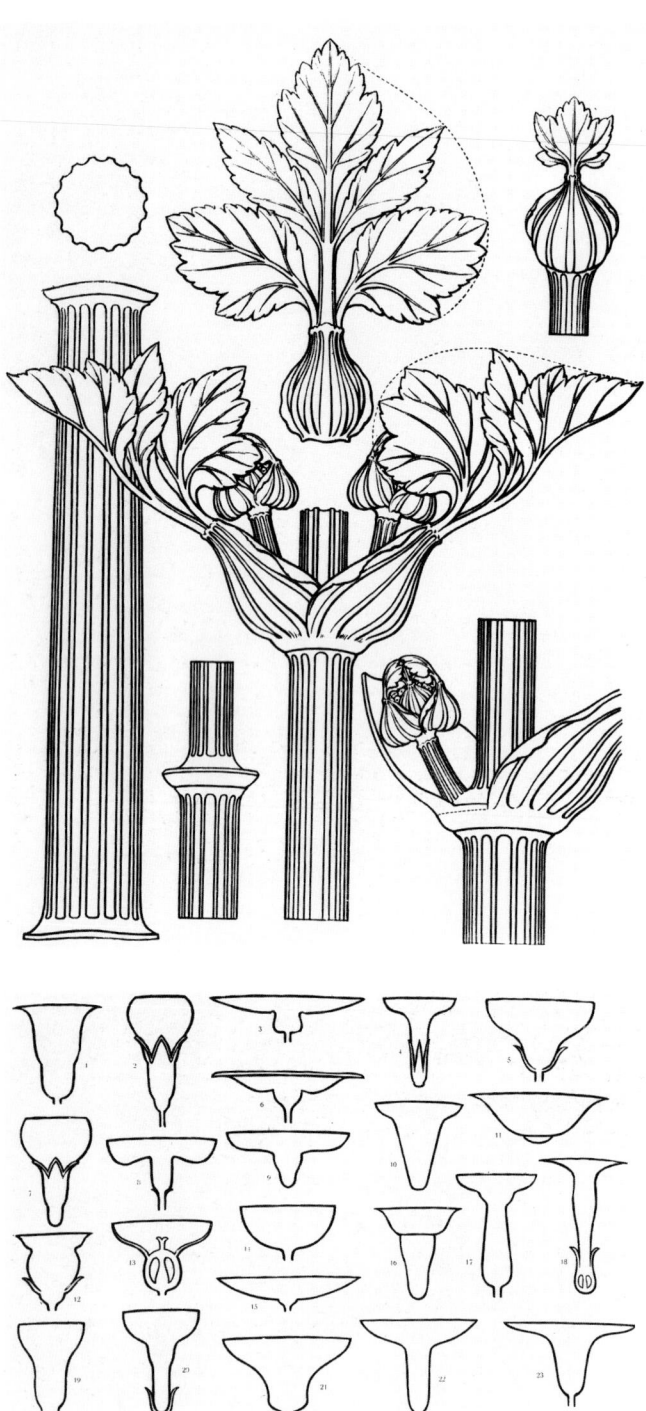

2.113 *Left* M. MEURER: **Analysis of the form of** *Smyrnium oliastrum.* *Pflanzenbilder Ornamental*, n.d. (*c.* 1910).

Like Dresser, Meurer stresses the architectural qualities of the plant.

2.115 *Below* LOUIS H. SULLIVAN: **Composition for modelled Ornament.** *A System of Architectural Ornament according with a philosophy of man's powers*, 1924.

The materials from which Sullivan created his ornament are essentially those of the nineteenth century and he is closer to Pugin, Colling and Dresser than would at first appear to be the case. However, his organization of decorative forms—like grand Beaux-Arts plans—is unmistakable.

2.114 M. MEURER: **Profiles of flowers.** *Pflanzenbilder ornamental*, *c.* 1910.

Meurer was the teacher of Karl Blossfeldt, the plant photographer (see Plate 2.118).

2.117 *Right* ANONYMOUS: **Fabric printing block.** From Allan Smith's *Fabric Printing*, 1953.

A design which has the quality of folk art. It is faintly reminiscent of William Morris' 'bird' textiles.

2.116 *Above* T. A. STEPHENSON: **Study in spirals.** *Seashore Life and Pattern*, 1944.

T. A. Stephenson was interested in marine life from a decorative as well as zoological point of view, and began painting seashore subjects in about 1911.

2.118 *Right* KARL BLOSSFELDT: **Early development of a plant.** Photograph. *Urformen der Kunst*, 1929.

Blossfeldt, like Meurer, his teacher, concentrated upon the architectural qualities of plants. He published a sequel to *Urformen der Kunst—Windergarten der Natur—*in 1932.

CHAPTER THREE
Geometrical Ornament

In most decorative design figurative and linear elements happily co-exist. However, this chapter is concerned with the development of specifically geometrical or mathematically generated ornament. It will be helpful first to look briefly at the evolution of geometry itself.

A reasonably advanced mathematical system is known to have existed in Mesopotamia, where multiplication tables and tables of squares dating from the time of Hammurabi (c. 1700 BC) have been found on baked earthenware tablets. The rudiments of geometry were also understood in Mesopotamia and were used in connection with land surveying. Greek tradition, however, attributed the invention of geometry to the Egyptians. The first true geometrical treatise was Euclid's *Elements*, which became known in Europe during the Middle Ages through an Arabic translation. Later, an understanding of Euclid was considered to be an essential part of a liberal education. Writing in 1773, the great Orientalist and jurist William Jones (1746–94)—a correspondent of Edmund Burke and Benjamin Franklin—declared that Euclid would reveal 'the principles of all natural knowledge' to the student.[1]

Both Egyptian and Greek ornament contain geometrical elements—the key-pattern, in some form or other, being the most obvious. But some of the earliest complex geometrical designs are found in ancient Rome. The Domus Augustana on the Palatine Hill, which was built by Domitian between AD 81 and 96, contains mosaic decorations based upon a grid of equilateral triangles which are combined to make an overall pattern of hexagons. K. A. C. Cresswell has drawn attention to the importance of this discovery.[2] Similar geometrical designs are found in Pompeii and in the Great Temple at Palmyra. Roman craftsmen were expert in setting out geometrical designs and were in possession of almost all the drawing instruments known to us, including dividers, proportional dividers, compasses and set squares. Even in a remote province such as Britain, mosaic floors of a fair degree of geometrical complexity are to be found. Samuel Lysons (1763–1819), the pioneer of Romano-British studies, illustrated the fine geometrical mosaic floors in the Roman villa at Woodchester.[3] Some of Owen Jones' designs for mosaics suggest an acquaintance with Lysons' work.

Cresswell has claimed that the full development of geometrical ornament belongs to the art of Islam. The prohibition on the representation of human and animal forms largely explains the concentration on purely geometrical ornament, but as Cresswell points out, the earliest Islamic geometrical decoration—to be seen in the window grilles in the Mosque of Ibn Tulun in Damascus (AD 879)—was based upon late Roman geometrical design. Islamic geometrical ornament was imitated in Europe as early as the thirteenth century, as Baltrušaitis has shown.[4] Mosaic pavements based on Islamic models have been found in Palermo and Pisa, and certain Islamic interlacing patterns are even to be seen in medieval English cathedrals. The shrine of St Dunstan at Canterbury, for instance, has diaper work at its base as well as an iron grille in the choir, both of which are apparently derived from an Islamic source.[5] Another striking example of Islamic influence is the Cosmati work floor of the Henry VII chapel in Westminster Abbey.

3.1 *Opposite* Edward B. Edwards: **All-over pattern based on mathematically generated spirals.** *Dynamarhythmic Design*, 1932.

With great skill, Edwards transforms spirals of the kind proposed by Hambidge into a complex all-over pattern.

The Hispano-Moresque and Mudejar traditions, too, furthered the development of geometrical ornament in Europe. In sixteenth-century Venice elaborate damascened arabesque ornament was produced by craftsmen from the Islamic world. The impact of Venetian-Saracenic work is reflected in some of the published decorative designs of such artists as Pellegrini (fl. 1530), Jean Gourmont (d. 1551) and Balthasar Sylvius (1515–80).[6]

Western geometrical decoration, by contrast to the intricate Islamic work, was far less complex. Walter Geddes' *Booke of Sundry Draughtes* (1615), intended for glaziers and plasterers, contains geometrical grids of only the very simplest type. But in 1704 a Carmelite priest, Father Sébastien Truchet, presented a paper to the Académie Royale des Sciences in Paris, describing a method of designing tile floors by permutation (see Plates 3.6 and 9). The method was simplicity itself. Square tiles were to be divided diagonally into two colours. Each tile could be rotated about an imaginary axis, thus producing four variant designs. Sixteen tiles arranged in a square—with four on each side, exactly in the manner of a child's box of pattern bricks—could produce an immense variety of designs. Large grids of tiles would produce a veritable infinity of designs. Truchet's ideas, however, appear to have made no impact on the practice of design and his book[7] has never been more than a mathematical curiosity.[2]

The language of descriptive geometry and the use of drawing instruments had been perfected, it should be mentioned, by the end of the eighteenth century, Gaspard Monge's *Geometrie Descriptive* (1795) being the key work. William Dyce, as we have seen, taught his students the practical geometry necessary for the design of ornament—how to construct simple grids, to be filled in with decorative motifs, how to divide and subdivide angles and the like. But his exercises do not constitute a real introduction to the study of geometrical decoration. His method is expounded in full detail in the *Drawing Book of the Government School of Design* of 1842–3 (see Plates 2.21–4; 3.10).

Owen Jones' and Jules Goury's *Plans, Elevations, Sections and Details of the Alhambra* (1834–45) with its magnificent chromolithographic plates of Moorish stucco and mosaic ornament undoubtedly helped to reawaken interest in geometrical decoration, particularly in Britain (see also Chapter Six). Girault de Prangey's two studies of the Alhambra and its decorations (the first published between 1836 and 1837 and the second in 1842), though less well known than Jones' and Goury's work, also helped to increase interest in the subject. A work by the German architect and antiquarian F. M. Hessemer, *Arabische und alt-Italienische Bau-verzierungen* ('Arabian and Early Italian Building Decorations'), also concentrated on geometrical decoration. It, too, is discussed in Chapter Six.

Owen Jones capitalized on his study of the ornament of the Alhambra with his *Designs for Mosaic and Tessellated Pavements* (1842). The book was published in order to advertise a process for making mosaic tiles which had been invented in 1840 by Richard Prosser of Birmingham. Prosser claimed that if flint and clay—the materials used for making porcelain—were compressed into a quarter of their original bulk, by means of an ingenious press, a satisfactory and inexpensive substitute for mosaic could be produced. Minton & Co. of Stoke-upon-Trent seem to have experimented with Prosser's process. Jones took full advantage of the complex and varied shapes that could be manufactured by this means. Some of his ten designs for floors are inspired by Roman geometrical models. One plate of a mosaic floor is adapted from an Islamic interlocking design while the final plate in *Tessellated Pavements*, though admittedly owing something to the decoration of the Alhambra, is a most original design which establishes Jones as one of the most accomplished designers in the geometrical idiom. The Print Room at the Victoria and Albert

3.2 GEORGE PHILLIPS: '**The application of the spot to decorative purposes.**' *Rudiments of Curvilinear Design* (1838–40).

Phillips was one of the earliest authorities to attempt to understand the phenomena of repeat pattern. He suggested that woven fabrics—when magnified—would serve as sources of inspiration for the making of patterns composed of spots.

Museum, London, possesses many examples of his geometrical designs.

David Ramsay Hay (1796–1866), a successful Edinburgh house-decorator who in his youth had been employed by Walter Scott in the decoration of Abbotsford, appears to have been influenced by the designs illustrated in Jones' *Alhambra*. Hay's *Original Geometric Diaper Designs* (1844)[8] contains a number of fairly complex geometric designs obviously inspired by Islamic originals (Plates 3.11–14). These designs, however, are not actually intended as decoration in themselves, but to serve as grids to contain or regulate ordinary floral ornament. Hay was an interesting figure who moved in Edinburgh's intellectual and scientific circles. His publications include works on the theory of proportion, as well as on colour theory; he assisted the great Clerk Maxwell in some of his experiments with colour.

Jules Bourgoin (1838–1907), one-time professor of ornament at the Ecole des Beaux-Arts in Paris, was the author of one of the most original studies of geometrical ornament, *Théorie de l'Ornement* (1873) (Plates 3.18–19). Bourgoin was a keen student of Islamic design and was fascinated by their complex geometrical patterns. He published two important books on the subject, *Les Arts Arabes* (1873) (Plate 3.17), and *Les Elements de l'Art Arabe* (1879) (Plate 3.21), which is probably still the most comprehensive study of its kind. However, Bourgoin went further than merely revising or paraphrasing the Islamic system of geometrical ornament. He appears to have been interested in the way in which plant cells are grouped together and to have applied this knowledge towards an understanding of tessellation. The cell theory, which dates from the late 1830s, would have been well known in cultivated circles in the 1870s.[9]

While D. R. Hay's and Bourgoin's essays in geometrical design were comparatively complex, a simple form of geometrical design was taught to young schoolchildren in Britain from the late 1880s. Such exercises were used widely by educationalists until they were replaced by a more imaginative programme of handwork teaching some time before the First World War.[10] Geometrical design was taught under the heading of 'hand-and-eye training'. This had first been suggested by Friedrich Froebel (1782–1852), whose ideas were well received in British educational circles. The introduction of hand-and-eye training can be seen as a response to the increasing pace of industrialization. Froebel believed that enthusiasm for work must be encouraged from early childhood, so that 'the hand should be no less dextrous, and the eye no less accurate, than the judgment is sure'. It is said that the American architect Frank Lloyd Wright played with Froebel blocks in his nursery. G. Ricks, a London School Inspector, was the first influential British exponent of Froebel's methods. He believed hand-and-eye training should 'take its place side by side with arithmetic, reading, writing and drawing'. In his *Hand-and-Eye Training* (1889) he demonstrated how children could make very simple geometrical designs with the aid of square grids (Plate 3.29). The intention was not so much to encourage artistic expression, but rather to develop the manipulative skills of children so that they would be equipped to cope with the world of industry.

Ricks' Froebel-inspired method was soon extended to teaching children brush-work. By dipping brushes into solutions of colour and then applying them to sheets of squared paper using various combinations of brush-strokes and intervals as directed by the teacher, an almost infinite variety of chequered patterns could be constructed. A class would produce identical patterns which varied only according to the neatness of the executant. Brush-work—as an aspect of hand-and-eye training—must have been widely taught to judge from the number of surviving textbooks that deal with the subject. E. C. Yeats' *Brush-Work* (1896) and *The Practical Teacher's Art Monthly* (1898–

3.3 ANONYMOUS: **Cut-out paper design.** From an album titled '100 Paper Cuts and Circles' given by the Textile Council to the Royal College of Art in the 1970s.

This is a design which achieves its effect through radiating symmetry. The design probably relates to the work of F. Cizek, whose ideas on paper cutting were published in *Papier—Schneide und Klebearbeiten* in Vienna in 1916. Cizek was a professor in the Kunstgewerbeschule des K. K. Oesterreichischen Museums für Kunst und Industrie. E. H. Gombrich in *The Sense of Order* (1979) illustrates two similar designs by pupils of Cizek.

1904) are typical. Both supply examples of simple pattern-making with brush-strokes.

In 1910 an ingenious work on mechanically produced design entitled *Multi-Epicycloidal and other Curves* was published by Edwin W. Alabone. Alabone used a machine described as 'an epicycloidal geometric chuck' (Plates 3.33–5) which was made by the firm of Holzapffel & Co.[11] The machine had an elaborate system of eccentrically mounted gears whereby a pen could be made to draw a continuous locus of great complexity and very considerable length; sometimes a design would take up to five hours to complete. Alabone's book, like Truchet's, remains a curiosity, although mechanically generated decoration of a not dissimilar type is used on banknotes in order to make counterfeiting more difficult. Holzapffel's machine was derived from his lathes, which are still used today by wood-turners.

Another delightful curiosity was *Projective Ornament* (1915) by the American Claude Bragdon—a great admirer, incidentally, of the ornamental system of the architect Louis Sullivan. Bragdon invoked the Fourth Dimension, from whence 'the decorative motifs of the new aesthetic may appropriately be sought'. More directly he based his ideas upon the 'magic squares' of the Swiss mathematician Leonhard Euler (1707–83). The 'magic square', which, it was once believed, could ward off evil or disease, was in fact brought to Italy from Byzantium in the fifteenth century. The magic square in Dürer's engraving *Melancholia* is almost certainly the best-known example.

This is the magic square of three:

8	1	6
3	5	7
4	9	2

The three numbers added together in the vertical columns or in the horizontal lines will produce 15. So, too, will the diagonal numbers. Similarly with all magic squares. The magic square of four is as follows:

9	7	14	4
6	12	1	15
3	13	8	10
16	2	11	5

The vertical horizontal and diagonal product is 34. Magic squares of five, six or seven would introduce more elaborate designs.

Bragdon's method of originating designs from magic squares is as simple as it is ingenious. All that is required is to trace the sequence of numbers in their boxes by a line—in either their ascending or descending order (Plate 3.41). Bragdon could have acquired all the knowledge he needed for his designs from a source no more recondite than the *Encyclopaedia Britannica* where, in the renowned ninth edition, there is an excellent account of magic squares.

Another American, Edward B. Edwards, was the author of *Dynamarhythmic Design* (1932), one of the most attractive and ingenious studies of geometrical ornament. Edwards was inspired by the teachings of Jay Hambidge, who asserted in *The Elements of Dynamic Symmetry* (1926) that the 'basic principles underlying the greatest art . . . may be found in the proportions of the human figure and in the growing plant'. Hambidge's 'Dynamic Symmetry' is a form of analysis of proportion based primarily on a study of Greek architecture and vases.[12] Edwards applied it to decorative design. His system made use of elegant curvilinear or straight-line spirals which are contained within rectangles of given proportions or ratios. He was particularly interested in the 1.618 rectangle—the 'Golden Mean' rectangle (Plate 3.4). Groupings of Edwards' spirals produce 'all-over' patterns which possess an

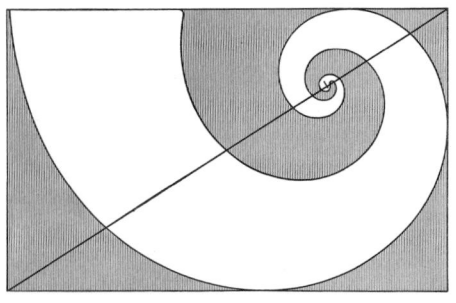

3.4 EDWARD B. EDWARDS: **1.618 rectangle (the Golden Mean rectangle) enclosing a spiral.** *Dynamarhythmic Design*, 1932.

Edwards met Jay Hambidge at Yale University in 1917 and began applying his 'Dynamic Symmetry' to decorative design. Although taken very seriously in their day, Hambidge's extremely ingenious theories have now fallen largely into abeyance.

ordered and satisfying complexity that is superficially reminiscent of Islamic geometrical design.

Some contemporary artists whose work has affinities with geometrical decoration deserve a mention here. The French artist François Morellet, a member of the Groupe de Recherche Visuel, produced in the late 1950s a number of art-works which, at first glance, could be mistaken for geometrical decoration (Plate 3.56). One of his preoccupations was to create works which depend for their effect upon the serendipitous geometrical forms brought about by the arbitrary superimposition of squared grids one upon another at different angles (Plate 3.57). Kenneth Martin, who abandoned figurative painting in the late 1940s, and who produced some of the earliest British mobile sculptures, has made drawings based upon arbitrary 'moves' within a squared grid (Plate 3.59). These are often close in their visual effect to the work of Bragdon, although Martin's work is of a more penetrating and philosophical nature. In 1972 the Arts Council of Great Britain mounted a major exhibition called 'Systems' which showed the work of a number of artists working in a manner which more or less corresponded with Kenneth Martin's.[13] Richard Allen, for example, played on the theme of mathematical variations (Plate 3.60).

Probably 'Systems' artists would assert that there was a clear distinction between their work and mere pattern-making, but the fact remains that the resemblances between many works of abstract art and ornament are of a more than superficial kind.

During the 1970s, when there was a good deal of interest in Islamic mysticism, several books were published which dealt with the arcane aspects of Islamic geometrical design. One such work was *The Language of Pattern. An inquiry inspired by Islamic Decoration* (1974).[14] The book, besides containing an analysis of Islamic geometrical design, gives examples (Plate 3.61) of new designs which bear a more than passing resemblance to the work of 'Systems' artists.

An impressive development in geometrical design was the Altair system, which was developed in the 1960s by a biologist, Ensor Holiday. Holiday took Islamic design as his starting point, but with the aid of a computer was able to draw regular grids of a complexity previously undreamed of (Plate 3.58). Holiday's designs were published in pads described as 'exciting pattern-sheets everyone can colour in'. Although Altair pads are especially popular with young children there is no doubt that Holiday's designs—with suitable colourways—could be used for ceramic tile decorations and carpet and fabric designs.

Geometrical ornament, however elaborate, must have a rational mathematical or geometrical origin. One may choose to impute arcane significance to geometrical patterns made by skilled craftsmen anxious to display their virtuosity—this has been particularly the case with Islamic work—but such interpretations are invariably made long after the creation of such ornament. As Holiday was one of the first to establish, the computer can now generate geometrical ornament of a baffling visual complexity. The computer has de-mystified geometrical design, but the eye may still enjoy unravelling its complexities.

3.5 A geometric pattern taken from drapery represented in a painted Attic vase in the British Museum. 6th–5th century BC. Archibald H. Christie, *Traditional Methods of Pattern Designing*, 1910.

Simple geometric patterns are of the greatest antiquity and can be found in prehistoric, ancient and primitive cultures.

3.6 *Left* FATHER SÉBASTIEN TRUCHET: **Permutations of tiles.** Father Dominique Douat, *Méthode pour faire une infinité de desseins differens*, 1722.

3.7 *Below* GEORGE PHILLIPS: **Neo-Classical foliage regulated by diagonals.** *Rudiments of Curvilinear Design* (1838–40).

Although simple geometry had always played an important part in regulating the design of all sorts of ornament, it was largely a matter of practice rather than of theory. Phillips' demonstration of the use of a diagonal is thus of particular interest.

3.9 *Above* FATHER SÉBASTIEN TRUCHET: **Tile panel composed of identical tiles divided diagonally.** Father Dominique Douat, *Méthode pour faire une infinité de desseins differens*, 1722.

A design using a grid of twenty-four by twenty-four identical diagonally divided tiles. The tiles were designated A, B, C and D according to their position, as if rotated about an imaginary axis. The number of variations theoretically possible with a grid of this size was almost infinite. Truchet, a Carmelite priest, appears to have been the earliest authority to have understood the importance of permutation in pattern designs.

3.8 *Left* LEONARDO DA VINCI: **Interlacing design based on a sketch in the *Codice Atlantico*.** Archibald H. Christie, *Traditional Methods of Pattern Designing*, 1910.

Leonardo would no doubt have seen examples of contemporary damascened work by Muslim craftsmen working in Venice.

3.10 *Left* WILLIAM DYCE: **Simple geometric design exercises.** *Drawing Book of the Government School of Design*, 1842–3.

Dyce was appointed Director of the Government School of Design—the earliest official British design teaching institution—in 1838. His *Drawing Book*, which stresses the importance of geometry, represents one of the earliest attempts to formulate a design teaching method. Dyce was strongly influenced by continental, in particular Prussian, ideas on design teaching. A painter himself, he considered ornamental design to be a half-mechanical activity—greatly inferior to fine art.

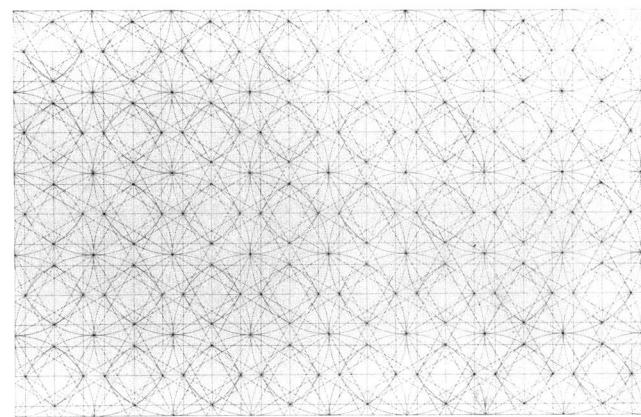

3.11 *Above right* DAVID RAMSAY HAY: **Design of intersecting grids.** *Original Geometric Diaper Designs*, 1844.

Hay was the Principal of a successful firm of Edinburgh decorators. He moved in Edinburgh's scientific and intellectual circles and published a number of works on the proportions of the human form, on vases and on colour harmony. From this design, it seems likely that Hay had studied Islamic geometric design.

3.12 *Right* DAVID RAMSAY HAY: **Design of intersecting grids.** *Original Geometric Diaper Designs*, 1844.

Viewed out of context this design appears to resemble certain twentieth-century geometrical designs. However, Hay's true intention was to devise new and more complex forms of repeat ornament.

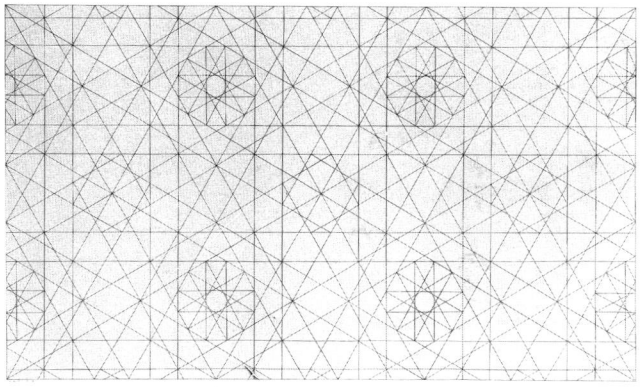

3.13 DAVID RAMSAY HAY: **Floral ornament arranged within a geometric grid.** *Original Geometric Diaper Designs*, 1844.

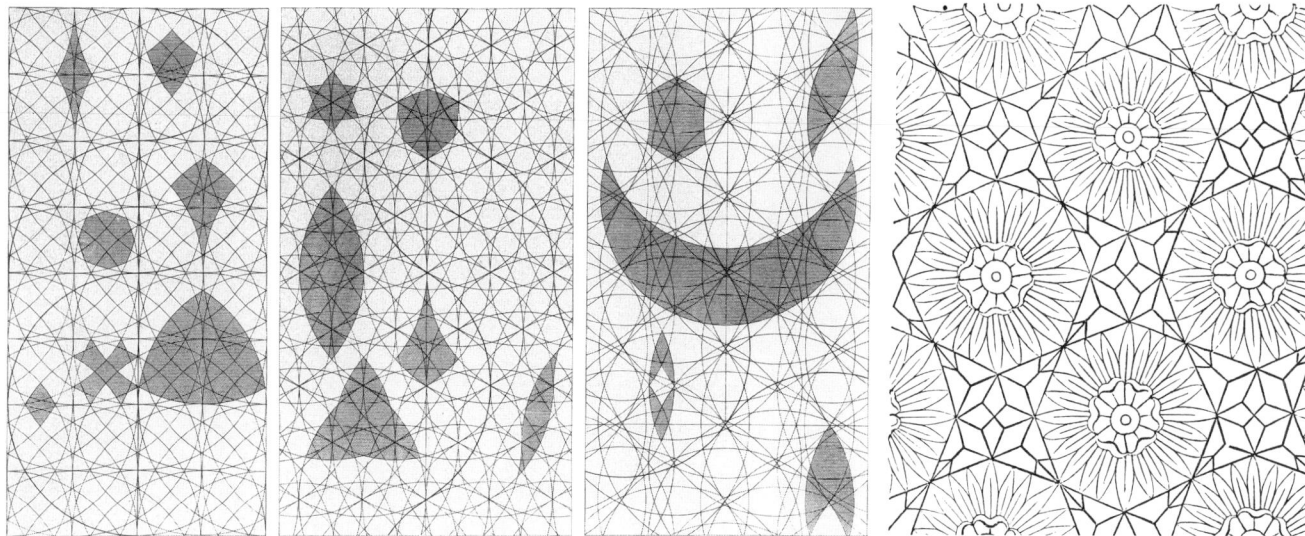

3.14 *Above* DAVID RAMSAY HAY: **Intersecting circles with configurations derived from these.** *Original Geometric Diaper Designs,* 1844.

Hay's discovery of agreeable decorative shapes (the shaded areas) within a grid of intersecting circles relates to his belief that all pleasing forms were governed by precise geometrical rules.

3.15 ANONYMOUS: **Example of design for printed muslin.** Richard Redgrave, *Manual of Design* (1876).

Redgrave's views on the teaching of design were very important in the period after the Great Exhibition of 1851. He was a keen champion of 'conventionalized', or non-naturalistic, design. 'Geometry . . . is the basis of symmetry,' he wrote, 'leading the way to those arrangements which best govern the general distribution of form.'

3.16 *Above* H. STEVENS: **Glass mosaic table-top.** *The Art-Journal Illustrated Catalogue. The Industry of All Nations, 1851,* 1851.

This design is apparently based upon Italian mosaic flooring of the kind to be seen in the Basilica of San Marco in Venice.

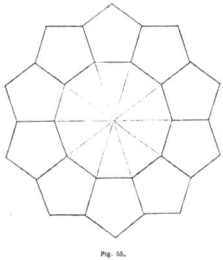

Fig. 55.

Cas particulier. — Décagone et pentagone (fig. 55).

On peut assembler 1 décagone et une couronne de 10 pentagones. L'angle du décagone étant égal à ⁸⁄₅, celui du pentagone à ⁶⁄₅, on a : ⁸⁄₅ + ⁶⁄₅ + ⁶⁄₅ = 4 droits.

On ne peut, avec ces figures, couvrir une surface illimitée.

3° *Polygones de trois formes.*

3.17 JULES BOURGOIN: **Analysis of Islamic geometric pattern.** *Les Arts Arabes,* 1873.

Bourgoin, an architect by training, was the first European authority to produce an analysis of Islamic geometrical decoration. He spent several years in Cairo collecting details of architecture and decoration for this book.

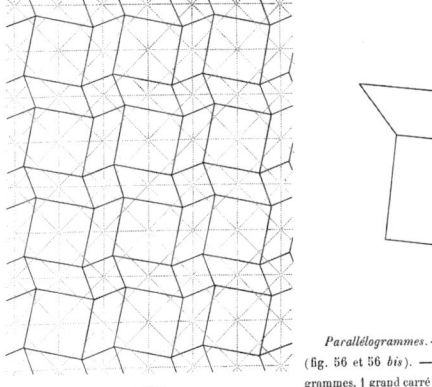

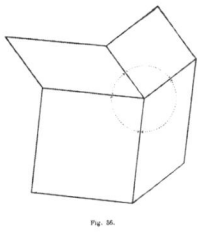

Fig. 56 bis.

Fig. 56.

Parallélogrammes. — Grand carré. — Petit carre (fig. 56 et 56 *bis*). — On peut assembler 2 parallélogrammes, 1 grand carré et 1 petit carré. — Les angles du parallélogramme, étant supplémentaires, valent 2 droits; en y ajoutant les angles droits du carré, on a 4 droits. — Les centres de figure déterminent un réseau quadrillé.

5

3.18 *Below* Jules Bourgoin: **The grouping of circles.** *Théorie de l'Ornement*, 1873.

Bourgoin's groups of circles—classified according to three types of agglomeration (see upper line)—suggest that he understood the cellular structure of plants.

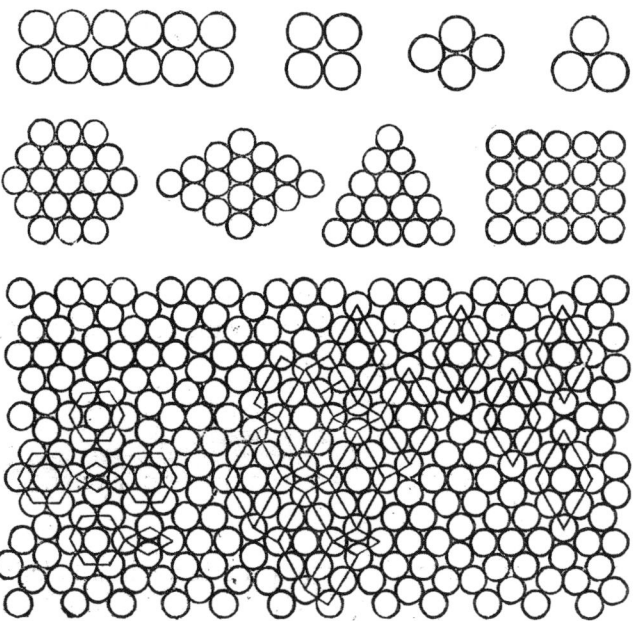

3.19 Jules Bourgoin: **Grouping of circles with geometric figures derived from their centres.** *Théorie de l'Ornement*, 1873.

Within this complex agglomeration of circles Bourgoin discovered a variety of geometric figures—squares, rectangles, lozenge shapes and hexagons. When joined they produce geometric ornament which is similar to simple Islamic work.

3.20 *Below* Archibald H. Christie: **Indian lattice design and its construction.** *Traditional Methods of Pattern Designing*, 1910.

Simple geometrical decoration in India dates back to the Mohenjo-Daro and Harappa civilizations of 1000 BC. Complex geometrical decoration is to be found on the base of a monument at Sarnath, near Benares, which dates from Buddhist times. This design, however, is clearly of Islamic origin.

3.21 Jules Bourgoin: **Analysis of Islamic geometric pattern.** *Les Elements de l'Art Arabe*, 1879.

This is a more complex pattern than the one shown in Plate 3.19. It is based on circles divided into twenty-four segments and subsidiary circles divided into eighteen segments. Designs of this degree of complexity require accurate drawing instruments for their setting out. Mathematical instruments in the form of celestial globes and astrolabes had been made in the Islamic world—notably in Persia—since the ninth century AD. They were greatly superior to instruments produced in Europe at the time.

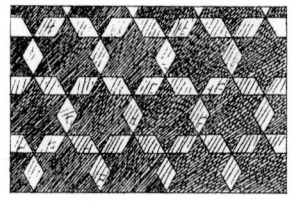

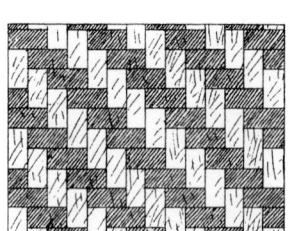

3.22 *Left* F. Edward Hulme: **Geometric tessellation.** *Principles of Ornamental Art* (1875).

These simple geometric patterns were mainly taken from medieval or Islamic sources. Hulme was a tireless collector of motifs and this book is among the most comprehensive of late nineteenth-century collections of design in black and white. He was also the author of a standard textbook on drawing instruments.

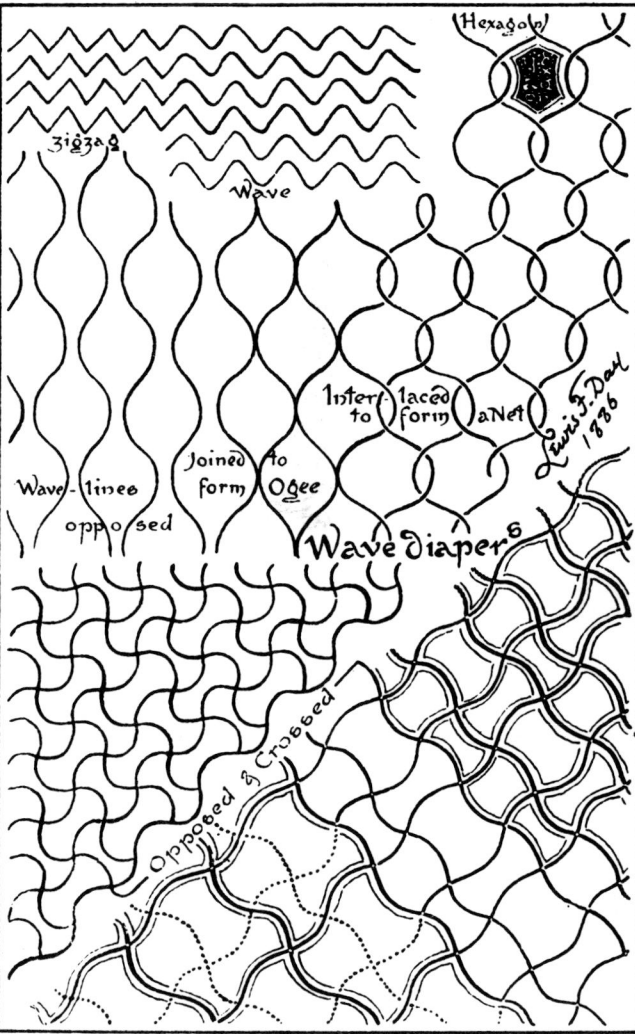

3.23 Lewis F. Day: **'Wave diapers'.** *Anatomy of Pattern*, 1898 (4th ed.). The plate is dated 1886.

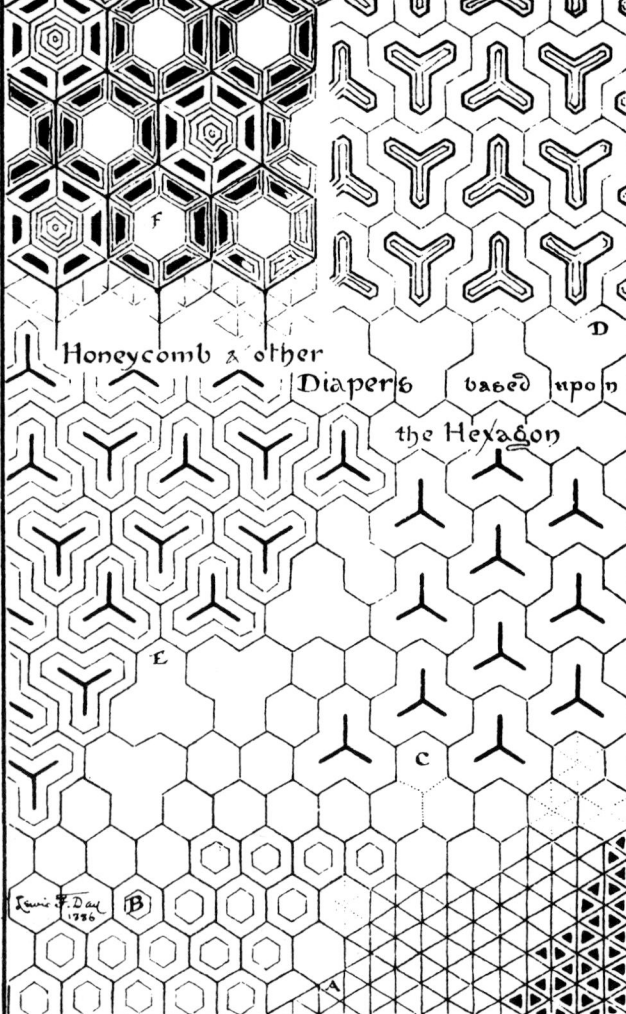

3.24 Lewis F. Day: **'Honeycomb and other diapers based upon the hexagon'.** *Anatomy of Pattern*, 1898 (4th ed.). The plate is dated 1886.

Like the majority of his contemporaries, Day was greatly influenced by Japanese geometrical and floral design, as this plate shows.

3.25 *Right* FRANK G. JACKSON: **Designs regulated by simple grids.** *Lessons on Decorative Design*, 1900.

This illustration shows how repeat patterns can be constructed with the aid of easily drawn grids. Jackson was the author of several manuals for schools.

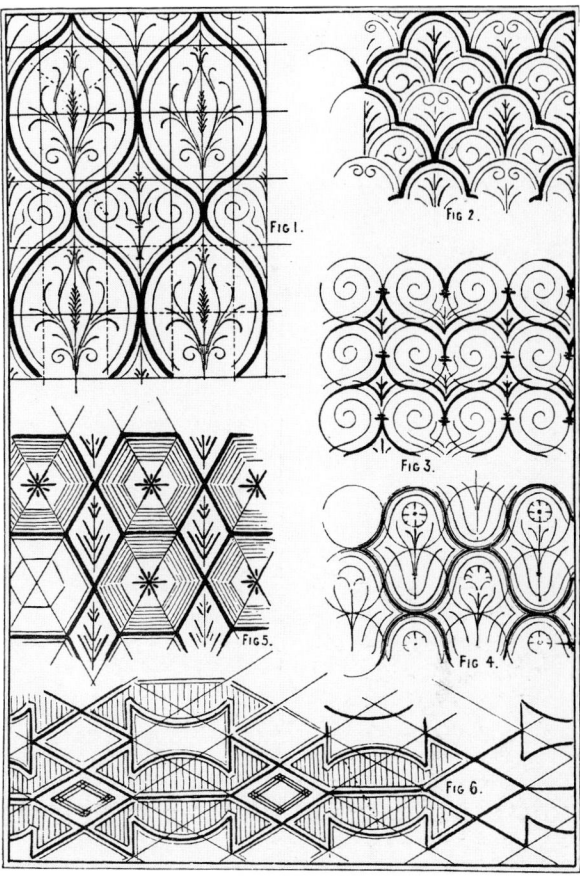

3.26 *Above* RICHARD GLAZIER: **Historic frets.** *Manual of Historic Ornament*, 1899.

Frets—geometrical interlacings—are the most important part of geometrical design.

3.27 *Right* LEWIS F. DAY: **'Diapers on the lines of intersecting circles'.** *Anatomy of Pattern*, 1898 (4th ed.). The plate is dated 1886.

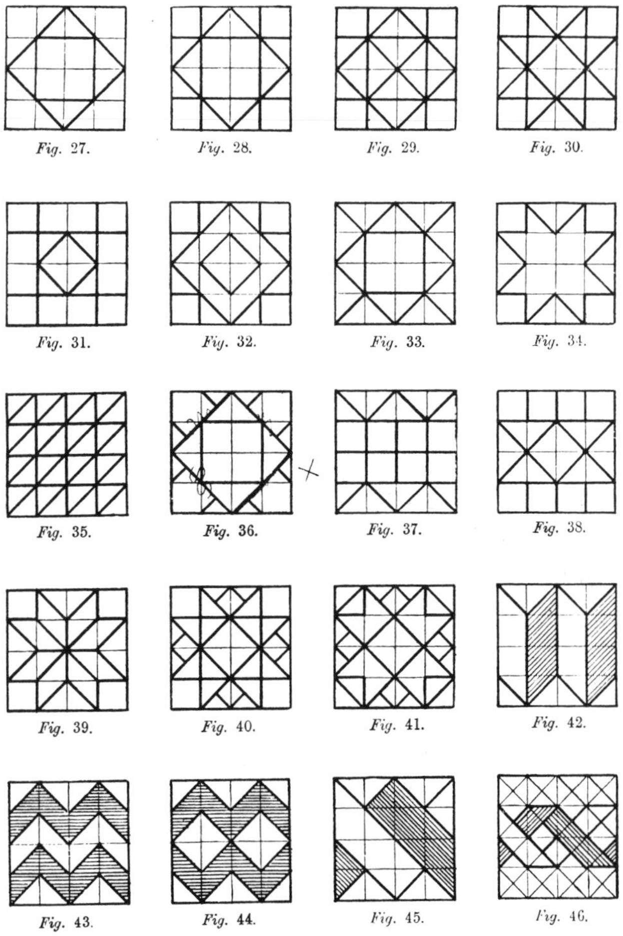

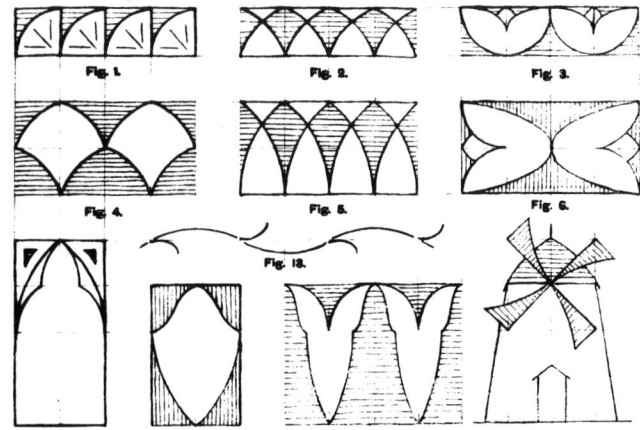

3.28 *Above left* GEORGE RICKS: **Simple drawing exercises on squared paper.** *Hand-and-Eye training*, 1889 (2nd ed.).

These simple exercises were intended primarily to encourage the manual co-ordination of children in the London Board Schools.

3.29 *Above* GEORGE RICKS and JOSEPH VAUGHAN: **Simple pattern making on squared paper.** *Hand-and-Eye training. Being a development of the Kindergarten occupations for junior and senior students*, 1894 (2nd ed.).

3.30 *Above* ANONYMOUS: **Industrial drawing, Stage II.** *The Practical Teacher's Art Monthly*, October 1898.

Designs such as this were drawn by the teacher on the blackboard and copied—as closely as their skills allowed—by the pupils. The importance of geometry in the designing of simple motifs is clearly shown.

3.33 *Right* **Alabone with his 'epicycloidal geometric chuck',
manufactured by Holzapffel & Co.** Photograph: Edwin W.
Alabone, *Multi-Epicycloidal and other Geometric Curves*
(1910).

Alabone, a Highbury doctor specializing in the cure of
tuberculosis, belonged to the Victorian tradition of the scientific
amateur. His costly machine, with its interchangeable gears, was
able to trace complex locii with the aid of a pen of the kind used
in barometers or seismographs. The descendants of the various
Victorian machines for drawing patterns—now produced in
plastic—are enjoyed by children today.

3.34 *Above* **Design drawn by Alabone's 'epicycloidal
geometric chuck'.** Edwin W. Alabone, *Multi-Epicycloidal and
other Geometric Curves* (1910).

This design must have involved at least five separate operations.

3.31 and **3.32** *Opposite far left and left* Denman W. Ross:
Arrangement of simple outlines. *A Theory of Pure Design*,
1907.

Ross's study of the phenomena of design antedated
Kandinsky's, or Kupka's, early experiments with abstract
painting as well as the development of the Gestalt theory of
perception. Ross was lecturing on these lines as early as 1901, for
E. A. Batchelder in his *Principles of Design* (1904) mentions
having assisted him at this date.

3.35 *Above* **Design drawn by Alabone's 'epicycloidal
geometric chuck'.** Edwin W. Alabone, *Multi-Epicycloidal and
other Geometric Curves* (1910).

This continuous locus design is of fairly considerable complexity
and could take up to five hours to complete.

3.36 *Left* UGO ZOVETTI: **Bookplate.** A. S. Levetus, 'The Imperial Arts and Crafts Schools, Vienna', *The Studio*, January 1907.

Zovetti, who came from Dalmatia, was a pupil of Koloman Moser, one of the leading Viennese graphic designers. Moser taught at the important Kunstgewerbeschule. Like Otto Wagner, Josef Hoffmann and Josef Maria Olbrich, he had a great enthusiasm for design governed by geometry. This modest bookplate epitomizes contemporary Viennese fondness for bold, simple design.

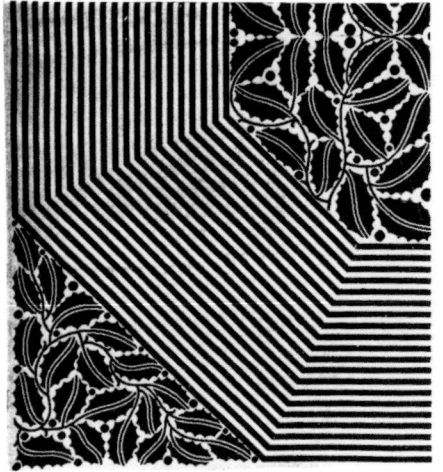 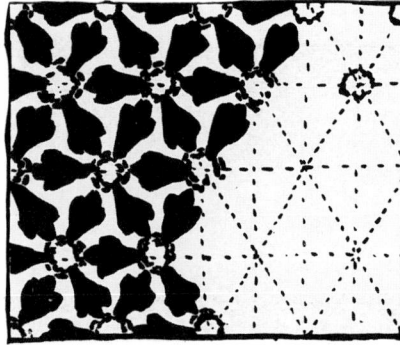 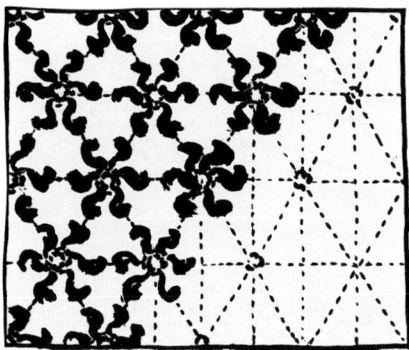

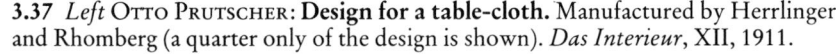

3.37 *Left* OTTO PRUTSCHER: **Design for a table-cloth.** Manufactured by Herrlinger and Rhomberg (a quarter only of the design is shown). *Das Interieur*, XII, 1911.

Prutscher, a leading Viennese architect and designer, combines stylized leaf-motifs and stripes arranged in an octagonal form with considerable skill.

3.38 *Above* GASTON QUENIOUX: **All-over patterns based on simple grids.** *Elements de Composition Décorative*, 1912.

Quenioux, with Eugène Grasset and M. P. Verneuil, was one of the leading French teachers of ornament in the early twentieth century. Here are illustrated two exercises calling for no great dexterity. The clear geometrical structure of the grids gives the roughly executed motifs an authority they would otherwise lack.

3.39 *Left* GASTON QUENIOUX: **Exercise in composition within a circle.** *Elements de Composition Décorative*, 1912.

Circular compositions are of particular importance in ceramic decoration. The elements in this design—little more than blots—are organized within a circle divided into twelve equal segments.

PATTERNS FROM EULER'S KNIGHTS-MOVE SQUARES

MAGIC LINES IN MAGIC SQUARES

8	1	6
3	5	7
4	9	2

MAGIC SQUARE OF 3

9	7	14	4
6	12	1	15
3	13	8	10
16	2	11	5

MAGIC SQUARE OF 4

30	39	48	1	10	19	28
38	47	7	9	18	27	29
46	6	8	17	26	35	37
5	14	16	25	34	36	45
13	15	24	33	42	44	4
21	23	32	41	43	3	12
22	31	40	49	2	11	20

MAGIC SQUARE OF 7

47	10	23	64	49	2	59	6
22	63	48	9	60	5	50	3
11	46	61	24	1	52	7	58
62	21	12	45	8	57	4	51
19	31	25	40	13	44	53	30
26	39	20	33	56	29	14	43
35	18	37	28	41	16	31	54
38	47	34	17	32	55	42	15

CHESS-BOARD PATH OF KNIGHT

THE MAGIC LINE IN A MAGIC SQUARE IS DISCOVERED BY TRACING THE NUMERALS IN THEIR ORDER FROM CELL TO CELL, AND BACK TO THE BEGINNING NUMBER

MAGIC LINE OF 3

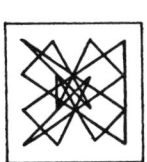

MAGIC LINE OF 4

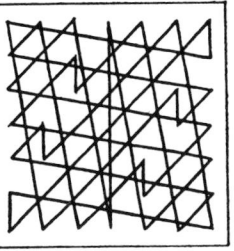

MAGIC LINE OF 7

THE "KNIGHT'S" TOUR

3.40 *Above left* CLAUDE BRAGDON: **'Pattern from Euler's knights' move squares'.** *Projective Ornament*, 1915.

These two motifs bear a resemblance to Celtic knotwork of the kind found on Irish crosses or illuminated manuscripts.

3.41 *Above* CLAUDE BRAGDON: **Magic squares.** *Projective Ornament*, 1915.

Although 'magic squares' are of considerable antiquity Bragdon seems to have been the first to realize that they had any potential as decoration.

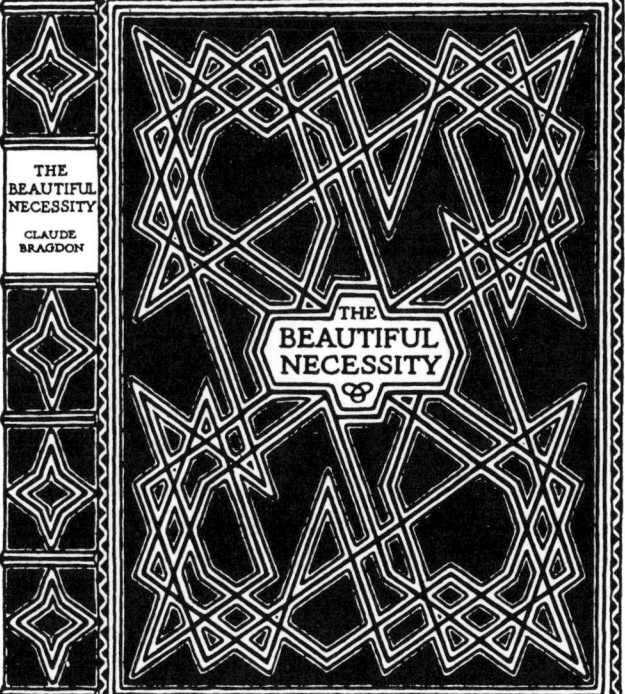

THE BEAUTIFUL NECESSITY

CLAUDE BRAGDON

THE BEAUTIFUL NECESSITY

3.42 CLAUDE BRAGDON: **Design for book-cover based on Euler's 'knight's move' squares.** *Projective Ornament*, 1915.

Das geradlinige Ornament.

1. Der Punkt und die Gerade.

Der Punkt · alleinstehend

Zwei Punkte : vertikal übereinander gestellt   Zwei Punkte ·· horizontal nebeneinander gestellt   Zwei Punkte ·˙ schräg zueinander gestellt

Die Gerade | in Vertikalstellung   Die Gerade — in Horizontalstellung

Zwei Gerade ✕ ✕ ✕ in schräger Lage sich schneidend

Zwei Gerade ┼ ┰ ┤ ┣ ┼ ┌┘ ┐┖ im rechten Winkel sich schneidend

Das Bandornament.

Durch verschiedenartige Aneinanderreihung dieser Geraden, verbunden mit Punkten in verschiedenen Lagen, entstehen seitwärtsstrebende oder auf- und abstrebende Band-ornamente oder Bandmuster.

Punkte

Gerade

Punkte und Gerade

Als weitere Übung reihe man eine beliebig gebrochene Linie, wie nebenstehend, mit kleinen

Es folgen hier noch einige Beispiele von Bandmustern, die auf Grund der bisher besprochenen Möglichkeiten entstanden sind.

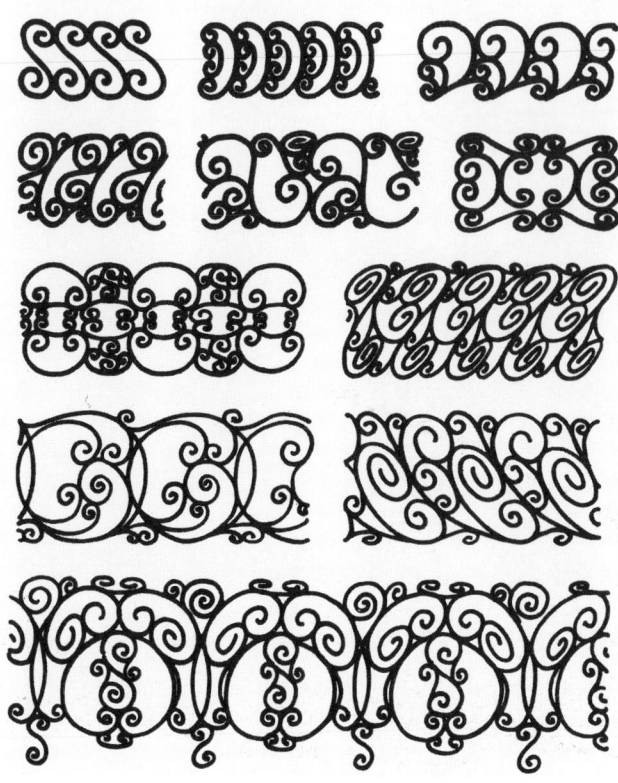

3.43 *Above left* PAUL DOLEZEL EZEL: **The combination of simple elements.** *Elementare Entwicklung des Ornaments*, n.d. (*c.* 1920).

Ezel demonstrates how combinations of straight lines and spots can produce an endless variety of border ornament.

3.44 *Above* PAUL DOLEZEL EZEL: **The arrangement of curvilinear elements.** *Elementare Entwicklung des Ornaments*, n.d. (*c.* 1920).

The simplest calligraphic element can be transformed by ingenious geometrical arrangement and/or repetition into pleasant decoration.

3.45 JOSEPH GAUTHIER: **Exercises in the combination of simple devices.** *Douze Leçons de Composition Décorative*, 1920.

Gauthier, like Ezel, demonstrates in these exercises how the fundamental geometric shapes can be combined and recombined to produce an endless variety of ornament.

3.47 *Right* EDWARD B. EDWARDS: **All-over design based upon rectangles.** *Dynamarhythmic Design*, 1932.

This is one of the few examples of European geometric design to rival Islamic work in complexity.

3.46 *Below* CLARENCE PEARSON HORNUNG: **Variant lattice designs.** *Handbook of Designs and Devices*, 1932.

Hornung was a designer who had a particular interest in trade marks. This led him to collect easily perceived motifs and patterns. Many of his devices were taken from Japanese sources.

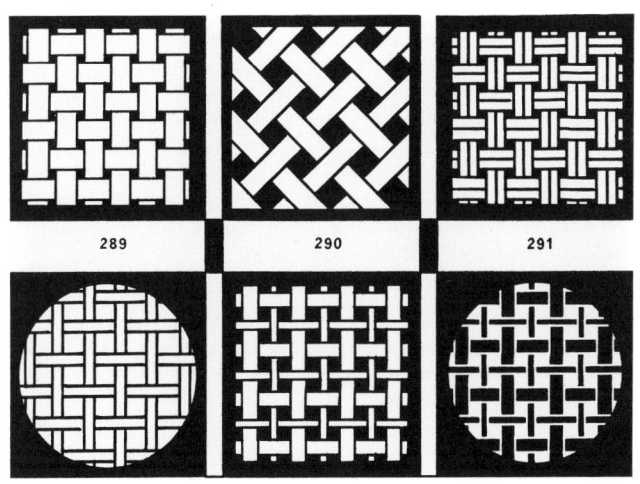

3.48, 3.49, 3.50 *Left and above* CLARENCE PEARSON HORNUNG: **Hexagonal and interlaced designs.** *Handbook of Designs and Devices*, 1932.

The designs on the left were largely based on snow crystals. The earliest study of the subject seems to have been that of Father Donato Rossetti, published in Turin in 1688. J. Glaisher's well-illustrated article on snow crystals as sources for designers appeared in the *Art Journal* in 1857.

The Circle

Some combinations.

3.51 BERNARD SLEIGH: **Circles and combinations of circles.** *A Handbook of Elementary Design*, 1934.

Sleigh's simplified designs belong in spirit to the Arts and Crafts tradition in its immediate pre-1914 war and post-war phases.

3.52 *Below left* ANONYMOUS: **All-over patterns and borders.** *Dryad Handicraft Instruction Leaflet No. 17. Pattern-Making with Simple Shapes* (this edition *c.* 1943).

The idea that everyone could create art—albeit simple art—was an important part of the teachings of the Arts and Crafts Movement. This illustration indicates how pleasing even the simplest regular groupings of geometric shapes can be.

3.53 *Below* ALAN SMITH: **All-over patterns produced by different arrangements of the same block.** *Fabric Printing*, 1953.

Many books of the kind from which this illustration is taken were published. By the 1950s, however, pattern-making was becoming less important in art and design education. It was being superseded by 'basic design' which was believed to develop a student's creative faculty more efficiently.

SQUARES

LEAF SHAPES

TRIANGLES

TRIANGLES AND CIRCLES

UNIT

3.54 *Below* RICHARD LANE: **'A student exercise square lattices, circular elements . . .' 1963.** *ULM 12/13. Zeitschrift der Hochschule für Gestaltung*, March 1965.

This design is composed of circles of three sizes. When viewed at an appropriate distance a tilted square—itself subdivided—will be seen within the large square. This design appeared as an illustration to William S. Huff's article 'An Argument For Basic Design'. Huff was particularly interested in Gestalt theory.

3.55 *Above* FRED WATTS, PETER HOTZ, RICHARD LANE: **Student exercises. 'Parquet deformations'**, 1961–3. *ULM 12/13. Zeitschrift der Hochschule für Gestaltung*, March 1965.

These exercises are reminiscent of Bauhaus methods, in which simple tessellated shapes are transformed sequentially, by deformation, into more complex forms.

3.56 *Left* FRANÇOIS MORELLET: **Random design of isosceles triangles.** *Morellet, Membre du Groupe deRecherche d'Art Visuel*, Catalogue of an Exhibition held at the Galerie Denise René, Paris, 1967.

This design is based upon a fixed grid of triangles. Numbers are taken randomly from a telephone directory—those ending with an even number are represented by a black triangle, those ending with an odd number by a white triangle. Morellet appears to be the earliest artist to have experimented with randomness in this way.

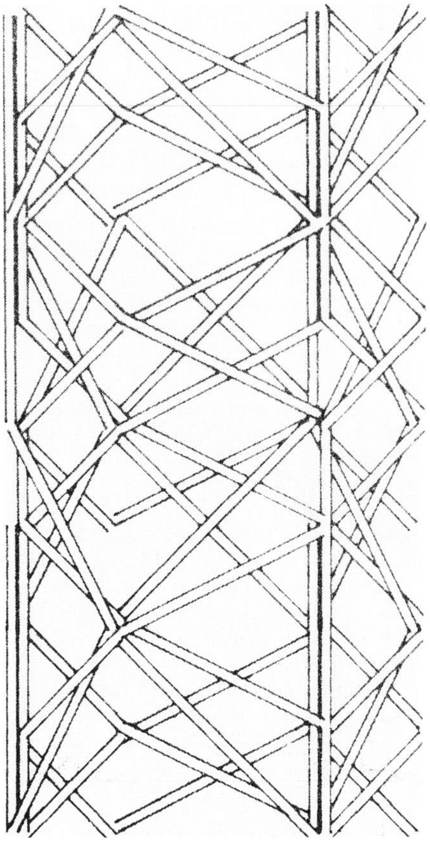

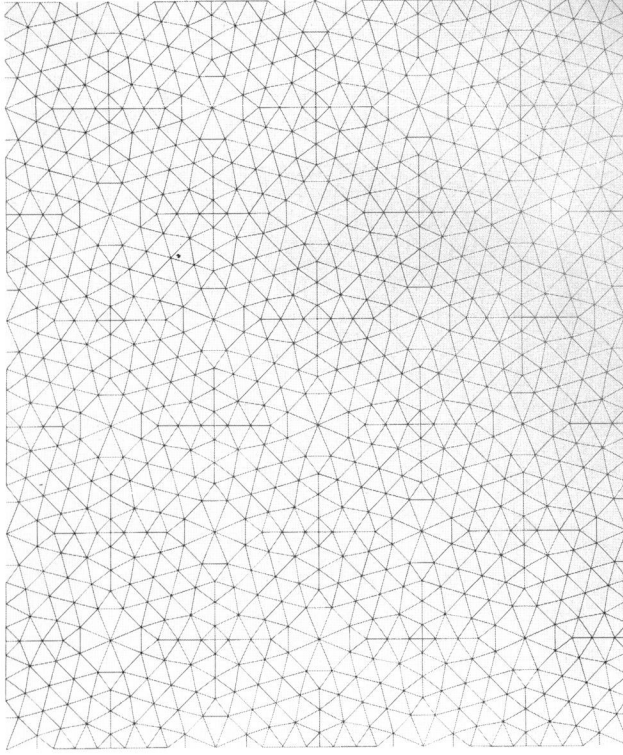

3.57 *Top left* FRANÇOIS MORELLET: **Design of two differently aligned grids.** *Morellet, Membre du Groupe de Recherche d'Art Visuel*, Catalogue of an Exhibition held at the Galerie Denise René, Paris, 1967.

Two superimposed grids are intentionally misaligned by two or three degrees from the right angle and the accidental distortions thus induced make this one of the most subtle and puzzling of Op Art works.

3.58 *Left* ENSOR HOLIDAY: **An Altair geometric design.** *Altair Design Pad 1*, 1970.

The designs of Holiday, a biologist, derive from Islamic geometrical decoration and are intended primarily for children.

3.61 KEITH ALBARN, JENNY MIALL SMITH, STANFORD STEELE and DINAH WALKER: **Permutations based on triangles, squares, pentagons and seven and eight-sided figures.** *The Language of Pattern*, 1974.

The authors—all of whom are designers——have made a detailed study of the mathematics of Islamic geometrical design and architecture.

3.59 *Opposite above* KENNETH MARTIN: **From a sequence of Nine Chance and Order Drawings**, 1974. *Kenneth Martin. Drawings and Prints. An Arts Council 'Working Methods' Exhibition*, 1977.

Martin is interested in the visual interpretation of the effects of chance.

3.60 *Opposite* RICHARD ALLEN: **'Three sets, eighteen variations'.** Drawing. *Systems*, Catalogue of an Arts Council Travelling Exhibition, 1972–3.

Allen is here demonstrating the effect of 'variations' of sequences of six double-square tiles which have been divided diagonally into black and white halves.

3.62 VALERIE JAUDON: **'Yazoo City'.** Painting, 1975. *Dekor.* Catalogue of an Exhibition shown at the Mannheimer Kunstverien, Mannheim, the Amerika Haus, Berlin, and the Museum of Modern Art, Oxford, 1980.

This geometrical painting is intentionally decorative in its effect. The resemblance to an Islamic geometric design is largely superficial.

Chapter Four

The Gothic Revival

Classicism died in the nineteenth century, killed, said Thackeray, by Romanticism. The truth is not so simple. But the Romantic Movement's discovery of the Middle Ages did have the most profound influence upon all the arts. The simple faith and pageantry of the Middle Ages were immeasurably more attractive to moralist and aesthete alike than the high commerce and materialism of the nineteenth century.

The idealized view of the Middle Ages is a comparatively recent one. Vasari, in his *Lives* of 1550, called Gothic architecture 'monstrous'. It had contaminated Europe. As Renaissance ideals spread the cathedrals of the Middle Ages came to seem alien. Redolent of superstition, Gothic was no style for the Age of Reason. It lay beyond the pale of good taste. In his *Cyclopaedia* of 1727, Ephraim Chambers defined Gothic as 'that which deviates from the proportions, characters etc. of the antique'. A Greek building, declared Chambers, has not a single ornament that does not enhance the whole—'everything is simple, measured and restrained'. A Gothic building was characterized by an 'abundance of little, whimsical, impertinent ornaments'.

Ruins, menacing landscapes and cataclysms became part of the literary paraphernalia of Gothicism. It is no coincidence that Horace Walpole (1717–97), author of *The Castle of Otranto* (1765)—the first Gothic novel—also built Strawberry Hill, which became the most renowned Gothic house in Europe. Walpole's Gothic has been derided for its tinselly theatricality, but the fame that Strawberry Hill brought him encouraged many landowners to build in the Gothic manner.

Walpole and his friends—his 'Committee of Taste'—went to some trouble to achieve a degree of authenticity in the Gothicizing of Strawberry Hill. Sir William Dugdale's *History of St Paul's Cathedral* (1716), with its engravings of the medieval St Paul's, served as a useful reference. Another valuable source was Batty and Thomas Langley's *Gothic Architecture, improved by Rules and Proportions* (1747). The title is all-revealing, for the Langleys sought no less than to tame and re-model Gothic on Vitruvian lines. They even tried to establish five Gothic Orders. Such effrontery has offended later authorities, but the Langleys' efforts were nonetheless a triumph of ingenuity. The book demonstrates, above all else, the all-pervading power of Classicism. For all its alleged deficiencies, this was the first Gothic pattern-book.

Interest in the Middle Ages was an inevitable accompaniment to the awakening of the Romantic spirit, with its search for the picturesque. At the end of the eighteenth century, William Beckford (1760–1844), who was rich enough to indulge his wildest fantasies, built a medieval abbey on Salisbury Plain—the ill-fated Fonthill. Fonthill Abbey outdid Strawberry Hill, not only in its vast scale, but also in the correctness of its architectural features. James Wyatt, Beckford's architect, took particular pride in his antiquarian knowledge. But Fonthill quickly crumbled and was remembered only as the folly of a megalomaniac and not entirely lovable eccentric.

The progress of the Gothic Revival went hand-in-hand with the development of a tradition of Gothic archaeology. The first Gothic architect-

4.1 *Opposite* John Ruskin: **Details from the West Gate at Rouen. Intersectional mouldings.** *The Seven Lamps of Architecture*, 1883 edition.

'The exhibition of technical dexterity, in work of this kind, is often marvellous, the strangest possible shapes of sections being calculated to a hair's breadth . . .'

antiquarian of importance was John Carter (1748–1817), a passionate believer in the value of ancient monuments, who began publishing his *Specimens of the Ancient Sculpture and Painting now remaining in this Kingdom* in 1780. An efficient, if unprepossessing draughtsman, Carter had been employed from 1774 by the *Builder's Magazine*. He later made drawings for the Society of Antiquaries, and he engraved his own illustrations for his publications. For the decorated frontispiece of the first of the two volumes of *Specimens* he engraved a scene of medieval splendour—a romantic composition of Piranesi-like complexity (Plate 4.8). The frontispiece of the second volume (Plate 4.9) is more significant. An abbot is shown refusing to surrender his abbey during the time of Henry VIII. The abbot and his monks become 'the miserable spectators of sacrilege' as armed men deface statues and paintings. Much later, A. W. Pugin was to say: 'Everything glorious about the English churches is Catholic, everything debased and hideous, Protestant.' Pugin generously praised Carter for his efforts to prevent the mutilation of ancient monuments. Through his zeal Carter gave new impetus to the Gothic Revival.

Among other early architect-antiquarians interested in medieval architecture was James Cavanah Murphy, an Irishman. In 1795, he published a fine folio volume on the medieval church at Batalha, in Portugal—the first work devoted entirely to the architecture of a single Gothic building (see Plate 4.10). Murphy was equally interested in Moorish buildings, as his *Arabian Antiquities of Spain* (1813–16) testifies, and was not so committed to the revival of the Gothic as Carter. Also in 1795, Joseph Halfpenny published *Gothic Ornaments in the Cathedral Church of York* (see Plate 4.12). Halfpenny was clerk of the works to John Carr, the architect responsible for the restoration of York Minster. Like Murphy's book, *Gothic Ornaments* is mainly noteworthy as a curiosity from an early stage in the development of the Gothic Revival.

The first standard work on Gothic was Thomas Rickman's *An Attempt to Discriminate the Styles of Architecture in England* (1817), which referred to over three thousand buildings. His book, not too greatly changed, remained in print for well over sixty years. Rickman's division of the Gothic into its various developmental phases—Norman, Early English, Decorated and Perpendicular—had an enormous influence on both architects and historians. Another important antiquarian who helped further the cause of Gothic by supplying good and copious illustrations was John Britton, whose *Architectural Antiquities of Great Britain* came out in forty parts between 1807 and 1826.

Gothic archaeology was becoming progressively more scientific. Augustus Charles Pugin (1762–1832), father of A. W. Pugin, was responsible for several books which contain measured drawings of medieval buildings. *Specimens of Gothic Architecture* (1821–3) was the earliest of such works. The elder Pugin's drawings far surpass in accuracy any which had been published previously. As a boy, A. W. Pugin assisted his father—he could have had no better training in Gothic design.

The young Pugin developed an enthusiasm for Gothic architecture which transcended mere antiquarianism. Gothic architecture and the restoration of England to the Roman Catholic faith became passionate causes. In 1836, when he was twenty-four, he published *Contrasts* (Plate 4.14). Here, not without wit, he contrasts contemporary architecture with that of the Middle Ages. Besides caricaturing flabby Neo-classicism, Pugin also attacked modern society. He was entirely disenchanted with his own times.

The intense and occasionally bigoted Catholic fervour of *Contrasts* makes it a difficult book for us to take entirely seriously. Nevertheless, it remains one of the most compelling examples of architectural propaganda. In 1844 Pugin produced another book which also had a great deal of influence,

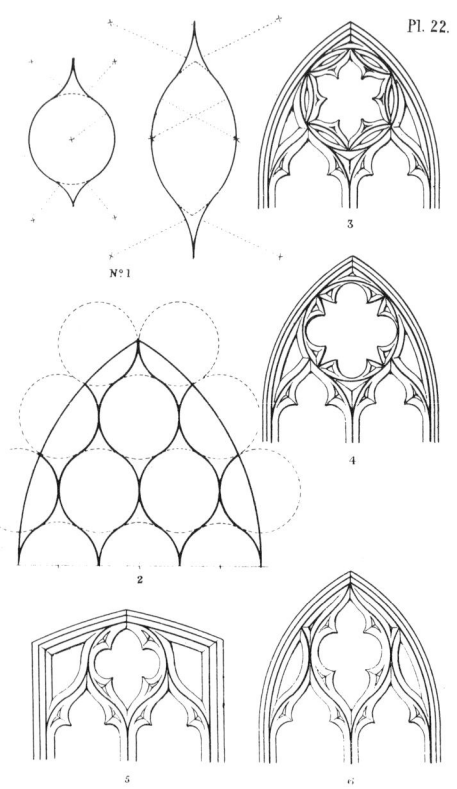

Pl. 22.

4.2 Edward A. Freeman: **Geometrical and reticulated tracery from St Cross, Everdon and Rothersthorpe, Northants.** *An Essay on the Origin and Development of Window Tracery in England*, 1851.

Freeman, an amateur, was the author of a *History of Architecture* and the *Architecture of Llandaff Cathedral*. His modestly produced handbook contains nearly four hundred diagrams of tracery of different periods and varying complexity. The architect R. W. Billing's *The Power of Form applied to Geometric Tracery*, also published in 1851, was a comparable work.

not as a tract but as a pattern-book. This was his *Glossary of Ecclesiastical Ornament* which supplied architect and cleric alike with a dazzling selection of archaeologically correct Gothic ornament. It was among the earliest of British books to be lithographed in colour and ran into several editions. Pugin's second pattern-book, *Floriated Ornament* (1849), contains ornaments derived from familiar plants and is considered in Chapter Two.

Pugin was the most accomplished designer of Gothic ornament of his generation. He designed wallpaper (Plate 4.20) and tiles (Plate 4.21) as well as ecclesiastical and secular architectural ornament in the Gothic style. Working in collaboration with him was another fervent Roman Catholic, John Hardman (1811–67), whose firm Hardman & Co. produced 'medieval' ecclesiastical and domestic plate to designs by Pugin. Hardman and his partner William Powell also produced work for the Gothic Revival architect and designer William Burges (1827–81), some of whose designs verge on the fantastical (see Plate 4.43).

The most prolific of all Gothic Revivalists, George Gilbert Scott (1811–78), exhibited even excessive boldness in his additions and restorations of medieval buildings (see Plate 29). Scott also designed the Albert Memorial in London with its Gothic gabled canopy and pinnacle encasing the serene figure of Prince Albert. Bruce Talbert (1838–81) produced detailed drawings for the gates of the Memorial from Scott's designs but later abandoned Gothic in favour of the modish Queen Ann style. However, his book *Gothic Forms* (1867) had considerable influence on designers of the day (Plate 4.46). It was dedicated to a most important Gothic architect, George Edmund Street (1824–81), the architectural mentor of Philip Webb and William Morris. Talbert exploited the market for Gothic furniture and ornament which had been largely created by the popular Medieval Court (Plate 4.35) at the Great Exhibition of 1851 and its successor the International Exhibition of 1862. His Gothic furniture has something of the overstated and even aggressive quality of William Butterfield's designs. Butterfield (1814–1900), a High-Church Gothic Revivalist, believed in making his designs robustly practical.

Pugin's propaganda was too much associated with Roman Catholicism for Protestant Britain. John Ruskin, on the other hand, was the ideal Protestant champion of the Gothic. He saw architecture as the measure of a nation's moral development. The 'Lamps' in his *Seven Lamps of Architecture* (1849), the first of his two great books on architecture, are: Sacrifice, Truth, Power, Beauty, Life, Memory and Obedience. These could almost serve as headings for a sermon. Ruskin insists upon the superiority of hand-work over machine-work, 'to those who love Architecture, the life and accent of the hand are everything', and stresses the importance of individual expression (see Plates 4.24–9). Here, in seminal form, is the philosophy of the Arts and Crafts Movement.

In *The Stones of Venice* (1852–3) Ruskin pursues his theme of the liberty of the workman and extols the virtues of Gothic architecture at the expense of the Venetian Renaissance, which he sees as born out of corruption. In the chapter 'The Nature of Gothic' he catalogues the characteristics—or 'moral elements'—of a Gothic building: 'Savageness, Changefulness, Naturalism, Grotesqueness, Rigidity, Redundance'. By 'redundance' Ruskin meant superfluity of display. This is among the most extraordinary analyses in the whole literature of architecture. He admires 'the fantastic ignorance of the old sculptors ... those ugly goblins and formless monsters ... stern statues, anatomyless and rigid', for these are the 'signs of the life and liberty of every workman who struck the stone; a freedom of thought ... which it must be the first aim of all Europe ... to regain for her children.'

The Stones of Venice is invariably discussed as polemic or vision, but it also served as a pattern-book. Many of Ruskin's own drawings are repro-

4.3 EDWARD A. FREEMAN: **Rayonant and decorated tracery from Barnwell St Andrews, Portishead, Chipping Norton and Market Harborough.** *An Essay on the Origin and Development of Window Tracery in England*, 1851.

With the aid of clear illustrations of this kind the setting-out of comparatively complex tracery would have posed no difficulties for the competent draughtsman.

duced in gentle but sombre aquatint. He never shows buildings in their totality, but rather concerns himself with details and ornament (see Plates 4.30–3). For him, ornament brought a building to life.

Ruskin's ideas were to be put into practice in the University Museum, Oxford. Henry Acland, a distinguished Oxford physician and a friend of Ruskin's, was the prime mover in the scheme. Acland believed that science teaching had for too long been conspicuous by its absence in Oxford and wanted to set up a new institution to advance the sciences and medicine. The Dublin architectural partnership of Deane and Woodward won the competition for the new museum with a Gothic design which, if not entirely Venetian, had Venetian affinities. Benjamin Woodward, the junior partner, was its author. Tragically he died of consumption before it was completed. Ruskin was involved with the museum project from its inception, and claimed it was 'the first building raised in England since the close of the fifteenth century which has fearlessly put to new trial the old faith in nature and in the genius of the unassisted workman'. The O'Shea brothers, Dublin stonecarvers, were the 'unassisted' workmen. Nearly every capital in the museum—and there are many—was carved by the O'Sheas with decoration derived from native British plants and animals. The very museum structure itself was intended to educate—like its contents. The O'Sheas were competent, naturalistic carvers, but their efforts have neither the protean vigour nor the endearing innocence of the medieval work Ruskin admired. Woodward's Oxford Museum, however, was one of the greatest buildings to have come out of the Gothic Revival.

While Ruskin delighted in the naïve ebullience of Gothic, Viollet-le-Duc, the greatest European exponent of Gothic, saw it as a striving after rationality. Viollet-le-Duc spoke as a man of science. He excelled in the geometrical organization of ornament and in the decorative treatment of structural metalwork. Examples of his plant-like structural metalwork can be seen in his *Entretiens sur l'Architecture* (1863 and 1872), a work which has come to be seen as the most important nineteenth-century contribution to architectural theory (Plate 4.34).

However, it is not primarily as a Gothic propagandist or designer that Viollet-le-Duc should be revered, but as the most distinguished theorist to exploit Gothic in the search for a scientific architecture for the nineteenth century. Viollet-le-Duc did not, in the event, make the final imaginative leap and come happily to terms with the all-metal and non-historicist structure.

Of the three major theorists of the Gothic Revival discussed in this chapter—Pugin, Ruskin and Viollet-le-Duc—Viollet-le-Duc had, as a restorer, by far the greatest historical and practical understanding of medieval architecture. But in many ways the wonder is that the Gothic Revival produced theorists of this calibre at all. Rather than a revolution in theory, the Gothic Revival was a transformation of architectural practice—and that almost wholly confined to Britain. Its true impetus came not from theoretical works but from the example of buildings by architects passionately enamoured with medievalism.

By the mid-1880s the Gothic tide had turned. Pugin was long since dead. Dead too were Gilbert Scott, George Edmund Street and William Burges. Ruskin was withdrawing from the world and had said all he could about Gothic thirty years before. The great age of church building was over. Religion was being supplemented by aesthetic experience. But the Gothic Revival was not so much in its death throes as metamorphosing. From it sprang the Arts and Crafts Movement (see Chapter Nine).

3.63 OWEN JONES: Design for mosaic pavement. Watercolour and ink (late 1830s or early 1840s). From a volume of drawings 'Designs for mosaic tiles'. The Print Room, Victoria and Albert Museum, London.

3.64 OWEN JONES: **Design for mosaic pavement.** *Designs for Mosaic and Tessellated Pavements*, 1842.

Based partly on Islamic models. Jones may also have been experimenting with M. E. Chevreul's theory of the simultaneous contrast of colours.

3.65 OWEN JONES: **Design.** Watercolour and ink. From a volume of designs for wallpapers and textiles. The Print Room, Victoria and Albert Museum, London.

3.66 *Above* **Floor coverings:** from J. B. Waring, *Masterpieces of Industrial Art and Sculpture at the International Exhibition, 1862*, 1863.

3.67 A STUDENT OF YACOV CHERNIKOV: **Ornamental composition.** Yacov Chernikov, *Ornament Kompozutzionno-klassicheskiye postroyenya*, 1930.

The Russian constructivist architect Chernikov taught his students geometrical ornament for the same reasons as later teachers taught 'basic design'.

4.4 Eugène-Emanuel Viollet-le-Duc: **Details of decoration for a side chapel in Notre-Dame.** *Peintures Murales des Chapelles de Notre-Dame de Paris*, 1870.

Although much of Viollet-le-Duc's decoration for Notre-Dame survives, the original brilliance of the colouring is entirely lost.

4.5 John Carter: **Painting of Arthur, Prince of Wales, son of Henry VII,** from a window in the Priory Church of Great Malvern, Worcestershire. *Specimens of the Ancient Sculpture and Painting now remaining from the earliest period to the reign of Henry VIII*, 1780–94.

4.6 JAMES K. COLLING: **Details of a painted rood screen,** Dickleburgh Church, Norfolk. *Gothic Ornaments*, 1861.

4.7 W. AND G. AUDSLEY: **Bands of decoration.** *Polychromatic Decoration as applied to buildings in the medieval styles*, 1882.

4.8 *Right* JOHN CARTER: **Frontispiece** to Volume I of his *Specimens of the Ancient Sculpture and Painting now remaining from the earliest period to the reign of Henry y. VIII*, 1780–94.

Carter was the earliest authority to depict the Middle Ages in such a fanciful and romantic way. Edward III, Matilda, his queen, and Edward the Black Prince are shown here—all were 'copied exactly from the statues on their several monuments'.

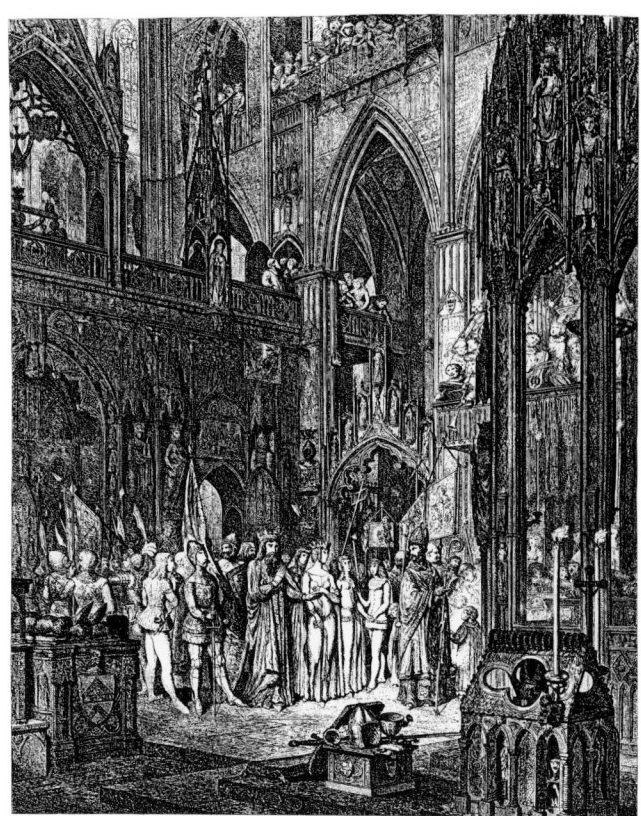

4.9 *Left* JOHN CARTER: **Frontispiece** to Volume II of his *Specimens of the Ancient Sculpture and Painting now remaining from the earliest period to the reign of Henry y. VIII*, 1780–94.

'The design represents the first wound that the Ancient Sculpture and Painting . . . received in the reign of Henry VIII.' Thomas, Lord Cromwell, is shown presiding over the sacking of an abbey while the distressed abbot and his monks look on.

4.10 JAMES CAVANAH MURPHY: **A section of the Chapter House at Batalha.** *Plans, Sections and Views of the Church of Batalha*, 1795.

Murphy's folio volume on Batalha was the earliest detailed study of a medieval building. The book was widely used as a source of reference by architects attempting to design in the Gothic style.

4.11 Sir James Hall: **Miniature cathedral of branches.** *Essay on the Origin, History and Principles of Gothic Architecture,* 1797.

Sir James Hall, an amateur theorist, put forward the idea that medieval church builders had simply copied the crude forms of huts made of willow branches and the like. As late as 1859 Christopher Dresser echoed this idea in an article in the *Art-Journal* in which he suggested that Gothic tracery might have been inspired by the intersecting branches of trees in forests. Gothic was long thought of as an essentially 'organic' style.

4.12 *Below* Joseph Halfpenny: **Quatrefoil carving showing Sampson and the lion.** *Gothic Ornaments in the Cathedral Church of York,* 1795.

Halfpenny worked under John Carr on the restoration of York Minster.

4.13 George Phillips: **Composition in the Gothic style.** *Rudiments of Curvilinear Design,* 1838–40.

Gothic was among the many styles that George Phillips attempted. In the late 1830s there was a demand for interiors and decoration in the Gothic manner, but little call for a correct archaeological approach.

4.14 A. W. PUGIN: **Vignette.** *Contrasts*, 1841 edition.

Pugin weighs nineteenth-century architecture—represented by such figures as Charles Barry, Decimus Burton, George Dance, John Nash, Robert Smirke and Sir John Soane—against fourteenth-century architecture and finds it wanting.

4.15 GEORGE PHILLIPS: **Composition in the Gothic style.** *Rudiments of Curvilinear Design*, 1838–40.

Phillips' Gothic is as elegant and accomplished as Pugin's adolescent work. But Phillips tamed Gothic and transformed it into a drawing-room style.

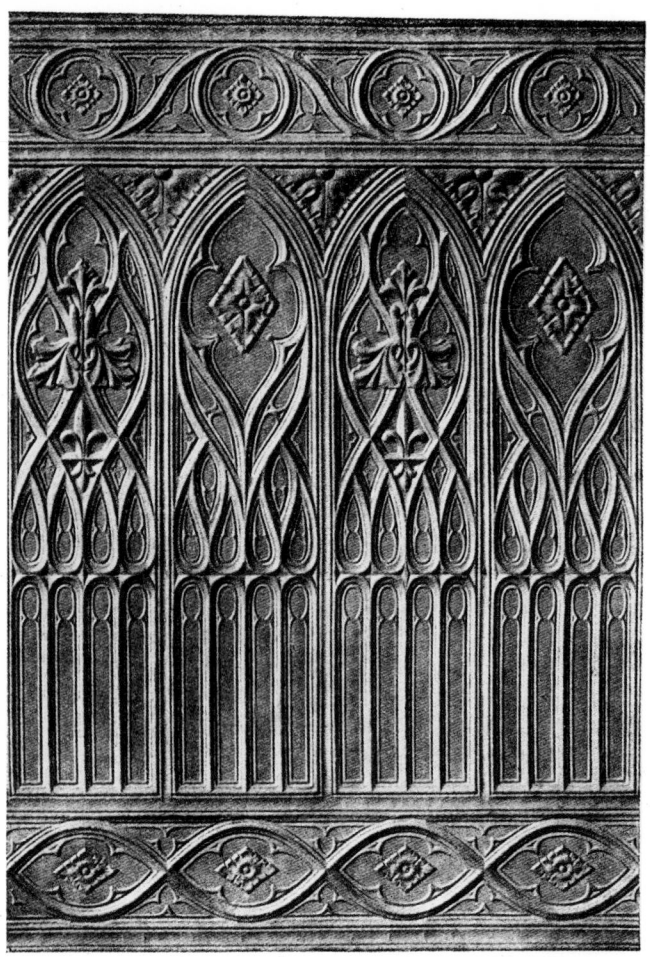

4.16 *Above left* F. ELLINGHAM: **'Lignomur' wallpaper,** 1912. Alan Victor Sugden and John Ludlam Edmondson, *A History of English Wallpaper, 1509–1914* (1925).

'Lignomur' was the trade name of a patent embossed wallpaper with a simulated wood finish.

4.17 *Above* ROBERT HORNE: **Wallpaper with Gothic tracery,** *c.* 1849. *Journal of Design and Manufacture*, June 1849.

Pugin ridiculed illusionistic designs such as this.

4.18 JOHN RUSKIN: **'Wall veil decoration'. A 'Renaissance' detail contrasted with a Romanesque treatment at S. Pietro, Pistoia.** Aquatint by T. Boys, after Ruskin. *The Stones of Venice,* 1852–3.

Ruskin contrasts a bland 'Renaissance' window with a rich, potent, medieval equivalent. The inference is clear. The idea of using comparisons of details to reinforce an aesthetic or moral argument was probably borrowed from Pugin.

4.19 A. W. Pugin: **Wallpaper design for the Houses of Parliament.** From Alan Victor Sugden's and John Ludlam Edmondson's *A History of English Wallpaper, 1509–1914* (1925).

Pugin's vigorous decoration rises above the mere historical pastiches of almost all his contemporaries. Like William Burges, he was fascinated by heraldic devices.

4.20 A. W. Pugin: **Wallpaper for the Houses of Parliament,** 1848. Alan Victor Sugden and John Ludlam Edmondson, *A History of English Wallpaper, 1509–1914* (1925).

The wallpaper incorporates the shamrock and the thistle—the emblems of Ireland and Scotland. Pugin sought to create a decorative language which was rich in symbolism.

4.21 *Right* A. W. Pugin: **Group of four encaustic floor tiles.** Richard Redgrave, *Manual of Design*, 1876.

Pugin appears to have begun designing tiles for Minton & Co., Stoke on Trent, the first of the great Victorian tile manufacturers, in about 1843. The appearance of an early Pugin design in the 1870s indicates the esteem in which his decorative design was still held.

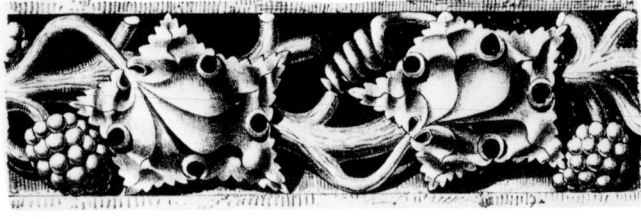

4.22 *Top left* J. K. COLLING: **Bands of foliated ornament from Henry VIIth Chapel, Westminster.** *Gothic Ornaments*, 1861.

Although a practising architect, Colling is best known as an architectural draughtsman—he was one of the founding members of the Association of Architectural Draughtsmen.

4.23 *Above left* J. K. COLLING: **Carvings in stone from a cornice at the back of the altar, Beverley Minster, Yorkshire.** *Gothic Ornaments*, 1861.

Colling, a tireless collector of ornamental details, presented an accurate picture of medieval ornament and did not minimize its grotesque aspects. Ruskin preferred to concern himself with medieval naturalism.

4.24 *Left* JOHN RUSKIN: **Details from a church in St Lo.** *The Seven Lamps of Architecture*, 1883 edition.

Ruskin claimed that this plate was intended 'to show the greater beauty of the natural weeds than of the carved crockets, and the tender harmony of both'.

4.26 JOHN RUSKIN: **Capital from the lower arcade of the Doge's Palace, Venice.** *The Seven Lamps of Architecture*, 1883 edition.

Ruskin described this capital as belonging to 'the noblest period' of Venetian Gothic. 'What is done by the Venetian, with a power as irresistible as that of the waves of his surrounding sea, is done by the masters of Cis-Alpine Gothic, more timidly, and with a manner somewhat cramped and cold, but not less expressing their assent to the same great law.' The 'great law', of course, is the law of nature.

4.25 *Opposite* JOHN RUSKIN: **Ornaments from Rouen, St Lo, and Venice.** *The Seven Lamps of Architecture*, 1883 edition.

The main message of this book was that architecture could exert a moral influence upon society. Medieval buildings, with their ebullient ornament, allowed individual expression. (This, and Plates 4.26–9, were copied by an engraver from Ruskin's own etchings in the first edition.)

4.27 *Far left* JOHN RUSKIN: **Pierced ornament from Lisieux, Bayeux, Verona and Padua.** *The Seven Lamps of Architecture*, 1883 edition.

'The spandrel is from the south western entrance of the Cathedral of Lisieux . . . Its work is altogether rude, but full of spirit . . .'

4.28 *Left* JOHN RUSKIN: **Window from the Ca' Foscari, Venice.** *The Seven Lamps of Architecture*, 1883 edition.

Ruskin praised this window for its 'purity of form'.

4.30 *Right* John Ruskin: **The Decoration of Bases.** Aquatint by T. Boys, after Ruskin. *The Stones of Venice*, 1852–3.

Writing of the purpose of this book Ruskin declared in his Preface of February 1851 that 'The principles it inculcates are universal'.

4.29 *Left* John Ruskin: **Portions of an arcade on the south side of the Cathedral of Ferrara.** *The Seven Lamps of Architecture*, 1883 edition.

Ruskin admired work such as this for its innocent display of virtuosity.

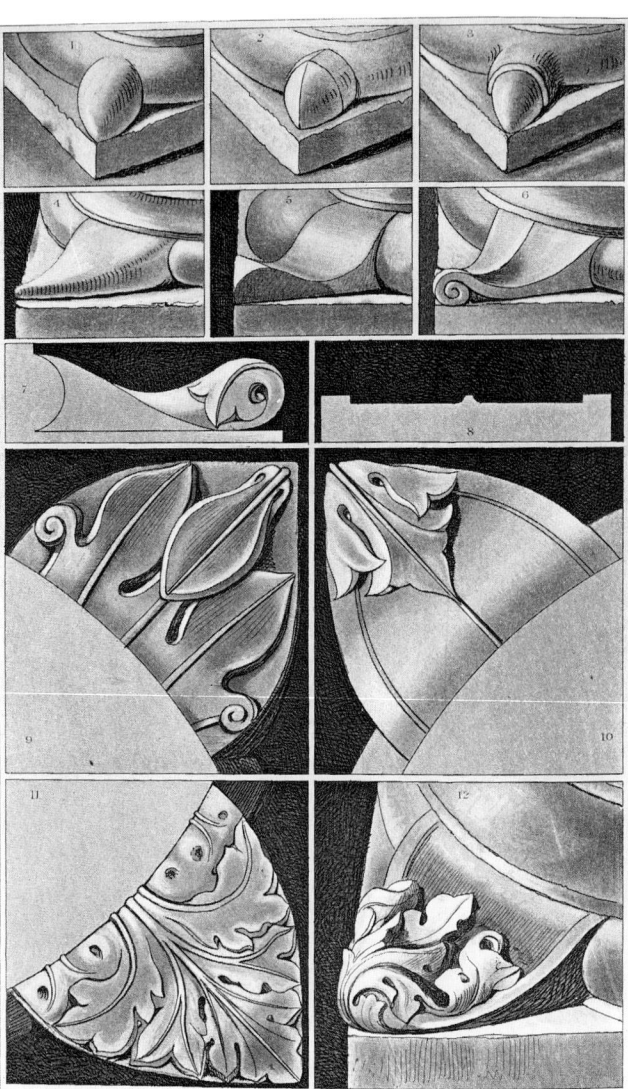

4.31 *Left* John Ruskin: **Cornice decoration.** Engraving by G. Allen, after Ruskin. *The Stones of Venice*, 1852–3.

Many of Ruskin's plates are of the pattern-book variety and would have been useful to architects as sources of reference. However, Ruskin declared in the Preface to the Third Edition (1874) that 'two thirds' of the book had been 'resolutely ignored'.

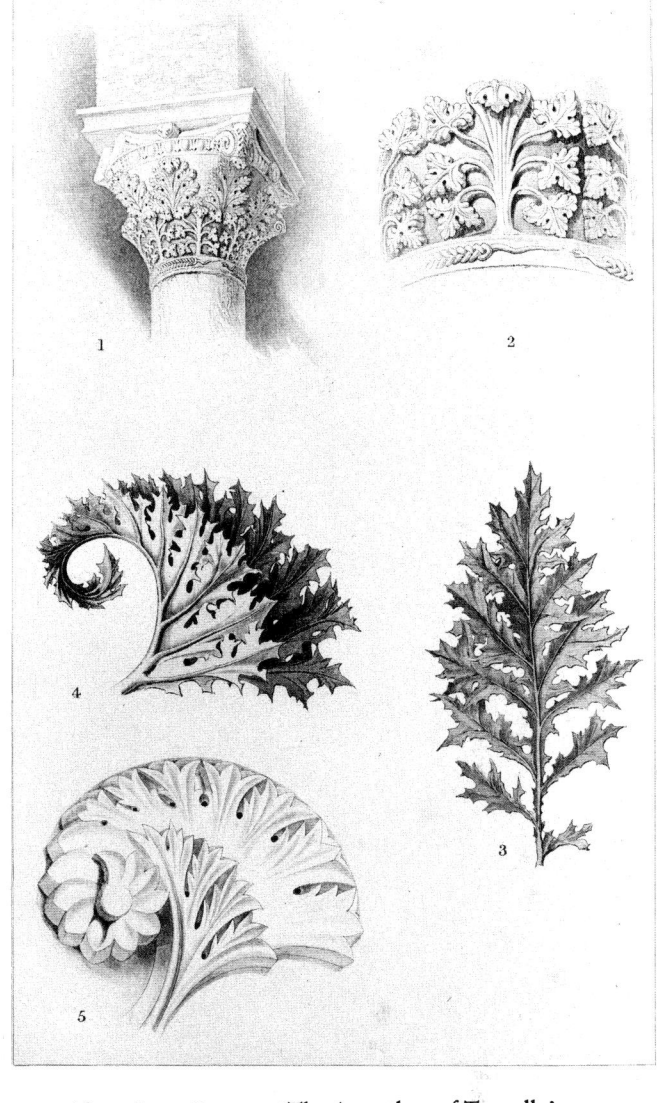

4.32 *Above* JOHN RUSKIN: 'The Acanthus of Torcello'.
Engraving by G. H. Le Keux, after Ruskin. *The Stones of Venice*, 1852–3.

Ruskin delighted in the variety of the capitals at Torcello, a basilica-type church seven miles north of Venice, but complained: 'It is not . . . to be expected that . . . the delicate fancies of the Gothic leafage springing into new life, should be read, or perceived, by the passing traveller who has never been taught to expect anything in architecture except the five orders.'

4.33 JOHN RUSKIN: **Details of foliated ornament from capitals of the Ducal Palace, Venice.** Engraving by G. H. Le Keux, after Ruskin. *The Stones of Venice*, 1852–3.

In this plate, Ruskin invites his readers to compare Renaissance carving—the two right-hand examples on the bottom line— with the earlier work illustrated.

4.34 *Left* Eugène-Emanuel Viollet-le-Duc: **Cast-iron fan vaulting.** From the Atlas which accompanies his *Entretiens sur l'Architecture*, 1863–72.

Viollet-le-Duc published several projects designed according to medieval principles but which used modern materials.

4.36 *Below* A. W. Pugin: **The Medieval Court at the Great Exhibition, 1851.** *The Art-Journal Illustrated Catalogue, The Industry of All Nations, 1851*, 1851.

The Medieval Court was almost entirely the work of Pugin and his last major gesture as a designer before his death in 1852.

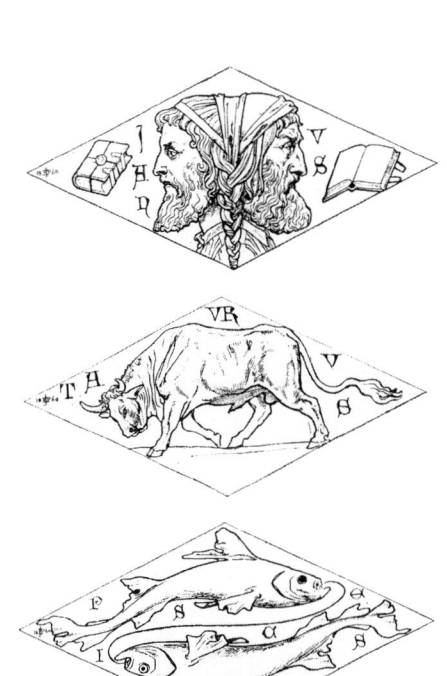

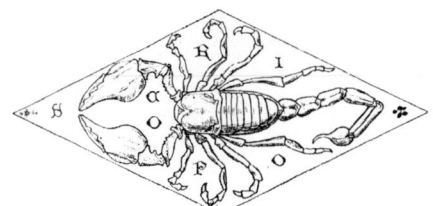

4.37 *Right* Edward John Poynter: **Drawings of the Signs of the Zodiac.** For William Burges' restoration of Waltham Abbey, 1859. Herbert Sharp, 'A short account of the work of Edward John Poynter, RA', *The Studio*, February 1896.

Burges' scheme for the ceiling of the nave at Waltham was full of elaborate symbolism— 'The Economy of the World', the Four Elements, the Past and Future, the Signs of the Zodiac and the Labours of the Months (see Plate 4.40). Like the Pre-Raphaelites with their painting, Burges sought to produce architecture charged with meaning.

4.38 *Right* Richard Norman Shaw: **Pulpit in the Frauenkirche, Nuremberg.** *Architectural Sketches from the Continent*, 1858.

Shaw won the Royal Academy Gold Medal in 1854 for his drawings of medieval buildings executed in 1853 during a tour in France, Italy, Bavaria, Bohemia and Belgium. He became George Edmund Street's principal draughtsman in 1859, in succession to Philip Webb.

4.35 *Opposite* **The Medieval Court at the International Exhibition,** London, 1862. *The Illustrated London News*, 30 August 1862.

The Medieval Court at South Kensington was a splendid show-case for the achievements of the Gothic Revival at its zenith. Here was shown the furniture and metalwork of architects like William Burges, William Butterfield and George Gilbert Scott. Nevertheless, Gothic was never entirely successful as a secular style.

4.39 *Left* Mr Hedgeland, London: **Stained and painted glass window.** *The Art-Journal Illustrated Catalogue. The Industry of All Nations, 1851*, 1851.

Although in the Decorated style of the fourteenth century this window did not accord with correct mid-nineteenth-century 'medieval' principles. It was far too approximate in its archaeological references, and furthermore the figure was over-naturalistic.

4.40 *Above* Edward John Poynter: **Drawings for the Labours of the Months and the Four Elements.** For William Burges' restoration of Waltham Abbey, 1859. Herbert Sharp, 'A short account of the work of Edward John Poynter, RA', *The Studio*, February 1896.

4.41 *Above* Messrs Newton, Jones & Willis, Birmingham: **Portion of Archbishop's cope.** *The Art-Journal Illustrated Catalogue. The Industry of All Nations, 1851*, 1851.

The design of vestments formed an important part of Pugin's *Glossary of Ecclesiastical Ornament*. Inevitably, this design reflects its influence.

4.42 *Left* GEORGE GILBERT SCOTT: **Screen for Hereford Cathedral.** Manufactured by Skidmore's Art Manufacturer's Co., Coventry. *The Illustrated London News*, 30 August 1862.

There is no real medieval precedent for the Hereford screen, although it bears a certain resemblance to French thirteenth-century small-scale ecclesiastical metalwork of the kind used in the making of elaborate reliquaries, or croziers and the like.

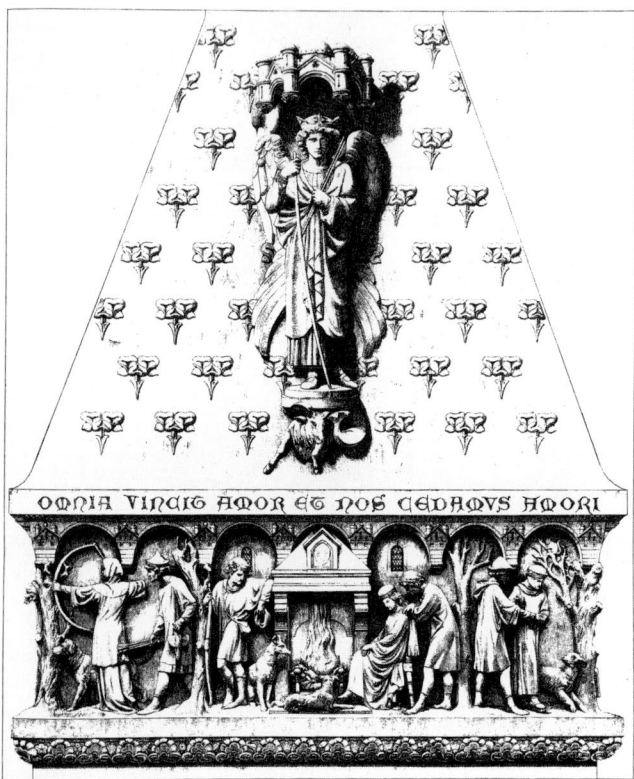

4.43 WILLIAM BURGES, designer, THOMAS NICHOLLS, sculptor: **Upper part of the chimneypiece in the Winter Smoking Room, New Tower, Cardiff Castle,** 1870–3. Richard Popplewell Pullan, *The Architectural Designs of William Burges,* 1883.

Cardiff Castle, like Viollet-le-Duc's Château de Pierrefonds (1857), was part restoration and part imaginative re-creation. Lord Bute, Burges' patron, was one of the richest men in Britain. Burges was thus able to indulge his sense of high fantasy. He employed Nicholls in many of his schemes.

4.44 WILLIAM BURGES, designer, THOMAS NICHOLLS, sculptor: **Evangelistic emblems from the West Window, St Finbar's Protestant Cathedral, Cork,** 1862–76. Richard Popplewell Pullan, *The Architectural Designs of William Burges,* 1883.

Burges' French thirteenth-century treatment is neither pedantic nor overbearing.

4.45 *Right* WILLIAM EDEN NESFIELD: **Title-page** of his *Specimens of Medieval Architecture*, 1862.

Nesfield's book was among the many collections of drawings of medieval buildings published during the Gothic Revival. Nesfield was a fine draughtsman—almost the equal of his early partner Richard Norman Shaw. The figures are by the painter Albert Moore.

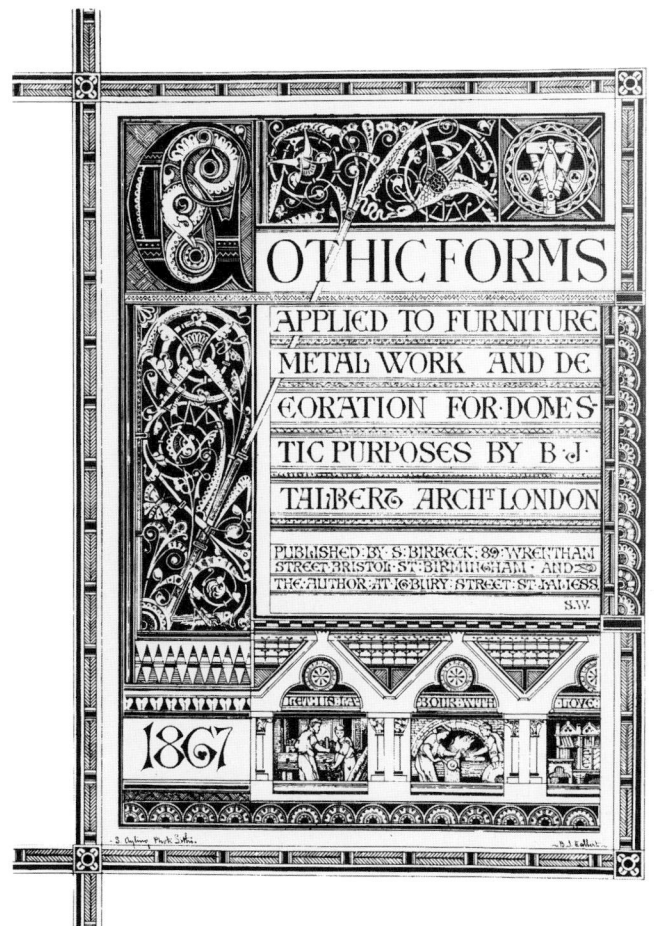

4.46 BRUCE J. TALBERT: **Title-page** of his *Gothic Forms*, 1867.

Talbert's book had a considerable influence. Its impact can be seen in the work of Christopher Dresser, J. Moyr Smith and Frank Furness, the Philadelphia Gothic Revival architect, who produced some handsome ornament in a manner very like Talbert's. In the sequel to this book—*Examples of Ancient and Modern Furniture* (1876)—Talbert revealed an attachment to the modish Queen Anne style and an ability to design in the Japanese manner.

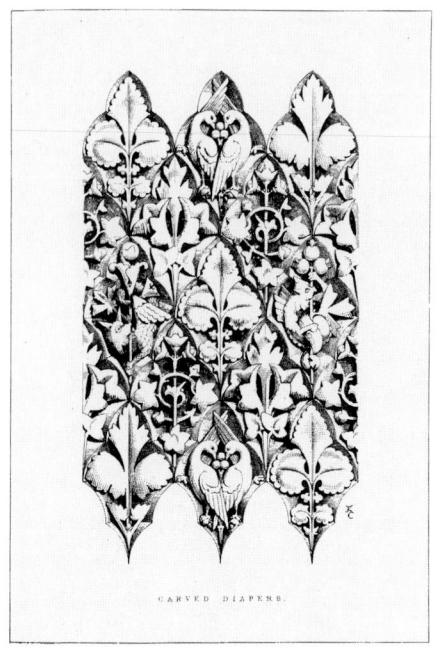

COUPLED CAPITAL.
Fern, Celandine and Grevillea Acanthifolia.

BRACKET FOR
CHURCH LETTERN.

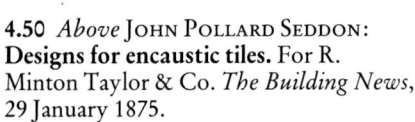

4.50 *Above* John Pollard Seddon: **Designs for encaustic tiles.** For R. Minton Taylor & Co. *The Building News,* 29 January 1875.

4.51 *Right* W. Galsworthy Davie: **Medieval tiles from Laon Museum.** *The Building News,* 19 May 1876.

The contrast between the mechanical perfection of J. P. Seddon's tiles (see above) and the joyous simplicity of the medieval examples illustrated here is apparent.

4.47 *Opposite far left* J. K. COLLING: **Carved diaper.** *Art Foliage for Sculpture and Decoration*, 1865.

While Colling's two-volume *Gothic Ornaments* was the main published collection of English medieval carved ornament, *Art Foliage* was a work devoted to original designs.

4.48 *Opposite centre left* J. K. COLLING: **Coupled capital.** *Art Foliage for Sculpture and Decoration*, 1865.

Colling based the foliation of this capital upon ferns. The design should be compared with Ruskin's drawing of a capital in the Doge's Palace from *Seven Lamps of Architecture* (see Plate 4.26).

4.49 *Opposite left* J. K. COLLING: **Bracket for church lectern.** *Art Foliage for Sculpture and Decoration*, 1865.

The small inlaid motif on the right is in the manner of Christopher Dresser's 'conventionalized'—or stylized—method of transforming drawings of plants into conventional ornament.

4.52 *Right* CHRISTOPHER DRESSER: **Studies for wall decorations.** *Studies in Design*, 1874–6.

Dresser was no more than a competent designer of Gothic ornament and it is possible that this design is by Moyr Smith.

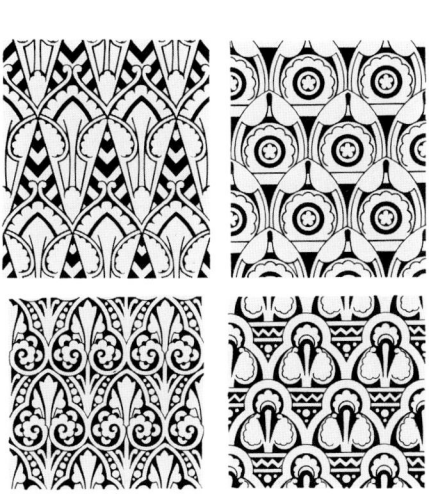

4.54 *Left* CHRISTOPHER DRESSER: **All-over Gothic decoration.** *Studies in Design*, 1874–6.

The top left and right designs appear to have been taken straight out of Bruce Talbert's *Gothic Forms*.

4.53 *Far left* W. AND G. AUDSLEY: **Decoration 'suitable for wall spaces of moderate dimensions'.** *Polychromatic Decoration as applied to buildings in the Medieval Styles*, 1882.

The Audsleys' book was intended primarily to show what could be done with stencilling, a form of decoration which was widely practised during the nineteenth and early twentieth centuries.

4.55 CHRISTOPHER DRESSER: **Design for a painted glass window.** *Modern Ornamentation*, 1886.

Although this design is based on an earlier design of the pattern of frost upon a window pane, it is loosely Gothic in spirit. Dresser also published a frieze and all-over pattern of a very similar type in *Studies in Design*.

4.56 LEWIS F. DAY: **German Gothic tracery patterns.** *The Planning of Ornament*, 1887.

Day was particularly skilled in simple geometric design. Here he turns tracery into an ingenious repeat pattern—something no Gothic purist would have tolerated.

5.1 GEORGE AITCHISON: **Details of a drawing room.** For E. H. Mann, Berkeley Square, London. Watercolour and gouache, *c.* 1880. The Royal Institute of British Architects, London.

5.2 Eugène Grasset: **Design for a stained-glass window.** *Dekorative Kunst*, Vol. II, 1899.

5.3 Owen Jones: **Design for a door in the Egyptian style.** For Lord Ashburton. Gouache. The Print Room, Victoria and Albert Museum, London.

Here Jones adapts the Egyptian style for modern purposes.

5.4 MARGARET MACDONALD MACKINTOSH: **Cover.** For *Deutsche Kunst und Dekoration*, Vol. V, 1902.

5.5 CHRISTOPHER DRESSER: **Band of decoration.** *Studies in Design*, 1874–6.

Although this is in Dresser's 'new style', Egyptian elements are easily detectable.

5.6 THOMAS CRANE: **Design for a cushion.** M. S. Lockwood and E. Glaister, *Art Embroidery, A Treatise on the practice of decorative needlework*, 1878.

Crane's designs, with their muted colour schemes, are representative of the eclectic spirit of the Aesthetic Movement of the 1870s.

5.7 GEORGE ASHDOWN AUDSLEY AND MORRIS ASHDOWN AUDSLEY: **Friezes.** *The Practical Decorator and Ornamentist,* 1892.

5.8 OWEN JONES: **Design for ceiling.** Watercolour and gouache. The Print Room, Victoria and Albert Museum, London.

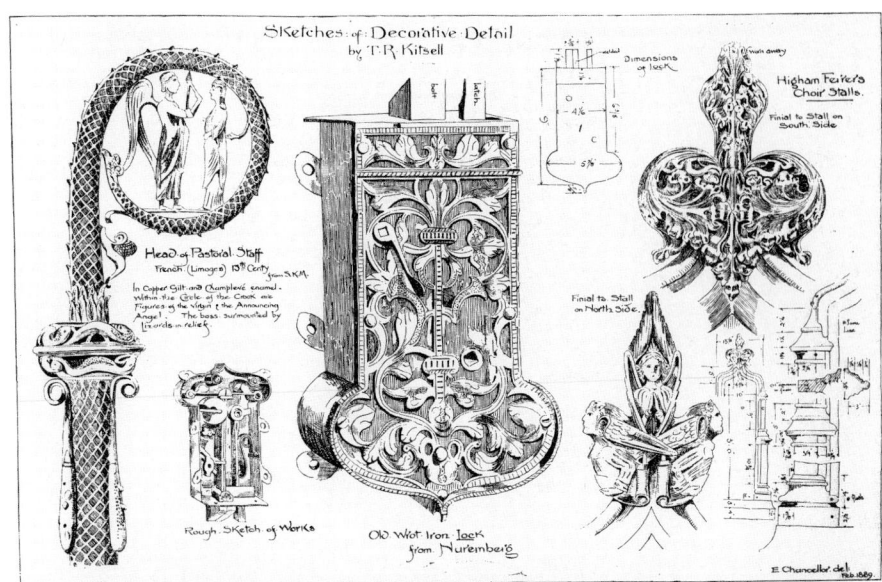

4.57 T. R. KITSELL: **Sketches of decorative detail.** *The Building News*, 22 February 1889.

The collection of authentic medieval detail was an important activity throughout the Gothic Revival. Although by 1889 this was transforming itself into the Arts and Crafts Movement many architects and amateurs continued to publish their findings.

4.58 RICHARD NORMAN SHAW: **Green altar-cloth of All Saint's, Leek, Staffordshire.** Kineton Parkes, 'The Leek Embroidery Society, with illustrations of its work', *The Studio*, July 1893.

This design, though not in the strictest archaeological sense Gothic, shows a command of the idiom. All the materials used here were manufactured locally; Wardle, William Morris' one-time adviser on dyeing, was responsible for the colouring.

114

CHAPTER FIVE
Eclecticism

Eclecticism has often been harshly judged. During the years of the Modern Movement's ascendancy it came to be associated with sentimental borrowings from the past, intellectual vacuity and, above all, creative bankruptcy. But despite all the opprobrium heaped upon it, eclecticism has a perfectly respectable history. Vasari praised Raphael for the skill with which he embodied in his own work the best of the art of those who had gone before. Sebastiano Serlio's great work, *L'Architettura*, published between 1537 and 1551, was a work of compilation and Serlio was in the truest sense an eclectic. *L'Architettura* provided builders and architects with a vast repertory of motifs and was by far the most influential architectural source-book of the sixteenth and seventeenth centuries.

In the eighteenth century Johann Fischer von Erlach (1656–1723), the leading Baroque architect in Austria, published the earliest engravings of non-Western buildings—including Egyptian and Chinese examples—in *Entwurff einer historischen Architectur* ('An Outline of Historical Architecture') (1721). Von Erlach's book was a harbinger of later eclecticism and exoticism. Giovanni Battista Piranesi (1720–78) was a keen advocate of a new style of architecture based upon the free adaptation of Roman models. His *Diverse maniere d'adornare i cammini* ('Diverse manners of ornamenting chimney-pieces') (1769), which includes designs for chairs, vases, picture frames and clock-cases as well as chimney-pieces, showed his borrowings from Egyptian, Tuscan and Greek styles, in addition to Roman.

Like Fischer von Erlach, Jean-Louis Nicolas Durand (1760–1834) shows examples of non-Western buildings. His *Recueil et Parallèle des édifices en tout genre* ('A Selection and Comparison of all Types of Buildings') of 1800 fulfils the promise of its title. But Durand, who was the principal architectural theorist in France and Germany during the early years of the nineteenth century, was not so much concerned with picturesque effect as with establishing the rational principles which he believed were to be found underlying all architectural systems. Aimé Chenavard (1798–1838), also an architect, includes designs for furniture, tapestry, carpets and stained glass as well as architecture in his *Recueil des Dessins* (1828) and illustrates Chinese, Egyptian and Turkish styles together with Renaissance and Gothic examples.

The architect who subscribes to eclecticism aims to achieve a synthesis of styles in his works. But much ornament is ephemeral—and intended only to be so—and not constrained by the physical and practical realities of architecture. The eclectic approach to ornament, in consequence, often ends merely in the production of pastiches. It is only the finest eclectic ornament which rises above the level of imitation.

An early and important designer of eclectic ornament was George Phillips. Little is known about his life, although on the evidence of his *Rudiments of Curvilinear Design* he was as accomplished a designer of ornament as anyone of his generation and was among the earliest authorities to write on theoretical aspects of ornamental design. Phillips was also interested in the science of perception, which in the 1830s had not even been given a name and had very little in the way of a literature.[1]

His book includes Egyptian (Plate 5.13), Grecian, Roman, Byzantine,

5.9 W. S. Black: 'The Seasons'. **Wallpaper with frieze.** For Jeffrey & Co. *Art et Décoration*, Vol. III, 1898.

An accomplished design which, though superficially resembling Crane's (see Plate 5.42), is less concerned with evoking a specific historical style.

Gothic, Arabian, Persian and 'Hindoostanee' examples. Eleven plates in all are given over to Oriental styles and, unexpectedly, especially for the late 1830s, styles in the Japanese and 'Japanese ornament in the Chinese Manner' are illustrated. Phillips' experiments in eclectic design are moderated by a kind of Neo-classical restraint, possibly derived from Sir John Soane.

In 1840, the year in which *Rudiments of Curvilinear Design* was completed, H. W. and A. Arrowsmith, decorators to Queen Victoria, published *The House Decorator and Painter's Guide*, which illustrates schemes for rooms in the Elizabethan, Pompeian, Moorish, Louis XIV, François I, Louis XV, Gothic and the modern French styles. But the Arrowsmiths' designs, though not without elegance, amount to no more than pastiches.

No less an authority than Owen Jones championed eclecticism. In *The Journal of Design*, which appeared in June 1851 shortly after the opening of the Great Exhibition, he wrote:

> Each civilization in the ascendant goes to nature for its principles, and enriches its own invention with the choicest conceptions of antecedent ages; while . . . declining civilizations substitute only a series of decrepit, disordered and fruitless caprices.
>
> We possess the inestimable advantage of living in an age when nothing of the past remains a secret; each stone of any monument of every clime has told its tale, which is now brought within reach of our fire-sides; yet, hitherto, how little have we shown ourselves worthy of this great privilege! The ease with which our knowledge might be obtained has made us indifferent to its acquirement, or has led us to substitute an indolent and servile imitation for an intelligent and imaginative eclecticism.[2]

Jones' 'intelligent and imaginative eclecticism' called in effect for the synthesis of ornamental styles in order to create a new style. It would seem to have been an appropriate aesthetic philosophy for an age which sought its own identity and which was surfeited with an immense variety of architectural and ornamental styles to choose from.

As noted in Chapter One, John Leighton's *Suggestions in Designs* shows both Western and Oriental styles and has the hallmarks of an eclectic pattern-book. But Leighton is all too often heavy-handed as an ornamentalist and is more appropriately described as a designer of pastiches.

Christopher Dresser, one of the most successful of nineteenth-century designers of ornament, was able to recognize the pluralistic nature of the culture of his times with refreshing realism. His views derived largely from Owen Jones. Writing in February 1868 in *The Chromolithograph*,[3] the first magazine to be printed in colour, Dresser set out his case for eclecticism:

> Variety has at no period been so much sought as at the present. Persons vary in opinions, hold different faiths, and seek different results. And with this mixed state of feelings, variety in all things must be achieved. Unlike past periods the present has no national architecture. We erect one building in the Gothic style, another in imitation of the classic Parthenon, and the third in the form of an Egyptian temple; variety in architecture being sought as well as variety in other things. With ornament it is similar.

Dresser's ideas on designing ornament in different styles (Plates 5.28 and 31) may now strike us as rather oddly affected. In *Studies in Design* (1874–6) he observed:

> My success in production largely depends upon the extent to which I become, in feeling, for the time a Chinaman, or Arabian. . . . In order

5.10 FRANK M. JONES: **Design for a menu card.** *The Studio*, Vol. XVII, 1899.

This design is reminiscent of Aubrey Beardsley, though more pedestrian. It was the work of a student at the Royal College of Art, London, and was entered in the National Competition, 1899.

that I enter into the spirit of the Oriental, I often find it necessary to inform myself of the religion, mode of government, climate and habits of a people, for it is only by understanding their faiths and usages that I can comprehend the spirit of their ornament and become for a time one of them in feeling.

Dresser's last book of designs, *Modern Ornamentation* (1886), shows designs in adapted styles, mixed styles and styles of his own invention (Plates 5.35, 50, 51). Throughout the book he demonstrates an unequalled virtuosity in eclectic designing.

The great majority of nineteenth-century designers were in fact eclectics in practice, if not in theory. Even Pugin's Gothic ornament is a distillation of several medieval stylistic phases. The same is true of the Gothic ornament of George Gilbert Scott, William Butterfield, William Burges, Philip Webb and Viollet-le-Duc. Burges was prone to incorporate Islamic and even Japanese features in his ornament; some of Viollet-le-Duc's designs for the wall decorations of the side chapels of Notre-Dame in Paris have elements evidently borrowed from Islamic sources. It should come as no surprise that Gothic revivalism had its eclectic side, for both the Gothic Revival and eclecticism were ramifications of the same historicism that was so characteristic of the nineteenth century.

As we have seen, the architect and ornamental designer Bruce Talbert began his career as a Gothicist and ended it as an eclectic. Despite his premature death at the age of forty-three, he became, with Christopher Dresser, the most influential trade designer in Britain during the 1860s and 1870s (see Plate 5.29).

By 1876, as evinced by his second book, *Examples of Ancient and Modern Furniture*, Talbert had thrown aside Gothic in favour of a modified Jacobean style which better suited the currently fashionable 'Queen Anne' architecture. Like so many of his contemporaries, he was also influenced by Japan and his ornament was, by now, unashamedly eclectic in character. Talbert's renunciation of Gothic coincides precisely with its general decline in importance as a domestic style.

During the 1870s the 'Queen Anne style' became particularly popular with the cultivated and prosperous middle classes for their new houses.[4] Nineteenth-century Queen Anne is, in fact, an eclectic style, and bears little relationship to the architecture produced during the reign of Queen Anne. It combines elements from vernacular building, mid-seventeenth-century Dutch-influenced brick architecture and eighteenth-century Neo-classicism. Paradoxically, Queen Anne façades were quite often composed in a bold, asymmetrical way which harked back to the recent Gothic Revival past. W. Eden Nesfield (1835–88) and Richard Norman Shaw (1831–1912)—both initially Gothicists—played a major part in formulating the vocabulary of Queen Anne architecture and decoration. Fashionable artists were especially fond of the style—Whistler, Luke Fildes and Kate Greenaway all had Queen Anne studios or houses. The 'aesthetes' suburb at Bedford Park, West London, founded in the mid-1870s, was built entirely in the Queen Anne style.

The Aesthetic Movement, which blossomed in the 1870s under the influence of Ruskin and Walter Pater, brought in its wake a lively interest in the design of ornament. Designers of ornament acquired a status which had been previously reserved for academic artists. Christopher Dresser even claimed that 'ornamentation is not only a fine art, but . . . it is even a higher art than that practised by the pictorial artist, as it is of wholly mental origin.'[5] Such extreme claims, however, were taken none too seriously by Dresser's contemporaries.

5.11 KOLOMAN MOSER: **Decorative design.** *The Studio*, November 1904.

Moser was among the most influential of the artists associated with the Vienna Secession. His work was first publicized in the Secessionist journal *Ver Sacrum* in 1898. This design, which presumably could be repeated infinitely, combines Mucha-like figures with highly stylized wintry trees. A band of figures in a similar style once decorated the exterior of Olbrich's Secessionist building.

5.12 HELEN HAY: **Almanac.** *The Evergreen. A Northern Seasonal. The Book of Autumn,* 1895.

The Evergreen review was founded by the young Patrick Geddes (later a pioneer townplanner and sociologist), and published in Edinburgh in 1895 and 1896. Its four volumes—Spring, Summer, Autumn and Winter—possess an air of Yeatsian, Celtic mysticism and exhale a naive optimism. Its many vignettes and devices are for the most part amateurish, but suggest the existence of a lively, highly eclectic, Scottish school of ornament.

During this period decorative designers were invariably eclectic in their approach. This was an inevitable and sensible response to the vast quantity of visual data—whether found in museums, exhibitions or books—which confronted them. Less tangibly, eclecticism fitted the prevailing psychological mood of the Aesthetic Movement in which sensual delight became more important than moral improvement. The cult of beauty became a surrogate for religion. 'Art,' said Walter Pater, in his conclusion to *The Renaissance* (1868), 'comes to you proposing to give you nothing but the highest quality to your moments as they pass, and simply for those moments' sake.' The aesthete, brought up during the high-minded years of the Gothic Revival, had necessarily to underplay the moral associations of historical or national decorative styles. In a strictly nineteenth-century sense—the sense in which it would have been understood by Pugin and Ruskin—eclecticism savours faintly of the amoral.

Lewis F. Day's several excellent practical manuals of design, his *Instances of Necessary Art* (1880) and *Every-Day Art* (1882), most perfectly epitomize the decorative style of the Aesthetic Movement (see also Plate 5.34). Walter Crane, although well known as an illustrator (Plates 5.36 and 43), published nothing on the practice of design until *The Claims of Decorative Art* (1892)—a collection of essays on Arts and Crafts themes. His illustrated manuals, *The Bases of Design* (1898) and *Line and Form* (1900), combined the idealism of the Arts and Crafts (see Chapter Nine) with the vivacity of the Aesthetic Movement.

The Ecole des Beaux Arts in Paris, the earliest as well as—in the nineteenth century at least—the foremost school of architecture, encouraged an eclectic approach to design. Here an attempt was made to forge a new architectural style for the century; the Neo-Greek style was the principal outcome of such efforts. France produced, with greater success than other nations, progressive, eclectic architecture,[6] but established no school of eclectic ornament comparable with that of Britain during the period of the Aesthetic Movement, although these were many accomplished designers.

François-Désiré Froment-Meurice (1802–55) catered to the tastes of wealthy Parisian aristocrats with his silverware and elaborately decorated jewellery, drawing on both the Rococo and Gothic styles for inspiration. The bronze founder and furniture manufacturer Ferdinand Barbedienne (1810–92) produced bronze and silverware in a variety of styles and had a number of fashionable artists working for him. Some of his designs reflect the interest in *chinoiserie* and *japonaiserie*. At one point he employed three hundred men in order to meet the demand for his work. Albert-Ernest Carrier-Belleuse (1824–87) established a reputation in England and Paris as a decorative sculptor. He is remembered today mainly for his caryatids, often supporting bronze *torchères*. From 1875 until his death he was artistic director at the Sèvres porcelain factory. Also working in both France and England was Marc Solon (1835–1913), a very successful porcelain decorator. He published a set of ornamental designs, *Inventions décoratives*, in 1866 in Paris, and subsequently wrote a number of books on ceramics which were published in London. He was primarily influenced by classical models but he was not painstakingly archaeological in his approach and in many ways he epitomizes nineteenth-century French eclecticism.

That eclecticism should have been so widely debated during the nineteenth century was the outcome of the universal faith in historicism—that is, the fixation with the art and architecture of the remote and more recent past. Eclecticism can be understood as no more than an offshoot of this, but more positively it can be seen as a rational response to an unparalleled inrush of visual information.

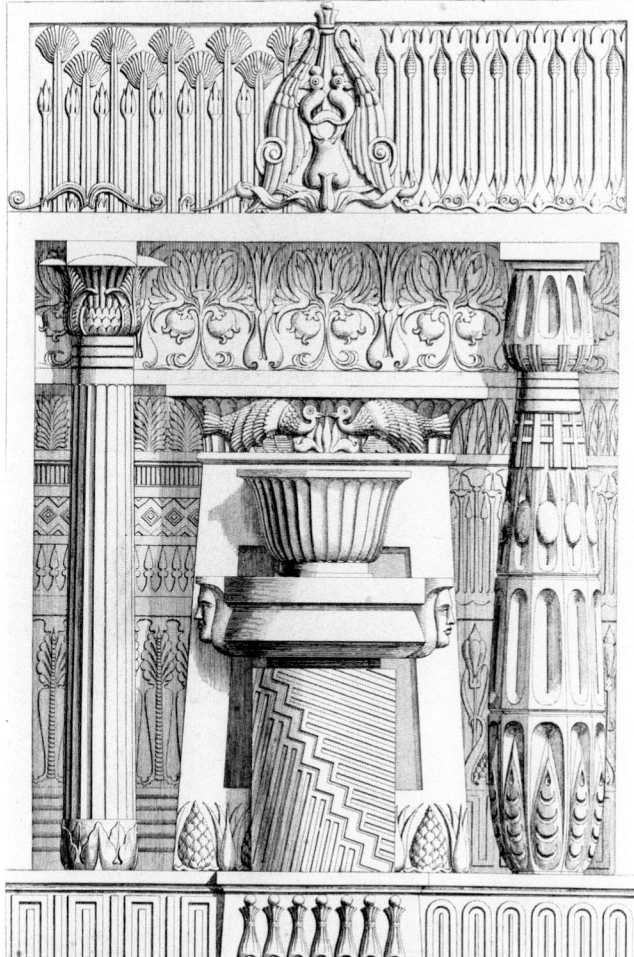

5.13 *Left* GEORGE PHILLIPS: **Ornamental composition in the Egyptian style.** *Rudiments of Curvilinear Design* (1838–40).

Phillips was among the earliest British ornamental designers to publish a collection of designs in a wide range of styles. 'As the Poet embellishes his verse with allusions to bygone scenes . . . so may the imagination of the Artist embody new inventions from among the accumulated treasures of ancient and modern precedent.'

5.14 *Below* **Carpet.** Manufactured for Jackson & Graham. *The Art-Journal Illustrated Catalogue. The Industry of All Nations, 1851,* 1851.

This design is predominantly Rococo in style. It is possibly based on engravings by Jean François de Cuvilliés (1695–1768), but the naturalistic floral swags and the garland in the centre of the design establish it unmistakably as a work of the 1850s.

5.16 LUDWIG GRUNER: **Table-cloth.** Executed by Mrs Purcell and her assistants. *The Art-Journal Illustrated Catalogue. The Industry of All Nations, 1851,* 1851.

The naturalistic wreath of flowers is unsuited to a design which is Renaissance in character, although, of course, there is no Renaissance precedent for an embroidered table-cloth of this kind.

5.15 Carpet. Manufactured by H. Brinton & Sons, Kidderminster. *The Art-Journal Illustrated Catalogue. The Industry of All Nations, 1851,* 1851.

The design is composed of Rococo scrolls and naturalistic palm leaves. It would have been the despair of reformers like Owen Jones, Richard Redgrave and Pugin.

5.17 CAPTAIN FOWKE: **Section through the South Court, the South Kensington Museum.** *The Building News*, 24 March 1865.

Henry Cole's South Kensington Museum—now the Victoria and Albert Museum—was the centre of British official art education. The early parts of the building were intended as object lessons in design. The principal influence in its decoration was Alfred Stevens (1817–75), but principally through the work of his pupil Godfrey Sykes (1824–66) and, in turn, through Sykes' own pupils. There were many earlier decorated metal structures including Karl Etzel's Dianabad, Vienna (1841–3), Skidmore's covered court for Deane and Woodward's Oxford Museum (1855–9), and Henri Labrouste's Bibliothèque Nationale (1862–8).

5.21 *Opposite* F. W. MOODY: **Faience decorations for the South Kensington Museum,** 1866. *Lectures and Lessons on Art*, 1875.

Moody's modernized Renaissance decorations can still be seen at the Victoria and Albert Museum. Moody was a vociferous opponent of Christopher Dresser's views on ornament.

5.18 FORMIGE: **Detail of window in the Palais des Beaux Arts at the Paris Universal Exhibition,** 1889. F. G. Dumas and L. De Fourcaud, *Revue de l'Exposition de 1889*, n.d.

During the heyday of the Modern Movement the idea of a rational iron structure clad with irrational decoration—in this case a mixture of Louis Quatorze and nineteenth-century naturalism—seemed ludicrous. Nevertheless, Formige exhibits very considerable skill in fusing two decorative styles and transforming structure itself into decoration.

5.19 *Left* Alfred Stevens: **Spandrel.** F. W. Moody, *Lectures and Lessons on Art*, 1875.

Stevens, a sculptor, worked in an accomplished Italianate manner. His virtuosity was legendary. His students Godfrey Sykes, F. W. Moody, Reuben Townroe and James Gamble all emulated his style, but with a certain Victorian rigidity. Stevens designed a number of cast-iron pieces.

5.20 *Top right* Godfrey Sykes and Reuben Townroe: **Mosaic panels illustrating the arts and sciences 'in their application to manufactures', for the quadrangle of the South Kensington Museum.** *The Building News*, 30 June 1876.

The panels depict Fine Art, Design, Building, Agriculture, Pottery and Glass, Commerce, Textile Fabrics, Mining, Engineering and Steel Smelting.

5.22 *Above* F. W. Moody: **Chapter heading.** *Lectures and Lessons on Art*, 1875.

5.23 and **5.24** *Below left* Godfrey Sykes and Reuben Townroe: **Mosaic decorations for the exterior of the quadrangle, the South Kensington Museum.** *The Building News*, 3 March 1876.

The quadrangle is conceived in a late medieval North Italian style—a style half Gothic, half proto-Renaissance. The profusion of representations of figures in contemporary dress savours far more of Gothic than Renaissance practice.

5.25 *Left* ALBERT MOORE: **Design for a mosaic panel for the Central Hall of the Houses of Parliament,** *c.* 1860. *The Studio,* May 1900.

The panel shows St Andrew attended by two female figures representing fortitude and faith. Moore was unworried by anachronisms or conflicting styles in his paintings—he would even show figures in draped Classical costumes holding Japanese fans.

5.26 *Above* WILLIAM BURGES: **Room in Cardiff Castle for the Marquess of Bute** (1870s). Richard Popplewell Pullan, *The Architectural Designs of William Burges,* 1883.

Burges' exteriors are mainly in a scholarly, though inspired, thirteenth-century French Gothic style. His interiors, however, are often eclectic. The ceiling in this comparatively modest room is borrowed from an Islamic source.

5.27 RICHARD NORMAN SHAW: **Chimneypiece in alabaster and marbles for the picture gallery at Cragside, Northumberland.** Drawn by W. R. Lethaby, *c.* 1880. W. Shaw Sparrow, ed., *The British Home of To-Day,* 1904.

This design has elements which appear to have been taken from late sixteenth-century Italian or Flemish strapwork which are combined with French seventeenth-century details—perhaps adapted from the engravings of Jean Le Pautre.

5.28 CHRISTOPHER DRESSER: **Grotesque design.** *Studies in Design,* 1874–6.

A free adaptation of either the eleventh-century Cluniac or Celtic manuscript styles—no attempt has been made to achieve archaeological precision. It is possible that this design is by J. Moyr Smith, who worked for Dresser, probably in the late 1860s, and produced work in a very similar manner.

5.29 *Far right* BRUCE J. TALBERT: **Design for border,** *c.* 1870. The Print Room, Victoria and Albert Museum, London.

As a decorative designer Talbert was an eclectic. This design has floral elements which seem Japanese, while the background foliage is typical of contemporary British work.

5.30 *Below* RICHARD NORMAN SHAW: **Chimneypiece at Dawpool, Cheshire,** 1882–4. R. Phene Spiers, *Architectural Drawings,* 1892.

Shaw's work never descends to the level of pastiche or turgid archaeological exercises. Here he combines late medieval and Renaissance details.

5.31 *Above* CHRISTOPHER DRESSER: **Wall decorations.** *Studies in Design,* 1874–6.

Studies in Design proclaimed Dresser's eclecticism and shows designs in a wide range of more or less 'pure' styles. Some, however, are in mixed styles, or are very free interpretations of historical and national styles. The main design on this plate is loosely Islamic in character, although the roundel is reminiscent of Gothic Revival Geometrical design.

5.32 *Above left* OWEN W. DAVIS: **Door decorations.** *Art and Work*, 1885.

An adaptation of High Renaissance, Raphaelesque decoration. The seven-panelled door (bottom right-hand panel), however, is eighteenth-century in its proportions.

5.33 *Above* THOMAS CRANE: **Decoration for an embroidered table-cloth.** M. S. Lockwood and E. Glaister, *Art Embroidery*, 1878.

Thomas Crane's designs for secular embroideries epitomize Aesthetic Movement taste. Here the leaf and blossom motif appears to have been adapted from Greek vase painting. The radiating suns, however, are suggestive of Japanese design. Thomas Crane was the brother of Walter Crane.

5.35 *Above* CHRISTOPHER DRESSER: **Decorative panel.** *Modern Ornamentation*, 1886.

The design is composed of arabesques which have been borrowed from an Islamic source. (Dresser would have known Owen Jones' *Alhambra*, and could have used it as a reference.) The organization of the design, however, is typical of the late nineteenth century.

5.34 *Left* LEWIS F. DAY: **Door decorations.** *The Planning of Ornament*, 1887.

Day combines a floral arrangement, which appears to have been inspired by Japanese decoration, with Greek key patterns. He had a particular ability to synthesize unrelated styles and was one of the most accomplished of eclectic designers. His textbooks are still used by designers and students.

5.36 *Right* WALTER CRANE: **An illustration** from his *Mrs Mundi, At Home*, 1875.

In Crane's allegorical poem the Sun, the Moon, the Seasons, the Elements, the Nations etc. are invited to a grand ball given by Mrs Mundi—an Aesthetic hostess. The clouds and sun are represented in the Japanese manner, the potted plants in Neo-Greek style, the male figure—the Sun—is dressed in eighteenth-century fashion, and the female figure—Spring—appears to be in Pre-Raphaelite costume. The book encapsulates the enthusiasms of the Aesthetic Movement.

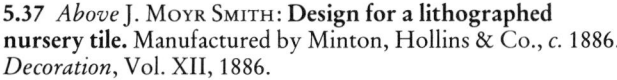
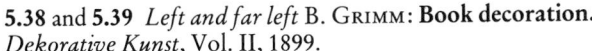

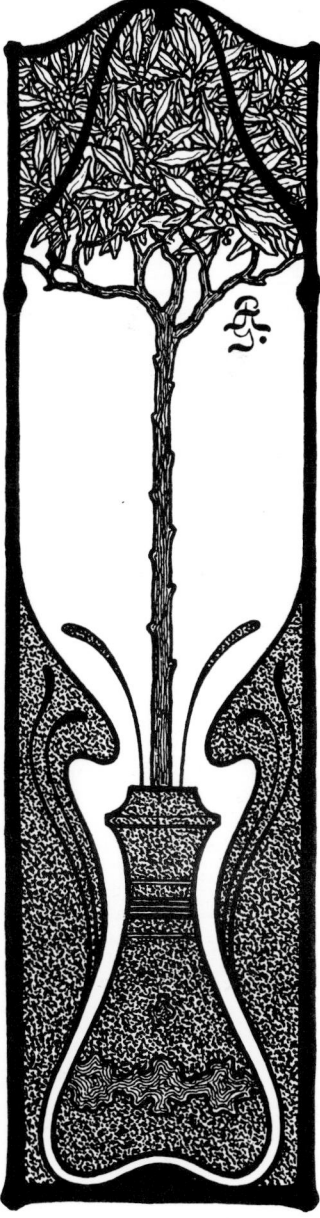

5.37 *Above* J. MOYR SMITH: **Design for a lithographed nursery tile.** Manufactured by Minton, Hollins & Co., *c.* 1886. *Decoration*, Vol. XII, 1886.

Moyr Smith was evidently inspired by Walter Crane's nursery wallpapers (see Plates 5.42, 43). Moyr Smith was the editor and principal contributor of *Decoration*, a well-produced magazine which epitomized the eclectic tastes of the 1880s.

5.38 and **5.39** *Left and far left* B. GRIMM: **Book decoration.** *Dekorative Kunst*, Vol. II, 1899.

These designs, though yet more mannered, recall the elegant 'Classical' vases with flowers which graced the decoration associated with the Aesthetic Movement in Britain. Nevertheless, Grimm's design belongs unquestionably to the period of the Jugendstil.

5.41 WALTER CRANE: **Sgraffito spandrel.** *The Building News*, 31 December 1886.

Crane was enthusiastic about reviving *sgraffito* decoration. The technique (*sgraffito* = 'scratched') was widely used during the Middle Ages and the Renaissance. The greatest British exponent of the technique was Heywood Sumner.

5.40 *Far left* H. OSPOVAT: **Book-plate for Walter Crane.** Gleeson White, 'Some recent bookplates, mostly pictorial', *The Studio*, March 1897.

Ospovat was born in Russia but studied at the National Art Training Schools, later the Royal College of Art, London. Here he paraphrases Crane's eclectic style.

5.42 WALTER CRANE: **'Sing a Song of Sixpence'.** For Jeffrey & Co., 1875. Alan Victor Sugden and John Ludlam Edmondson, *A History of English Wallpaper* (1925).

This was the earliest of Walter Crane's many wallpaper designs. The figures are clad in a variety of costumes—some in the Pre-Raphaelite or 'Reformed' dress of the 1870s. The borders separating the illustrations are in a Raphaelesque manner. (The nursery-rhymes illustrated include: The Queen of Hearts, Little Boy Blue, Bo-Peep and Four-and-Twenty Blackbirds.)

5.43 *Above* WALTER CRANE: **'The House that Jack Built'.** For Jeffrey & Co., 1886. *The Studio*, December 1894.

Crane's nursery wallpapers are in the same eclectic style as his 'toy-books'. His influences included the Japanese print, linear figure drawings from Greek vases, and the South Kensington style of Godfrey Sykes.

5.44 C. J. P. MILLER AND H. CHILDS: **Ceiling corner.** *Decoration*, July 1886.

Miller's design (top right) is loosely based on late seventeenth-century French ornament. Childs' design (bottom left) consists almost entirely of an arrangement of Greek anthemions with the addition of rather inappropriate Adamesque swags or festoons.

5.45 GEORGE PRETTY: **Decoration for the lower panels of a door.** *Decoration*, October 1886.

A fairly free interpretation of the Italian or French Grotesque style.

5.46 ANDREW WELLS: **Painted frieze and dado band for the parlour of John P. Currie,** Pollokshields, Scotland. *Decoration,* October 1886.

Adamesque decoration, with some typically nineteenth-century sprays of naturalistic foliage in the frieze.

5.47 MRS COURTNEY-EDMONDS: **Decoration for a ceiling centre.** *Decoration,* November 1886.

The decorative motifs, which are derived from the Greek anthemion and stylized plant forms, are combined with considerable skill.

5.48 W. REYNOLDS: **Decorative panel.** *Decoration,* December 1886.

The grotesque birds are reminiscent of those found in Italian textiles of the fourteenth century—in particular those produced in Lucca. The remainder of the design is Renaissance in character.

5.49 *Left* OWEN W. DAVIS: **The 'King's College' wallpaper decoration.** For William Woollams & Co., 1890. Alan Victor Sugden and John Ludlam Edmondson, *A History of English Wallpaper* (1925).

This scheme is loosely seventeenth-century—particularly the strapwork—although its overall organization is typical of the late nineteenth century.

5.50 *Below* CHRISTOPHER DRESSER: **Fragment of a decorative panel.** *Modern Ornamentation*, 1886.

Dresser uses two principal styles in this design. The corner motif is geometric Gothic—of the kind favoured by Pugin or Colling. The adjacent borders are arabesques.

5.52 *Below* G. A. AUDSLEY AND M. A. AUDSLEY: **Scheme for wall decoration.** *The Practical Decorator and Ornamentist*, 1892.

The stylized plant motifs are of the type that Pugin illustrated in his *Floriated Ornament*. The dado rail, however, is of a Classical or Renaissance character.

5.51 CHRISTOPHER DRESSER: **Fragment of an all-over pattern.** *Modern Ornamentation*, 1886.

Although the elements in this design are almost wholly Gothic—of a distinctly nineteenth-century variety—the organization is of a most unmedieval kind.

5.56 ROBERT ANNING BELL: **Damask table-cloth.** Manufactured by John Wilson's Successors. *The Studio*, November 1899.

Anning Bell is best known for his illustrated books, coloured plaster reliefs, and his watercolours of women in Classical or Renaissance costume. This design illustrates Shakespeare's *A Midsummer Night's Dream*.

5.53 *Left* G. A. AUDSLEY AND M. A. AUDSLEY: **Ceiling decoration.** *The Practical Decorator and Ornamentist*, 1892.

This design is based almost wholly upon the Greek anthemion —a motif composed of radiating leaf or petal forms. Here, it is used in a manner which recalls that of Robert Adam, or his protégé George Richardson.

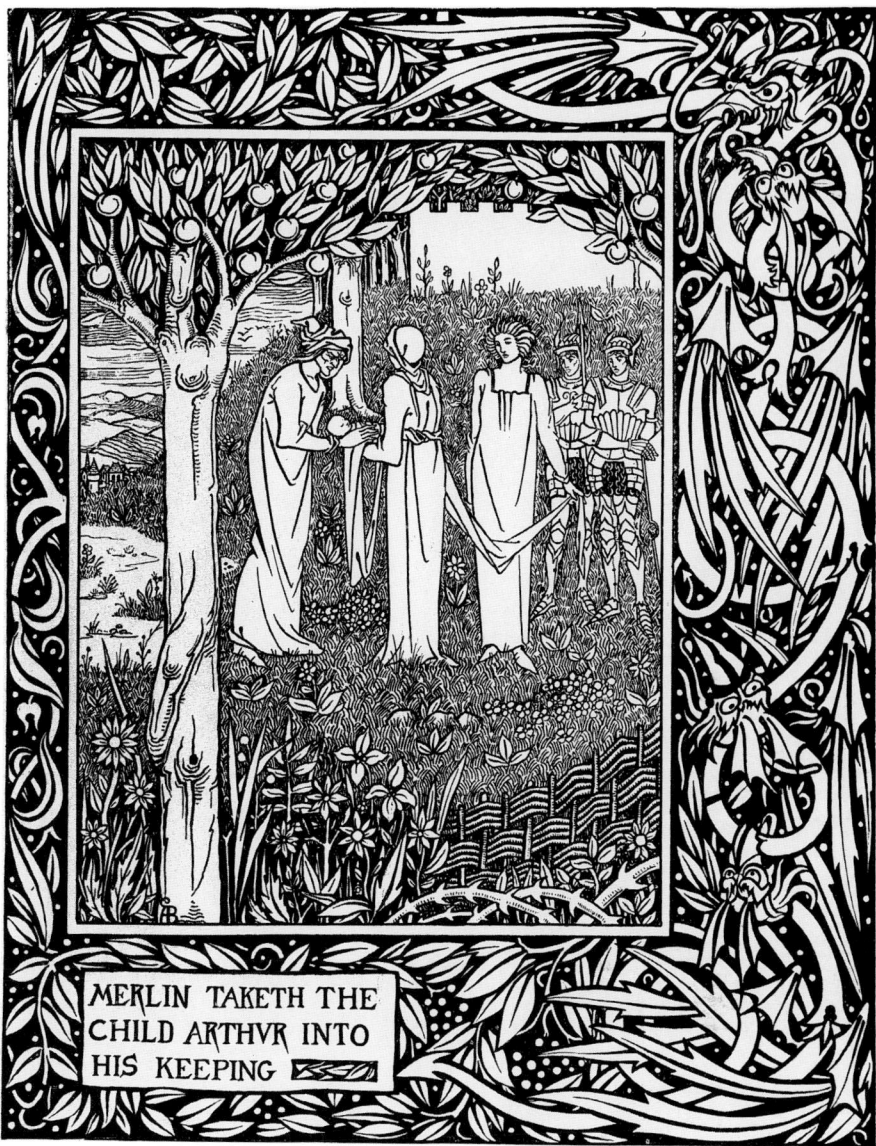

5.54 *Opposite* G. A. AUDSLEY AND M. A. AUDSLEY: **Decoration.** *The Practical Decorator and Ornamentist*, 1892.

This design, based on Greek motifs, is clearly intended for a dado. Its organization, however, is most unarchaeological and entirely a product of the late nineteenth century.

5.55 *Opposite* WALTER CRANE: **'Corona Vitae'. Wallpaper with frieze.** For Jeffrey & Co., 1890. *Art et Décoration*, Vol. IV, 1898.

Crane has taken as his principal model Italian woven textile design of the fourteenth century. But the idealized figures are in loose-fitting Classical dress. So skilful is Crane, however, that this juxtaposition is entirely pleasing.

5.57 AUBREY BEARDSLEY: **A page from Sir Thomas Malory's** *Morte D'Arthur*, 1893–4. Joseph Pennell, 'A New Illustrator: Aubrey Beardsley', *The Studio*, April 1893.

Beardsley assimilated several powerful influences, including the art of Burne Jones, William Morris' Kelmscott Press books, and the Japanese coloured woodblock print. The malevolent grotesque faces in the border may have been suggested by Celtic illumination.

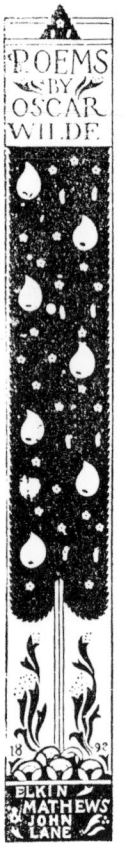

5.59 *Above* CHARLES RICKETTS: **Title-page for Michael Drayton's *Nimphidia and the Muses*,** published by the Vale Press in 1896. *The Studio*, October 1896.

Although Ricketts was acquainted with the work of the Kelmscott Press and Aubrey Beardsley, an important influence was early Venetian book illustration and decoration—in particular the *Hypnerotomachia Poliphili* (1499).

5.58 *Top left* CHARLES RICKETTS: **Design for the cover of Oscar Wilde's *Poems*,** 1892. *The Studio*, Vol. IV, 1894.

The formality of this design suggests the influence of Renaissance Venetian printing, while the sinuous plants are reminiscent of William Blake. There is also a distinct affinity with Beardsley's decorative work.

5.60 *Left* WILL BRADLEY: **Cover of the prospectus of Bradley's magazine *Will Bradley, his book*.** *The Studio*, June 1896.

Bradley (1868–1962), an American book illustrator and poster designer, fell under the spell of the Kelmscott Press and Beardsley. His Beardsleyesque poster designs of the 1890s are among the most memorable graphic works of the 'black and white' era.

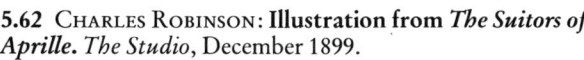

5.61 LAURENCE HOUSMAN: **Illustration from *The Field of Clover.** The Studio*, February 1899.

Like Ricketts, Housman was influenced by early Italian printed books. In the border of this design, however, there is an almost excessive complexity which is reminiscent of Morris' Kelmscott borders.

5.62 CHARLES ROBINSON: **Illustration from *The Suitors of Aprille.** The Studio*, December 1899.

Charles Robinson, the brother of Heath Robinson, was to become one of the most successful book illustrators during the Edwardian period. The foliage motifs in the border of this design are linked by the simple device of two sets of adjoining circles—the effect is rich and less frenetic than that of many Kelmscott borders.

5.63 CHRISTOPHER DRESSER: **Textile design,** 1895–1900. *The Architectural Review*, 1937.

This is probably the work of an anonymous member of the Dresser Studio, rather than Dresser himself, who by the 1890s was concerned almost entirely with selling designs. The figures are borrowed from Aubrey Beardsley.

5.64 CARLOS SCHWABE: **Illustration for Catulle-Mendes'** *L'Evangile de l'Enfance*, 1892. *Art et Décoration*, January-June 1899.

Schwabe was a major exhibitor at the first salon of the Rose Croix—the Belgian Rosicrucian movement. Here he combines naturalism and stylization with the same facility as Burne Jones.

5.65 and **5.66** ANONYMOUS: **Headpieces.** For J. Arthur Thomson 'The Biology of Autumn' and Patrick Geddes 'The Sociology of Autumn', *The Evergreen. A Northern Seasonal. The Book of Autumn*, 1895.

The upper design is a grotesque bat. The lower design is an updated version of a Celtic interlaced device—borrowed from a cross or an illuminated manuscript.

5.67 *Right* JAN TOOROP: **Theatre programme cover.** Gabriel Mourey, 'Some French illustrated theatre programmes', *The Studio*, May 1897.

Toorop spent his early years in Java. The figures in his symbolist compositions of the 1890s have the attenuated quality of Javanese shadow-puppets—this is especially the case with his famous drawing 'The Three Brides' which was illustrated in the September 1893 issue of *The Studio*. The flame-like motifs in this programme cover may also relate to shadow-puppet (Wayang) decoration.

5.68 *Left* CHARLES RENNIE MACKINTOSH: **Poster for The Scottish Musical Review.** Gleeson White, 'Some Glasgow Designers and their Work', Part I, *The Studio*, July 1897.

The dreaming—or brooding—face was perhaps inspired by the drawings of the Belgian Symbolist Fernand Khnopff, whose work Mackintosh could have seen in W. Shaw Sparrow's article in the March 1894 issue of *The Studio*. The singing birds could have come from Morris, or Voysey. Mackintosh was also evidently influenced by the decorative style of *The Evergreen*.

5.69 *Above* JAMES ALLAN DUNCAN: **Design for a book-cover.** *The Studio*, December 1898.

Duncan was trained in Glasgow, although he was not part of the Mackintosh circle. Here he has adapted interlacing patterns of the type found in the Book of Kells, the Lindisfarne Gospels and the Book of Darrow.

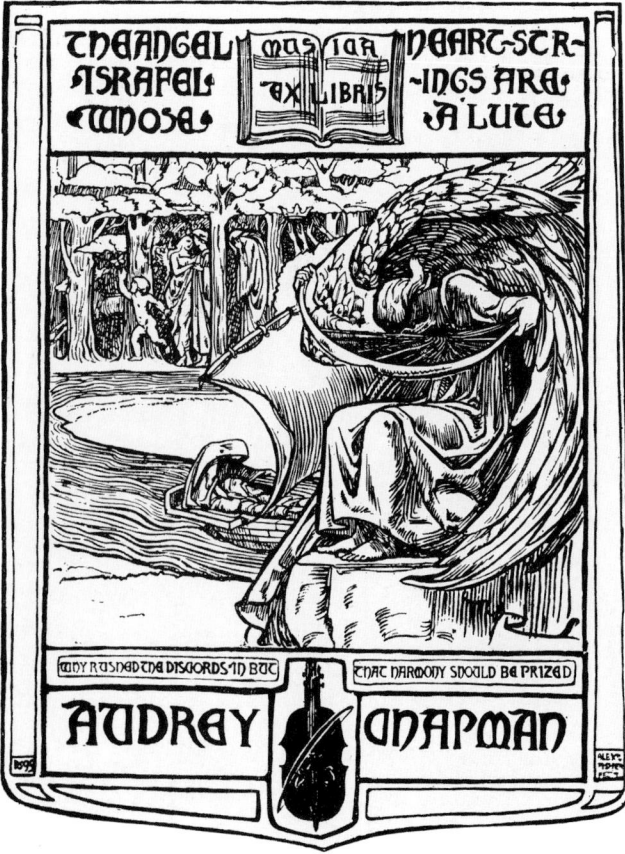

5.70 *Left* ALEXANDER FISHER: **Book-plate for Audrey Chapman**, 1899. *The Studio*, May 1900.

The design is a complex allegory: the Angel Azrafel, 'whose heart strings are a lute', makes sweet music; 'behind . . . there are figures typical of love, youth and youthful sorrow'. A boat bearing the dead body of an old man floats down the River of Time to the Unknown.

5.71 CHRISTINE ANGUS: **Design for an initial letter.** *The Studio*, August 1900.

Christine Angus was a Liverpool art student and a pupil of the Glasgow-trained Herbert McNair—a close friend of Mackintosh. The ethereal standing figure is reminiscent of the Glasgow style—in particular the work of the Macdonald sisters. The Burne Jones-like figures in the upper half of the letter are reflected in its lower part, thus producing a curiously disturbing effect.

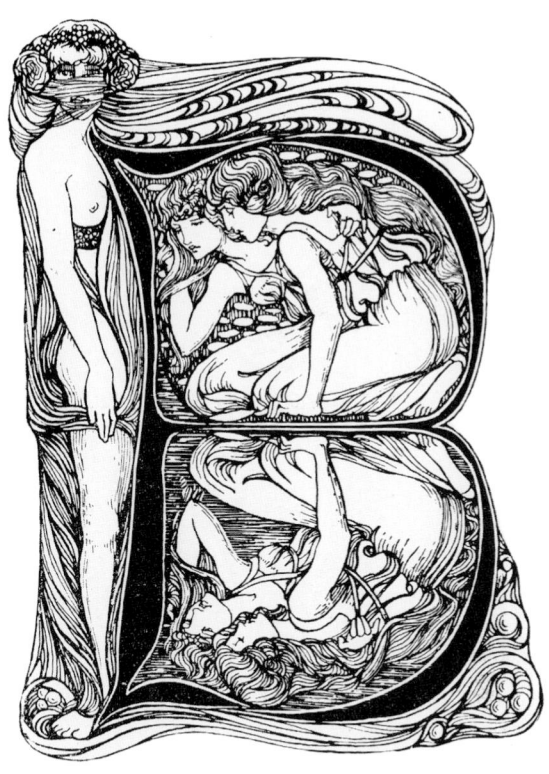

5.72 H. WIJDEVELD: **Design for a calendar.** *The Studio*, April 1907.

Wijdeveld, a Dutch architect, was twenty-two when this design was executed. He had recently spent some time studying British decoration and architecture in London. He was later to become editor of the avant-garde Dutch architectural journal *Wendigen* and a champion of Frank Lloyd Wright. The pastoral images in this design are characteristic of the British Arts and Crafts movement. Floral and foliage design was widely taught in Holland.

CHAPTER SIX

Orientalism

The West has long been drawn to the East. During the Middle Ages, Islamic decorative ideas were so thoroughly absorbed that their presence has only been recognized comparatively recently. The arabesque is an example of what was originally a Graeco-Roman motif returning home, so to speak, via the Islamic World. The ogee arch (or four-centred arch), which was so characteristic a feature of the Decorated Style of the thirteenth and fourteenth centuries, is now thought to be of Indian Buddhist origin. Chinese decorative motifs—the peacock, the dragon or the phoenix—are to be found, shorn of their symbolism, in medieval manuscripts. Engraved ornament by Jean Berain sometimes exhibits Chinese features and Chinese ceramic wares were copied in the early eighteenth century. Thomas Chippendale's *Gentleman and Cabinet-Maker's Director* (1764) contains numerous designs inspired by Chinese models. In 1757, William Chambers (1723–96), in many ways the most influential British architect of his day, who had spent some time in Canton, published *Designs of Chinese Buildings, Furniture, Dresses, Machines and Utensils . . . from the originals drawn in China*.[1]

The fashion for *chinoiserie* as a decorative style reached its height in the eighteenth century. Chinese motifs appeared on textiles, furniture, wallpaper, ceramics and silverware. Frequently whole rooms were decorated in the Chinese style. But by the end of the century the craze began to die down. Later, *japonaiserie* became the fashion. This will be considered in the chapter on Japan.

In general, early interest in Oriental art was of a more or less romantic kind and not based upon scholarly understanding. Certainly Western imitations were rarely accurate. By the middle of the eighteenth century, however, serious archaeological study had become a passion among the intelligentsia. The East India Company had always been able to count men of culture in its ranks and archaeological pursuits were taken up in India by company officials. Warren Hastings (1732–1818) encouraged the study of Indian culture, in particular of Sanskrit literature. Among his protégés were Sir Charles Wilkins (1749?–1836), a senior merchant in the East India Company and the first European translator of the Bhagavad Gita, and Sir William Jones (1746–94), first president of the Asiatic Society of Bengal, judge and one of the greatest students of Oriental languages. Jones made the suggestion that accurate drawings be made of Indian architecture, that they 'may furnish our own architects with new ideas of beauty and sublimity'.[2]

The best-known examples of Indian architectural influence in Britain are Sezincote in Gloucestershire and the Royal Pavilion at Brighton. Sezincote was built in about 1805 by Samuel Pepys Cockerell (1753–1827) for his brother, who had made his fortune in India. The Royal Pavilion, a skilful and amusing pastiche of 'Hindoo' (more correctly Mughul) architecture, was largely the work of John Nash (1752–1835).

This interest in Indian buildings had been inspired to a very considerable extent by the accurate and detailed aquatints of Indian mosques and temples supplied by Thomas Daniell (1749–1840) and his nephew William Daniell (1769–1837), whose *Oriental Scenery* (1795–1815) won the greatest admiration. The Daniells were working at the time when the enthusiasm for

6.1 Wallpaper based on the decorations of the Alhambra. Messrs Woollams, manufacturers, London. *The Art-Journal Illustrated Catalogue. The Industry of All Nations, 1851*, 1851.

the Picturesque was at its height and they often present India as a kind of Elysium. The architects Thomas Hope and Sir John Soane were both interested in Indian architecture. Hope's designs for his house in Duchess Street, London, included Indian elements, and Hope, of course, was highly influential in matters of contemporary taste.

In 1811 and 1821 the French Orientalist Louis Langlès brought out a two-volume work which is probably the most important nineteenth-century study of Indian antiquities, art and iconography. Entitled *Monuments Anciens et Modernes de l'Indoustan* ('Ancient and Modern Monuments of Hindustan') Langlès' study was a synthesis of current writings on India and showed that he knew the work of the Daniells well.

The findings of an Indian historian, Rám Ráz, published by the Royal Asiatic Society in 1834 under the title *Essay on the Architecture of the Hindus* gave Europeans their first opportunity of examining the liturgical principles which governed Hindu temple building. Rám Ráz's achievement was the more remarkable because of the very great difficulty in translating early Sanskrit treatises, which abounded in obscure technical terms. His illustrations, which may well have been the work of an Indian draughtsman, were of architectural decoration as well as complete temples—all were South Indian (Plates 6.21 and 23). Rám Ráz's untimely death deprived India of her first modern historical scholar. His *Essay* remained the standard work on Hindu architecture for many years until replaced by James Fergusson's *History of Architecture in All Countries* (1867) which considers India in greater detail (Plate 6.24). Fergusson also played an early and important role in the photographic documentation of Indian architecture.

During the eighteenth century, interest in the architecture of the Islamic world began to develop. There was an especial fascination with the Alhambra at Granada in southern Spain and other comparatively accessible Moorish remains.[3] Apart from being in accord with the antiquarian enthusiasm of the age, this interest may also be seen as a ramification of the cult of the Picturesque. Durand's influential and widely studied *Recueil et Parallèle des Edifices de tout genre* contains passable engravings of the Alhambra and confirmed the status of the building as a major work of architecture.

James Cavannah Murphy began publishing his *Arabian Antiquities of Spain* in 1813 (Plates 6.7 and 8).[4] His plates illustrate Moorish buildings in Cordoba, Spain, as well as the Alhambra. Matthew Digby Wyatt, while conceding that Murphy's *Arabian Antiquities* had given the British public their first opportunity to study the intricacies of the decoration of the Alhambra, still felt inclined to describe it as a 'singularly inaccurate work'.[5]

By far the most impressive study of the Alhambra was Owen Jones' and Jules Goury's *Plans, Elevations, Sections and Details of the Alhambra*, which was completed in 1845. As a young man Jones had embarked on a grand tour, visiting Greece, Constantinople, the Holy Land, Alexandria, Cairo and Thebes. It was during this journey that he acquired his lifelong admiration for Islamic architecture and ornament. In 1834, in the company of Jules Goury, a most able young French architect and draughtsman, Jones visited the Alhambra. The two resolved to publish a detailed account of the building, its decorations and history. Unfortunately, Goury died during the cholera epidemic of 1834. The loss of a valued friend and collaborator prompted Jones to think for a time of abandoning the immense project. However, with the help of two experienced lithographers, he set up his own lithographic press to reproduce the Alhambra's decorations in colour. The earliest chromolithographic plate in the *Alhambra* is dated '1 March 1836' and must surely be one of the earliest examples of British colour printing.

Jones went to great lengths to ensure the accuracy of his Alhambra details and actually brought back to London impressions of its ornament made with

6.2 EDWARD WILLIAM LANE: **Soffit of a projecting window showing geometric ornament.** *An Account of the Manners and Customs of the Modern Egyptians*, 1860 edition.

Like many Western artists Lane was greatly impressed by Islamic geometrical decoration.

the aid of plaster or unsized paper. The *Alhambra* went into two folio-sized volumes. The first of these, completed in 1842, is in many ways typical of the tradition of books on antiquarian subjects which had begun in the eighteenth century. Jones' fine colour printing and transcriptions of inscriptions in Arabic and Kufic script and their translations in English and French, together with a historical account of the Alhambra by the Spanish Arabist Pascual de Gayangos, make the first volume of the *Alhambra* one of the noblest of nineteenth-century antiquarian works, certainly of those treating of a single building.[6] The second volume is far less satisfactory and consists solely of fifty chromolithographic plates devoted to fragments of decoration which are never shown in their architectural setting. Jones' intention in publishing this second volume was to supply manufacturers and designers with examples of Alhambra ornament to copy or study. In *The Stones of Venice* (1852–3), Ruskin called the decorations of the Alhambra 'vile' and 'detestable'. This reaction to an art he considered mechanical and inhuman was entirely predictable.

Although Jones virtually bankrupted himself in publishing his *Alhambra*—he was obliged to sell family property in Wales—it won him a reputation as an Orientalist, an authority on ornament and the producer of the most sumptuous book of the 1840s. I. K. Brunel, the engineer, and Pugin were among its subscribers. Jones was known as 'Alhambra Jones' for a generation.

An Orientalist who has been somewhat overshadowed by Owen Jones is Edward William Lane (1801–76). Lane did as much as anyone in Britain to arouse enthusiasm for the study of modern Islamic cultures and to dispel the romantic idea that they were medieval societies. He first visited Egypt in 1825.[7] He was a competent draughtsman and made drawings with the aid of a *camera lucida*, the precursor of the photographic camera.

The Egypt which fascinated Lane was modern Egypt. He learned Arabic, lived the life of a cultivated Egyptian and immersed himself in the contemporary culture of Cairo. In 1836 he published *An Account of the Manners and Customs of the Modern Egyptians*, which was illustrated with numerous wood-engravings after his own drawings (Plates 6.25–6). The book caused something of a sensation on its publication and is said to have sold out within a fortnight. As a comparatively inexpensive work, *Modern Egyptians* reached a far larger public than Owen Jones' costly *Alhambra*. Lane's second book, a scholarly translation of *The Thousand and One Nights*, published in monthly parts between 1838 and 1840, was illustrated with wood engravings after delightful drawings by William Harvey (Plates 6.27–30) and must also have done much to further enthusiasm for Eastern art.

A number of painters, too, were attracted to the East. Eugène Delacroix (1798–1863) responded to the sights and colours of North Africa and produced many sketches of Oriental dress and ornament. John Frederick Lewis (1805–1876) lived in the Middle East for some years and painted harem scenes there. Their Oriental sensuality caused a sensation when they were exhibited in London. Many of the painters took great pains to get the details of costume and setting exactly right, filling their studios with appropriate models and bric-à-brac. William Holman Hunt (1827–1910) may have borrowed some of his details from Prisse d'Avennes's *Histoire de l'Art Egyptien* or Lane's *Modern Egyptians*. Lawrence Alma Tadema (1836–1912) meticulously reproduced the background details of ancient Egypt in such pictures as *An Egyptian Widow*.

The German Orientalist F. M. Hessemer (1800–60) has, like Lane, been rather neglected by historians. He was trained as an architect and accompanied the English historian Henry Gally Knight as a draughtsman when he visited Italy and Egypt between 1827 and 1830. His *Arabische und alt-Italienische Bau-verzierungen* ('Arabian and early Italian Building

6.3 Kashmir scarf. Mr Blakeley, manufacturer, Norwich. *The Art-Journal Illustrated Catalogue. The Industry of All Nations, 1851*, 1851.

An elegant and economical design which is closer in spirit to Kashmiri work than many European imitations. This scarf was purchased by Queen Victoria at the Great Exhibition.

Decorations'), published between 1836 and 1842, illustrates the decoration of mosques, tombs and private houses in Cairo and Alexandria in the first part, and in the second part concentrates on decorations in Italy. Like the illustrations in Jones' work Hessemer's drawings are reproduced by chromolithography. The book is, however, more a portfolio of design models than an archaeological study in the manner of the *Alhambra*.

France produced several of the most important nineteenth-century students of Islamic architecture and decoration. Pascal Coste, an architect and antiquarian from Marseilles, whose *Architecture Arabe et Monuments du Caire* ('Arab Architecture and Monuments of Cairo'), was published between 1837 and 1839, was among the earliest of serious students of Islamic design. Coste also published *Monuments Modernes de la Perse* ('Modern Monuments of Persia') in 1867. This was the first comprehensive study of Persian building, although the archaeologist Charles Texier's *Description de l'Arménie, la Perse et la Mésopotamie* ('Description of Armenia, Persia and Mesopotamia') of 1842–5 contains some illustrations of Islamic buildings. Coste's accounts of his travels were published, in two volumes, in 1878.

The perplexing Prisse d'Avennes has generally been seen as a larger-than-life extravagant figure. Egyptologist, Arabist, soldier, diplomat and artist, he was also the author of one of the most sumptuous of all the great chromolithographic books, *L'Art Arabe d'après les monuments du Kaire* ('Arab Art according to the Monuments of Cairo') of 1869–77 (Plate 6.36). Achille-Constant-Théodore-Emile Prisse d'Avennes (1807–79) was born in Avesnes-sur-Helpe, Nord, near the Belgian frontier. His father was an inspector of forests. Prisse d'Avennes qualified as an 'architect–engineer' at the age of nineteen and almost immediately left home to take part in the Greek War of Independence in 1826. He subsequently spent some time in the Holy Land, but later travelled to Egypt. There he became involved in various ambitious schemes, one of which was for moving the obelisk at Luxor. He studied hieroglyphics, learned Arabic and for a time even styled himself Edris-Effendi. He spent many years in Egypt and numerous wild tales were circulated about him. He died in France in some poverty. His fine library was sold in London by his widow. There is a striking contrast between the circumstances in which Prisse d'Avennes spent the last years of his life and the splendour of the four-volume *L'Art Arabe* which was completed just two years before his death. The book has been criticized because Prisse d'Avennes did not indicate all his sources or take into account current research, and even borrowed descriptions without acknowledgement from Saint-Genis' accounts of Islamic antiquities which had been published between 1818 and 1829.[8] There is some justice in such criticisms. But *L'Art Arabe* was written before the high standards of scholarship of the 1870s had been established, and it is more generous to judge it as a book of the 1840s.

Jules Bourgoin, whose work is also discussed in Chapter Three, spent some time in Cairo in his youth collecting and drawing examples of decorations, details and façades. He began publishing his findings in 1867 in *Les Arts Arabes* (Plate 6.37), to which Viollet-le-Duc contributed a preface: 'M. Bourgoin's book is not merely one of those agreeable collections of reproductions to skim through, which grace the libraries of architects and decorators, but which one seldom consults', wrote Viollet-le-Duc, 'rather, it is a practical and complete treatise which reveals a whole new order of composition.' Liberty & Co. of London possessed a copy of Bourgoin's *Les Arts Arabes*. It very likely served as the main source of reference for the Liberty Studio when they were designing their 'Moorish' interiors, which were fashionable in the 1880s and 1890s.

Viollet-le-Duc also contributed a preface to another book on Islamic design—Léon Parvillée's *Architecture et Décoration Turques au XVe siècle*

6.4 Ornament worn by Tibetan women. Illustrated in 'Tibetan Art', an article by Mrs Lilian Le Mesurier. *The Studio*, May 1904.

Tibetan art was discovered later than that of any other Eastern country. The metalwork of the 'Forbidden land', remarked Mrs Le Mesurier, 'remains veiled like a purdah woman'. Her article was published at a time when *The Studio* was filled with accounts of the doings of members of the Arts and Crafts Movement. Its illustrations were no doubt intended as suggestions for contemporary craft workers.

('Turkish Architecture and Decoration since the Fifteenth Century') of 1873. Viollet-le-Duc was deeply interested in Islamic design. He incorporated Islamic details in some of his own projects, for example, the tiled façade of the draper's emporium which appears in *Entretiens sur l'Architecture* ('Discourses on Architecture') of 1863–72. Some of the geometrical decoration in his designs for the murals for Notre-Dame were also inspired by Islamic motifs.

In his second book, *Théorie de l'Ornement* ('Theory of Ornament') of 1873, Bourgoin attempted to formulate a comprehensive and universal system of repeat pattern or tessellation. His ideas, though far from being wholly dependent upon Islamic geometry, do owe much to it. In *Les Elements de l'Art Arabe. Le trait des entrelacs* ('The Elements of Arab Art. The nature of interfacing') of 1879, he illustrates nearly two hundred examples of Islamic geometrical ornament and gives an analysis of the geometrical structure which is superimposed upon each design. Bourgoin was one of the most original thinkers to have directed his attentions to the subject of ornament. His approach is dispassionate and, in this respect, is in contrast to several more recent works, which are all too inclined to attribute mystical significance to Islamic decoration.[9]

An important episode in the history of the influence of Oriental design was the Great Exhibition in London of 1851. The East India Company displayed many Indian fabrics at the exhibition which were greatly admired by those most involved with the Government School of Design, in particular Henry Cole, Owen Jones and Richard Redgrave (Plate 6.35). Of the £5000 which the Treasury allocated from the profits of the exhibition for the purchase of objects of 'excellence in design' or 'rare skill in art workmanship' for Henry Cole's new Museum of Manufacture, just over £1500 was spent on articles exhibited by the East India Company. Owen Jones' remarks in the catalogue make interesting reading. He spoke of the Indian products as

> the works of a people who are still faithful to their art as to the religion, habits and modes of thought which inspired it: whilst those objects in the Collection which are of European workmanship exhibit only the disordered state of art at which we have now arrived; we have no guiding principles in design, and still less unity in its application. ... In the Indian Collection, we find no struggle after an effect; every ornament arises quietly and naturally from the object decorated, inspired by some true feeling, or embellishing some real want.

To a very considerable extent, Jones' views were echoed by two distinguished German authorities, the art historian Dr Gustave Waagen and the architect Gottfried Semper. Later compilers of encyclopedias of ornament—such as Racinet and Dolmetsch—also shared Jones' enthusiasm for Oriental designs. Indeed, with the advent of the encyclopedias of ornament, Oriental motifs and designs became part of a subconscious repertoire, and can be seen in the work of men as remote from each other as William Morris and Léon Bakst, or Antonio Gaudí and Gustav Klimt.

6.5 Designs on a copper Tibetan tea-pot. Illustrated in 'Tibetan Art', an article by Mrs Lilian Le Mesurier. *The Studio*, May 1904.

Tibetan metalwork was here described as 'almost Gothic in character'. Mrs Le Mesurier had evidently visited Sikkim and Western Tibet.

6.6 *Left* **Detail from the Alhambra:** Don Pablo Lozano, *Antiguedades Arabes de España*, 1804.

The Alhambra was the earliest important Islamic building to be known in the West. Numerous eighteenth-century writers make reference to it. The architectural theorist J.-N.-L. Durand illustrated it in his treatise of 1801. It thus gained an important place in architectural history.

6.7 *Above* JAMES CAVANAH MURPHY: **Hall of the Abencerrages, The Alhambra.** *The Arabian Antiquities of Spain*, 1813–16.

Murphy was a fine draughtsman. His somewhat romantic drawings, however, did not please the Victorians, who were obsessed with archaeological precision. Matthew Digby Wyatt compared Murphy's efforts unfavourably with those of Owen Jones.

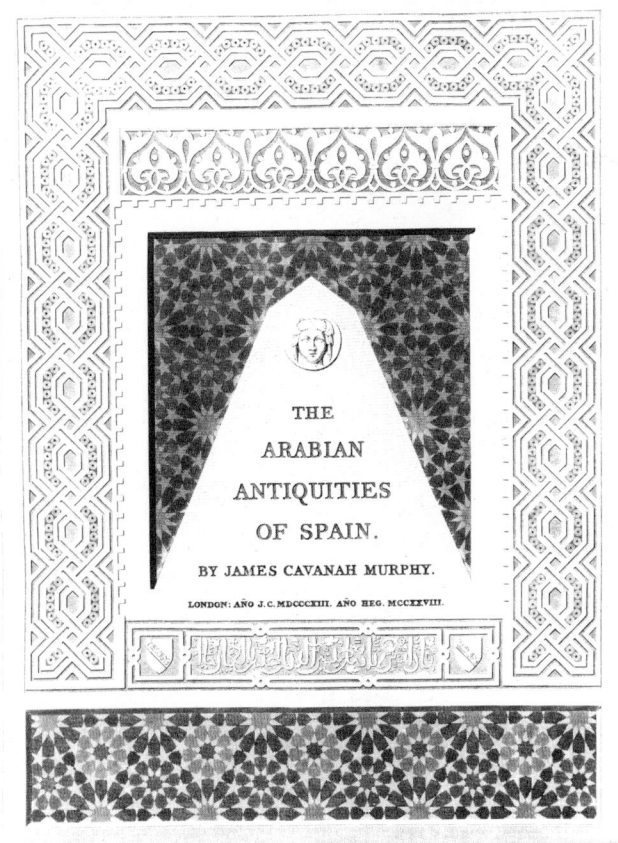

6.8 *Left* JAMES CAVANAH MURPHY: **Title-page** of *The Arabian Antiquities of Spain*, 1813–16.

James Murphy was the earliest English-speaking authority to make a detailed study of Islamic architecture—although Thomas and William Daniell had provided superb illustrations of Mughul and Hindu architecture in their *Oriental Scenery*.

6.9 GEORGE AITCHISON: **Design for the Arab Hall,** Leighton House, London, 1880. Watercolour and gouache. The Royal Institute of British Architects, London. Designed for Frederick Leighton, the painter. (The frieze is by Walter Crane.)

6.10 JULES BOURGOIN: **Entrance to the Fountain of Kaïd-Bey,** Cairo. *Les Art Arabes*, 1868–73.

The enthusiasm for patterned brickwork which was widespread in France in the 1870s and 1880s may well have been prompted by the 'discovery' of Islamic architecture.

145

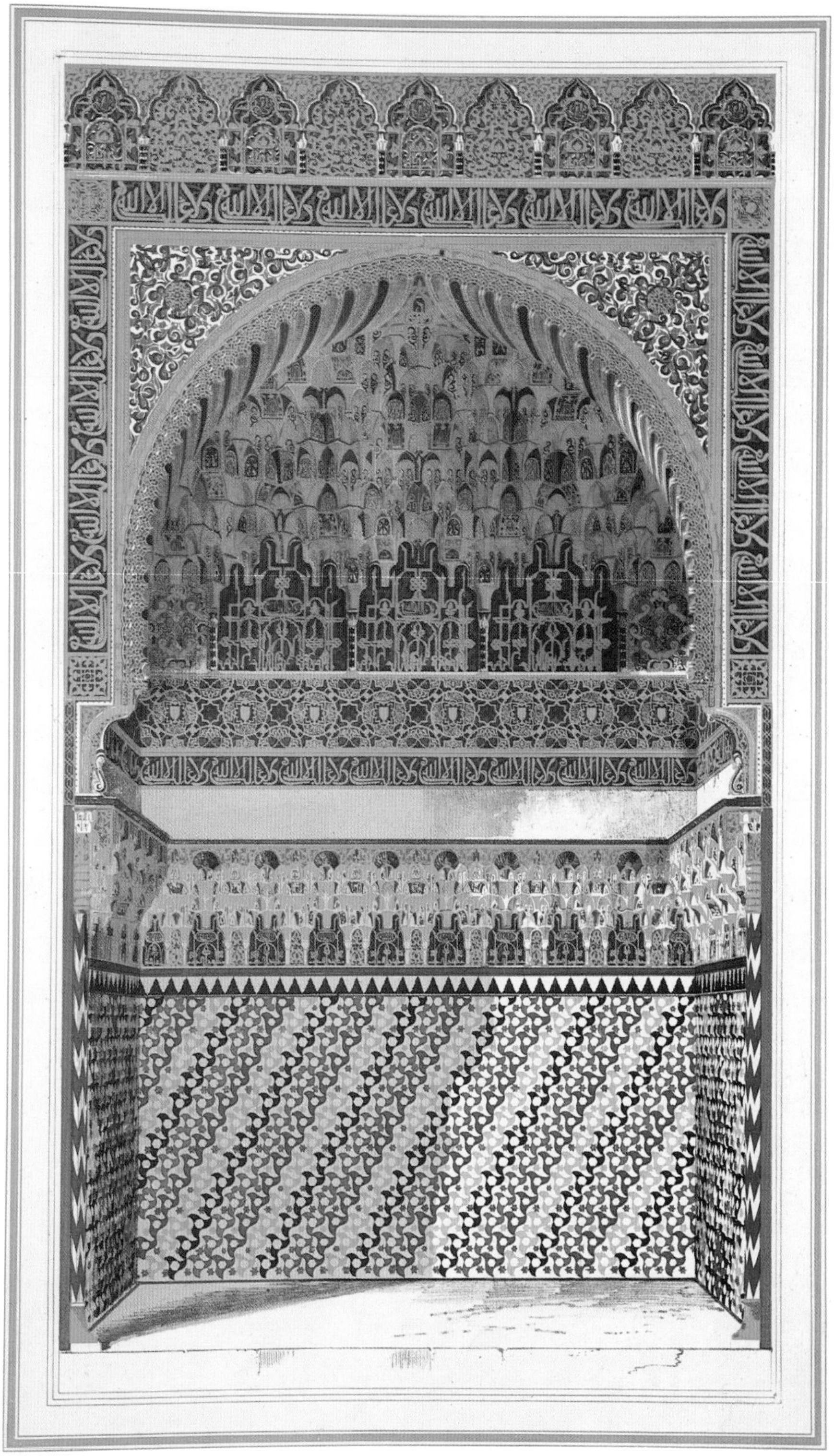

6.11 *Left* N. SIMAKOFF: **Details of moulded ceramic decoration from the Tomb of Khadji-Toglou,** Samarkand. *L'Art de l'Asie Centrale, 1879–83.*

6.12 *Below left* N. SIMAKOFF: **Details of Central Asian silk embroideries.** *L'Art de l'Asie Centrale, 1879–83.*

6.13 *Bottom left* FRIEDRICH M. HESSEMER: **Mosaic decorations from Cairo.** *Arabische und alt-Italienische bau-Verzierungen, 1936–42.*

6.14 *Below* OWEN JONES AND JULES GOURY: **Detail from the Alhambra.** *Plans, Elevations, Sections and Details of the Alhambra, 1842–5.*

6.16 *Right* Charles Texier: **Ornament from a porch in Tabriz,** Iran. *Description de l'Arménie, la Perse et la Mésopotamie,* 1842.

6.15 N. Simakoff: **Decorative details.** *L'Art de l'Asie Centrale,* 1879–83.

6.17 *Below* M. A. Racinet: **Persian decoration.** *L'Ornement Polychrome,* 1869.

6.18 *Below right* E. Prisse d'Avennes: **Textile fragment,** 14th century. *La Décoration Arabe,* 1885.

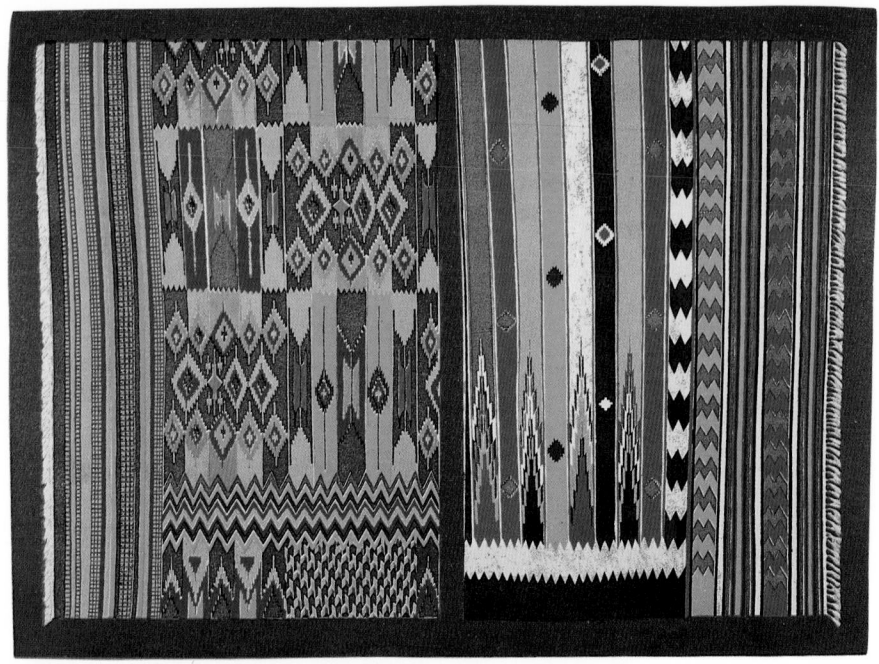

6.19 An inexpensive cotton carpet from India: J. B. Waring, *Masterpieces of Industrial Art and Sculpture at the International Exhibition, 1862, 1863.*

6.20 Scarf from Kashmir: M. D. Wyatt, *The Industrial Arts of the Nineteenth Century at the Great Exhibition, MDCCCLI, 1851–3.*

Indian design was much admired at the Great Exhibition.

6.21 *Right* RAM RAZ: **Details of South Indian columns and entablature, with Sanskrit nomenclature.** *Essay on the Architecture of the Hindus*, 1834.

Ram Raz's knowledge of Sanskrit enabled him to understand texts describing the principles of Hindu architecture which were inaccessible to European students.

6.22 *Above* GEORGE PHILLIPS: **Indian decorative details.** *Rudiments of Curvilinear Design* (1838–40).

Phillips does not disclose the reference sources for his neo-Hindu designs. The cusped arches suggest late South Indian Mughul-influenced architecture—the Palace at Tanjore, for example. He could have taken his ideas from the illustrations in Thomas and William Daniell's *Oriental Scenery*. The columns, however, suggest that he may have known Ram Raz's book.

6.23 *Right* RAM RAZ: **Entablatures, or prastaras.** *Essay on the Architecture of the Hindus*, 1834.

There is a certain stylized quality in the illustrations to Ram Raz's book which hints that they were the work of an Indian draughtsman. Ram Raz does not identify the majority of his examples, but all were in South India.

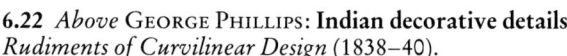

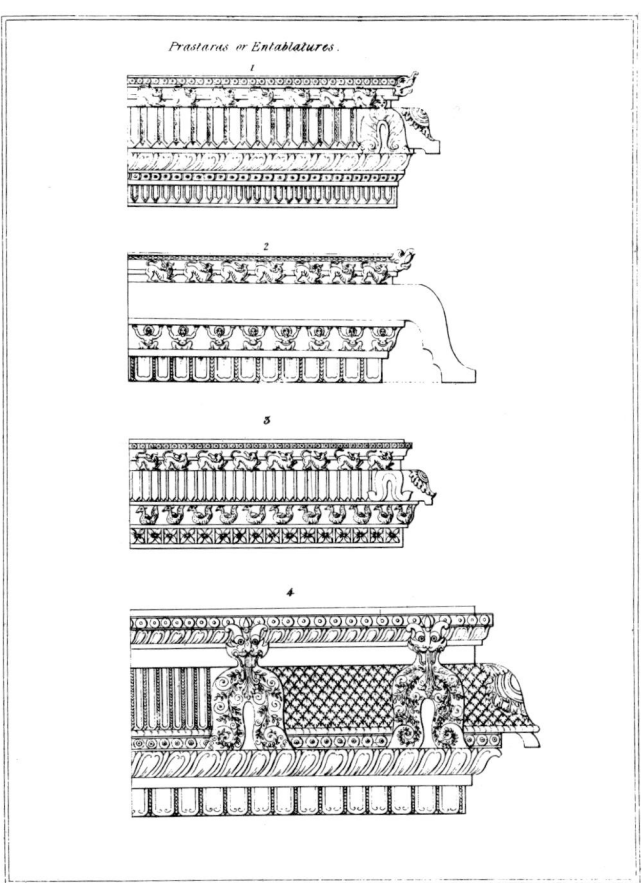

6.24 *Left* JAMES FERGUSSON: **Window in Ahmedabad.** After a photograph by Colonel Biggs. *History of Indian and Eastern Architecture*, 1891.

Photographs, copied by highly skilled wood-engravers, made possible the accurate illustration of all manner of subjects in comparatively inexpensive works such as this.

6.25 *Below left* EDWARD WILLIAM LANE: **Examples of panelling.** *An Account of the Manners and Customs of the Modern Egyptians*, 1860 edition.

The book is illustrated with wood-engravings after Lane's own drawings— some of which were made with the aid of a 'camera lucida' (a lens and prism which projected a faint image onto a drawing-board).

6.27 *Right* WILLIAM HARVEY: **Chapter heading** from Edward William Lane's *The Thousand and One Nights*, 1838–40. Engraving by Mason Jackson.

6.28 *Below* WILLIAM HARVEY: **Chapter heading** from Edward William Lane's *The Thousand and One Nights*, 1838–40. Engraving by Mason Jackson.

6.26 *Opposite left* EDWARD WILLIAM LANE: **Examples of lattice work.** *An Account of the Manners and Customs of the Modern Egyptians*, 1860 edition.

Lattice work screens and grilles, of the kind illustrated here, were an especially prominent feature of the 'Moorish' style of decoration introduced by Liberty & Co. of London in the 1880s.

6.29 *Left* WILLIAM HARVEY: **Chapter heading** from Edward William Lane's *The Thousand and One Nights*, 1838–40. Engraving by Landells.

The decoration is probably based upon an Islamic illuminated manuscript, although Harvey's design has a certain Rococo feel to it. He could well have found his model in the British Museum, or in the Bodleian Library, Oxford.

6.31 *Opposite* RICHARD GLAZIER: **Kashmir scarf.** *Manual of Historic Ornament*, 1899.

The elegant stylization of this Kashmir scarf should be compared with the clumsy naturalism of a Paisley shawl shown at the Great Exhibition (see Plate 6.32). Glazier's admirable and inexpensive book, in black and white, was a standard work for a generation of art students.

6.30 WILLIAM HARVEY: **Chapter heading** from Edward William Lane's *The Thousand and One Nights*, 1838–40. Engraving by Mary Ann Williams.

Harvey has here interpreted Islamic decoration very freely.

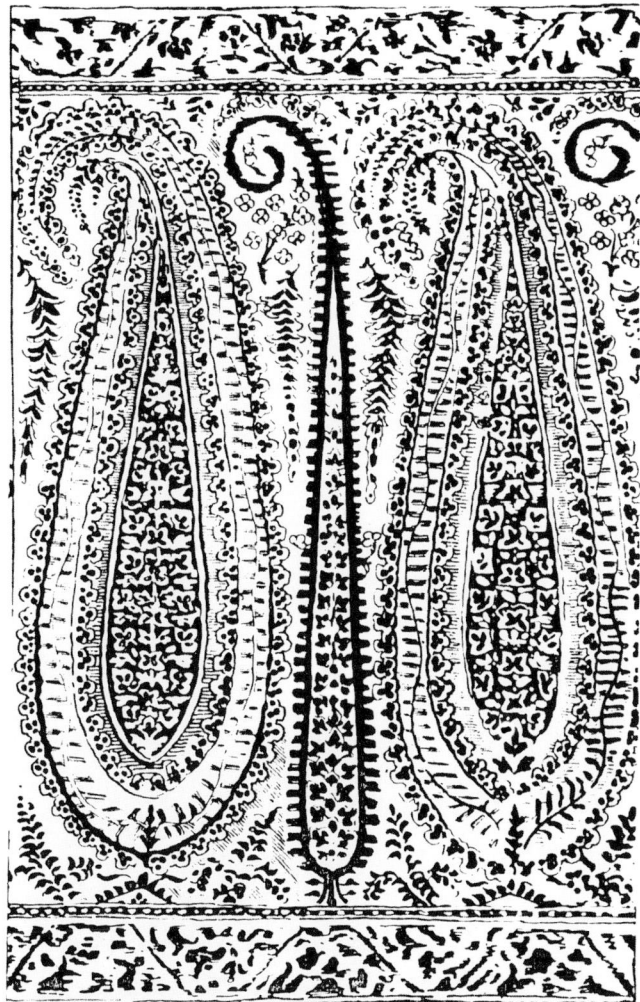

CASHMERE SCARF WITH THE PATTERN
FORMED OF PINES SCARLET GROUND. S K M.

6.32 *Above* **Shawl.** John Morgan & Co., manufacturers, Paisley. *The Art-Journal Illustrated Catalogue. The Industry of All Nations, 1851,* 1851.

An exaggeratedly naturalistic interpretation of traditional Kashmiri shawl design.

6.33 *Left* **Damask hanging.** Ackroyd and Son, manufacturers, Halifax. *The Art-Journal Illustrated Catalogue. The Industry of All Nations, 1851,* 1851.

A design adapted from the decorations in the Alhambra. As early as 1844, however, D. R. Hay, the Edinburgh house decorator, remarked that the Alhambra had become 'too familiar' through 'constant repetition'.

6.34 RALPH NICHOLSON WORNUM: **Decoration from the Alhambra.** *Analysis of Ornament*, 1855.

Wornum's book was based upon a series of lectures on ornament which he delivered at the Government School of Design in 1848.

6.35 RICHARD REDGRAVE: **Indian decoration.** Shown by the East India Company at the Great Exhibition of 1851. *Supplementary Report on Design*, 1852.

With the founding of the Department of Practical Art, after the Great Exhibition of 1851, Redgrave, a painter, was made responsible for official design-teaching methods. Greatly influenced by Owen Jones' enthusiasm for Oriental design and impressed by the East India Company's magnificent display in the Crystal Palace, he encouraged students to study Indian decorative design.

6.36 EMILE PRISSE D'AVENNES: **A Cairo interior of the seventeenth century.** *L'Art Arabe d'après les Monuments du Kaire*, 1869–77.

The magnificence of Prisse d'Avennes's book, and of several other contemporary books on Islamic architecture and art, is a measure of its enthusiastic reception in the West.

6.37 JULES BOURGOIN: **Entrance to the doorway of the Fountain of Kaïd Bey, Cairo.** *Les Arts Arabes*, 1873.

Bourgoin spent several years studying and drawing Islamic buildings in Cairo. He was a fine draughtsman and he became particularly interested in the geometry of Islamic abstract decoration. His *Elements de l'Art Arabe* is still the richest compilation of Islamic geometrical designs. Viollet-le-Duc was greatly impressed with Bourgoin's researches.

6.38 OWEN W. DAVIS: **Modern Indian ornament.** Lithographed by the artist. *The Building News*, 26 August 1870.

The Building News regularly published plates of ornament. Such plates were intended to serve as inspiration for architects designing interiors or decorated furniture. Because collections like Owen Jones' *Grammar of Ornament* and Racinet's *L'Ornement Polychrome* were so well known, designers sought to supply illustrations from previously untapped sources.

6.39 JOHN LEIGHTON: **Indian motifs.** *Suggestions in Design*, 1880.

Leighton published the first edition of this work in 1852–3. A considerable enthusiasm for Indian design had been aroused by the East India Company's magnificent collection of textiles shown at the 1851 Exhibition, and it was only in the 1870s, with the 'discovery' of Japan, that Indian ornament was supplanted as the premier exemplar of non-Western design.

6.41 *Below* RICHARD GLAZIER: **Glazed earthenware dish.**
Made by Persian potters working in Rhodes during the fifteenth
or sixteenth centuries. *Manual of Historic Ornament*, 1899.

Glazier described all the designs in his *Manual* as in the Rhodian
style. His sources of inspiration would have been museum
specimens, or illustrations in publications such as *The Grammar
of Ornament*, Prisse d'Avennes's *L'Art Arabe* and W. & G.
Audsley's *Outlines of Ornament*.

6.40 *Above* CHRISTOPHER DRESSER:
**Four studies in the manner of Persian
(Rhodian) ceramic decoration.** *Modern
Ornamentation*, 1886.

Dresser considered that an accomplished
ornamental designer should be able to
design in many styles. In *Studies in Design*
he declared that his success in designing in
a particular national style depended 'upon
the extent to which I become, in feeling,
. . . a Chinaman, or Arabian or such as the
case requires. . . . I often find it necessary
to inform myself of the religion, mode of
government, climate and habits of a
people, for it is only by understanding
their faith and usages that I can
comprehend the spirit of their
ornament . . .'

6.42 CHRISTOPHER DRESSER: **Decorative panel 'in the purest old Persian style'.**
Modern Ornamentation, 1886.

This is very likely to be a design by an assistant or a pupil, but its extremely precise
organization demonstrates the powerful influence Dresser exerted on his studio.
Although Dresser was an ardent enthusiast of Japanese art, he never lost his early
admiration for design from the Islamic world and India.

6.43 Turkish Tobacco Pavilion at the Paris Universal Exhibition, 1889. F. G. Dumas and L. De Fourcaud, *Revue de l'Exposition Universelle de 1889*, n.d.

The Turkish Tobacco Pavilion and the Persian Pavilion were the two neo-Islamic buildings at the 1889 Exhibition.

6.44 Entrance to the Pavilion of Cochin China at the Paris Universal Exhibition, 1889. F. G. Dumas and L. De Fourcaud, *Revue de l'Exposition Universelle de 1889*, n.d.

The Cochin China Pavilion—or 'Palace' as it was called—was one of the several Oriental buildings erected at the exhibition by the French authorities, who were anxious to demonstrate France's prowess as a colonial power.

6.45 Tonkinese embroiderers at the Paris Universal Exhibition, 1889. F. G. Dumas and L. De Fourcaud, *Revue de l'Exposition Universelle de 1889*, n.d.

Many craftsmen from the colonial East were to be seen at work in the 1889 Exhibition and their sophisticated skills were widely admired. Le Douanier Rousseau gained much of his knowledge of the exotic world from the Exhibition.

6.46 A Javanese dancer wearing a batik sarong at the Paris Universal Exhibition, 1889. F. G. Dumas and L. De Fourcaud, *Revue de l'Exposition Universelle de 1889*, n.d.

The Javanese Kampong with its villagers and dancers was a very popular feature of the 1889 Exhibition. Debussy was entranced by the small gamelan orchestra which accompanied the dancers. Here many Europeans would have had their first chance of admiring batik fabrics.

6.47 A Javanese batik maker at work at the Paris Universal Exhibition, 1889. F. G. Dumas and L. De Fourcaud, *Revue de l'Exposition Universelle de 1889*, n.d.

The batik maker is seen here drawing a traditional design in wax kept liquid by a small charcoal stove. In the 1890s Dutch artists were to begin experimenting with batik.

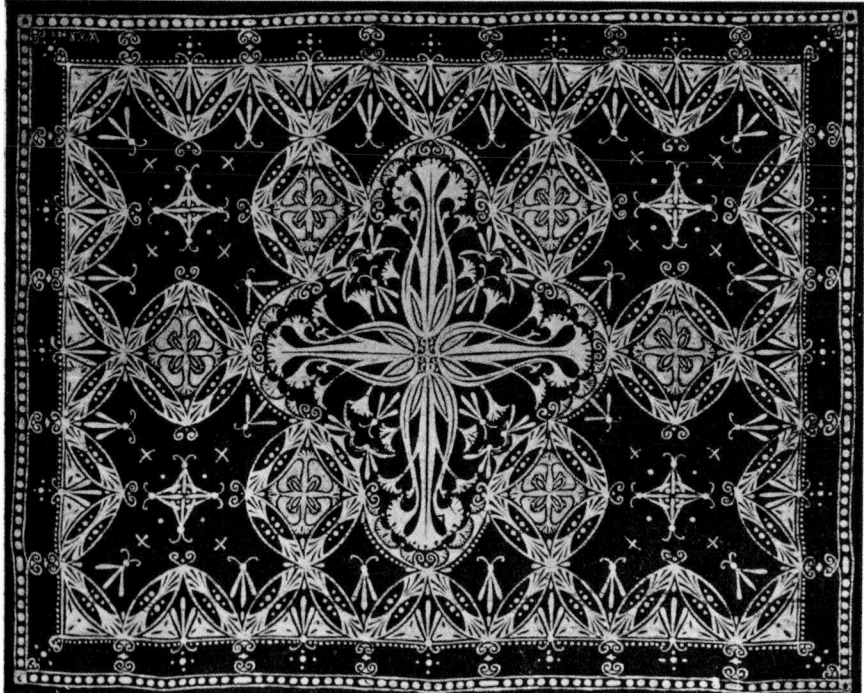

6.48 W.-K. REES: **Batik hanging on silk.** Illustrated in an article on batik by M. P. Verneuil, *Art et Décoration*, July-December 1905.

By 1905, Dutch-produced batiks were attracting attention abroad. The design illustrated here is composed partly of adaptations of Javanese motifs. The central motif, however, is very like the motifs found in Dutch ceramics of this period.

6.49 ALBERT REIMANN: **Batik design on cambric.** *The Studio*, January 1909.

A German batik. The repeated motifs are not unlike those found in Javanese work. The principal motif of peacocks admiring a bouquet of flowers is characteristic of the Jugendstil graphic style.

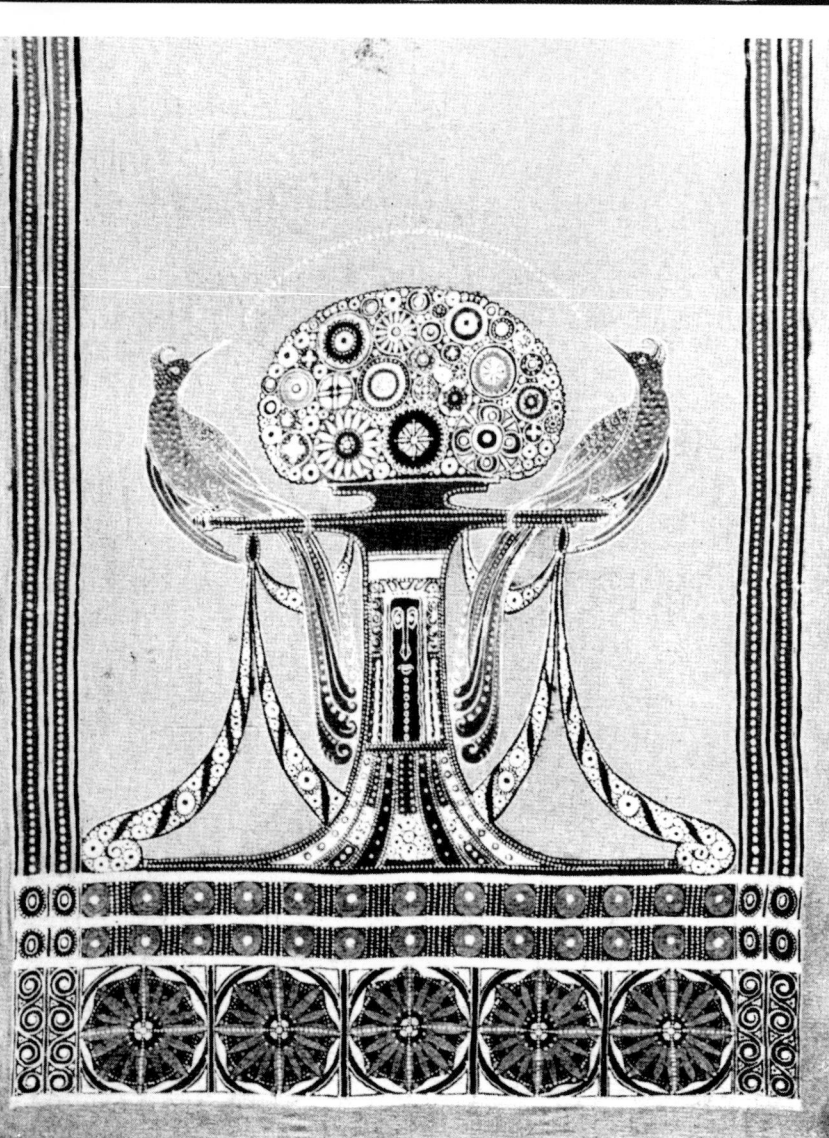

6.50 *Opposite* LE BEAU, OF HAARLEM: **Portière, or door hanging.** Illustrated in an article on batik by M. P. Verneuil, *Art et Décoration*, July-December 1905.

The grotesque cats have no equivalent in traditional Javanese batik design. However, their stylization does have a certain affinity with the extreme formalization found in Javanese *wayang* puppet figures.

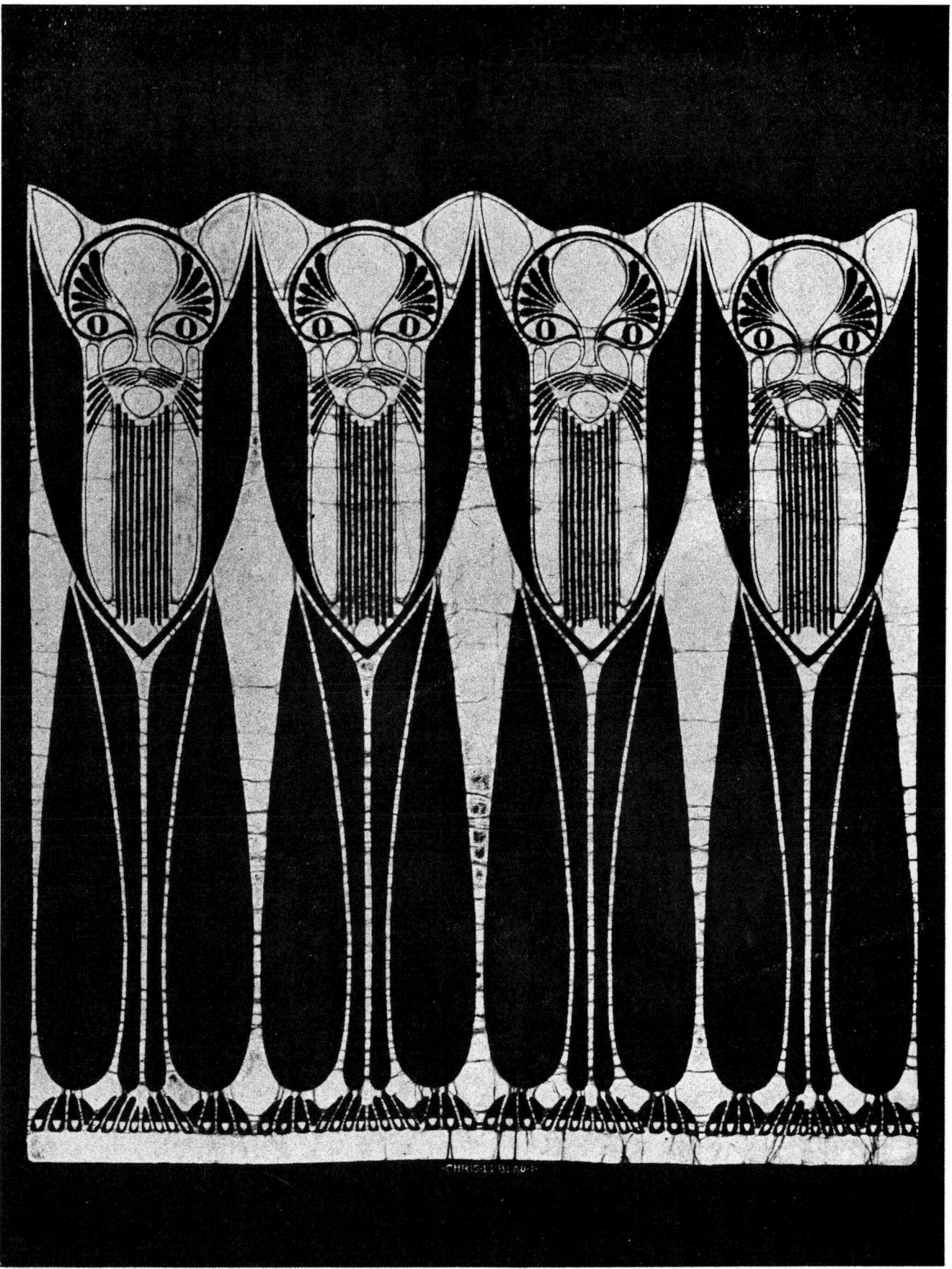

'The Cult of Japan'

Long before the US Commodore Perry's 'Black Ships' were seen in the Bay of Yedo, in July 1853, there had been European commercial and cultural intercourse with Japan. The Portuguese had arrived in Japan in 1542 or 1543 as missionaries and traders—only to be expelled in 1637. In the same year they were replaced by the Dutch, who were grudgingly permitted to set up a trading post at Deshima, in Nagasaki harbour. It was from the Dutch that the Japanese acquired a knowledge of the rudiments of Western science and the art of perspective, but the Tokugawa Shoguns, hereditary military dictators, deliberately set out to isolate Japan from the rest of the world: 'Let them think no more of us; just as if we were no longer in the world.'[1] Little hard information about Japan—or her arts and manufactures—filtered through to the Western world.

In 1728, an English translation of the *History of Japan*, by Engelbert Kaempfer (1651–1716), appeared—but Kaempfer said little about the wonders of Japanese art. M. Titsingh's *Illustrations of Japan*, a translation from the French, came out in 1821. This probably gave the British public their first opportunity of gauging the qualities of Japanese pictorial art through a few passable hand-coloured engravings which were copied from Japanese originals. But, in a sense, public curiosity concerning Japan was satisfied by the available literature on China—Japan being viewed mistakenly as a nation possessed merely of Chinese culture. This view persisted long after the 'opening up' of Japan.

Even in the 1830s, however, there was a burgeoning recognition of the quality of Japanese art. George Phillips' *Rudiments of Curvilinear Design* showed two compositions in the Japanese style (Plates 7.16 and 17), one of which he described as 'Japanese ornament in the Chinese manner'. It is this latter composition which is, in fact, the more convincingly Japanese and suggests that Phillips had seen Japanese lacquer-work—most likely imported indirectly via Holland. In 1852, Henry Cole's Museum of Manufactures in London thought sufficiently well of Japanese works to acquire a couple of examples. Other European museums also possessed modest collections of Japanese objects.

William Burges, who as one of the most gifted of all the Gothic Revival architects was discussed in Chapter Four, was an early and enthusiastic collector of Japanese prints. He must have delighted in the hieratic, angular qualities of the figures in Japanese woodblock prints. They would have reminded him of the bold simplifications of the figure drawings of the thirteenth-century French builder Villard de Honnecourt, whose work he admired. Burges saw an affinity between the art of his beloved thirteenth-century France and Japan. Indeed he was to claim, when writing of the London International Exhibition of 1862: 'Truly the Japanese Court is the real medieval court of the exhibition.'[2] 'The Cult of Japan'[3] bore a distinct relationship, at least in its early stages, to the Cult of the Medieval.

The album in which Burges mounted his Japanese prints—now in the Print Room of the Victoria and Albert Museum—was catalogued by Burges as 'Polychromy' and dated 'October 18th, 1858'. If Burges actually began collecting Japanese art at this date, he was one of the earliest private British

7.1 Japanese stencil plate—'Birds and Waves'. From the collection of Wilson Crewdson. *The Studio*, Vol. 40, 1907.

7.2 Sir Rutherford Alcock: **A Japanese fan.** *Art and Art Industries of Japan,* 1878.

An illustration of a characteristic Japanese manner of designing in which a series of isolated decorative designs is applied to a single object 'rich in fancy, all servile repetition of the parts of a design is interdicted as an offence against good taste ... betraying a poverty of invention'.

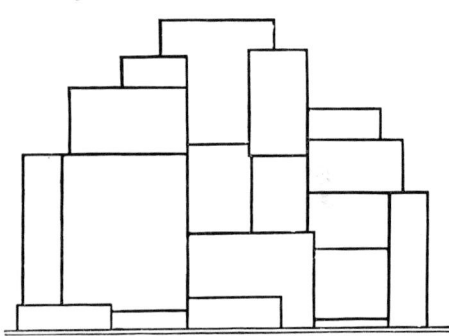

7.3 Sir Rutherford Alcock: **The arrangement of shelves in a Japanese eltagère.** *Art and Art Industries of Japan,* 1878.

Westerners were particularly puzzled by the studied asymmetry of Japanese design. Alcock thought it must have derived from a careful study of nature where rigid symmetry is seldom found.

collectors to do so. However, it is more plausible that his interest in Japan began, as it did for so many other British artists, with the 1862 exhibition.

The Japanese Court at the exhibition (Plate 7.18) was the outcome of the enterprise of Rutherford Alcock (1809–97), first British Ambassador to Japan, who volunteered to lend his collection of Japanese art and artefacts. The collection included lacquer-ware, straw baskets, china and porcelain, 'quaint forms of earthenware', bronzes, cutlery and craftsman's tools, arms and armour, imitation leather, textiles, coloured woodblock prints, science books, scientific models and instruments 'chiefly copied from the Dutch' as well as Japanese medicines.[4] Alcock claimed that the aim of his collection was to show 'a fair sample of the arts of the Japanese, and their capabilities'. It was his hope that it would 'throw some light on the competitive powers of production, as well as the progress in civilization of a people who have been nearly unaided by contact, or any interchange of ideas, with the European race'.

In his book *Art and Art Industries in Japan* (1878), Alcock looked back on the time when he had assembled his collection:

I determined to undertake the task myself ... my self-imposed duty became a labour of love which long survived the immediate object of providing the International Exhibition with such a varied collection as should make known in England, and through England to the rest of the world, an unexpected source of instruction as well as delight. ... Within a few years ... I found Japanese fabrics, silks, and embroideries, Japanese lacquer, china, faience, bronzes, and enamels exhibited for sale in the shops of every capital in Europe ... Superior alike in taste, design and workmanship, they could be sold at a price far below European articles of a similar kind.

There is much justice in Alcock's claim that his collection was of paramount importance in spreading knowledge of Japanese art. It inspired John Leighton to write his *On Japanese Art* (1863), the earliest British account of the subject, with a handsome Japanese woodblock print serving as a frontispiece. Like many contemporaries, Leighton was fascinated by the asymmetry often found in Japanese decoration and he observed how studiously repetition was avoided. But he was pessimistic about the effect of the West on Japanese art: 'The Japanese are a clever people ... I hope they may be richer and happier for their intercourse with Europe though I doubt it ... A people so sensitive will copy many of our defects, as the natives of British India have done, degrading themselves to meet the wants of European taste.'

Christopher Dresser was also impressed with Rutherford Alcock's collection. He made many sketches of the exhibits and managed to acquire what he described as a 'fair selection' of them. These were to form the nucleus of what was to become a large Japanese collection. His enthusiasm for Japan and Japanese art was fuelled by the magnificent collection of objects sent by the Shogun to the Paris Universal Exhibitions of 1867. Here were displayed major works of Japanese art which far eclipsed Alcock's collection (Plate 7.28). Dresser may also have met the craftsmen who built the Japanese village at Alexandra Park, London. Certainly he actively cultivated Japanese acquaintances in his desire to learn more about Japan.

In 1876 Dresser went on a semi-official visit to Japan. He took with him a collection of contemporary British art manufactures, to be given to the Tokyo Museum to replace a collection of European work—purchased at the Vienna International Exhibition of 1873—which had been lost in a shipwreck.[5] He also made arrangements with Tiffanys in New York to purchase a representative collection of Japanese work. It was sold on his return to New York, but at a considerable loss.

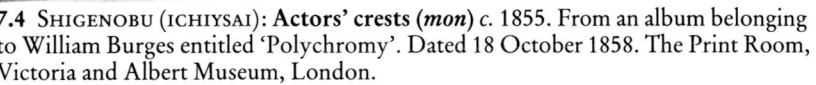

板芝山 重宣童ひと庄ん毛板新

7.4 SHIGENOBU (ICHIYSAI): **Actors' crests (mon)** *c.* 1855. From an album belonging to William Burges entitled 'Polychromy'. Dated 18 October 1858. The Print Room, Victoria and Albert Museum, London.

7.5 Book wrapper by an anonymous Japanese designer, *c.* 1850. From an Album belonging to William Burges entitled Polychromy. Dated 18 October 1858. The Print Room, Victoria and Albert Museum, London.

7.6 George Ashdown Audsley and Maurice Ashdown Audsley: **Wall decoration in the Japanese manner.** *The Practical Decorator*, 1892.

7.7 Bruce Talbert: **Design for a textile.** Gouache on cotton (1870s). The Print Room, Victoria and Albert Museum, London.

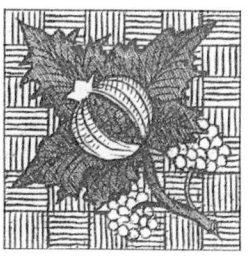

7.8 ANONYMOUS: **Designs for ceramic tiles.** From a manual for amateur pottery painters, *c.* 1878.

7.9 Lacquered and enamelled wares. From the collections of Sir Rutherford Alcock and Messrs Remi, Schmidt & J. B. Waring, *Masterpieces of Industrial Art and Sculpture at the International Exhibition, 1862*, 1863.

7.10 *Left* EUGÈNE-EMANUEL VIOLLET-LE-DUC: **Wallpaper for a dining room.** *Histoire d'une Maison*, 1873.

The cranes are evidently derived from a Japanese source.

7.11 *Right* ANONYMOUS: **Suggestions for decorative brush drawing for children.** *The Practical Teacher's Art Monthly*, Vol. II, 1899–1900.

Some of these designs are based upon Japanese models.

7.12 HECTOR GUIMARD: **Title-page.** *Le Castel Béranger*, 1898. Guimard's decorative style owes much to Japanese influence.

Dresser travelled some 2800 kilometres in Japan. He was received by the Emperor—surely a rare honour—and visited some sixty-eight potteries, and a hundred or so Shinto and Buddhist shrines. He reported upon everything he saw and was himself reported on by his government interpreters, who were required to study his every action as Western response to Japan. He described his visit in *Japan, its Architecture, Art and Art Manufactures* (1882), which presents a vivid and sympathetic picture of early Meiji Japan and warrants a place at least as a minor classic in nineteenth-century travel literature (see Plates 7.44–7). More significantly, *Japan* also contains the most detailed account of Japanese manufacturing which had so far been published.

Despite all the enthusiasm for Japanese art there were those who saw danger in its influence. Among them, inevitably, was Ruskin. Writing in 1867 on a company of Japanese jugglers who had recently visited London, he described the masks they wore as 'inventively frightful, like fearful dreams', and observed: 'There has long been an increasing interest in Japanese art, which has been very harmful to many of our own painters.'[6]

William Morris also shared some of Ruskin's prejudices. 'Clumsy-handed as the European or Aryan workman is . . .', he declared in his essay on 'The Lesser Arts of Life',[7] 'as compared with his Turanian [i.e. Chinese and Japanese] fellow, there is a seriousness and meaning about his work that raises it as a piece of work far above the deftness of China and Japan.' But Ruskin and Morris were exceptions. The real difficulty exists in finding mid- to late-nineteenth-century artists who were not, in one way or another, influenced by Japan.

Edward William Godwin (1833–86) was among the earliest British designers to work in a Japanese idiom. He designed a sideboard—now to be seen in the Victoria and Albert Museum, London—which has a distinctly Japanese air about it, although it resembles no known article of Japanese furniture. Godwin appears to have incorporated features of Japanese architecture in his design—possibly found in the prints owned by his friend Burges.[8] In the 1870s he designed a range of comparatively inexpensive furniture for the London furniture manufacture William Watt in a style which he described as 'Anglo-Japanese'. Godwin also designed textiles and wallpaper (Plates 7.21 and 22) in a Japanese manner; his Japanesery is particularly delightful and fanciful in his purely decorative designs.

Another architect, W. Eden Nesfield (1835–88), one-time partner of Richard Norman Shaw, also borrowed decorative ideas from Japan. His entrance lodge to Kew Gardens, London, incorporated motifs borrowed from a Japanese source in a decorated external stucco cove. An ebonized wood screen of 1867, almost certainly by Nesfield and now in the Victoria and Albert Museum, demonstrates a fluent understanding of Japanese decoration.[9] Nesfield's and Godwin's appropriation of Japanese motifs was a harbinger of future developments.

Thomas Jeckyll (1827–81), a somewhat obscure and eccentric architect and designer, should also be mentioned in connection with the early spread of Japanesery. A group of furniture he designed for Edward Green of Heath Old Hall, Wakefield, Yorkshire, probably between 1866 and 1870, makes use of low relief carving which is inspired by Japanese work.[10] Later designs by Jeckyll, including an elegant cast-iron pavilion which was shown at the Philadelphia Centennial Exhibition of 1876, reveal that he possessed an extensive vocabulary of Japanese decorative motifs.

The principal source of Japanese motifs would seem to have been Japanese prints or books. The coloured woodblock prints of Kiyonaga, Utagawa Kunisada, Kuniyoshi, Nishemura Shigenaga, Shuncho, Shunko, Toyonobu and Utamaro all make skilful use of the patterns of costume fabrics in a way which was entirely new to European art. In France Claude Monet,

7.13 Fritz Hellmuth Ehmke: **Decorative composition.** *Kunst und Handwerk* (bound volume for 1903–4).

A design which appears to have been inspired by Japanese stencils. Ehmke designed the Cologne Werkbund poster of 1914.

169

7.14 Gold lacquer box in the form of a lute. From the collection of Charles Ephrussi. Louis Gonse, ed., *L'Art Ancien à l'Exposition de 1878*, 1879.

Western collectors were greatly attracted by Japanese lacquer. By the 1870s there were many comparatively well-informed connoisseurs of the Japanese applied arts.

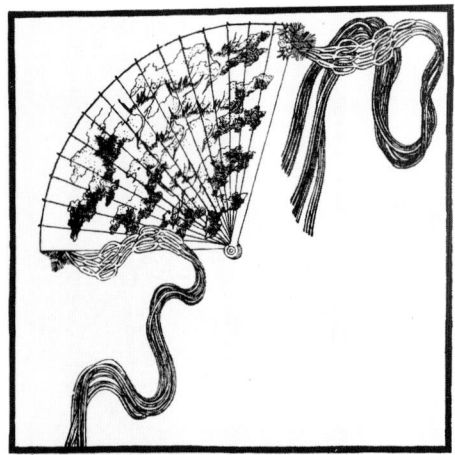

7.15 Fan of a court lady. From the *Isai gwa shiki*. William Anderson, *The Pictorial Arts of Japan*, 1886.

Anderson, an amateur, was medical officer to the British legation in Japan. His two-volume book—splendidly produced like so many books on Japanese art published in the 1870s and 1880s—was the first scholarly account of the subject in English.

Edouard Manet, Paul Gauguin, Toulouse Lautrec and Van Gogh were among those who responded to the flat patterns and two-dimensional quality of the Japanese print. The artist and designer Joseph Bracquemond (1833–1914) became interested in Japanese art after coming across some woodcuts by Hokusai. He designed textiles, bookbindings and silver in the Japanese style, and a table service he decorated in the Japanese manner with asymmetrically arranged birds and beasts was shown at the Paris Exhibition of 1867. In England the influence of Japanese art can be seen in the work of Dante Gabriel Rossetti, J. A. M. Whistler, Aubrey Beardsley and Walter Crane, to name but a few.

R. Wallace Martin of the Martin Brothers—'art potters' of the late 1870s and 1880s—was in possession of Japanese design books in 1874.[11] Similar Japanese woodblock books of *mon* (heraldic insignia) were sold in the 1880s by Batsfords as 'Japanese Encyclopedias of Design' at two shillings a volume. The *Grammar of Japanese Ornament and Design* (Plates 7.34, 37–41), by the architect Thomas Cutler, which was published in parts between 1879 and 1880, is based almost entirely on material culled from Japanese books.

Some of the finest of all late nineteenth-century colour printing was devoted to Japanese art—a real measure of the fervour which it generated. George Ashdown Audsley,[12] a successful Liverpool architect, and James Lord Bowes published the first major study of Japanese ceramics, *Keramic Art of Japan* (Plates 7.31–3), in 1875. Our views on Japanese ceramics have changed greatly since its publication and we are now likely to find Audsley and Bowes all too drawn to the vulgar or meretricious. But the book deserves re-appraisal, not merely because it was the first of its kind or because of its splendour, but because it reveals so much about the nature of nineteenth-century haut-bourgeois taste.

Audsley's *Ornamental Arts of Japan* (1882–4) and Louis Gonse's *L'Art Japonais* (1883) both contain sumptuous chromolithographs[13] illustrating exotic and ornate aspects of Japanese design. William Anderson's *Pictorial Arts of Japan* (1886) would at first sight seem outside the compass of the present study. But Japanese pictorial art is rich in decorative details and Anderson's fine two-volume work could have served well as a source-book (see Plates 7.48–51). Anderson was medical officer to the British legation in Japan and, though an amateur by present standards, was very well informed on his subject. His preface contains a brief but interesting account of contemporary publications on Japanese art.

Samuel Bing—'Art Nouveau Bing'—whose first shop in Paris had been a meeting place for enthusiasts of Japanese art, published an extensive part-work called *Artistic Japan* (1889–91), which came out simultaneously in English, French and German. It supplied what one can safely assume was a very large public with an excellent selection of Japanese pictorial and decorative art.

Art magazines such as *The Studio* and *Art et Décoration* frequently contained well-illustrated articles on Japanese art. By the turn of the century it would have been possible to see a good deal of Japanese art, in museums, in private collections and in handsome coloured reproductions. Japanese art was no longer alien, nor even a novelty. The features of its compositional style and decoration had, by a rapid osmosis, become absorbed by the West. The 'Cult of Japan' had passed, but Western art—decorative and pictorial—had been enormously enriched.

7.16 George Phillips: **'Japanese ornament in the Chinese manner'.** *Rudiments of Curvilinear Design* (1838–40).

Phillips' decorative composition was intended to serve as a model for architects, designers and manufacturers. It was published when there was very little understanding of the real nature of Japanese applied art.

7.17 George Phillips: **Japanese ornament.** *Rudiments of Curvilinear Design* (1838–40).

It is uncertain how Phillips could have acquired his limited knowledge of Japanese design. Possibly he could have seen examples of lacquer imported via Holland, or he may have adapted designs from illustrations in the scant literature of the subject.

7.18 The 'Japanese Court' at the International Exhibition, London, 1862. Wood-engraving after a photograph by the London Stereoscopic Co. *The Illustrated London News*, 20 September 1862.

This appears to be the only published illustration of Rutherford—later Sir Rutherford—Alcock's 'Japanese Court'. Both Christopher Dresser and William Burges were impressed by Alcock's collection. Burges admired in particular the medieval qualities of the Japanese work. Dresser made numerous drawings of the exhibits as well as purchasing many of them.

ON
JAPANESE ART.
A
DISCOURSE
DELIVERED AT THE ROYAL INSTITUTION
OF GREAT BRITAIN &c.
MAY 1.
1863.
by
JOHN LEIGHTON~
F.S.A., M.R.I.,
&c.

LONDON:
PRIVATELY PRINTED~
(50. COPIES.)
ONLY.

7.19 JOHN LEIGHTON (LUKE LIMMER). **Title-page** of his paper *On Japanese Art*, 1863.

Leighton was particularly interested in the asymmetry frequently found in Japanese design. His paper was dedicated to Sir Rutherford Alcock.

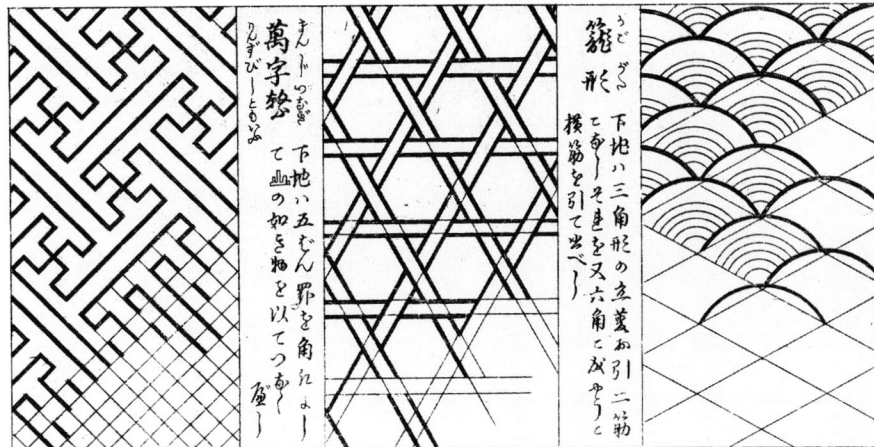

7.20 The setting-out of simple geometric patterns. From a Japanese manual, second half of the nineteenth century. (From the collection of Tim Imrie.)

Manuals such as this appear to have been fairly readily available in London and Paris from the early 1870s. By the 1880s, Batsfords were selling 'Japanese Encyclopaedias of Design' at two shillings a volume.

7.21 E. W. GODWIN: **'Peacock' wallpaper.** For Jeffrey & Co., 1873. Alan Victor Sugden and John Ludlam Edmondson, *A History of English Wallpaper, 1509–1914* (1925).

E. W. Godwin seems to have taken the all-over pattern and the phoenix used in this design from manuals published in Japan.

7.22 *Above left* E. W. GODWIN: **Butterfly brocade.** Silk. For Benjamin Warner, *c.* 1874. Victoria and Albert Museum, London.

The motifs used in this design appear to have been taken from a Japanese publication. The formal organization of the design, however, is characteristic of the 1870s.

7.23 *Above* BRUCE TALBERT: **Design for silk curtain.** For Cowlishaw, Nicol & Co., *c.* 1876. *Examples of Ancient and Modern Furniture*, 1876.

Talbert was a leading exponent of Gothic furniture in the 1860s. By 1876, however, he had taken up the modish Queen Anne style of R. Norman Shaw and W. Eden Nesfield. He became an expert textile designer in the Japanese manner.

7.24 BRUCE TALBERT: **Preliminary sketch for a textile with Japanese details.** Victoria and Albert Museum, London.

Like his contemporaries, Talbert was fascinated with the delicate, complex quality of Japanese pattern design. Presumably, he too had access to Japanese design manuals.

7.25 *Right* Bruce Talbert: **'Nagasaki'.** Silk damask. For Warner & Sons, *c.* 1880. Victoria and Albert Museum, London.

Seen out of context on the printed page this design appears unnecessarily complex—when hung as a curtain, however, the effect would be of great richness.

7.26 Sir Rutherford Alcock: **Lacquer boxes.** *Art and Art Industries of Japan*, 1878.

The lacquer box on the right shows the preferred method of dividing a space for decorative purposes. Sir Rutherford Alcock wrote as a well-informed amateur.

7.27 *Right* Bruce Talbert: **'Kingfisher'.** Silk damask. For Warner & Sons, *c.* 1880. Victoria and Albert Museum, London.

Western designers very frequently borrowed the bird and flower combination so frequently found in Japanese pictorial art (see Plate 7.40). It is possible that William Morris' use of this same motif owed its origin to Japan.

7.28 Carved wooden gateway to the Japanese farm at the Universal Exhibition, Paris, 1878. Louis Gonse, ed., *L'Art Ancien à l'Exposition de 1878*, 1879.

The Japanese farm was a popular exhibit at the 1878 Exhibition—it may well have set the fashion for the exotic villages which were to be such an important feature of the Paris Universal Exhibition of 1889. A Japanese 'village' had been created in England in 1874 at Alexandra Park, North London.

7.29 *Below left* **White lacquer box.** From the collection of Mme L. Cahen. Louis Gonse, ed., *L'Art Ancien à l'Exposition de 1878*, 1879.

7.30 Vignette. After a Japanese woodblock print. Louis Gonse, ed., *L'Art Ancien à l'Exposition de 1878*, 1879.

This is possibly adapted from a coloured woodblock by Katsushika Taito (1804–48).

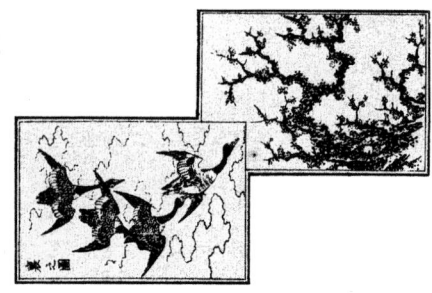

7.31 GEORGE ASHDOWN AUDSLEY AND JAMES LORD BOWES: **From a page of decorative vignettes.** *Keramic Art of Japan*, 1875–9.

Audsley and Bowes' magnificent two-volume work was the first major Western study of Japanese ceramics. It was evidently intended for collectors. The authors preferred the highly ornate wares—often intended for export—to the more austere work which was to become so admired in the twentieth century and which is reflected in the work of Bernard Leach and his followers.

7.32 George Ashdown Audsley and James Lord Bowes: **Representative Japanese all-over patterns.** *Keramic Art of Japan*, 1875–9.

Audsley and Bowes began their study of Japanese ceramics with a general examination of the principles of Japanese decoration. By the beginning of the twentieth century Japanese modes of decorative design had become so well absorbed that it is often difficult to detect their presence. Dufy's fabric of *c.* 1914–21 (see Plate 10.24) suggests an acquaintance with the kind of pattern seen in the bottom right-hand design.

7.33 George Ashdown Audsley and James Lord Bowes: **The juxtaposition of different patterns on a bowl of Ise Banko ware.** *Keramic Art of Japan*, 1875–9.

Early students of Japanese design were particularly interested in the frequent Japanese use of several patterns simultaneously—as a kind of patchwork.

7.34 *Right* Thomas W. Cutler: **Details from Japanese instructional manuals.** *Grammar of Japanese Ornament*, 1880.

It seems probable that this page was simply made up of four pages from two different Japanese design manuals which were reproduced by photo-lithography.

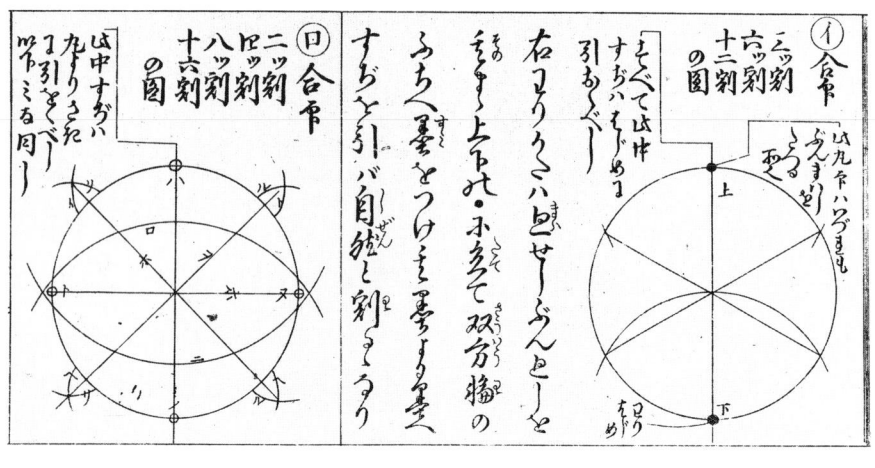

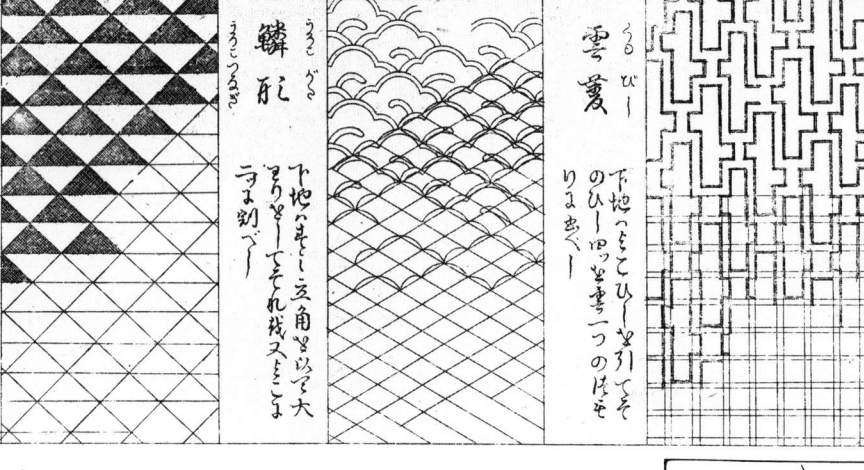

7.35 *Left* **The division of the circle into six parts.** From a Japanese manual of the second half of the nineteenth century. (From the collection of Tim Imrie.)

The division of the circle into six parts relates to the designing of crests or '*mon*'.

7.36 *Below left* **The setting-out of simple geometric patterns.** From a Japanese manual of the second half of the nineteenth century. (From the collection of Tim Imrie.)

7.37 *Bottom left* THOMAS W. CUTLER: **Studies of curves made with brushstrokes.** From a Japanese instructional manual. *Grammar of Japanese Ornament*, 1880.

Cutler's elegantly produced book was a compilation based almost entirely upon Japanese manuals. Cutler, an architect, made no claims to scholarship, but had an excellent understanding of the information required to design in the Japanese manner.

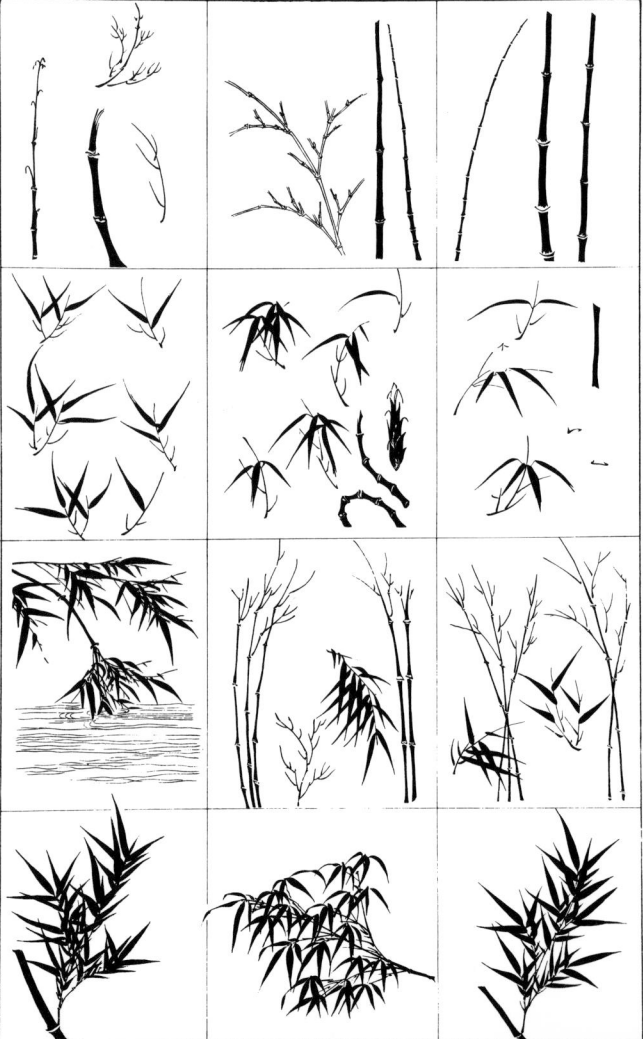

7.38 *Opposite* THOMAS W. CUTLER:
Graduated studies of the bamboo. From
a Japanese instructional manual.
Grammar of Japanese Ornament, 1880.

Painting with simple brushstrokes was a
highly esteemed art in Japan. The vogue in
Britain for teaching children brush
painting in the 1890s was very likely of
Japanese inspiration.

7.39 Japanese heraldic badges (*mon*). Thomas W. Cutler,
Grammar of Japanese Ornament, 1880.

Japanese heraldry was particularly popular with Western
designers. W. Eden Nesfield used *mon* on the exterior of a lodge
house at Kew Gardens in about 1866. They also appear in 1867
on a screen (now in the Victoria and Albert Museum) given to
his partner Richard Norman Shaw. This was probably designed
by Nesfield.

7.40 Bird and flowers. A wood-block illustration taken from an unacknowledged Japanese book. Thomas W. Cutler, *Grammar of Japanese Ornament*, 1880.

Western artists were invariably captivated by the unlaboured naturalism of Japanese prints and design, which must have been particularly refreshing to a generation of designers taught to design in a rigid, mechanical way.

7.41 'Plum and snow-laden fir, from a printed and embroidered crepe.' Thomas W. Cutler, *Grammar of Japanese Ornament*, 1880.

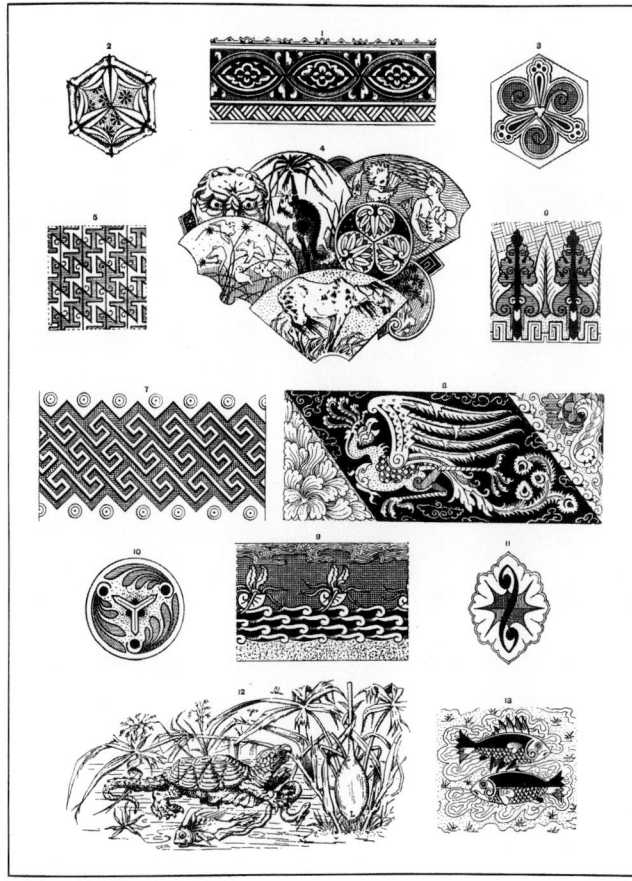

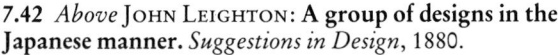

7.42 *Above* JOHN LEIGHTON: **A group of designs in the Japanese manner.** *Suggestions in Design*, 1880.

An earlier edition, the nucleus of this book, was published in 1852–3 under Leighton's nom-de-plume of 'Luke Limmer'. The text of the section on Japan is partly based on his 'Discourse upon Japanese Art', delivered at the Royal Institution, London, in 1863 (see Plate 7.19). By 1880, Leighton's conception of Japanese decoration looked decidedly old-fashioned.

7.43 *Above right* ATTRIBUTED TO CHRISTOPHER DRESSER: **Embossed dado wallpaper.** For Lincrusta Walton, 1881. Alan Victor Sugden and John Ludlam Edmondson, *A History of English Wallpaper, 1509–1914* (1925).

A wallpaper of very similar design manufactured in the United States, with Dresser's name printed on each piece, is in the Cooper Hewitt Museum, New York. The motifs in the design illustrated here are also somewhat similar to those in Bruce Talbert's silk damask 'Kingfisher' of about the same date (see Plate 7.27).

7.44 *Right* CHRISTOPHER DRESSER: **Title-page** of *Japan, Its Architecture, Art and Art Manufacturers*, 1882.

Dresser arrived in Japan on 26 December 1877. He visited manufacturers, craftsmen and Buddhist and Shinto shrines. His book is the earliest account of a visit to Japan by an artist.

JAPAN

ITS ARCHITECTURE, ART, AND ART MANUFACTURES

BY

CHRISTOPHER DRESSER
Ph.D., F.L.S., ETC.

LONDON
LONGMANS, GREEN, AND CO.
1882

7.45 *Left* **Detail of column and tie-beam from the Chion-in, Kyoto.** Christopher Dresser, *Japan, its Architecture, Art and Art Manufacturers*, 1882.

Dresser was fascinated by Japanese ecclesiastical and civil architecture. In his view, some temples rivalled the Alhambra, which Owen Jones had begun documenting in 1834. Dresser, it should be recorded, was among the most fervent admirers of Jones. This fine architectural drawing is by a Japanese draughtsman.

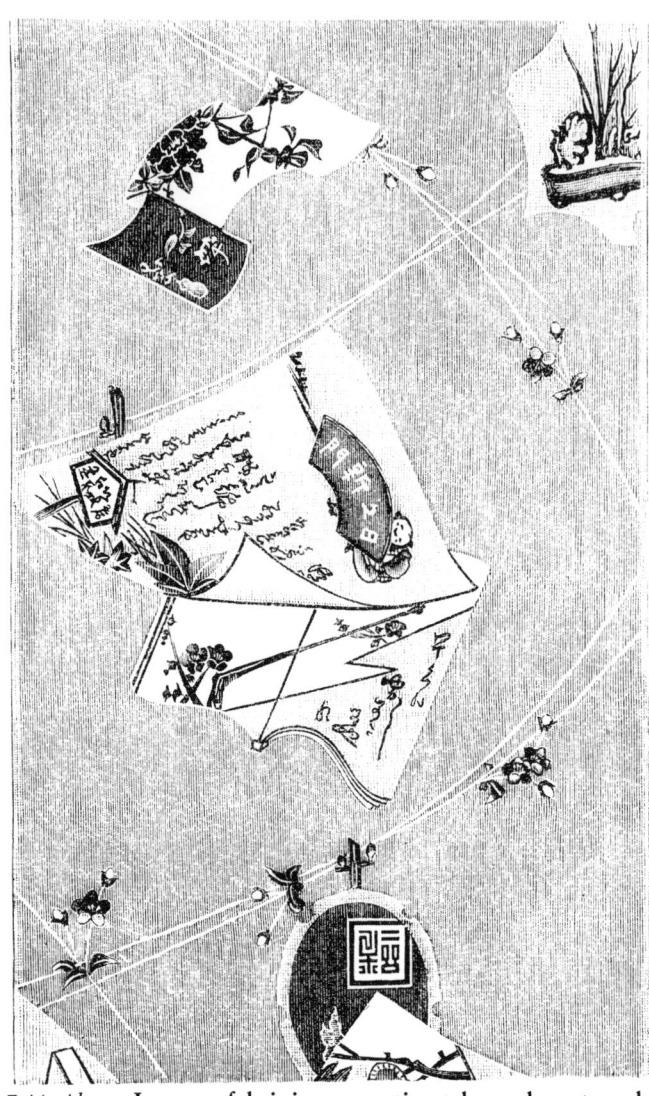

7.46 *Above* **Japanese fabric incorporating telegraph posts and insulators.** Probably late 1870s. Christopher Dresser, *Japan, its Architecture, Art and Art Manufacturers*, 1882.

The Japan Dresser visited in early 1877 was in the process of rapid transformation from a feudal to a modern state. He noted an efficient telegraph system, gas lighting and railways. The Japanese design of this fabric celebrated modern progress in a way quite unthinkable in Europe.

7.47 *Left* **A group of Japanese fabric designs.** Christopher Dresser, *Japan, its Architecture, Art and Art Manufacturers*, 1882.

Although Dresser was among the leading British ornamental designers of his era he devoted comparatively few illustrations to ornament in his book on Japan. No doubt he felt that black and white woodcut illustrations could not do justice to the subject.

7.48 *Left* **Page from the** *Takoro-mono.* William Anderson, *The Pictorial Arts of Japan*, 1886.

This shows the traditional emblems of good fortune—hat, mallet, key, purse, straw coat, sacred gem, and two formal designs called the Shippo and the Fundo, or weight used for balances.

7.49 *Above* **An illustration from a book of instruction in bamboo painting.** Reproduced from *Bokuchiku Hatsumo*, 1831, William Anderson, *The Pictorial Arts of Japan*, 1886.

7.50 *Above right* HOKUSAI: **Two designs for sword guards.** Illustrated in the Banshoku dzu-ko. William Anderson, *The Pictorial Arts of Japan*, 1886.

Hokusai was among the first Japanese artists to become widely known in the West.

7.51 *Right* **Decorative page taken from an unacknowledged Japanese book.** Anderson, *The Pictorial Arts of Japan*, 1886.

7.52 *Left* CHRISTOPHER DRESSER: **Decorative composition based upon a Japanese heraldic representation of a bird.** *Modern Ornamentation*, 1886.

This ingenious and curious design makes use of a bird motif taken from a Japanese book of crests. The organization of the motifs, however, is thoroughly Western and is an example of Dresser's sometimes desperate search for novelty.

7.53 *Below centre* SIDNEY HAWARD: **Design for a wallpaper frieze.** *The Studio*, Vol. II, 1893.

The swallows in silhouette were clearly inspired by Japanese work, but this frieze is probably not intentionally Japanese in its effect. Nevertheless, without at least a nodding acquaintance with Japanese decorative art, such elegance and fluidity would be inconceivable. The work was exhibited in the Arts and Crafts exhibition of 1893.

7.55 *Bottom right* TALWIN MORRIS: **Design for a book-cover.** *The Studio*, Vol. XV, 1898.

Like Plate 7.53, this is another example of what was probably an unconscious use of a Japanese decorative technique.

7.54 THE SILVER STUDIO: **Design for a ceiling paper.** *The Studio*, July 1894.

The complex, swirling organization of this design is clearly inspired by Japanese textile design.

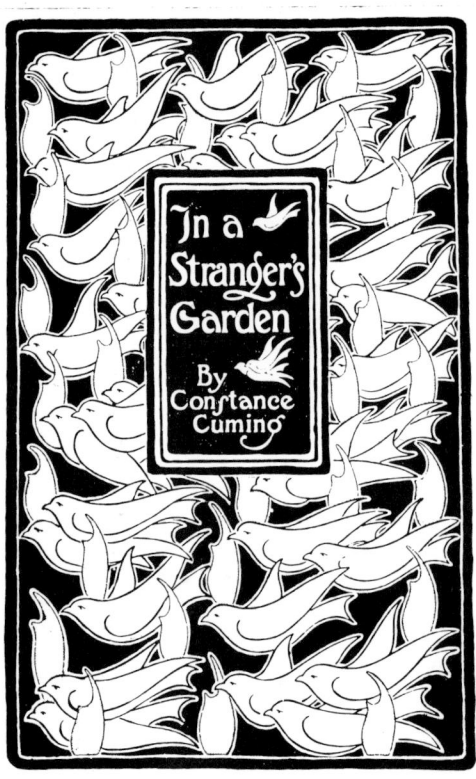

7.57 *Right* Christopher Dresser: **All-over pattern in the Japanese manner.** *Modern Ornamentation*, 1886.

Dresser often organized Japanese motifs in a highly formal way, perhaps because he had been taught to design in the late 1840s and early 1850s, when the somewhat rigid methods of William Dyce and Richard Redgrave prevailed.

7.56 Christopher Dresser: **All-over pattern in the Japanese manner.** *Modern Ornamentation*, 1886.

This is clearly an adaptation of a Japanese pattern of the 'Komai' type illustrated by Lewis F. Day (see Plate 7.58). Dresser, however, has rendered the pattern with a somewhat brutish mechanical precision not found in Japanese work.

7.58 Lewis F. Day: **'Panel in Niello. With geometric disposed in eccentric Japanese fashion'.** *The Planning of Ornament*, 1887.

Lewis F. Day's books on ornament were to exercise a considerable influence upon generations of art students. The design illustrated here is of a type known as 'Komai'. Messrs Elkington of Birmingham, manufacturers of silver and plate, made frequent use of such designs in the late 1870s and 1880s.

7.59 The exterior of the Japanese section at the Paris Universal Exhibition, 1889. F. G. Dumas and L. De Fourcaud, *Revue de l'Exposition Universelle de 1889*, n.d.

By 1889 Japan had adopted Western education and technology. Nevertheless, the qualities of its traditional culture and art were fully recognized. The philosopher Fukuzawa Yukichi suggested in his writings how traditional Japanese values and progressive Western ideas could be amalgamated. This building, part Western, part Japanese, seems to symbolize such attitudes.

7.60 *Below* **Japanese and Chinese houses in Charles Garnier's 'Habitations Humaines' section at the Paris Universal Exhibition,** 1889. F. G. Dumas and L. de Fourcaud, *Revue de l'Exposition Universelle de 1889*, n.d.

Charles Garnier, the architect of the Paris Opéra, took the idea of building houses representing the nations of the past and present from Viollet-le-Duc's book *Histoire de l'Habitation Humaine* of 1875. The Japanese house has affinities with some of the curious villas built in France during the Art Nouveau era.

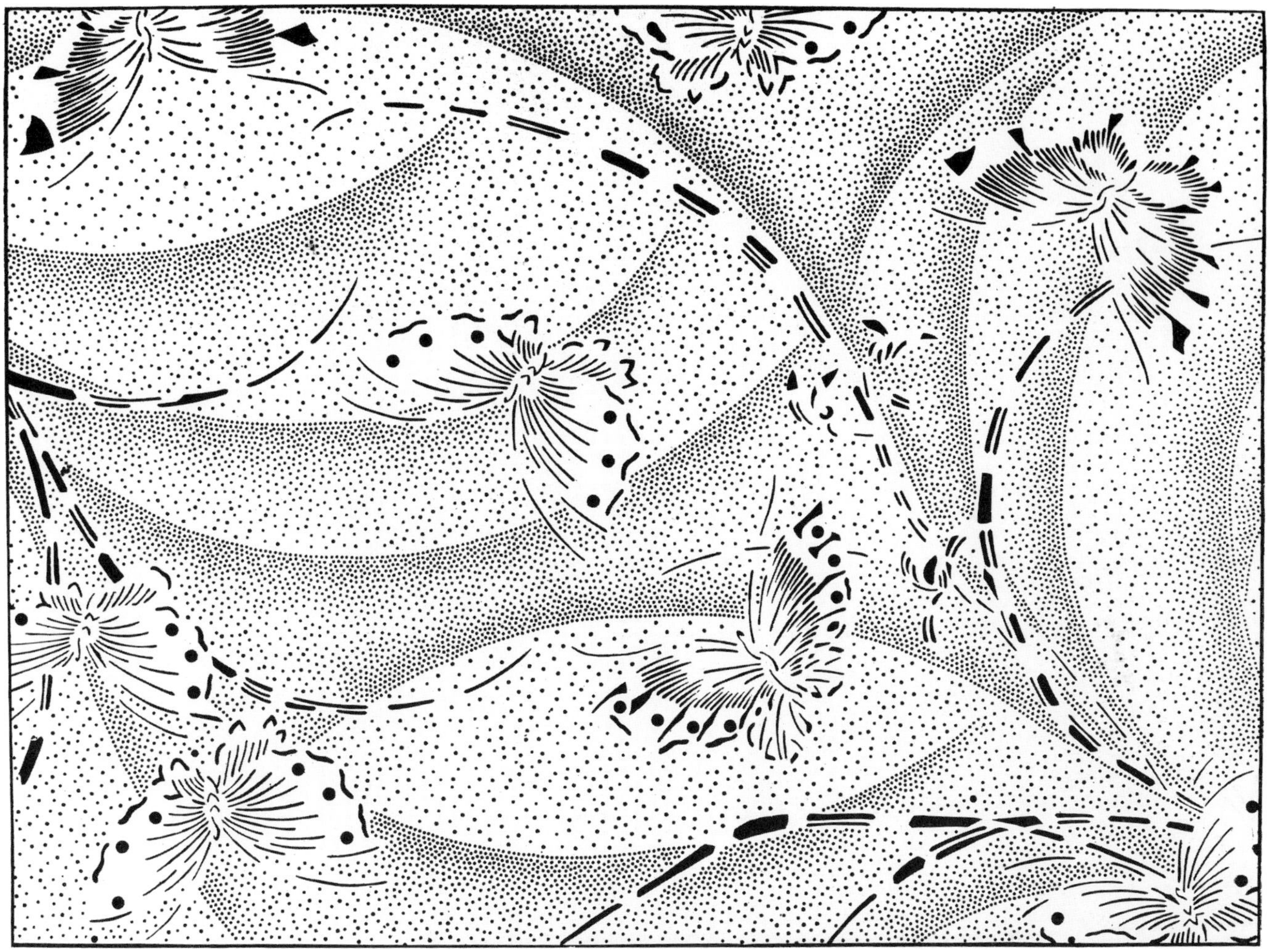

7.61 Japanese stencil design. Samuel Bing, *Artistic Japan*, 1888–91.

Bing's lavishly produced and comparatively inexpensive monthly work brought Japanese art and decoration to the notice of a very large public. Japanese compositional devices and decorative devices were henceforward to become part of the collective unconscious of Western designers.

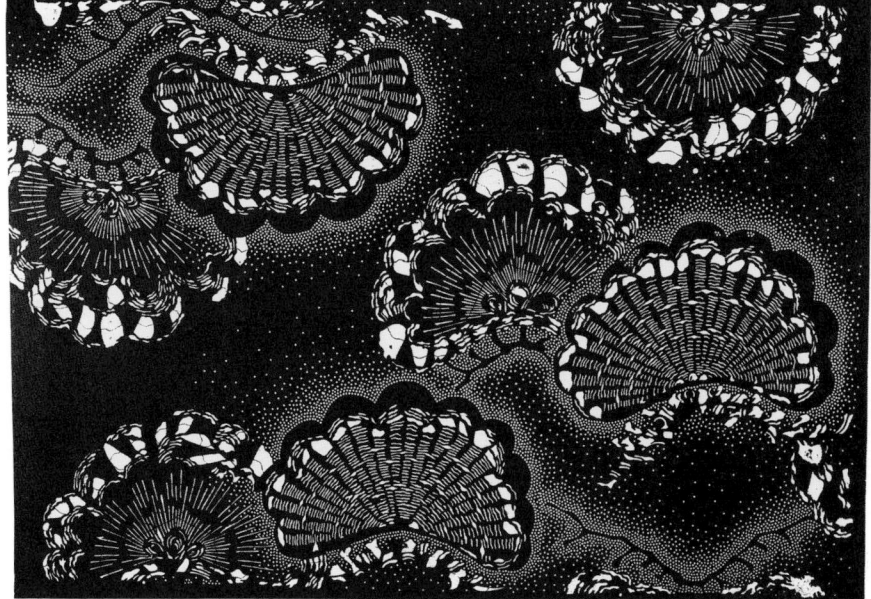

7.62 Japanese stencil design. Samuel Bing, *Artistic Japan*, 1888–91.

Japanese stencils were of a delicacy and refinement which astounded Western artists. They exerted a considerable influence on black and white decorations in books.

7.63 *Left* AUBREY BEARDSLEY: **'The Peacock girl'.** An illustration for Oscar Wilde's *Salome*, 1893. *The Studio*, February 1894.

The composition of this illustration obviously owes a great deal to the Japanese woodblock print. In addition, the decoration of the girl's skirt and the formalized peacock on her left seem to derive from Japanese stencils.

7.65 *Above* **A stencil plate.** From Andrew Tuer's *Book of Delightful and Strange Designs*, 1895, published in conjunction with Liberty & Co. William Crewdson, 'Japanese Art and Artists of To-Day: III Textiles and Embroidery', *The Studio*, October 1910.

This design makes an interesting comparison with Raoul Dufy's textile design 'Monuments de Paris, 1914–21' (see Plate 7.74). Both possess a similar, highly organized, though at first sight informal, structure.

7.64 *Top right* **Stencil cut from waterproof paper.** From an illustrated review of Mrs Ernest Hart's paper on crepe printers in the *Transactions of the Japan Society*, Vol. I. *The Studio*, February 1894.

Although Samuel Bing was probably the earliest European authority to have illustrated examples of Japanese stencil-work, Mrs Hart seems to have been the first British writer to have studied the subject.

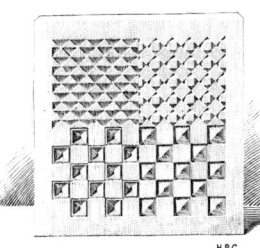

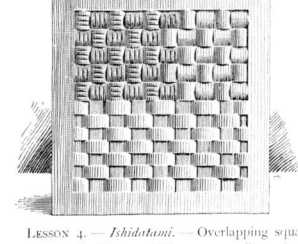

SET NO. 2.—LESSON 1.—*Kirikomi Sankaku.*—Triangular incisions. In this the line work present throughout the lessons of Set 1 are absent.

LESSON 4. — *Ishidatami.* — Overlapping square patterns. A slight modelling or rounding of the face occurs here for the first time.

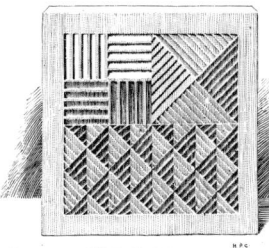

LESSON 2.—*Oikake Sankaku.*—Overlapping triangular patterns. A return to line work, showing some new developments in fine edge-cutting.

LESSON 5.—*Higaki.*— Interlacing patterns. A similar lesson to the last, but dealing with oblique work.

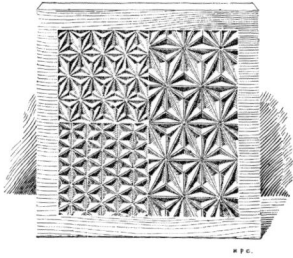

LESSON 3.—*Asanoha.*—Hemp-leaf pattern. Designs in which the incised work and fine edge-cutting of the last two lessons are incorporated.

LESSON 6.—*Kagome.*—Bamboo basket patterns. A more elaborate development of the preceding lessons.

7.66 CHARLES HOLME: **Illustrations from a Japanese course in wood-carving.** *The Studio*, May–September 1895.

Charles Holme, for many years editor of *The Studio*, was a great enthusiast of Japanese art. These illustrations were published at a time when the Arts and Crafts Movement was at its apogee and there was a widespread interest in wood-carving.

7.68 *Below* **Japanese stencil plate—'Birds and Waves'.** From the collection of Wilson Crewdson. *The Studio*, Vol. 40, 1907.

7.67 *Above* OGATA KORIN: **Plum blossom.** Charles Holme, 'Japanese flower painting', *The Studio*, April 1904.

Korin (1658–1716), the leading designer of pottery decoration and lacquer screens during the Edo period, was among the earliest Japanese decorative designers to be singled out by Western enthusiasts.

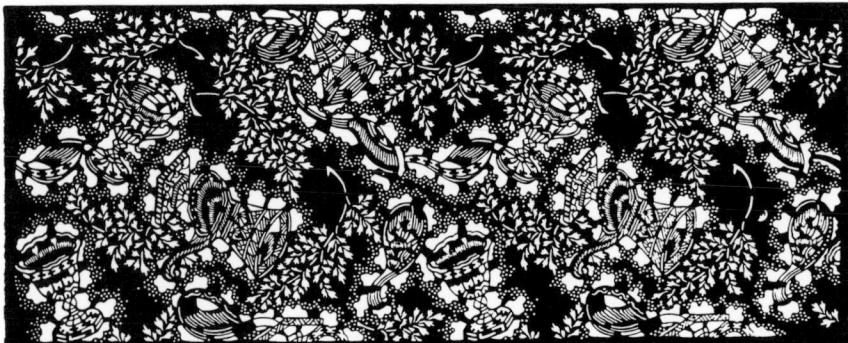

7.69 Stencil plate. From the collection of Charles Holme. William Crewdson, 'Japanese Art and Artists of To-Day, III Textiles and Embroidery', *The Studio*, October 1910.

A particularly accomplished design. Such elegant and relaxed organization of forms appealed particularly to Western designers.

7.70 Tengai Nao Onuma: **Design for a stencilled hanging**, 1910. William Crewdson, 'Japanese Art and Artists of To-Day, III Textiles and Embroidery', *The Studio*, October 1910.

Onuma was a Japanese student at Manchester. While the stencil technique he used was Japanese, the highly formal organization of this design is reminiscent of Walter Crane's decoration.

7.71 Japanese heraldic crests. Eugène Grasset, 'Armoires Japonaises', *Art et Décoration*, July–December 1912.

Eugène Grasset, the leading French authority on decorative design, took a keen interest in Japanese design.

7.73 STREET. **Designs for wallpapers.** After 1903. *Le Document du Décorateur.* Troisième série, n.d.

A design possibly taken directly from a Japanese source.

7.72 *Above* **Japanese stencil place—'Waterfall and Spray'.** From the collection of Wilson Crewdson. *The Studio*, Vol. 40, 1907.

Japanese stencils are of great delicacy and intricacy—the various elements being held together by a mesh of fibres or hairs. These were so fine that they would not leave any trace on the objects which were stencilled. Stencils were used in the making of crepes and other textiles, as well as for panels of inexpensive screens, papers for lining boxes and wallpapers.

7.74 RAOUL DUFY: **'Monuments de Paris'.** Fabric design, *c.* 1914–21. *Raoul Dufy, 1877–1953.* An exhibition organized by the Arts Council of Great Britain, 1983.

This design is organized in the fluent, but informal way of Japanese stencil designs (see in particular Plate 7.65). Dufy, like his contemporaries, would have had innumerable opportunities to see examples of Japanese design in actuality, or in journals like *Art et Décoration*, and the numerous French and foreign publications devoted to the subject.

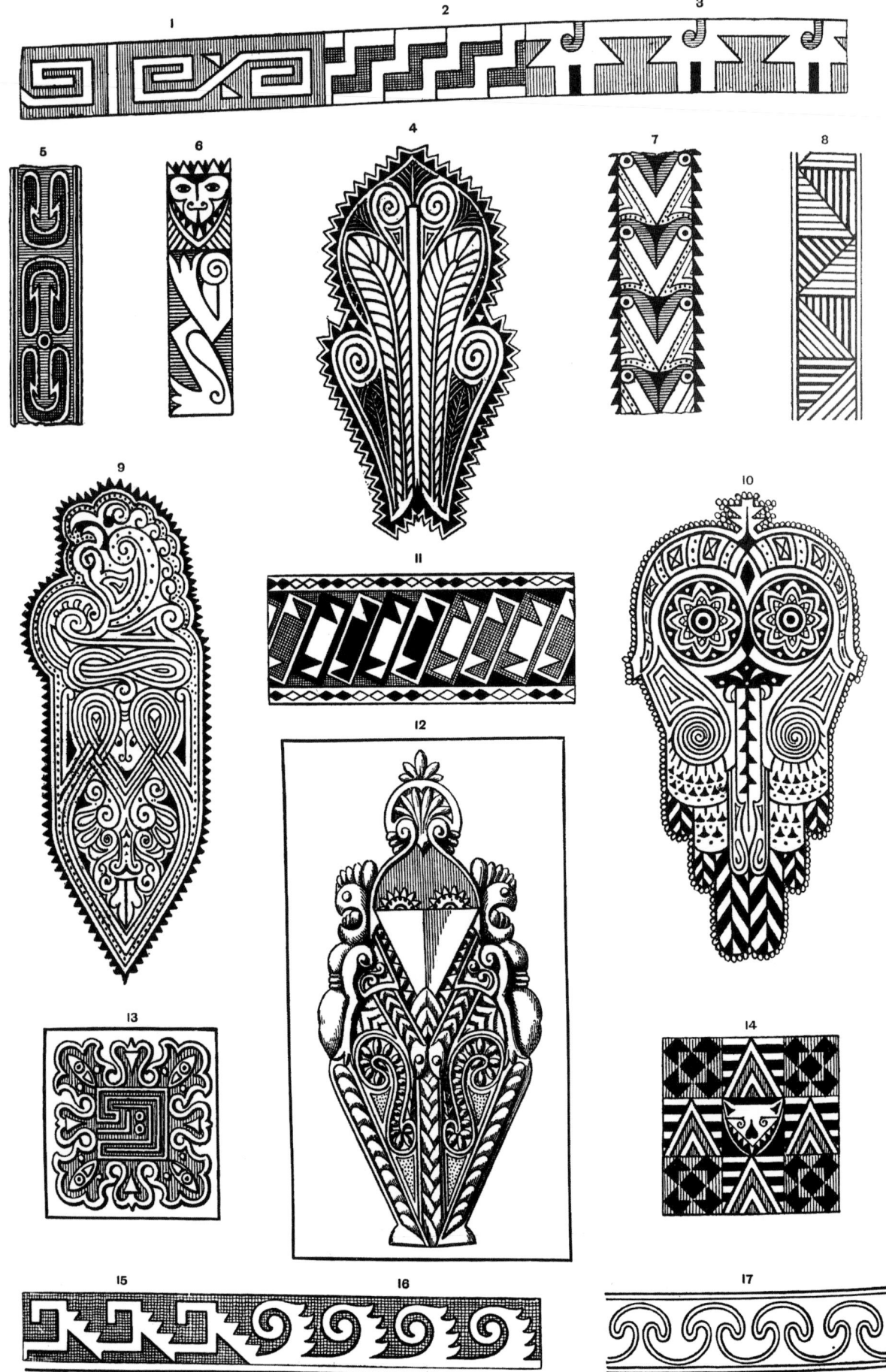

CHAPTER EIGHT
'Primitivism'

Only in recent times have we come to admire the arts of those pre-literate and remote cultures which, for want of a more suitable term, art historians have called 'primitive'. The nineteenth century, as did antiquity, could admire—albeit with reservations—the great Oriental civilizations, but had little but contempt for what was spoken of slightingly as 'savage'. Darwinism encouraged the belief that culture and art developed in a progressive evolutionary sequence. Primitive cultures were, it was believed, at a low evolutionary stage. Primitive art was like the art of children—unformed, and immature in its techniques.

The thought of studying primitive art did not occur to writers on art until well into the nineteenth century, although several important museums—such as the British Museum—had modest collections of primitive artefacts. However, these were generally seen as little more than curiosities, or looked at in much the same way as the products of nature. Yet, even in the eighteenth century, Jean-Jacques Rousseau had called for someone of the stature of Buffon, Diderot, or D'Alembert, who could study man throughout the world—that we might know ourselves the better.[1]

Owen Jones' discussion of the characteristics of primitive ornament in his *Grammar of Ornament* was the first of its kind. Jones believed that the primary impulse to create works of art sprang from man's desire to copy 'the works of the Creator'. But he also saw a functional value in the tattooed face of the warrior, in that it could be used to strike an enemy with terror. The most skilful warriors, he declared, would possess not only the most efficient, but also the most beautiful weapons.

The work of primitive peoples, despite its technical imperfections, possessed what Jones described as 'a grace and naïvete rarely found in mid-age and never in manhood's decline'. If we wished to return 'to a more healthy condition', he wrote, 'we must even be as little children or as savages—we must get rid of the acquired and the artificial, and return to and develop natural instincts.' Jones' thinking appears to be close to twentieth-centtury ideas on art teaching, in particular those of the Bauhaus. Modernist teaching has often insisted upon the expunging of inherited traditions in order that latent creativity can be unleashed. But Jones was seeking not so much to foster individualistic creative expression, but rather to establish a new school of design founded upon the principles which could be discovered through the study of universal art. Principle 36 from the *Grammar of Ornament* makes this quite clear: 'The principles discoverable in the works of the past belong to us, not so the results . . .' Jones' 'natural instincts' were not, then, matters of intuition, in which the process of reasoning had no part to play. He was, in fact, referring to the canons of design—which he thought existed throughout the world—which were based upon common craft practice. These were lost sight of when art was 'in decline'.

The Modernist belief that the love of ornament was a relic of barbarism found its most articulate spokesman in Adolf Loos (1870–1933), a leading Austrian architect and designer. Whereas Jones had asserted that the desire to ornament objects 'grows and increases' in proportion to progress in civilization, Loos in an article of 1898 wrote: 'the less civilized a people is, the more

8.1 *Opposite* JOHN LEIGHTON: **Decoration based upon Polynesian and South American originals.** *Suggestions in Design,* 1880.

Leighton was one of the few contemporary designers to have actually imitated Polynesian and South American design, and this plate is therefore of particular interest.

prodigal it will be with ornament and decoration.' And in his celebrated essay 'Ornament and Crime' of 1908, Loos went even further: 'The evolution of civilization', he wrote, 'is measured by the removal of ornament from objects of use.'

It should be remembered that anthropology—or ethnology as it was frequently called—was in its infancy in the nineteenth century.[2] Ignorance was therefore a factor which militated against the acknowledgement of qualities which could be admired in primitive art. An historically interesting book which is redolent of nineteenth-century prejudice and ignorance is G. G. Zerffi's *Manual of the Historical Development of Art* (1876) (Plate 8.9). 'The Oceanic Negro' [presumably he meant the Melanesian], he writes, 'never goes beyond geometrical ornamentation', while the Turanian, that is, Chinese and Japanese, man 'excels in technical ability, has great powers of imitation, can produce geometrical ornamentation of the most complicated and ingenious character' but 'is incapable of drawing the human form'. Zerffi's racial theory of art now seems singularly crude and has long since lost all credibility.

The views of W. G. Collingwood (1854–1932) generally accord more with twentieth-century ideas than Zerffi's. His ideas on primitive ornament are contained in *The Philosophy of Ornament* (1883) (Plates 8.5 and 11). Collingwood thought that much primitive ornament had its origin in basket-work, or plaiting. He considered that some of the shapes which arose from these processes often resembled natural forms. These were seized upon as motifs because of their resemblances to elements which were associated with nature-worship—a zig-zag suggested the waves of the sea, a circle the sun, a spiral a snake.

Collingwood appears to have been one of the earliest authorities to realize that lack of realism in representation did not necessarily signify an undeveloped technique. He noticed, for example, that extreme forms of stylization and realism were to be found side by side in the carving of the Maori house he had seen at the South Kensington Museum. 'Hideous' carved faces covered with spirals and feather-patterns were found next to 'lifelike . . . even pleasant portraits of actual men'. The distorted faces were associated with ritual or magic and were placed on the house 'not for love's sake, but for fear'. It was not until 1940, however, with the discovery of the realistic prehistoric pictures of animals on the walls of the caves at Lascaux, in the Dordogne, that the true antiquity of naturalism was realized.

Like Owen Jones before him, Collingwood admired the vigour of primitive art. His conclusion has a distinctly Ruskinian ring to it.[3] The 'barbaric or half-civilized tribes . . . put their soul into their work—we put only our capital into ours and as little of that as possible.'

Neither the Pre-Columbian cultures nor the arts of the west coast of South America are primitive in the sense that we now use the term. But in the nineteenth century these were seen to be outside the mainstream of historical development and were accorded a comparatively lowly place within the universal hierarchy of achievements.

Charles Wiener, a French anthropologist in charge of three official expeditions in Peru and Bolivia between 1875 and 1877, took a good deal of interest in Peruvian art. His account of his travels, published in *Pérou et Bolivie* in 1880,[4] is accompanied by many wood-engravings of textiles and pottery, together with some interesting observations on Peruvian decoration (Plates 8.36–9, 41). But, like his contemporaries, Wiener explained away the flat and stylized—or 'geometrical'—treatment of animals and figures in Peruvian work by saying it arose from an imperfect technical knowledge. However, he was able to recognize the grace and vitality inherent in Peruvian decoration.

In the early 1880s Christopher Dresser in his search for novel forms for

8.2 Hjalmar Stolpe: **A decorated club from Central America.** *Studier Amerikansk Ornamentik*, 1896.

Stolpe was a Swedish anthropologist. The meandering geometrical decoration is particularly sophisticated and indicates the universality of purely abstract geometrical design.

his designs for the Linthorpe Pottery borrowed Peruvian shapes and decoration. His source of inspiration was probably the Peruvian pottery in the British Museum which was by now beginning to build up its collection of artefacts from other cultures. It is worth citing here what was perhaps the earliest example of a building which borrowed an indigenous South American style. This was the Mexican pavilion at the Paris Universal Exhibition of 1889, which was designed by a Mexican architect—Antonio Anza—in a more or less archaeologically correct Aztec manner, with all the characteristic decorative motifs.[5]

Polynesian art, as we have seen, had its admirers in Owen Jones and Collingwood, but African art seems to have attracted little attention throughout most of the nineteenth century. At the Colonial and Indian Exhibition of 1886, the first major exhibition lit by electricity incidentally, which was held in Kensington, examples of West African arts were on view.[6] A gold ornament from Ashanti (Plate 8.6) was praised for the excellence of its design. Textiles and carvings from Nigeria were also displayed, but seem to have been thought of primarily as curiosities.

The main aim of the Paris Exhibition of 1889 was to show France's newly acquired industrial capabilities to the world. Besides Algerian, Tunisian, Madagascan, Tonkinese and Annamite 'villages', complete with their inhabitants, there were two African villages—one representing the French Congo, the other Senegal—to be seen in the Esplanade des Invalides. (It was at this same exhibition that the Javanese Kampong, or village—exemplifying Dutch colonialism—with its dancers, its gamelan orchestra and its batik-makers, made such an impression, not least upon the composer Debussy.) Observers noted, in particular, the work of the Congolese carvers and weavers. The Loango ivory carvers attracted some ridicule. They portrayed Parisians in frock-coats and top hats—the women with comically exaggerated posteriors. 'Despite their artistic taste', one critic observed, 'the sturdy Loangos made good porters, even cooks, washermen or tailors.'[7] Here, certainly, African art was taken none too seriously.

The writer Pol-Neveux treated the art of Senegal with more respect and sensed the potency of African sculpture.[8] King Tofa had sent to the exhibition a kind of carved retable—or altar—which represented a fantastic scene, a sort of 'religious nightmare'. More significantly, Dinah-Salifou, King of the Nalou, exhibited large figures in ebony: 'more hieratic, calmer, with a somewhat simplified anatomy, but more refined artistically'. Pol-Neveux noticed a mask—'Surely a portrait'. Its carver had all the sincerity of a medieval artist who had tried to portray a neighbour, or a friend known since childhood. Such sympathy for African art was rare in the nineteenth century.

The 1897 punitive expedition by the British against the Kingdom of Benin, in what is now Nigeria, had recently brought to light carving, and in particular bronze-casting, of a technical accomplishment previously undreamed of in African art. Its discovery prompted one of the first serious accounts of African art to appear in a popular magazine—H. Ling Roth's 'Primitive Art from Benin'—which came out in *The Studio* in December 1898.

In his article Ling Roth summarized the characteristics of Benin art: 'boldness, freedom, clearness in execution, originality, due perhaps as much to a grotesque mixture of subjects as to the method in which they are handled'.

In 1898 the Arts and Crafts Movement was in its ascendancy and its ideals were promoted by *The Studio* with more fervour than any other journal. Arts and Crafts workers sought to produce vigorous and unaffected work. Such qualities were undoubtedly felt to exist in Benin art, which may account for *The Studio*'s interest in a subject previously thought of as the preserve of the specialist.

8.3 ALFRED C. HADDON: **Decoration from a bamboo tobacco pipe,** probably from the mouth of the Fly River, in the Liverpool Museum. *Evolution in Art: as illustrated by the life histories of designs,* 1895.

The design appears to represent an aerial view of a man wrestling with a crocodile—the lozenge shapes indicating water.

195

Early twentieth-century issues of *The Studio* contained five articles on primitive art by C. J. Praetorius: 'Maori Wood Carving' (Plates 8.21, 27), 'Maori Houses' (Plate 8.29); 'Decorative Art in New Guinea' (Plates 8.28, 30); 'Art in British New Guinea' (Plates 8.31, 32); and 'Art in the Solomon Islands' (Plates 8.33–5).[9] Praetorius, an excellent draughtsman, drew his own illustrations—he was artist to the Society of Antiquaries of London for many years—and wrote with intelligence and acuity. His views on the work of the Trobriand Islanders, whose home is off the north-east coast of Papua New Guinea, seem to typify the thinking of the Arts and Crafts period. 'The work, free from restraint or rule, was full of human individuality, with a balance of line, savage beauty, and pleasant inaccuracies, qualities often wanting in designs by civilized and learned craftsmen, who, full of indistinct memories of the work of others, unconsciously produce an un-original echo, with uncertain meaning, and often without beauty.' This could almost be Morris.

Two early students of primitive art, and ornament in particular, were Henry Balfour and A. C. Haddon. Balfour was Curator of the Pitt-Rivers Museum from 1891 until his death in 1939.[10] In 1893 he published *The Evolution of Decorative Art. An Essay upon its Origin and Development as Illustrated by the Art of Modern Races of Mankind*. Works such as this are currently unfashionable, for as the study of anthropology has advanced, anthropologists have tended to concern themselves more with the study of individual cultures and the minutiae of individual cultures, than with the generalized studies of the kind Balfour embarked upon.

A. C. Haddon was Professor of Zoology at the Royal College of Science, Dublin. His *The Decorative Art of British New Guinea* was published in 1894 and his *Evolution in Art, as Illustrated by the Life-Histories of Designs* in 1895. Haddon held the current view that most primitive artists attempted to achieve realism in their work. He took a great interest in the way primitive drawings were executed and recorded how his friend Maimo, the Chief of Tud, drew a warrior by outlining the right-hand side of the figure with the right hand and the left-hand side with his left hand.

Balfour's and Haddon's pioneering work has been somewhat eclipsed by that of Franz Boaz, whose *Primitive Art* was not published until 1926. Boaz, who trained originally as a geographer, began his anthropological work in the 1890s among the Pacific Coast Indians of British Columbia. His detailed study of the phenomena of 'split representation' marked a deeper penetration into the real nature of primitive representation than anything previously published. Split representation is found in Haida and Tshimshian painting: animals, often bears, are shown as if 'cut in two from head to tail'.[11]

8.4 *Above* **'Leather bottle from the Niger'.** Frank Cundall, ed., *Reminiscences of the Colonial and Indian Exhibition*, 1886.

Exhibits from Nigeria at the Colonial and Indian Exhibition of 1886 included brassware, leatherwork, sword sheaths, mats and textiles. The bottle came from Sokoto, a Muslim kingdom in the north of Nigeria.

8.5 *Right* W. G. COLLINGWOOD **'Barbaric ideals'.** *The Philosophy of Ornament*, 1883.

The carving on the left is from New Zealand. Collingwood was interested in the evolution and influence of techniques, and noted the 'high degree of perfection' in New Zealand wood-carving. The gold figure, now in the Liverpool Museum, is from Central America and illustrates the use of wire and solder.

The impact of primitive art and decoration is not easy to establish, yet its power came to be increasingly admired as the twentieth century progressed. Exponents of Modernism were quick to read in it an anti-academic or anti-historicist message. 'Primitive' crafts—basket-making and coiled pottery—had been taught to children as part of the Arts and Crafts revolution that had begun in schools early in the twentieth century.[12] Herbert Read, in *Art Now* (1933), declared that 'it is impossible to exaggerate the significance of primitive art'. Certainly a large number of painters were affected by it. Gauguin's statues and vases were influenced by the art he had seen in Tahiti. Picasso drew inspiration from African masks and carvings. Roger Fry wrote with enthusiasm on the art of the Bushmen in the *Burlington Magazine* in 1910. Primitive elements are to be seen in the products of the Omega workshops which Fry founded in 1913. Paul Klee, the painters of the Brücke, the Cubists, the Fauvists, all responded to the vitality and energy of primitive art.

If our present re-assessment of the Western academic tradition continues, it seems likely that the influence of primitive art, which was so powerful during the era of Modernism, will wane. We understand better now that primitive works of art were often 'functional'—that is, they had a ritual or magical purpose—and were not produced by capricious or individualistic artists who saw themselves as seers, as artists in the West have so often seen themselves, at least since the age of Romanticism. The view of works of art as the outcome simply of an aesthetic impulse is receding.

8.6 *Left* **Gold ornament from Ashanti.** Drawn by Thomas Riley. Frank Cundall, ed., *Reminiscences of the Colonial and Indian Exhibition*, 1886.

This ornament had been given to the British Government by the King of Ashanti as part of the indemnity demanded after the Ashanti war of 1874.

8.7 *Below* **Canoe decoration from New Guinea.** Owen Jones, *Grammar of Ornament*, 1856.

Owen Jones illustrated a well-chosen selection of Polynesian and New Guinea ornament. He was a pioneer student in this field, but still held the belief that there was a clear-cut division between 'civilized' and 'savage' cultures.

8.8 *Above* **Canoe decoration from New Zealand.** Owen Jones, *Grammar of Ornament*, 1856.

Owen Jones had a particular admiration for Maori design, which he saw as a manifestation of a universal capacity to embellish according to sound aesthetic principles.

CHART
OF THE
HISTORICAL DEVELOPMENT OF ART.

A.D. 1200 - 1800
MODERN ART.

HIGH RENAISSANCE

BIZARRE · EARLY RENAISSANCE

CHINA

ENGLISH · GERMAN · FRENCH

SPANISH · ITALIAN

GOTHIC · ECCLESIASTICAL

MARBLE
BRICKS
WOOD
IRON
BRASS

A.D. 1-1200
CHRISTIAN ERA

KELTIC

FRANK · OSTROGOTHIC

NORMAN

MAHOMEDAN

ROMANESQUE

BYZANTINE

EARLY · CHRISTIAN

IRON
MARBLE
WOOD
BRICKS
MORTAR

ROME · ETRUSKAN

500 B.C.
HISTORICAL
CLASSICAL

1ST PERIOD · 2ND PERIOD · 3RD PERIOD · 3RD PERIOD · 2ND PERIOD · 1ST PERIOD

SCULPTURE · ARCHITECTURE

GREECE

MARBLE

TIME ABSOLUTE
6000 - 500 B.C.

ROCK
HEWN
TEMPLES

EGYPT

ASSYRIA
PERSIA · BABYLON

BUDDHA

HEBREW
PHŒNICIAN

IRON
BRONZE
STONE

NEGRO ART

MANU

10,000 - 600
B.C.

THE VEDAS

FLINT
WOOD

SAVAGE ART

TIME RELATIVE
000000 - 000,000 B.C.

NEGRO · ARYAN · TURANIAN

HUTS
CAVES
CAVERNS

8.9 *Left* G. G. ZERFFI: **'Evolutionary' chart.** *Manual of the Historical Development of Art*, 1876.

Zerffi was committed to a characteristically nineteenth-century racial theory of art. 'Aryan' art had progressed, through 'savagery', to Classical art and had culminated in the art of the High Renaissance. 'Turanian'—Chinese or Japanese—art had pursued its own separate course. Negro art, however, had remained at the developmental stage.

8.10 *Below* **State stool from the Gold Coast (now Ghana).** Drawn by Thomas Riley. Frank Cundall, ed., *Reminiscences of the Colonial and Indian Exhibition*, 1886.

The Colonial and Indian Exhibition held in London in 1886 was intended to popularize the idea of Empire. Although the West African section—Sierra Leone, Gambia, Gold Coast and Lagos—was comparatively small, there was modest praise for some African crafts, particularly woven textiles. The British public would have had few opportunities before the exhibition to judge the quality of African design for itself.

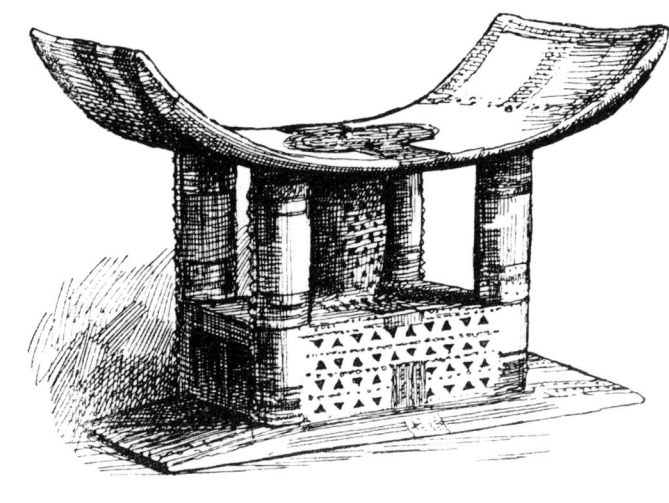

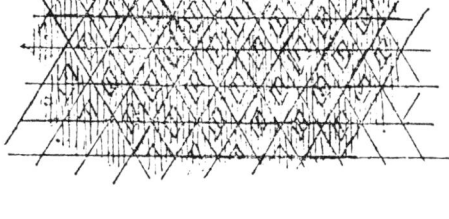

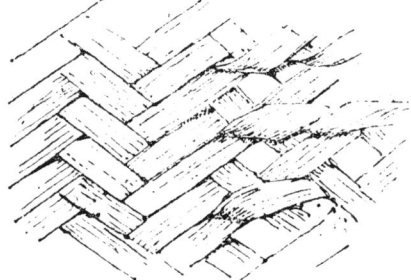

8.11 *Above* W. G. COLLINGWOOD: **'Asiatic contrasts'—Aryan and Turanian.** *The Philosophy of Ornament*, 1883.

Collingwood was particularly interested in the differences between 'Aryan' and 'Turanian' design. His mentor was Sir George C. M. Birdwood, author of *The Industrial Arts of India*, 1880, who had stressed the superior moral and intellectual qualities of Aryan art.

8.14 *Below* ALFRED C. HADDON: **Animal drawings from the Torres Straits.** From examples in the British Museum, Cambridge, Oxford and Berlin. *Evolution in Art: as illustrated by the life histories of designs*, 1895.

Haddon was especially interested in problems of the representation of humans and animals. He was the earliest serious student of New Guinea art.

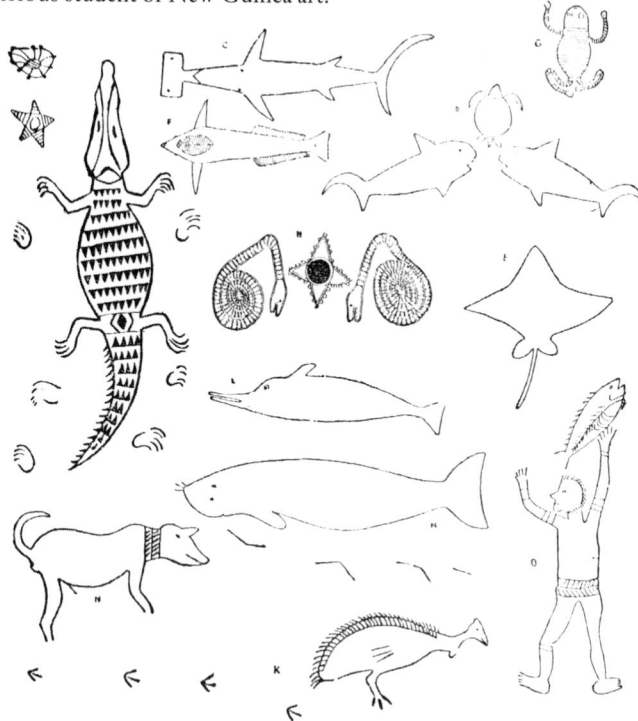

8.13 *Above* **New Caledonian 'village' at the Paris Universal Exhibition**, 1889. After A. LePère. Pol-Neveux, 'Le Village Canaque', in F. G. Dumas and L. de Fourcaud, *Revue de l'Exposition Universelle de 1889*, n.d.

Prominent at the Paris Exhibition of 1889 were the 'villages' from all parts of the French Colonial Empire. Pol-Neveux, who wrote with some sympathy about African carving, was less impressed by these New Caledonian images. He was struck not by the terrifying aspect of the figures, but by their 'sadness'.

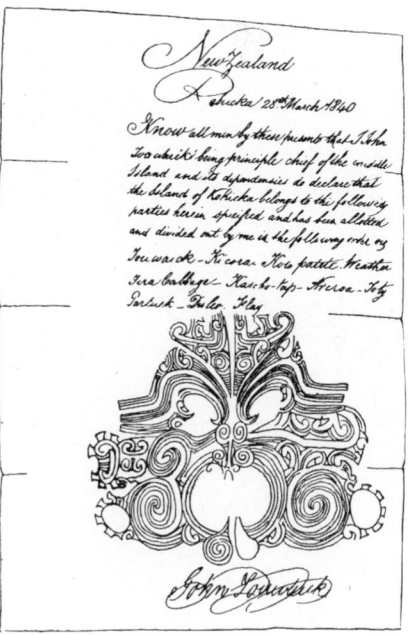

8.12 *Opposite* FRANK G. JACKSON: **'Modern savage plaited rush work'.** *Lessons on Decorative Design*, 1900.

Jackson's book was intended for junior art students. Plaiting and weaving were considered to be of great importance as sources of inspiration to early makers of pattern. Jackson probably took this idea from W. G. Collingwood.

8.15 *Above* H. G. ROBLEY: **Nose tattooing.** Drawn from a tattooed head in Robley's collection, *Moko, or Maori Tattooing*, 1896.

Robley was conscious that Maori tattooing was a dying art. Although he was no anthropologist, he was determined to document what remained of it before it was too late. His book is still of considerable value to the student of body decoration.

8.16 H. G. ROBLEY: **A Maori chief's drawing of his own facial decoration as a substitute for a signature.** *Moko, or Maori Tattooing*, 1896.

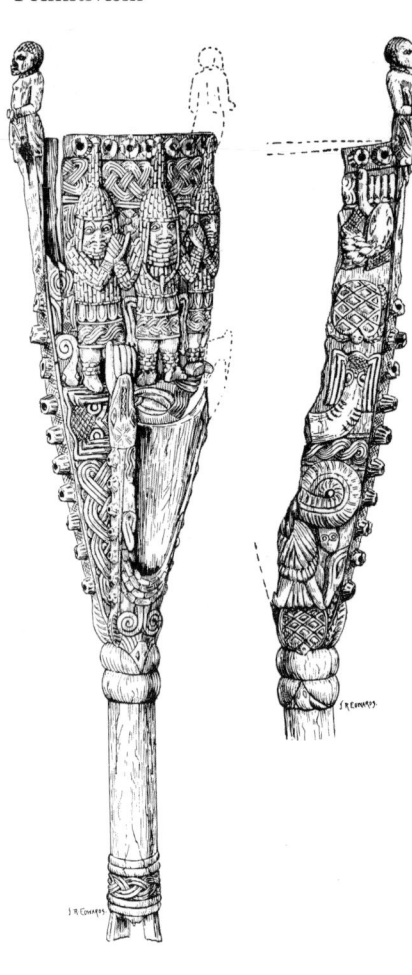

8.17 *Left* H. Ling Roth: **Details of a carved ivory sistrum.** 'Primitive Art from Benin', *The Studio*, December 1898.

In his article Ling Roth summed up the characteristics of Benin art as 'boldness, freedom, clearness of execution, and originality', which were, he said, 'due perhaps as much to a grotesque mixture of subjects as to the method in which they are handled . . .'.

8.18 and **8.19** H. Ling Roth: *below* **Carving on elephant tusk** and *centre* **Carving representing a double cat-fish.** 'Primitive Art from Benin', *The Studio*, December 1898.

The design of the cat-fish bears some resemblance to the 'split representations' of animals found in the Americas.

8.20 *Above* H. Ling Roth: **Top of a staff, carved in ivory.** From the collection of Miss M. H. Kingsley. 'Primitive Art from Benin', *The Studio*, December 1898.

8.21 *Opposite* C. J. PRAETORIUS: **Carved hand-club.** 'Maori Wood Carving', *The Studio*, October 1900.

The Maoris, according to Praetorius, had been in New Zealand for some four or five hundred years. Maori carving was reputedly 'invented' by the legendary figure Rauru. The penalty for deviation from the prescribed style was death. Praetorius felt that the Maoris had produced 'some of the finest art under barbaric conditions'. Little use was made, however, of animal, fish or plant motifs.

7.75 JIMBEI KAWASHIMA: **Silk brocade for curtains.** Manufactured by Kawashima & Co., Nishijih, Kyoto. *The Studio*, Vol. 51, 1910.

Fabrics of this kind were originally used for court costumes.

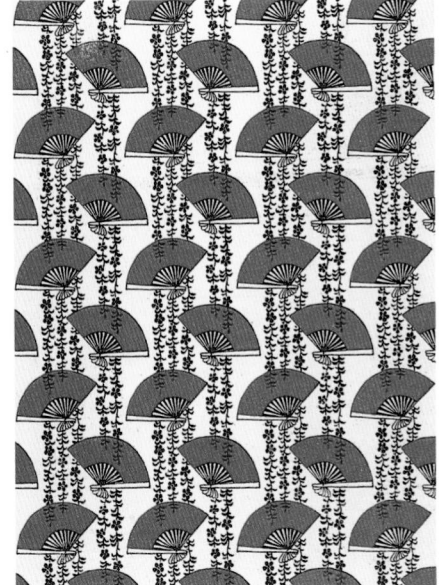

7.76 HENRI GILLET: **Decoration with Japanese fans.** *Nouvelles Fantasies Decoratives*, *c.* 1920.

8.23 Owen Jones: **Melanesian and Polynesian bark fabrics.** Original gouache illustration for *The Grammar of Ornament*, 1856. The Print Room, Victoria and Albert Museum, London.

8.22 *Opposite* M. A. Racinet:
Decoration from Oceania and Central Africa. *L'Ornement Polychrome*, 1869.

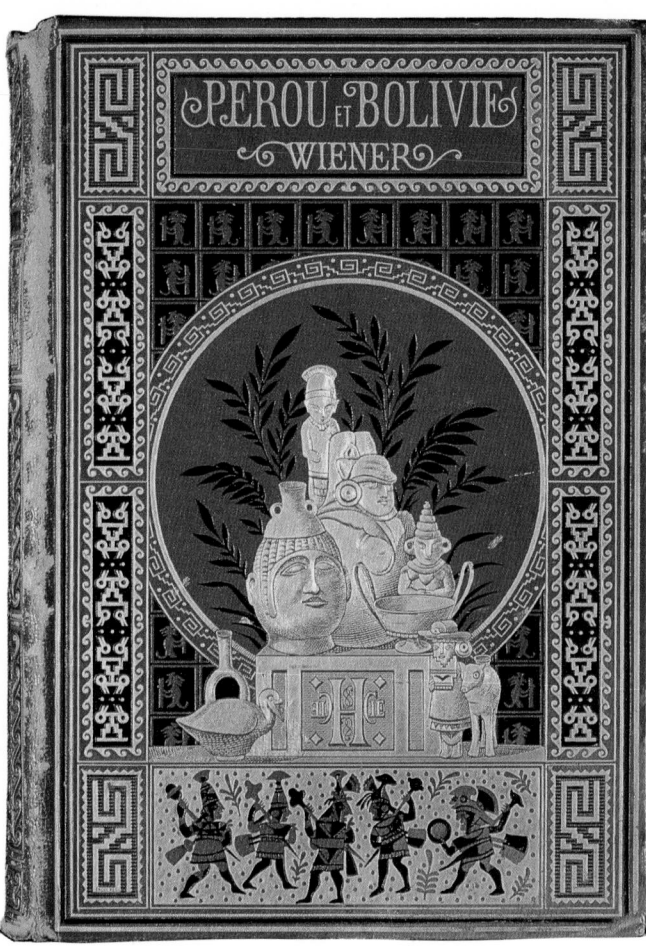

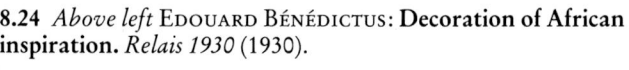

8.24 *Above left* EDOUARD BÉNÉDICTUS: **Decoration of African inspiration.** *Relais 1930* (1930).

8.25 *Above* A. SOUZE: **Publisher's binding for Hachette.** For Charles Wiener's *Perou et Bolivie*, 1880.

Souze designed a number of inventive decorative bindings including that of Viollet-le-Duc's *Histoire d'un Dessinateur*.

8.26 ANONYMOUS: **Design for textile.** Manufactured by Albert Godde, Bedin & Cie, Lyon & Mulhouse, *Art, Goût, Beaute*, 1923.

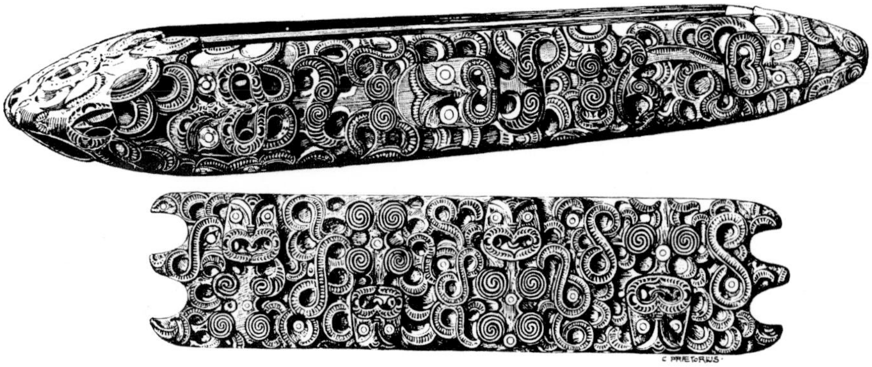

8.27 *Right* C. J. Praetorius: **Carved box.** 'Maori Wood Carving', *The Studio*, October 1900.

The box was intended for storing sacred 'Luai' feathers. 'On these boxes is found the most elaborate ornament, composed of human figures and curves, with many shell discs set in among the carving.' Since the introduction of European tools, wrote Praetorius, 'only inferior carving' was done, 'obviously for the market'.

8.28 *Right centre* C. J. Praetorius: **A frigate-bird depicted naturalistically compared with a New Guinea carving.** 'Decorative Art in New Guinea', Part I, *The Studio*, March 1902.

The frigate-bird was considered auspicious by the people of New Guinea. It was always rendered in 'grotesque style'.

8.29 *Right* C. J. Praetorius: **Carved lintel from the doorway of a Maori house.** 'Maori houses', *The Studio*, February 1901.

'All Maori patterns, demons and figures, have their particular meaning and proper name . . . one reason for so much repetition in their subjects and ornaments was the fear of "Aitua" or evil omen for he who was bold enough to introduce new ideas . . .'

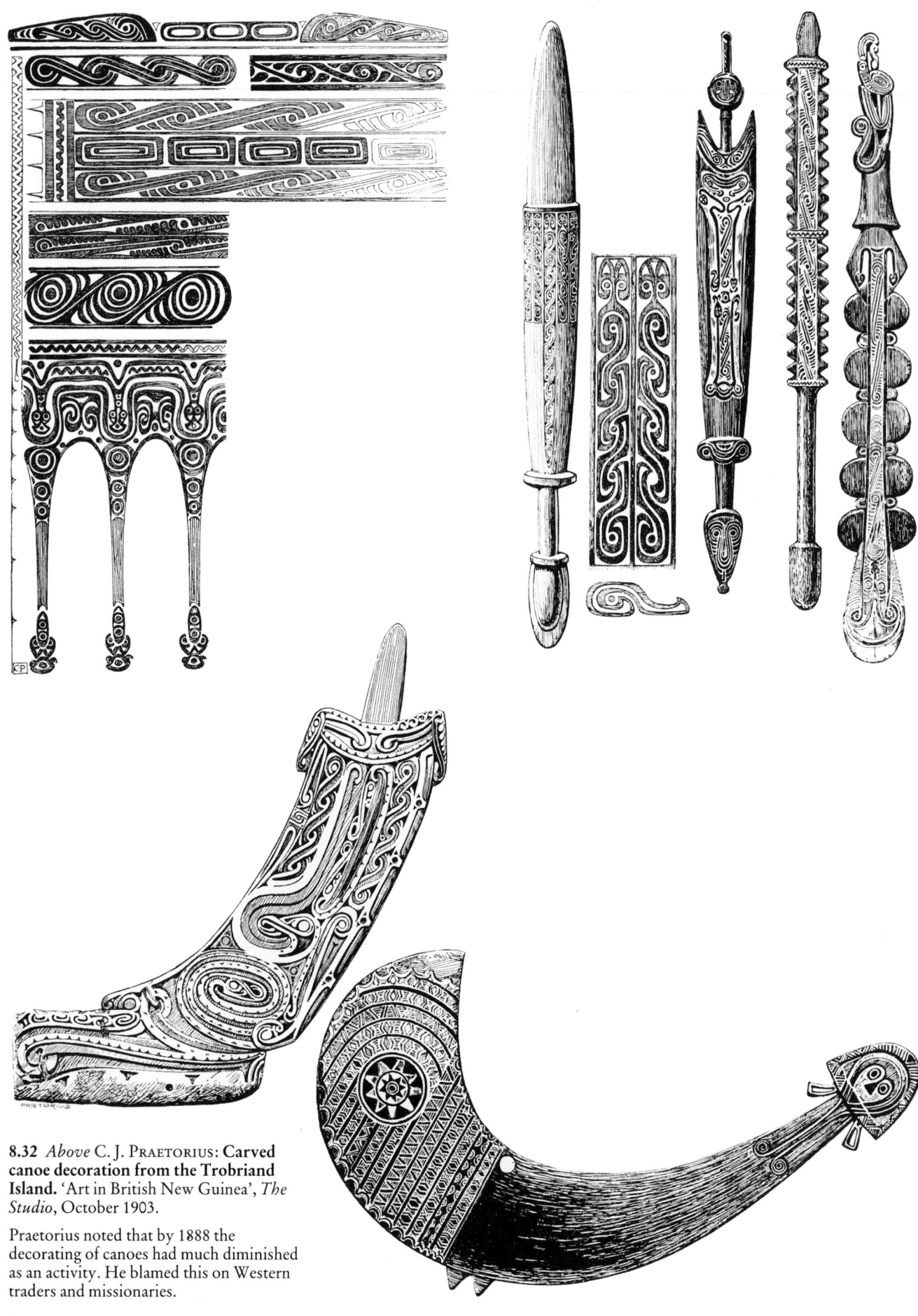

8.32 *Above* C. J. PRAETORIUS: **Carved canoe decoration from the Trobriand Island.** 'Art in British New Guinea', *The Studio*, October 1903.

Praetorius noted that by 1888 the decorating of canoes had much diminished as an activity. He blamed this on Western traders and missionaries.

8.30 *Opposite far left* C. J. Praetorius: **Patterns based upon traditional representations of the frigate-bird.** 'Decorative Art in New Guinea', *The Studio*, March 1902.

In a few years, remarked Praetorius, it would be impossible to produce such a work, so rapidly were conditions in New Guinea changing.

8.31 *Opposite left* C. J. Praetorius: **Decoration on a carved club from Trobriand Island.** 'Art in British New Guinea', *The Studio*, October 1903.

Praetorius observed that New Guinea decoration seldom impaired an object's utility. The combination of beauty with utility was sought during the Arts and Crafts era.

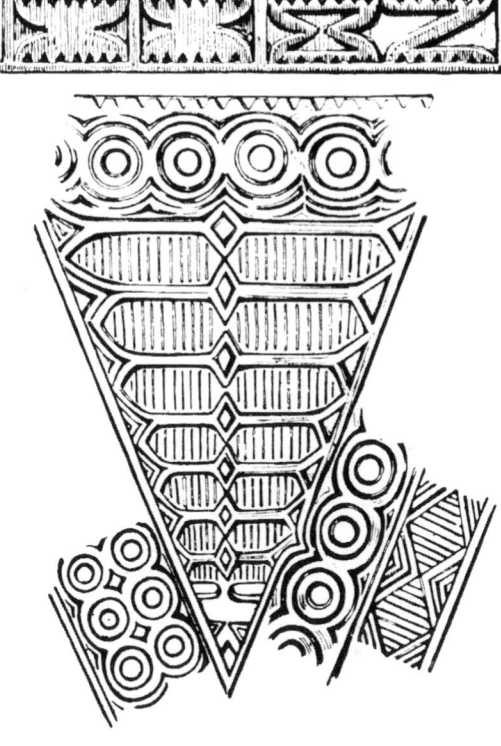

8.34 *Right* C. J. Praetorius: **Decoration from the Solomon Islands.** 'Art in the Solomon Islands', *The Studio*, March 1905.

Praetorius wrote of a 'quaint imaginative power' and 'sense of beauty' in the decorative work of the Solomon Islanders. Their efforts to represent the human form were, however, 'poor'.

8.35 *Bottom right* C. J. Praetorius: **Forehead ornaments of shell.** 'Art in the Solomon Islands', *The Studio*, March 1905.

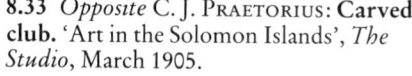

8.33 *Opposite* C. J. Praetorius: **Carved club.** 'Art in the Solomon Islands', *The Studio*, March 1905.

Praetorius noted that the Solomon Islanders drew the circles used in their decoration without the aid of compasses. However, they used templates of coarse shell for their zig-zag decorative designs.

8.36 and **8.37** CHARLES WIENER: *Left* **Poncho found at Ancon, Peru.** *Below* **Fabric found at Paramonga.** *Pérou et Bolivie*, 1880.

Wiener brought back some four thousand objects and textile samples from his three expeditions to Peru and Bolivia. Like many contemporaries, he explained away stylized representation as a matter of imperfect drawing technique. Nevertheless, he admired the ingenuity of Peruvian weavers.

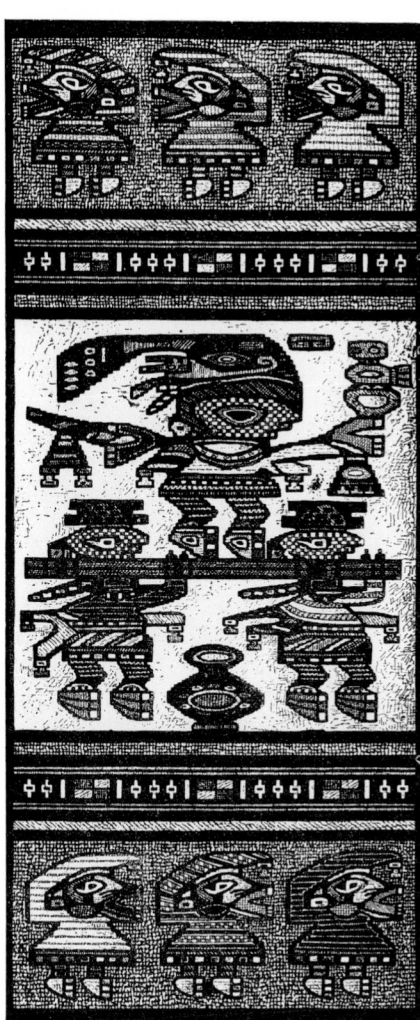

8.40 *Above* **'The Palaces of the Aztecs and Incas'.** In Charles Garnier's 'Human Habitations' section at the Paris Universal Exhibition, 1889. F. G. Dumas and L. de Fourcaud, *Revue de l'Exposition Universelle de 1889*, n.d.

Viollet-le-Duc's popular educational book, *Histoire de l'Habitation Humaine* (The Story of Human Habitation), was the starting-point of Garnier's re-creations of ancient houses. (One is also reminded of the reproductions of the architecture of historical styles at the Crystal Palace, Sydenham, in 1854.) Garnier, the designer of the Paris Opéra, was concerned with effect rather than with absolute accuracy.

8.41 *Below* CHARLES WIENER: **Design on a calabash found at Infantas, Peru.** Executed after the Spanish conquest. *Pérou et Bolivie*, 1880.

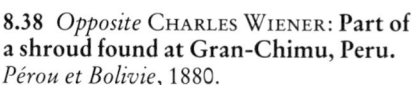

8.39 *Above* CHARLES WIENER: **Fabric found at Ancon, Peru.** *Pérou et Bolivie*, 1880.

Wiener called this a 'marvellous' fabric. He described it as representing a procession in which a chief is carried in a litter up a slope. That the slope is winding upwards is indicated by the directions of the profiles of the warriors in the upper and lower panels.

8.38 *Opposite* CHARLES WIENER: **Part of a shroud found at Gran-Chimu, Peru.** *Pérou et Bolivie*, 1880.

Gran-Chimu is an important archaeological site 500 kilometres north of Lima.

8.42 *Left* RICHARD GLAZIER: **Peruvian textiles.** From the Smithies' Loan Collection, Manchester. *Manual of Historic Ornament*, 1899.

Glazier's book was published when the Arts and Crafts Movement was at its apogee. Peruvian design was bold and unaffected—two qualities sought by Arts and Crafts workers.

8.43 *Below left* HANS HILDEBRAND: **Urn found in a Swedish dolmen.** *The Industrial Arts of Scandinavia in the Pagan Time*, 1883.

During the summer of 1882 a major exhibition of pre-Christian Scandinavian art was mounted at the South Kensington Museum, London. Hans Hildebrand, Royal Antiquary of Sweden, and J. J. Worsaae, Director of Royal Museums and Archaeological Monuments of Denmark, contributed accompanying handbooks. Hildebrand's and Worsaae's writings helped popularize the idea that 'barbaric' European art should be viewed as part of the mainstream of historical development. W. G. Collingwood, G. Jackson and J. Moyr Smith all knew Hildebrand's book.

8.44 *Below* HANS HILDEBRAND: **Part of a gilt harness from Gotland.** *The Industrial Arts of Scandinavia in the Pagan Time*, 1883.

This stylized bird bears a distant likeness to a New Guinea representation of a frigate-bird. Creatures such as this are also found in Celtic illuminated manuscripts.

8.45 J. Moyr Smith: '**Shakespearian Archaeology ... early Scandinavian. Hamlet, Act 1, Scene I'**. *Decoration*, Vol. 12, Christmas 1886.

Moyr Smith took his references from Hildebrand's *Industrial Arts of Scandinavia*. He was a protégé of Christopher Dresser and designed theatre sets and a number of interiors using Shakespearian themes.

8.46 Gerhard Munthe: **Chapter heading for the Saga of the Son of Magnus.** *Art et Décoration*, July–December 1904.

Munthe, like many contemporaries, sought to revive a national decorative style. (Viollet-le-Duc in *L'Art Russe* had suggested how the Russians could draw on their native decorative traditions.) Munthe would have found numerous examples of early Scandinavian art in the publications of Hildebrand and J. J. Worsaae.

CHAPTER NINE
The Arts and Crafts Movement

The ideas of the Arts and Crafts movement are rooted in the Gothic Revival. Champions of the Gothic, as part of their archaeological researches, had delved into medieval art in order to understand its role and function. Pugin believed the transcending factor had been faith: building a cathedral was a supreme act of devotion. Thus a new age of faith would call for Christian architecture—pointed Gothic architecture. For Viollet-le-Duc the development of scientific constructional principles by medieval craftsmen affirmed man's constant search for rationality. The desire for the expression of truth in building, common to both Pugin and Viollet-le-Duc, has affinities with Arts and Crafts ideals.

However, it is Ruskin's understanding of medieval architecture which contains within it the essential Arts and Crafts message: people deprived of the means of self-expression are brutalized. He argued that the Industrial Revolution had created an urbanized peasantry. Without the supportive structure of the village community and the clearly defined roles of village life, people became disoriented, fractious, even violent. Satisfying work by hand was an antidote to the deadly poisons of urbanization and mechanization.

The tone of Ruskin's writing is invariably paternalistic, and at the same time permeated with an irrational fear of impending apocalypse. William Morris, on the other hand, was by nature more optimistic. It is his thinking, not Ruskin's, which dominates the theory and practice of the Arts and Crafts movement during its apogee. Morris himself held Ruskin in the highest esteem; he had his Kelmscott Press print the chapter 'On the Nature of Gothic' from Ruskin's *The Stones of Venice* in an edition of five hundred copies, which was large by Kelmscott standards. This was a significant act of homage.

'On the Nature of Gothic' might well be described as the primer of the Art and Crafts movement. What is particularly important in this extraordinary and poetic piece of writing is that Ruskin sees the cathedral as a product of a better and more cohesive society than his own. This was a society to which everyone contributed according to his or her ability. It mattered not that medieval work was often coarse, clumsy or naïve—for it was, above all things, vital. The discipline of the Classical style demanded servility. In the cathedral, the ordinary workman had been allowed to give of himself and contribute to the totality. Out of 'fragments full of imperfection'—the crude carvings—could rise up 'a stately and unaccusable whole'. Ruskin, while never glorying in roughness of finish for its own sake, delighted in work which proclaimed that it had been made by men and women, not machines.

A glance at the illustrations in this chapter will reveal that no absolute boundary exists between Arts and Crafts ornament, on the one hand, and Gothic Revival ornament or the nature-inspired ornament that was so prevalent in the nineteenth century, on the other. It is true that Arts and Crafts designers of ornament revelled particularly in pastoral themes and favoured the representation of native plants and birds—the familiar and the pleasing. There is also an especial, though immeasurable, energy in the best Arts and Crafts ornament.

9.1 *Opposite* HENRY WILSON: **Wallpaper for Jeffrey & Co.** *Art et Décoration*, Vol. III, 1898.

Wilson, an architect who collaborated with Lethaby in the Liverpool Cathedral Competition of 1903, was also well known for his metalwork. His *Silverwork and Jewellery* of 1903 was a standard Arts and Crafts text. Here his indebtedness to Morris is very apparent.

Morris, in 'Some Hints on Pattern Designing', a lecture delivered at the Working Men's College in London in December 1881 and published posthumously in 1899, described good decoration as: 'Something that will not drive us into unrest or callousness; something which reminds us of life beyond itself, and which has the impress of imagination strong on it; and something which can be done by a great many people and without too much difficulty and with pleasure.' Morris was calling for the revival of authentic popular art. In addition, the welfare of the creators of ornament was of as much importance as the work itself.

Did, then, the philosophy of the Arts and Crafts—glimpsed in a vision by Ruskin and more practically stated by Morris—bring into being an entirely distinctive style of ornament? Morris saw that the act of making things, or devising patterns, could be socially beneficial and therapeutic in an age when the craftsman had been superseded by the machine-minder. The division of labour, the inevitable concomitant of mechanization, deprived the worker of the satisfaction of being able to take a pride in an end product. Arts and Crafts ornament is thus consistently anti-mechanistic—both in the sense that it portrays an aspect of nature, and in the sense that its creators studiously avoid the characteristics of machine-produced work.

Among the propagandists of the Arts and Crafts movement were the illustrator Walter Crane (1845–1915), and the architects and designers W. A. S. Benson (1854–1924) and C. R. Ashbee (1863–1942). Like Morris, Crane believed that 'genuine and spontaneous art is a pleasurable creation', but although committed to the Morris ideal he was also highly responsive to contemporary changes in fashion and as a designer was eclectic in spirit (see Plates 5.36, 42). Benson designed furniture and textiles for Morris' firm and set up a workshop for the manufacture of metalwork. Unlike many of his Arts and Crafts contemporaries he was quite willing to use the machine for the production of well-designed goods. Ashbee's work is often highly idiosyncratic and he was open to a number of influences (Plate 9.43). C. F. A. Voysey (1857–1941), today remembered principally for his contribution to the revival of English domestic architecture, designed a number of textiles, wallpapers and carpets (Plates 9.25–8, 31–2) in the pastoral spirit advocated by Morris, but did not share Morris' socialist beliefs.

The designs in Godfrey Blount's *Arbor Vitae* (1899) might be thought a trifle flaccid when compared with Morris' or Voysey's firm and polished design, but Blount is making it plain that handicraft must proclaim itself to be what it is, and not strive to emulate the precision of machine-made work. Blount, like many a good teacher, mildly over-states his case in order to emphasize it. *Arbor Vitae* (see Plates 9.49 and 50) has been undeservedly neglected by historians.

Arts and Crafts thinkers felt that a change for the better in society and the arts was impending. In his *Wood Carving*[1] of 1903 (Plates 9.4, 52) George Jack, the American-born architect and carver and a keen disciple of Morris, voiced the Arts and Crafts condemnation of the Renaissance attitude to the crafts, but ended on an optimistic note:

> To the Renaissance must be attributed the fatal separation of the crafts-man's function into the hands of designer and executant which has so completely paralysed the living spirit of individual invention. It has taken close upon four centuries to open the eyes of craftsmen to this inconsistency, and revive the medieval truth that invention and execution are strictly but one and the same thing. Let us hope that the present awakening to the importance of this fact may lead to what will be truly worthy of being called a Renaissance; not merely of outward forms, but of that creative energy which justifies the true meaning of the word.

9.2 GEORGE WRAGGE: **Lock plate.** *The Studio*, Vol. XIV, 1898.

This design may be the work of Edgar Wood, one of the most adventurous of Arts and Crafts architects, whom Wragge was later to commission to design a complete range of decorative metalwork. Wragge operated a successful metalwork business in Manchester which was run on Arts and Crafts lines.

Joyful confidence and moral certainty seem to be conveyed by the most successful Arts and Crafts decoration. Are these qualities somehow contained within the decoration itself? Or is it simply that one invariably associates Arts and Crafts work with the idealists who produced it?

In 1894, Morris, in an Address at the Distribution of Prizes at the Birmingham Municipal School of Art, talked about the sources which had inspired him. This lecture was given so late in Morris' career—he was to die some two years later—that it is a kind of valediction. Morris speaks out against 'manner', which I take to mean excessive dependence for ideas upon received, run-of-the-mill, commercial work—such work being 'mannered'. 'The corrective to overmuch manner is', he asserted, 'first, diligent study of Nature, and secondly, study of the work of the ages of Art. The third corrective is infallible if you have it . . . it is imagination.' These, then, are the sources of Morris' own inspiration: nature and the historical styles of which he approved—medieval, early Italian Renaissance and Persian.

Nature, as we have seen in Chapter Two, was thought of throughout the nineteenth century as the fountainhead from which all decorative inspiration could flow. Interpretations of nature might be infinitely varied, but 'nature the designer' was a rallying-call throughout the century in which scientific materialism had deposed God. In stressing the primary importance of the study of nature, Morris is entirely typical of his age. So, too, is his counselling of the selective study of history—'the ages of Art'; for he saw his own times as possessing no art. Morris' ornament, dependent as it is upon these two principal sources of motifs, is thoroughly Victorian. It is because of his psychological understanding of the malaise and alienation of his age—explicit in his writings and implicit in his designs—that Morris rises above his fellows.

W. R. Lethaby (1857–1931) was in many ways the apostolic successor to Morris, although he was far less active politically and operated on what could be described as an 'aesthetico-moral' plane. In his Preface to George Jack's *Wood Carving* he discussed ornament in unmistakably Morris-like tones: 'Most design will always be the making of one thing like another, with a difference, but always with some guidance as to treatment, from an example known to be fine. I would say, for instance, "Do a panel like this, only let it be oak foliage instead of vine, and get a thrush or a parrot out of the Bird Book".' In emphasizing that the representation of nature should be guided by an intelligent understanding of past practice Lethaby's theme is the same as Morris'. Ornament was 'a language addressed to the eye . . . pleasant thought expressed in the speech of the tool'. For the Arts and Crafts evangelists it was an art form that was accessible to everyone. It could soothe, like a balm, those whose psyche had been traumatized by the destruction of their now half-remembered pastoral world and the failure of industrialization to improve their lot.

Ornament held a very important place in Arts and Crafts theory. But the founding fathers of the Modern Movement, whose ideas often stem from the Arts and Crafts, were to anathematize it. Adolf Loos, with humour, and Le Corbusier, with deadly seriousness, ridiculed ornament. They relegated the ornamented object to a lower plane, a lower evolutionary phase, than the unornamented object in which pure unadulterated form was all-important. Did Arts and Crafts theorists anticipate the crisis of ornament?

Lethaby—and again I quote from his Preface to George Jack's *Wood Carving*—expressed a view which hints at the difficulties: 'Mere structure will always justify itself, and architects who cannot obtain living ornament will do well to fall back on structure well-fitted for its purpose and as finely finished as may be without carvings and other adornments.' By 'living ornament' Lethaby clearly meant ornament made by living craftsmen. But Lethaby had no doubts about the validity of ornamenting buildings, although

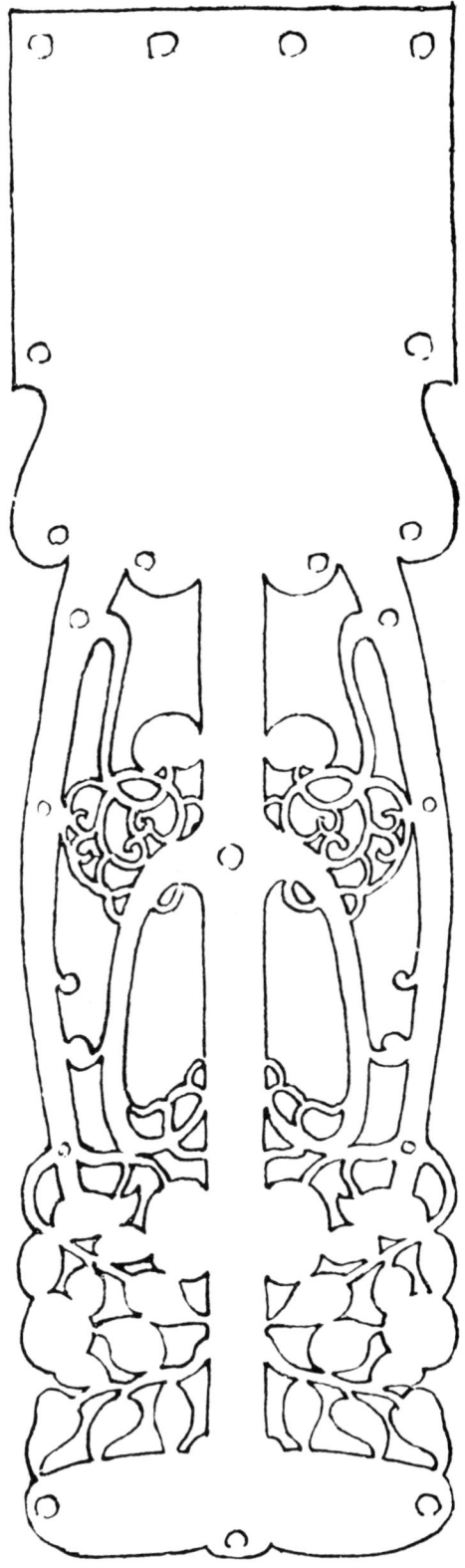

9.3 George Wragge: **Hinge.** *The Studio*, Vol. XIV, 1898.

Arts and Crafts designers invariably seized any opportunity to decorate hinges. Again, this design may be the work of Edgar Wood.

he was very discreet in applying ornament to his own. He continued: 'It would be better still if architects would make the demand for a more intellectual code of ornament than we have been accustomed to for so long.' This 'intellectual code of ornament' was never established theoretically, although many Arts and Crafts architects were fine ornamentalists in practice. One has simply to recall the work of C. R. Ashbee (Plate 9.43), Baillie Scott (Plates 9.36–8), C. R. Mackintosh (Plates 10.15, 18), Harrison Townsend (Plates 9.34, 41, 45) or Edgar Wood (see Plates 9.2, 3).

Yet the idea of an 'intellectual code of ornament' remains a tantalizing prospect. Is Lethaby, however, concerned about the potential capacity of ornament to convey meaning, or is he merely concerned with the visual etiquette of ornamenting a structure?

The thought of infusing ornament with meaning was attractive to Arts and Crafts workers. Nineteenth-century study of medieval art, Oriental art and the burgeoning science of anthropology had served to show that ornament was able to contain and to convey complex meanings. Lethaby, an accomplished historian, was deeply interested in universal symbols but the times were against the development of a richly symbolic and significant language of ornament. The emergence of an evolved and confident industrial culture towards the end of the nineteenth century and an increasing degree of secularization militated against the creation of ornament charged with any kind of symbolism.

One of Lethaby's last publications, *Designing Games* (1929), issued by Dryad Handicrafts of Leicester, demonstrated how easy visual 'games' could serve to generate simple pattern. Quite evidently this little pamphlet was intended for amateur craftworkers. It is an admirable illustration of the lowly status ornament now had within the hierarchy of the arts. It had not achieved the exalted place which Morris, or Ruskin for that matter, had envisaged for it.

In any examination of Arts and Crafts ornament it is important to place Morris within a historical setting, if not as social reformer and politician, at least as designer. Lewis F. Day gives a compressed and canonical account of the development of nineteenth-century decorative art in his monograph on William Morris of 1899.[2] He sees Morris not so much as the initiator of reform, but as the culminating figure in a wider movement. Like many contemporaries, Day avoided discussing Morris' political commitments.

Morris was born just at the right moment: the way was prepared for him. Walter Scott, without really appreciating Gothic art, had called popular attention to its romance. Rickman had long since 'discriminated' the styles of English Architecture. Pugin had established his True Principles of Gothic Architecture and was designing all manner of medieval furniture; and by the time [Morris] came to take any heed of art, Gothic architecture was the fashion. [Henry] Shaw and others had published books on medieval antiquities and Viollet-le-Duc his famous dictionary; even Owen Jones, the Orientalist, had cleared the ground by creating a reaction of taste against mere naturalism pretending to be design. Fergusson, Semper, Wornum, Digby Wyatt and above all Ruskin had been writing about art until people were beginning to listen. Men like William Burges and E. W. Godwin were hard at work already ... the times were ready for the man and the man was William Morris.

There we have it: Goths, Orientalists and Eclectics had all paved the way for Morris. And all the elements found in their work are to be found in some admixture or other in the ornament of the major Arts and Crafts designers. But idealism, concern for the special role of art, intense passion for nature and tradition—why, these are the special preserve of the Arts and Crafts.

9.4 GEORGE JACK: Carving suitable for a small corner cupboard, showing two possible treatments. *Wood Carving: Design and Workmanship*, 1903.

Over-stated medievalism for didactic purposes seems almost to caricature Arts and Crafts practice.

9.5 WILLIAM MORRIS: **'Trellis' wallpaper,** 1864. Victoria and Albert Museum, London.

In 1864 Morris' decorative style was immature, although this design is forceful and original. The birds were drawn by Philip Webb, whom Morris had met in the office of George Edmund Street, the Gothic Revival architect. Morris was evidently particularly fond of the trellis theme and returned to it on other occasions: the embroidered curtains, of about 1893, around his four-poster bed at Kelmscott Manor, his Oxfordshire summer home, are distinctly reminiscent of this design. 'Trellis' is still produced by Arthur Sanderson and Sons Ltd., London.

9.6 WILLIAM MORRIS: **'Acanthus' wallpaper,** 1875. Victoria and Albert Museum, London.

Morris made rapid progress as a decorative designer, although his comparatively unsophisticated early work showed great promise. Here, with great skill, he suggests living forms, with depth and space beyond. Reformers like Pugin, Owen Jones and Richard Redgrave, however, were opposed to such illusionistic treatments. Decorations based upon the acanthus date back to Classical times. Morris, nevertheless, brings a new vitality to the ancient motif. 'Acanthus' was used in an interior in Old Swan House, Chelsea Embankment, built between 1875–7, which was one of Richard Norman Shaw's most influential 'Queen Anne' houses.

9.7 WILLIAM MORRIS: **'Apple' wallpaper,** 1877. Victoria and Albert Museum, London.

Morris' wallpapers and textiles invariably invoke the familiar countryside. The pastoral tradition has a long history in England. In much of his writing, Morris was an inheritor of this tradition, but he is the only designer who really can be said to belong to it.

9.8 WILLIAM MORRIS: **'Fritillary' wallpaper,** 1885. Victoria and Albert Museum, London.

The fritillary is a species of lily. This particular design has the graphic quality that can be seen in the borders of some of the pages of Morris' Kelmscott Press books.

9.9 SELWYN IMAGE: **Design, possibly for stained glass.** *The Studio*, Volume XIV, 1898.

From 'The Work of Mr Selwyn Image', an anonymous article. Selwyn Image was associated with the Century Crafts Co-operative venture which lasted from 1882 until probably 1888. Image was disciple of Ruskin and an admirer of Morris.

9.10 MAY MORRIS: **Embroidered panel for a screen.** Manufactured by Morris & Co. Executed in chain stitch. *The Century Guild Hobby Horse*, Vol. II, 1887.

May Morris was the younger of William Morris' two daughters. Her decorative design resembles her father's. In 1885, she became responsible for the embroidery executed by Morris & Co.

9.11 *Above* W. R. LETHABY: **Ornaments from Christian coffins, Constantinople.** *Lead Work, Old, Ornamental and for the most part English,* 1893.

Lethaby was to succeed Morris as the principal exponent of Arts and Crafts philosophy. Although an able architect, draughtsman and designer, he is best remembered as a teacher and theoretician. Like Morris, he was interested in the popular art of the past and saw hope for the future in the revival of a vigorous demotic tradition.

9.12 *Right* W. R. LETHABY: **Font, Brookland, Kent.** *Lead Work, Old, Ornamental and for the most part English,* 1893.

Lethaby thought that the commonplace and the familiar could provide suitable inspiration for the designer and craftsman. He sought to break down the barriers that existed between 'high art' and popular art. This medieval font, though clumsy, was an ideal model and it epitomizes Arts and Crafts attitudes.

9.13 *Left* GEORGIE (GEORGIANA) CAVE FRANCE: **Invitation card.** *The Studio,* Vol. II, 1893.

Georgie Cave France married Arthur Gaskin, a fellow student at the Birmingham School of Art, in 1894. She was a prominent member of the influential 'Birmingham School' which was firm in its adherence to the tenets of the Arts and Crafts Movement. The work of the Gaskins is commemorated in a detailed catalogue published by the Birmingham Museums and Art Gallery in 1981.

9.14 *Below* LOUIS FAIRFAX-MUCKLEY: **Chapter heading.** *The Studio,* Vol. IV, 1895.

The foliage in this design resembles the semi-naturalistic decoration of designers like E. W. Godwin, George Haité or Bruce Talbert. The pictorial elements are reminiscent of E. Burne Jones. Fairfax-Muckley was a product of the Birmingham School of Art.

9.15 WILLIAM MORRIS: **Printed fabric. 'Wandle'.** Registered 1884. Manufactured by Morris and Co. Aymer Vallance, *The Art of William Morris*, 1897.

9.16 *Left* WILLIAM MORRIS: **Wallpaper. 'St James's'.** Specially designed for St James's Palace, 1881. Manufactured by Morris and Co. Aymer Vallance, *The Art of William Morris*, 1897.

9.17 *Below left* HEYWOOD SUMNER: **'David'. Cartoon for sgraffito decoration.** *The Studio*, Vol. XIII, 1898.

Sumner decorated several churches using the *sgraffito* (incised or scratched) technique.

9.18 *Below* C. F. A. VOYSEY: **Design for a fabric.** Watercolour. About 1895. The Royal Institute of British Architects, London.

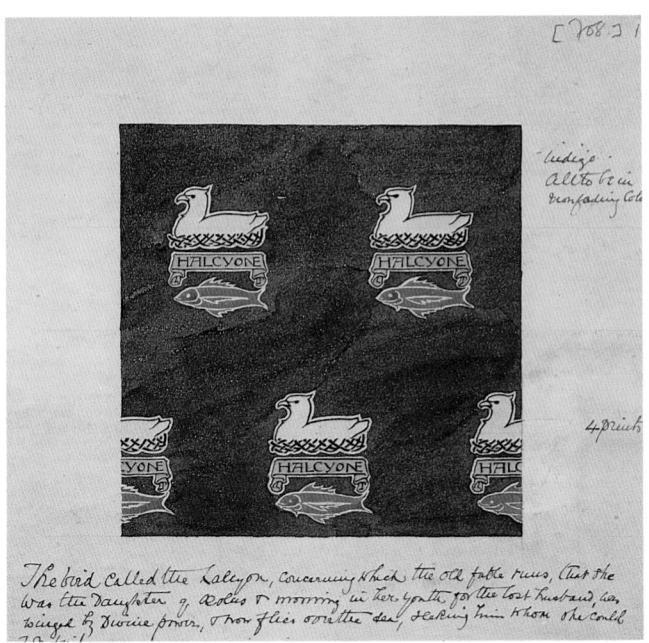

9.19 *Above* C. F. A. Voysey: **Design for a fabric. 'Halcyon'.** Watercolour. *c.* 1895. The Royal Institute of British Architects, London.

9.20 *Right* Jessie R. Newbery and Ann Macbeth: **Design for an appliqué banner.** *The Studio*, Vol. XXIV, 1902.

9.21 *Below* C. F. A. Voysey: **Design for a fabric.** Watercolour. *c.* 1898. The Royal Institute of British Architects, London.

9.22 *Below right* M. H. Baillie Scott: **Design for a piano case.** For the New Palace of the Grand Duke of Hesse in Darmstadt. *The Studio*, Vol. XVI, 1899.

The Grand Duke, Ernst Ludwig, was an enlightened patron of the arts. His artist's colony at Darmstadt—with buildings by J. M. Olbrich—was to become internationally famous.

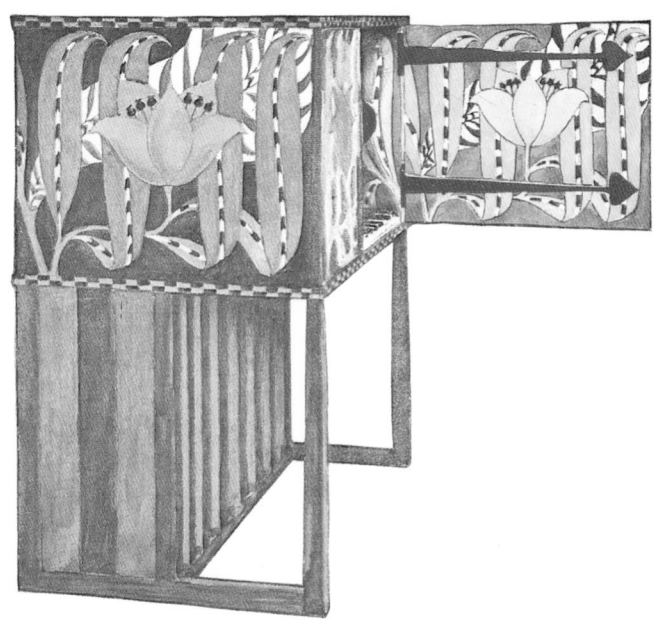

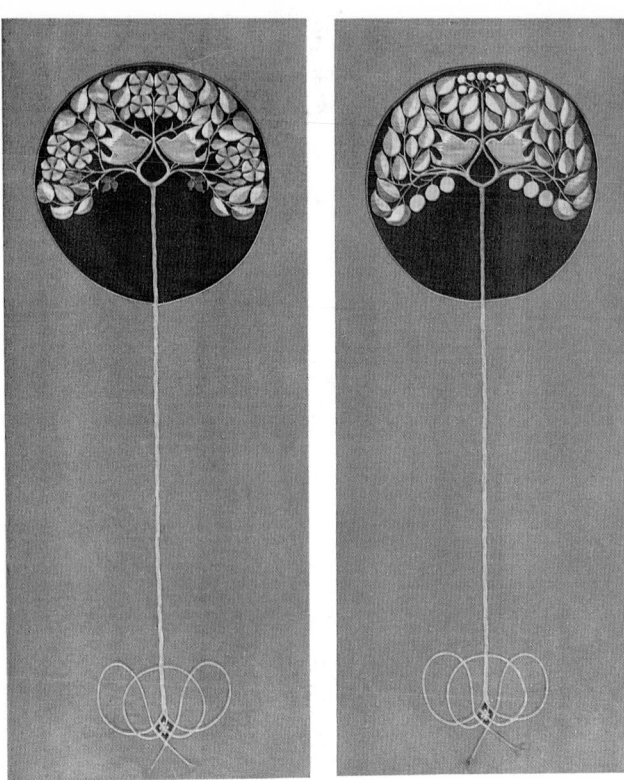

9.23 M. H. Baillie Scott: **Embroidered panels.** *The Studio*, Vol. XXVIII, 1903.

9.24 H. T. Wyse: **Design for an appliquéd and embroidered portière.** *The Studio*, Vol. XIV, 1898.

9.26 *Above* C. F. A. VOYSEY: **Wallpaper—'The Buttercup and Daisy'.** For Essex & Co., late 1890s. A. V. Sugden and J. L. Edmondson, *A History of English Wallpaper*, 1925.

Voysey designed many wallpapers for Essex & Co. as well as advertisements for the firm, which appear in contemporary journals.

9.25 *Above* C. F. A. VOYSEY: **Design for wallpaper—'Mimosa'.** *The Studio*, Vol. VII, 1896.

The Studio helped to make Voysey's work known to a wide public. His decorative style, though Morris-like in its imagery, is simple, forceful and immediately recognizable.

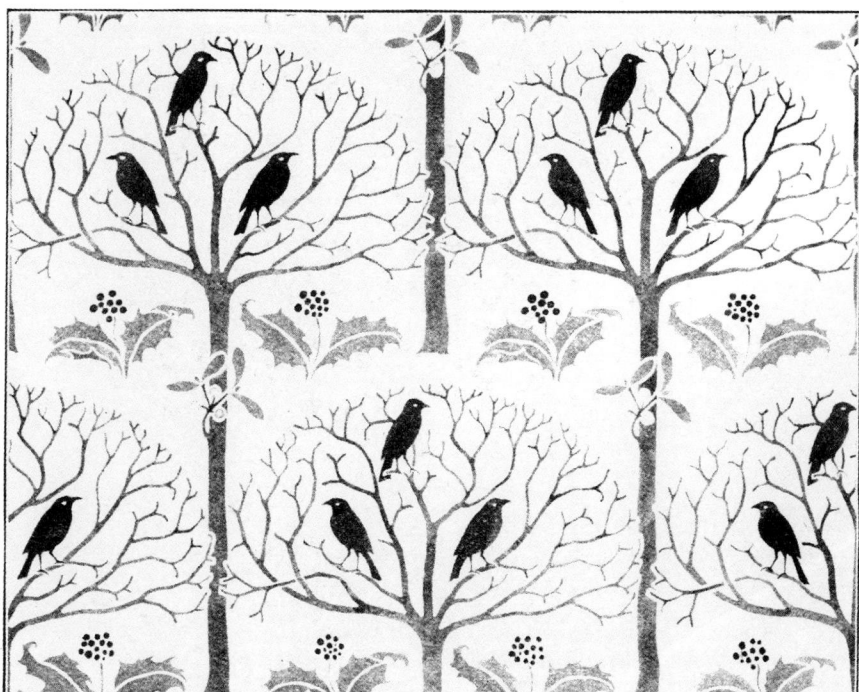

9.27 *Right* C. F. A. VOYSEY: **Design for chintz.** *The Studio*, Vol. VII, 1896.

Voysey was described by *The Studio* as 'an architect first and foremost', though 'particularly fecund in the invention of patterns'. The construction of his patterns is singled out for praise—construction was 'the science and essence of good architecture'.

9.28 *Left* C. F. A. VOYSEY: **Design for wallpaper.** *The Studio*, Vol. VII, 1896.

9.29 *Below* SELWYN IMAGE: **Tailpiece.** *The Century Guild Hobby Horse*, Vol. II, 1887.

Selwyn Image was an ordained priest in the Church of England, but resigned Orders in order to devote himself to art which, during the heyday of the Aesthetic Movement, had been elevated almost to the level of a new religion.

9.30 *Right* 'Lind': **Design for an end-paper.** *The Studio*, Vol. XXVIII, 1903.

'Lind' was the pseudonym of an entrant in one of the many competitions organized by *The Studio*. 'Lind', whose name was not revealed, was accorded an 'Honourable Mention'.

9.31 C. F. A. Voysey: **Wallpaper—'The Squire's Garden'.** For Essex & Co., 1898, A. V. Sugden and J. L. Edmondson, *A History of English Wallpaper*, 1925.

Voysey was an accomplished designer of heraldry and the peacocks here have a markedly heraldic quality. Here he seems to have been influenced by the pictorial wallpapers of Crane.

9.32 *Above* C. F. A. VOYSEY: **Original decorative design,** 1907. Voysey's ability to simplify nature was impressive.

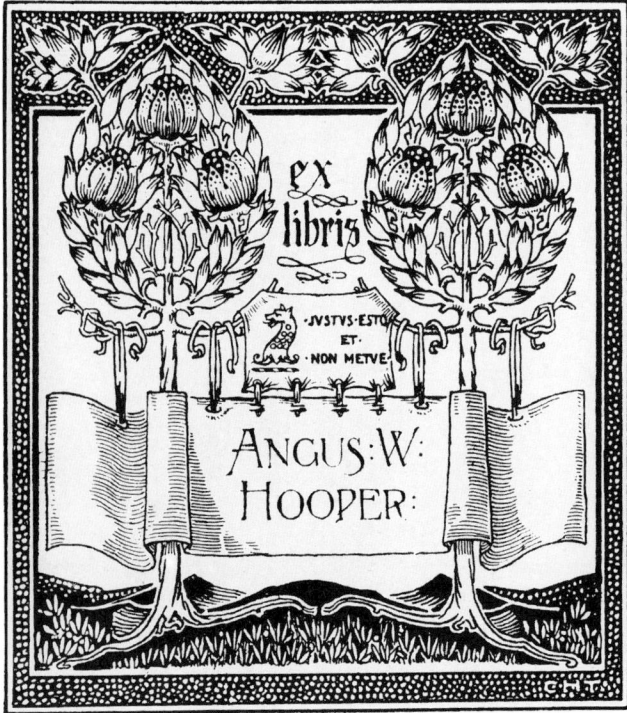

9.33 *Below* 'MADDER BROWN': **Design for tapestry.** *The Studio*, Vol. II, 1893.

This won second prize in a *Studio* competition, but 'Madder Brown' will remain anonymous for he or she omitted to give a name, or address. The style called for by the organizers was 'Italian Renaissance', and it is interesting to see how Madder Brown's interpretation owes more than a little to Morris' version of fifteenth-century Italian design.

9.34 *Left* C. HARRISON TOWNSEND: **Design for a book-plate.** *The Studio*, Vol. IV, 1895.

Although Harrison Townsend was the archetypal Arts and Crafts architect—involved with every aspect of design—he was more susceptible to modish influences than contemporaries in his decorative design. Here, one can detect the impact of Aubrey Beardsley's *Morte d'Arthur* of 1891–2.

9.36 *Left* M. H. BAILLIE SCOTT: **'Apple-Tree' wall decoration.** *The Studio*, Vol. V, 1895.

This design appears in Baillie Scott's article, 'The Decoration of the Suburban House'. He declared that the decoration 'could be carried out in various schemes of colour, but a golden yellow for the flowers with a quiet shade of green for the leaves and stems might be suggested—the leaves would then form a good background for pictures . . .'. Baillie Scott's ideas were widely influential on the Continent. His earliest major Continental commission was to decorate the palace of the Grand Duke of Hesse, at Darmstadt, which was completed in 1898.

9.37 *Below* M. H. BAILLIE SCOTT: **Leaded window with ornamental shutters.** *The Studio*, Vol. V, 1895.

Perhaps because of his particular fondness for decoration, which is far less restrained than Voysey's or Mackintosh's, Baillie Scott has been accorded a lower place in the hierarchy of proto-Moderns. Now that the history of the Modern Movement is being revised, Baillie Scott's real importance may come to be acknowledged. In his indebtedness to vernacular building and in his love of pastoral decoration he is the ideal Morrisian architect.

9.35 *Opposite* C. H. B. QUENELL: **Design for a cushion cover** · *The Studio*, Vol. II, 1894.

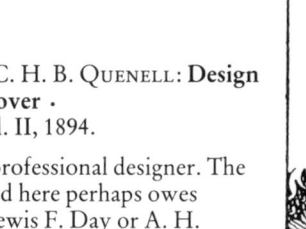

Quenell was a professional designer. The design illustrated here perhaps owes something to Lewis F. Day or A. H. Mackmurdo.

9.38 M. H. BAILLIE SCOTT: **'Landscape' frieze.** *The Studio*, Vol. V, 1895.
Landscape friezes were popular in the 1890s and 1900s.

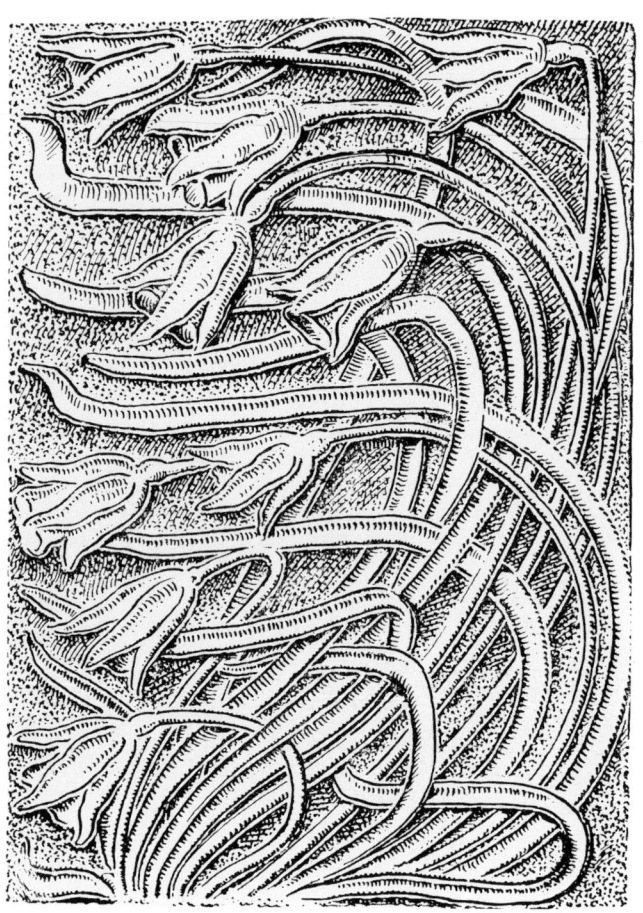

9.39 *Above* GLEESON WHITE: **Design for embossed leather.** *The Studio*, Vol. VI, 1895.

Gleeson White was founder and editor of *The Studio*. Until his untimely death in 1898 he did much to publicize the Arts and Crafts Movement. His interpretation of daffodils seems to owe something to William Blake's *Songs of Innocence*, 1789, or *Songs of Experience*, 1794.

9.41 C. HARRISON TOWNSEND: **Carved stone capital for the Horniman Free Museum.** *The Studio*, Vol. XXIV, 1901.

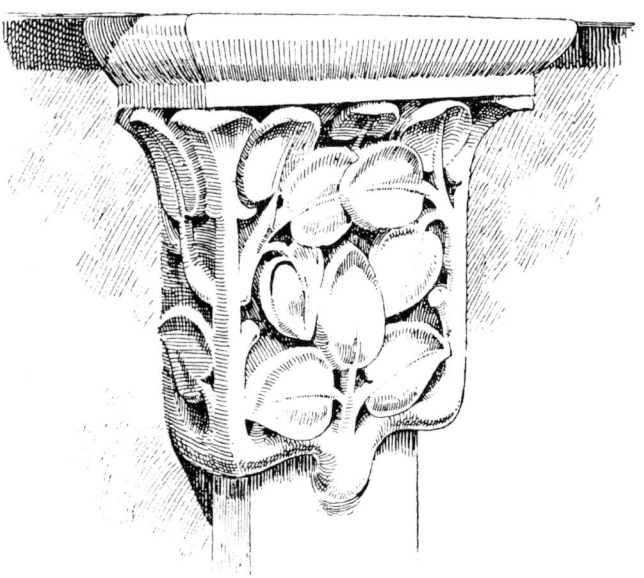

9.40 TALWIN MORRIS: **Design for publisher's binding.** *The Studio*, Vol. XV, 1898.

Talwin Morris was Art Director of Blackie & Sons of Glasgow.

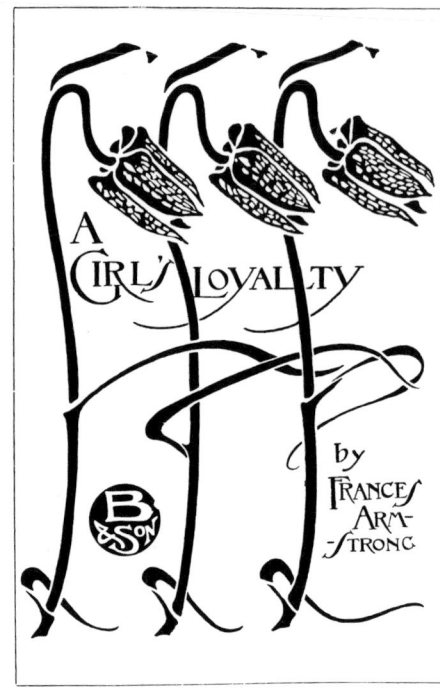

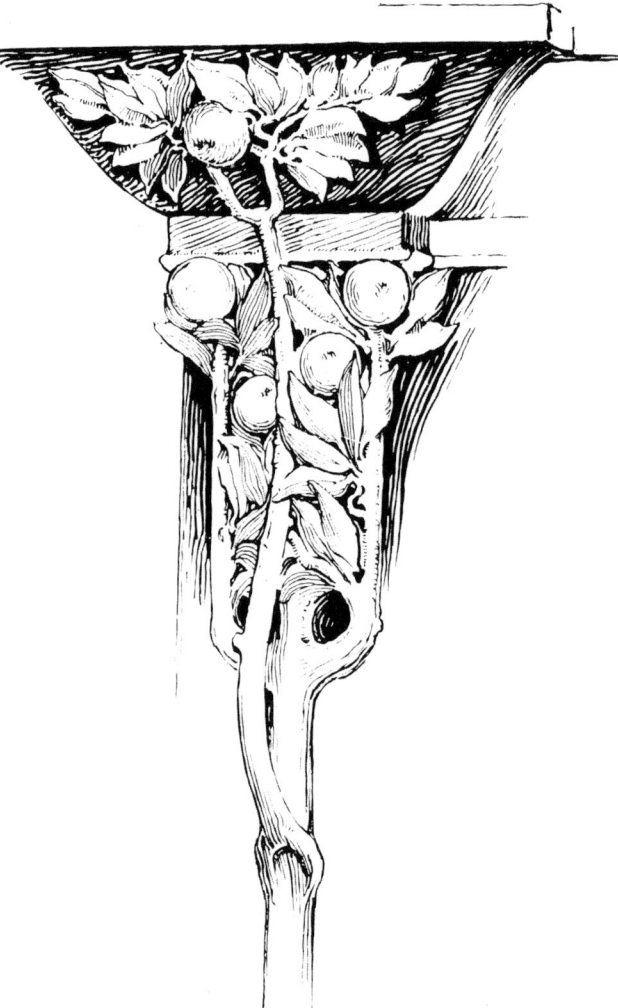

9.43 *Right* C. R. ASHBEE: **Embossed leather wall-hanging.** *The Studio*, Vol. XII, 1897.

This was executed at Essex House, the premises of the Guild of Handicraft, founded by Ashbee in 1888. The technique of embossed leather was also used by Morris & Co.

9.44 *Below* JOHN WILLIAMS: **Panel of fender.** Executed by Patrick Roche, Fivemiletown (Co. Tyrone). *The Studio*, Vol. XI, 1897.

This was exhibited at the Home Arts and Industries Association Exhibition held at the Albert Hall, London, in 1897. The Association strove 'to re-instate the lost industries and crafts of [Britain's] villages, and to interest townspeople in making things comely as well as useful'.

9.45 *Below right* C. HARRISON TOWNSEND: **Drawing-room wallpaper.** *The Studio*, Vol. XIII, 1898.

This wallpaper was specially designed for Cliff Towers, Salcombe, South Devon. The house, ambitious and inventive, was never built. With Baillie Scott, Ernest Newton and Voysey, Harrison Townsend was one of a group whose work was much publicized by *The Studio*. The stylized orchard is distinctly reminiscent of Morris.

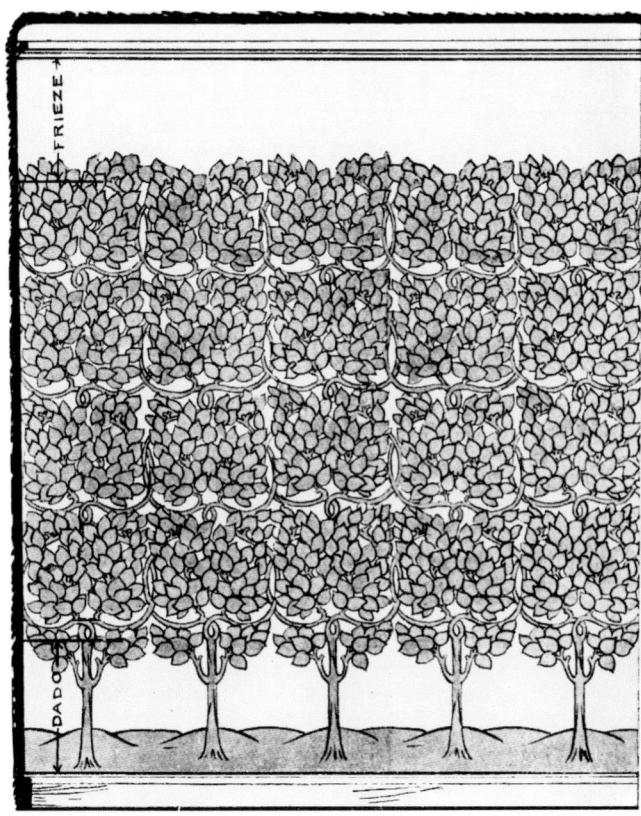

9.42 *Opposite* GEORGE FRAMPTON: **Capital and corbel.** *The Studio*, Vol. XII, 1898.

Frampton, though most popularly remembered for his Peter Pan statue, Kensington Gardens (1912), was a prominent figure in the Arts and Crafts movement. His lively naturalism is here far removed from the often pedantic archaeological exercises of the Gothic Revivalists of the previous generation.

9.46 *Above* HEYWOOD SUMNER: **Wallpaper for Jeffrey & Co.**
Art et Décoration, Vol. III, 1898.

Heywood Sumner is probably best known for his church
decoration, although he was also a painter, etcher, book-
designer and archaeologist.

9.47 *Above right* MRS G. F. WATTS: **Altar carried out by the
pupils of the 'Compton Class'.** Drawn by Louis R. Denchars.
The Studio, Vol. XVII, 1899.

This can be seen at the Watts Memorial Chapel, Compton, near
Guildford. Mary Watts, wife of the painter George Frederic
Watts and an amateur architect, attempted to revive rural crafts.
Her little chapel, designed in 1896, was covered with richly
symbolic modelled decoration, which is part Celtic, part
Romanesque, part Byzantine in its inspiration.

9.48 *Right* ALFRED G. WRIGHT: **Design for tiles.** *The Studio*,
Vol. XI, 1897.

The ancient ships with their bird's head figureheads closely
resemble the ships in Walter Crane's *The Fairy Ship*, 1869, but it
is equally probable that William De Morgan, who used ancient
ships on his painted tiles, supplied the inspiration. Wright was a
student at the Nottingham School of Art and this design was
entered for the 1897 National Competition, South Kensington.

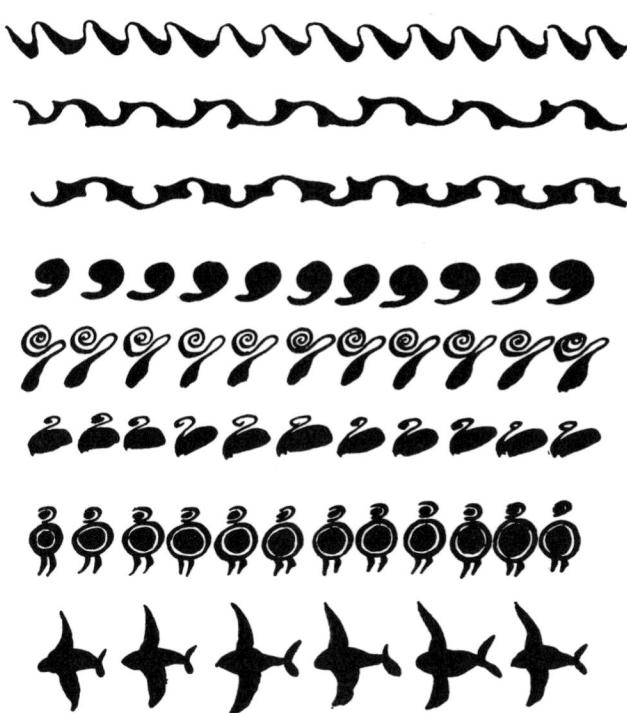

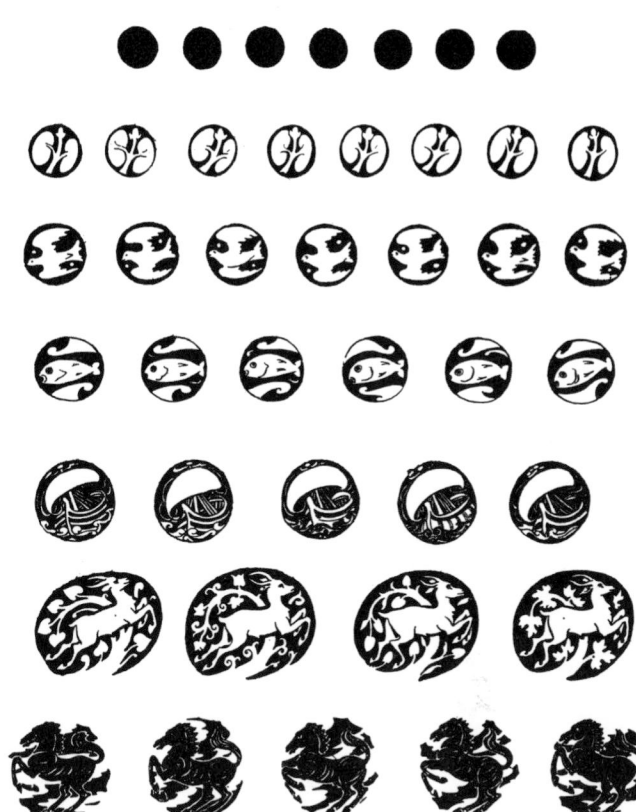

9.49 *Above* GODFREY BLOUNT:
'Independent developments of the spiral and the spot'. *Arbor Vitae*, 1899.

Blount's *Arbor Vitae* is one of the earliest Arts and Crafts primers. Here he demonstrates how simple calligraphic motifs can be transformed into ornament. If art was to become, as Lethaby put it, 'a normal mode of activities', simple creative techniques had to be developed and taught.

9.50 *Above right* GODFREY BLOUNT:
'Evolution of a frieze from a line of circles'. *Arbor Vitae*, 1899.

Blount was an idealist who endeavoured to revitalize rural life. He was founder of the Peasant Arts Society and in 1896 set up the Haslemere Peasant Industries. In his championing of easily executed decoration one is reminded of Morris' belief that decoration should be 'something which can be done by a great many people without too much difficulty and with pleasure'.

9.51 *Above* GEORGE JACK: **Details of carving.** *Wood Carving: Design and Workmanship*, 1903.

While always encouraging students to express themselves in their own way, Arts and Crafts teachers constantly advocated the diligent study of ancient work. Jack's *Wood Carving* was published in John Hogg's *The Artistic Crafts*, a series of technical handbooks, edited by W. R. Lethaby, which provided a comprehensive record of Arts and Crafts practice and theory.

9.52 *Left* GEORGE JACK: **Carved ornament suitable for a bread plate.** *Wood Carving: Design and Workmanship*, 1903.

Familiar symbols of the countryside were widely used in Arts and Crafts decoration.

233

9.55 *Above* GEORGE JACK AND PHILIP WEBB: **Book-cover carved in English oak.** For the *Tale of Troy*, 1892. George Jack, *Wood Carving: Design and Workmanship*, 1903.

Jack has adapted Webb's sketch of a lion (Plate 9.53) for a special cover for the first Kelmscott book to be set in Morris' Troy Type. Jack was close to both Webb and Morris—he became chief furniture designer for Morris & Co. in about 1890 and took over Webb's architectural practice in 1900 (he built nothing of note). This tight, cautious, design, to be pondered over and savoured, epitomizes the Morrisian approach to decoration.

9.53 *Top* PHILIP WEBB: **Sketch of a lion.** George Jack, *Wood Carving: Design and Workmanship*, 1903.

Webb's sketch was done for George Jack (see Plate 9.55). Arts and Crafts philosophy encouraged collaboration—Webb and Morris, for example, designed wallpaper together. Jack carved a memorial plaque commemorating Morris, after a sketch by Webb, which can be seen in the village of Kelmscott, Oxfordshire.

9.54 *Above* H. C. D. CHORLTON: **Initial letters.** *The Studio*, Vol. XXX, 1903.

Chorlton, a printer and typographical designer, was a member of the Northern Art Workers' Guild and a close friend of the Manchester architect Edgar Wood. His initial letters bear a passing resemblance to some of C. R. Ashbee's designs.

A String of Beads — Design consists of arrangement let us practise arrangement separately, and on its ✕ simplest terms. Take the simplest possible arranged form, and ✕ make all ornament spring from this, without, for a considerable ✕ time changing its character, or making any additions ✕ of a different character. If we are not then to do this what resource have we! we may change its direction. Proceed then to do so, observing a few very simple rules 1. Do the work in single "stitches" 2. & to each arm of the cross in turn. 3. keep a record of each ✕ step; that is, as soon as you ✕ have got any definite developement from your original form, put that down on ✕ paper and leave it, drawing it over again and developing from the second drawing. The fourth rule is the most important of all: 4. Keep "on the ✕ spot" as much as possible, i.e. take a number of single steps from the point you have arrived at, not a number of consecutive steps leading farther from ✕ it. For example: "b" here is a single ✕ step from "a", you do ✕ one thing. I do not ✕ want you to go on developing from it [fig. "b"] as c, d & e. until you have gone back to fig. "a" and made all the immediately possible steps to be taken from it, one of wh. is shown. fig "f".

Seed of design as applied to Craft & Material. Suppose you have three simple openings. (fig."a") garret windows, or ✕ passage windows, we will suppose, each ✕ ✕ with a central horizontal bar: and suppose you have a ✕ number of pieces of glass to use up already cut to one guage, and that six of these fill a window, can you get any little variety by arrangement on the ✕ following terms· 1. Treating both upper and lower ranges alike 2. Allowing yourself to halve them, vertically only. 3. Not wasting any glass. 4. Not halving more than two in each light. how is this, fig. "b" ✕ you despise it? ✕ so absurdly simple? ✕ It is the key to all ✕ simple ornament in ✕ leaded glass Exhaust all the possible varieties, there are at least nine. ✕ Do them. Thats all

A String of Beads

9.56 C. W. WHALL: **Details of a simple method of creating ornament.** *Stained Glass Work*, 1905.

Whall, like Morris and Lethaby, believed that anyone could create ornament if they took the trouble. The idea of 'High Art'—for an élite—was rejected in favour of an intelligent popular art.

9.57 PUPILS OF H. A. PAYNE, Birmingham School of Art: **Six 'quarries'—Day and Night, the Spirit on the Face of the Waters, the Creation of the Birds and Fishes, Eden and the Parable of the Good Seed** (2 designs). C. W. Whall, *Stained Glass Work*, 1905.

Payne's pupils were boys in their teens—these designs are typical of work produced by the 'Birmingham School', as it came to be known. One is reminded, in designs 4, 5 and 6, of the woodcuts produced by Arthur Gaskin, one of the most distinguished members of the Birmingham School, in the 1920s.

9.58 MARY L. NEWILL: **Study of the Scotch fir.** *The Studio*, Vol. V, 1895.

Mary Newill taught embroidery at the Birmingham School of Art and was a member of the Arts and Crafts Exhibition Society. Although this design is not strictly decorative, it is in accordance with the spirit of the Arts and Crafts Movement with its reverent treatment of nature. A degree of conventionalism, or stylization, prevails, but the harsh, almost mechanistic, approach of the 1850s and 1860s has been rejected in favour of a gentler naturalism.

9.59 PAUL ARNDT: **Design for a tablecloth.** *The Studio*, Vol. XXXV, 1905.

Paul Arndt was an art student at Battersea Polytechnic. This design was entered in the National Competition of the London Schools of Art, 1905. The representation of the Four Seasons, with their familiar associations, is typical of the imagery encouraged by the Arts and Crafts.

9.60 PUPILS OF C. W. WHALL: **Drawings from nature, made in preparation for designs.** C. W. Whall, *Stained Glass Work*, 1905.

Nature was the principal source of inspiration advocated by Morris. These meticulous drawings show a reverential attitude to nature that owes much to the teachings of Ruskin.

9.61 C. R. ASHBEE: **Embossed leather wall-hanging.** *The Studio*, Vol. XII, 1897.

Like Plate 9.43 this was executed at the Guild of Handicraft. With the Guild, Ashbee attempted to revive the medieval practice of co-operation between groups of craftsmen. The Guild met with some initial success and moved from London to Chipping Camden in the Cotswolds in 1902. However, it was unable to compete with purely commercial ventures like Liberty & Co. and went into voluntary liquidation in 1908. Ashbee was an innovative domestic architect, although he never had the popular appeal of other Arts and Crafts architects like C. F. A. Voysey, Ernest Newton and M. H. Baillie Scott.

CHAPTER TEN

Art Déco—The Evolution of a Style

One of the most influential, and possibly the most internationally renowned, of early twentieth-century architects was Josef Hoffmann (1870–1956), who can in many ways be seen as the precursor of Art Déco. A protégé of Otto Wagner (1841–1918), the doyen of Viennese architecture, Hoffmann possessed a highly developed skill in architectural composition and geometrical design, and underpinning even the slightest of his ornamental designs is the rigorous geometrical construction which is found in so much early twentieth-century Viennese design. (Another Wagner protégé, Joseph Maria Olbrich (1867–1908), actually had three of the Platonic forms—the square, the equilateral triangle and the circle—appliquéed on the curtains in his private office in Darmstadt.[1])

Hoffmann's earliest published schemes—for monumental entrances and interiors—which appeared in the Viennese journals *Ver Sacrum* and *Das Interieur*, are partly in the manner of Wagner and partly in a modish Art Nouveau style which somewhat resembles that of Henry Van de Velde. The earliest example of what could be said to anticipate Art Déco is his decorative relief above a doorway in the Secessionist Exhibition held in Vienna in 1902. Remarkably, this relief is seemingly entirely abstract in its conception and consists of an assemblage of apparently randomly placed blocks.[2]

The Vienna Secession was established by a group of artists and architects who broke away from the conservative Viennese academy in the late 1890s and played a considerable role in the development of the decorative arts in Austria. Apart from Hoffmann and Olbrich, its members included the graphic designer Kolomon Moser (1868–1918) and the painter Gustav Klimt (1862–1918).

The Palais Stoclet in Brussels, which was furnished and decorated by the Wiener Werkstätte[3] in 1905–11, was Hoffmann's most important essay in decorative architecture. (His large pavilion for the Austrian section of the Werkbund at the Werkbund Exhibition in Cologne of 1914 was in a modernized Classical style—besides, it was a temporary building.) Hoffmann's decoration is for the most part geometric, although the whole marble-clad building is edged with a moulding which bears some resemblance to the traditional 'egg and dart' of Classical architecture. The Palais Stoclet would not have looked out of place in the Paris Exhibition of 1825. The decoration of the interiors, though sumptuous, is a great deal more restrained than that which would have been found in a Morris and Company interior of a decade earlier.

The Franco-Belgian architect Robert Mallet-Stevens (1886–1945) was greatly influenced by the Viennese style and in particular by the work of Hoffmann. The Palais Stoclet was in fact built by his wealthy uncle, Adolf Stoclet. Mallet-Stevens' pre-1914 projects have an undeniably Viennese air about them, especially in their restrained and geometrical ornament which is directly reminiscent of Hoffmann.

Charles Rennie Mackintosh (1868–1928) was also attracted to Vienna and in 1900 he designed a sitting-room which was exhibited at the Secessionist Exhibition of 1900, and a year or so later designed a drawing-room for Mr and Mrs Fritz Wärndorfer. After the establishing of the Vienna connection Mackintosh's architecture and decoration (see Plate 10.18) always had a hint

10.1 *Opposite* Designer unknown: **Fragment of woven silk textile.** Designed for Bianchini-Ferier, Lyons, 1925. Victoria and Albert Museum, London.

This textile bears a resemblance to Dufy's more obviously 'commercial' designs.

of Vienna about them. This is especially true of his remodelled exterior rear elevation and interiors for Bassett-Lowkes's house at 78 Derngate, Northampton—his last executed architectural commission.

The Viennese decorative style of the early years of the twentieth century had many affinities with the style which has come to be known as Art Déco and one of the links was established by Paul Poiret (1879–1944), a couturier and gallery owner, and a disciple of Jacques Doucet (1853–1929), perhaps the most famous and successful of Parisian dress designers. Poiret visited Hoffmann in 1910 and became a great admirer of his work, although Vienna was not the only influence acting upon him. Like Doucet, Poiret was eclectic in his tastes. He shared the contemporary enthusiasm for Oriental, primitive and folk art as well as a liking for the eighteenth century. In 1911 he encouraged Raoul Dufy (1877–1953) to set up as a textile designer. A few years earlier Dufy had begun to try his hand at wood-engraving, and since this technique is very close to block cutting for fabric printing he was able to apply its lessons. His textiles (Plates 10.12–14, 24–7) are invariably bold and simple and sometimes show the influence of sixteenth- and seventeenth-century popular woodcuts. During the 1920s they were very fashionable and one can see a wide range of influences at work: Vienna, Japan, the Orient, the Russian Ballet, Cubism. Dufy's approach was joyously eclectic (Plates 10.38–40).

Other important Parisian designers of the period whose work is associated with Art Déco include Jacques Emile Ruhlmann (1879–1933), Edouard Bénédictus (1878–1930), and Sonia Delaunay (1885–1979). Bénédictus was particularly skilled at adapting the styles of currently fashionable painters, such as Picasso and Kandinsky, to decoration. The *Gazette du Bon Ton*, published in Paris between 1912 and 1914, and between 1920 and 1925, supplies an unequalled record of the modish and frequently delightful Parisian decoration of the era. A luxury bathroom by Ruhlmann was featured in an issue of 1920.

The London theatre designer and artist Claud Lovat Fraser (1890–1921) produced textile designs which have some affinities with those of the Parisian designers (Plate 10.30). There is a similar lightness of touch and occasionally something of their witty historicism in Lovat Fraser's decorative work. His colours, too, are brilliant and suggestive of folk art. Had he lived longer, he might well have produced textiles which would have vied with those of the Parisian designers.

The Art Déco style takes its name from the Exposition Internationale des Arts Décoratifs Industriels held in Paris in 1925. The declared aim of the exhibition was to encourage work 'of modern inspiration and real originality'.[4] According to the organizers, 'originality' could be 'displayed as much in the developing of existing art forms as in the invention of the entirely new'. Thus the Art Déco style is essentially eclectic and is distilled from a number of art movements. Although, inevitably, work by Parisian designers took pride of place at the exhibition, Art Déco can properly be described as an international style, though it was not as cohesive a style as the International Style which dominated architecture and design during the 1930s.

Art Déco, as we have seen, had its origins in the years before the 1914–18 war. The products of the Omega workshop (Plates 10.8–11), for instance, exhibit many Art Déco characteristics. It was created by, and for, a generation which was almost certainly better informed about art than any that had gone before it. Popular art magazines—well produced as a result of advances in printing technology—made it possible for new ideas to reach the public, or at least the middle-class public, in a way that had not been possible before. To turn the pages of *The Studio*, founded in 1893, *Art et Décoration* and *Deutsche Kunst und Decoration*, both of which were founded in 1897, and the other art

10.2 and **10.3** EMANUEL JOSEF MARGOLD: **Square-shaped vignette,** *c.* 1910. *Das Interieur*, XI, 1910.

Designing decoration to fit within a given format—a square, a rectangle, a triangle, a circle—was a frequent exercise in design schools throughout the nineteenth century and up until the 1930s. It was a simple matter to adapt such designs for repeats.

magazines which came into being about the turn of the century, is to see the Art Déco style in the process of evolution. (*The Studio*, committed as it was to the ideals of the Arts and Crafts Movement, had perhaps a rather less significant part to play in the development of Art Déco.)

To a somewhat lesser extent, two buildings by a British architect, Charles Harrison Townsend (1851–1928), can also be seen as presaging the Art Déco style. These are his Horniman Museum, Forest Hill, London, of 1896–1901 and the Whitechapel Art Gallery, of 1899–1901. It is not so much because of their details and decoration, which are entirely characteristic of the Arts and Crafts Movement, but for the daring of their façades, that these two buildings can be seen as what we might call 'proto-Art Déco'.[5] Townsend's facades are powerfully monumental, but comparatively plain. His decoration is compressed into smallish areas. Where it is to be found it is rich and ebullient. Louis Sullivan adopted a more or less similar practice in the United States. So, too, did Olbrich in his Vienna Secession Building of 1898. A seminal Jugendstil building, the Elvira Photographic Studio in Munich of 1897–8, by August Endell is in a similar vein. The separating of ornament, by such designers, from the columns, capitals and entablatures, with which it was traditionally associated, was to pave the way for a freer, more individualistic approach to its design. Art Déco ornament was dependent for its existence upon the experiments of the avant-garde designers of the turn of the century.

If one examines the work at the Paris Exhibition of 1925 one is struck immediately by the liveliness and ingenuity of the decoration of the exhibits, as well as by that of the pavilions which housed them. The future of the art of ornament seemed secure. Each pavilion was the work of a different architect: on occasion there was close collaboration between architect and craftsman—a practice which recalls the teaching of the Arts and Crafts Movement. The ceremonial gateway to the exhibition, La Porte d'Honneur, was by Henry Favier and André Ventre. Its 'forms . . . were new and curious—the piers were like strange trees—the grilles were florid but had an exotic beauty . . .' wrote H. C. Bradshaw in the British report. This gateway is, in fact, the ideal Art Déco study piece in terms of both architecture and decoration. With its aspirations to monumentality it resembles a grandiose Ecole des Beaux Arts student exercise. Its 'exotic beauty' is more precisely an Oriental beauty. Could Ankor Wat, the great twelfth-century Hindu-Buddhist temple complex in Cambodia—in 1925 administered by France—have been in the minds of the designers? The gateway also displayed the 'extraordinary' skills of the metalworker Edgar Brandt.

It is hardly remarkable, perhaps, that Oriental or 'exotic' elements are frequently found in Art Déco design. During the nineteenth century both designers and public had ample opportunity to study Oriental decoration in museums and in the extensive collections published by such authorities as Owen Jones and Racinet. The lessons of 'exotic' decoration had been well absorbed by the turn of the century. The Russian Ballet—with Diaghilev, Stravinsky, Nijinsky and the set designer Bakst—had burst upon Paris in 1909. Its decor, based upon Russian peasant art, but spiced also with motifs and colours borrowed from the Islamic peoples within greater Russia, helped to rekindle interest in Oriental decoration. Influential designers such as Dufy and Lovat Fraser were, on the evidence of their work, much impressed by the boldness and gaiety of the Russian designs.

Most of the pavilions at the exhibition which were in the style we have come to call Art Déco were French. They included the Pavilion of Nancy and Eastern France by P. Le Bourgeois and Jean Bourgon, the Pavilion of Lyons and St Etienne by Tony Garnier—renowned for his designs for an ideal industrial city published a decade and a half earlier, the Grand Palais by Charles Letrosne, and the Sèvres Factory Pavilion by P. Patout and André

10.4 Szabo, metalworker: **Mirror frame in wrought iron.** For Ed Delion. G. Henriot, *La Ferronnerie Moderne, c.* 1924.

Szabo again employs a distinctly graphic style. The frame of the mirror is very close to borders found in such elegant contemporary journals as *La Gazette du Bon Ton* and *Femina*.

Ventre. Commercial pavilions which accorded with the stylistic mood of 1925 were L. H. Boileau's Au Bon Marché, A. Laprade's Grands Magasins du Louvre and Henri Sauvage's Primavera.

Some foreign pavilions, though to a lesser extent, also displayed Art Déco characteristics. Austria, by Josef Hoffmann; Belgium, by Victor Horta—once one of the leading exponents of Art Nouveau architecture; Great Britain, by Easton and Robertson—internally Arts and Crafts, but externally rather frivolous and decidedly eclectic; Holland, by J. F. Staal; Poland, by Joseph Czajkowski; and Sweden, by Carl G. Bergstein—in a fey, updated, Neo-classical Style. Denmark's pavilion, by Kay Fisker, like Hoffmann's Austrian pavilion, was plain, symmetrical and monumental, but not in essence Modernist. Professor Armando Brasini's Italian pavilion, in a coarse Roman Baroque manner, was an exception to the rule. It made a most unfavourable impression. Robert Mallet-Stevens' Pavilion of Tourism savoured strongly of the style of Le Corbusier in its architecture, but its decoration with its splendid interior relief of an ocean liner and a Goliath biplane airliner—by the Martel brothers—represented Art Déco at its most urbane.

All in all, the decoration of so many of the pavilions in an Art Déco manner encourages one to take the view that the style was, if not primarily an architectural style, certainly one which lent itself especially well to architectural decoration. But the Modern Movement of architecture and Design, which was beginning to gather momentum at the time of the exhibition, was to despise decoration. The work of the Viennese school, however, proves that decoration could very happily co-exist with Modernist architecture. Mallet-Stevens understood this well and made use of decorated stained glass in his buildings. But Le Corbusier's extremist polemic relegated ornament to a lowly status. Art Déco became a term of contempt—a style associated with vulgar urban vernacular. Looking back some sixty years after the events of the 1925 Exhibition one can see that twentieth-century decoration was then well able to express the ideals of a highly industrialized and multifarious society.

10.5 PETER BEHRENS: **Design for linoleum.** For the Delmenhorster Linoleum Fabrik. *La Décoration Intérieure Allemande* (1910).

Behrens' geometric design suggests the influence of Viennese designers like Josef Hoffmann. The Delmenhorster Linoleum Fabrik was among the early members of the Werkbund, an association of manufacturers and designers which advanced the cause of German industrial design, founded in 1907.

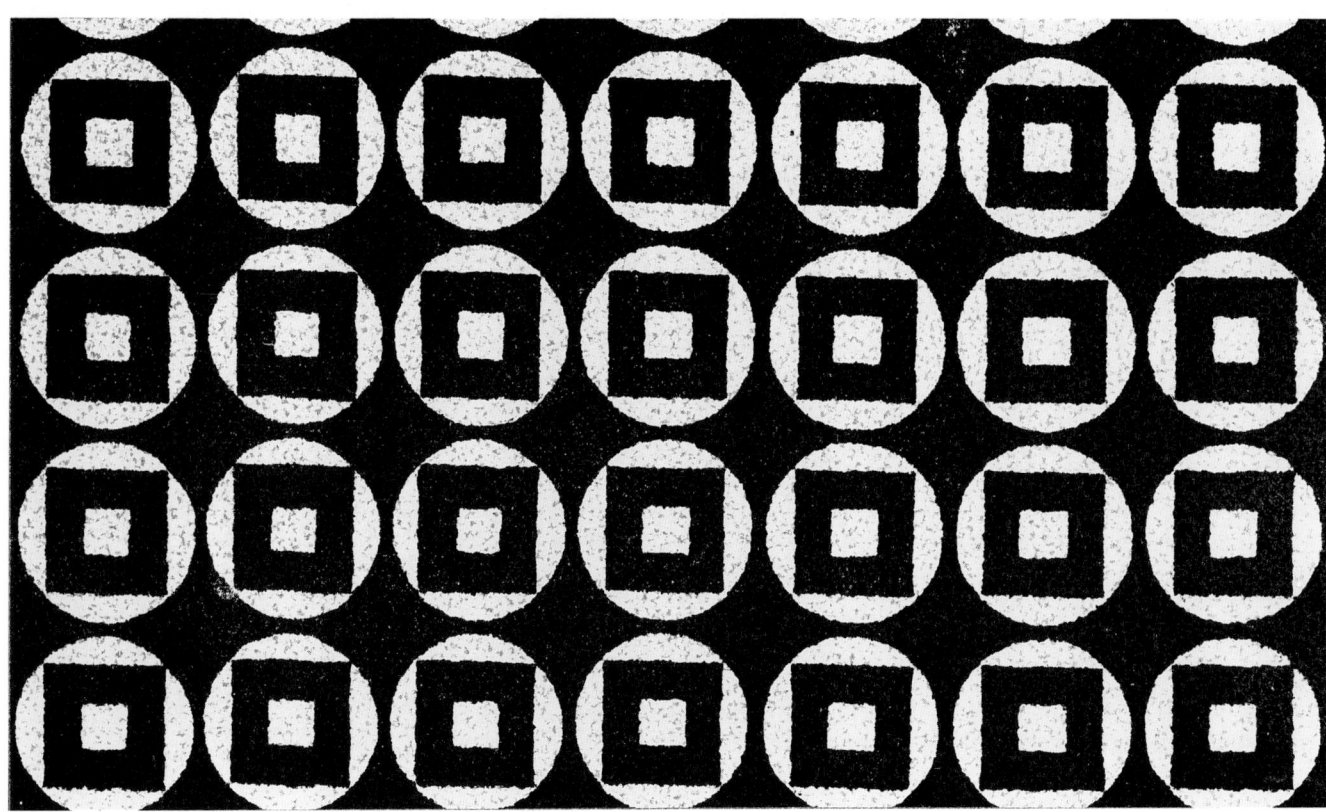

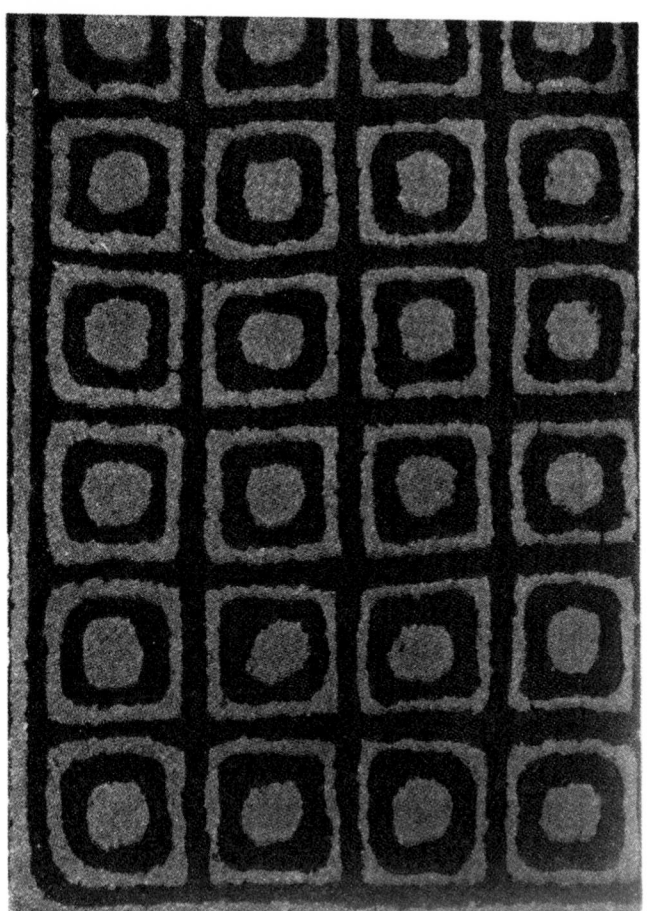

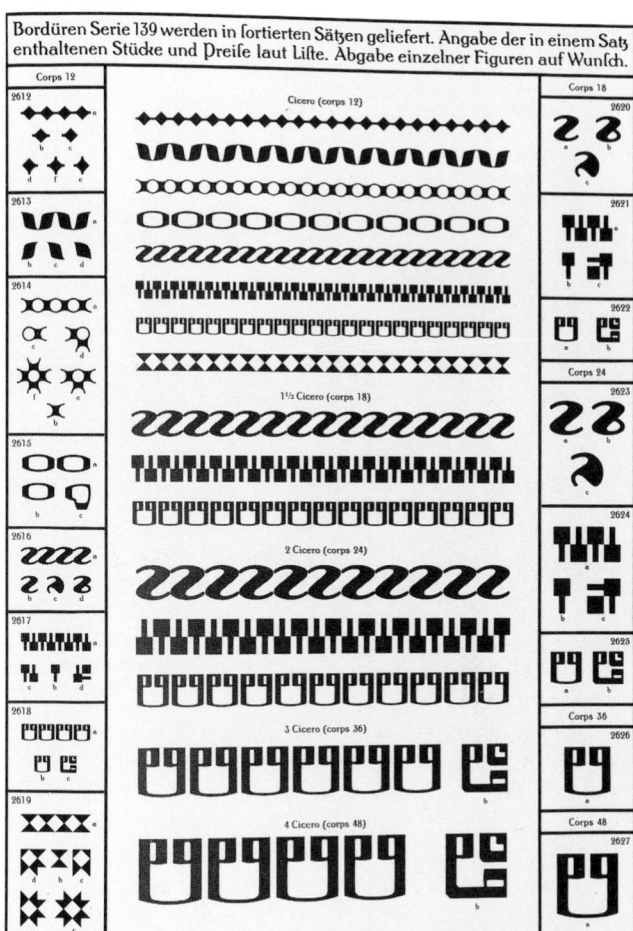

Bordüren Serie 139 werden in fortierten Sätzen geliefert. Angabe der in einem Satz enthaltenen Stücke und Preife laut Lifte. Abgabe einzelner Figuren auf Wunfch.

10.6 *Above* RICHARD RIEMERSCHMID: **Design for linoleum.** For the Deutschen Linoleum-Werke. *Jahrbuch des Deutschen Werkbundes*, 1912.

Riemerschmid, an architect and a versatile designer, was an influential member of the Werkbund. His decoration is generally rather restrained. Boldness and simplicity were, in fact, to become the principal characteristics of Art Déco design.

10.7 *Above right* LUDWIG SÜTTERLIN: **Typographical ornaments.** Catalogue of Emil Gursch, typefounders, Berlin, *c.* 1912.

Sütterlin's decorations, as well as his type-founts, have curvilinear Jugendstil characteristics. Yet their extreme simplicity is suggestive of later work, especially that of the early 1920s.

10.8 DUNCAN GRANT: **Design for wool rug.** *The Omega Workshops, 1913–19. Decorative Arts of Bloomsbury*, 1984.

Roger Fry praised the design for its 'sensual irregularities'. Wilful irregularity, derived from folk art, is sometimes a characteristic of Art Déco design.

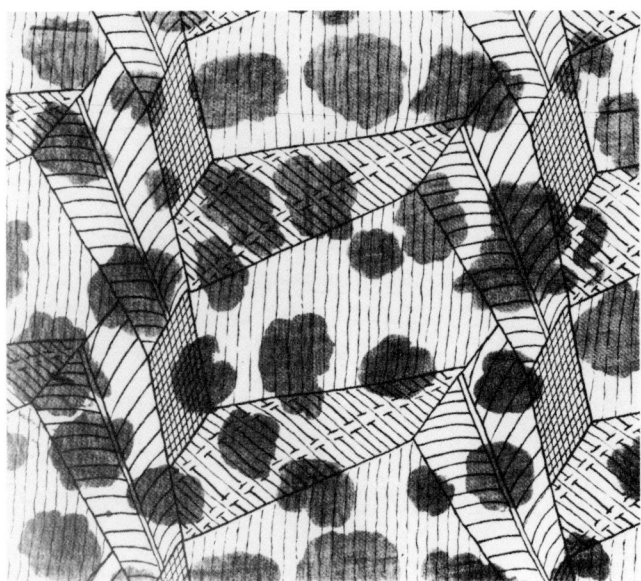

10.9 VANESSA BELL: **Printed linen. 'White Spring'.** For the Omega Workshops, 1913. *The Omega Workshops, 1913–19. Decorative Arts of Bloomsbury*, 1984.

It is possible to see in this design—possibly by Vanessa Bell—the influence of Cubism. One can also detect the influence of primitive textiles, perhaps bark cloth.

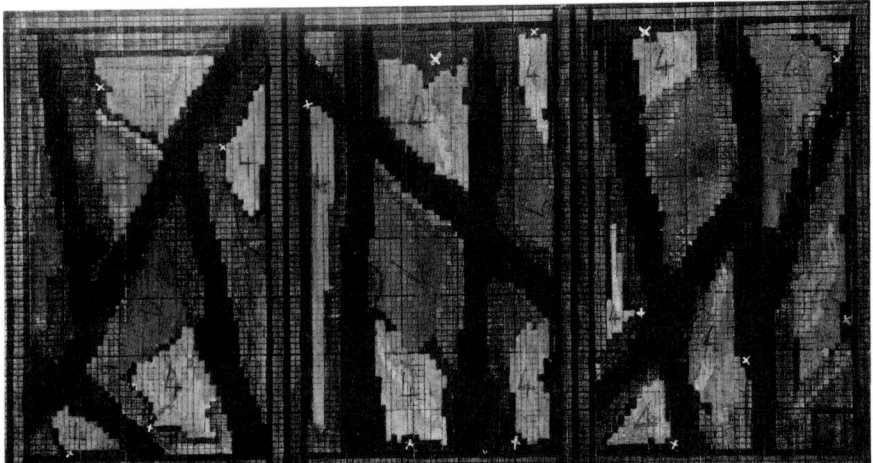

10.10 ATTRIBUTED TO FREDERICK ETCHELLS: **Rug.** *The Omega Workshops, 1913–19. Decorative Arts of Bloomsbury*, 1984.

There is a certain anarchic quality in Omega Workshops design. In this particular design a square grid, reminiscent of Hoffmann's work, has superimposed upon it an irregular and assertive geometric shape. This rug and Duncan Grant's (Plate 10.8) were exhibited at the Ideal Home Exhibition of 1913.

10.11 DESIGNER UNKNOWN: **Design for a rug.** For the Omega Workshops, 1913–14. The Print Room, Victoria and Albert Museum, London.

This is essentially a painter's design. Few decorative designers in the pre-1914 period were able to tolerate such asymmetry and apparent randomness.

10.13 *Above* RAOUL DUFY: **'Scale-pattern'.** Fabric design for Maison Bianchini-Ferier, Lyons, *c.* 1919. *Raoul Dufy, 1877–1953.* An exhibition organized by the Arts Council of Great Britain, 1983.

The scale-pattern is frequently found in Japanese decoration.

10.12 *Above left* RAOUL DUFY: **Fabric design.** For Maison Bianchini-Ferier, Lyons, *c.* 1919. *Raoul Dufy, 1877–1953.* An exhibition organized by the Arts Council of Great Britain, 1983.

Although textile designing was a secondary activity for Dufy, his skills as a decorative designer were of the highest order. When hung in folds this fabric is particularly successful.

10.14 *Left* RAOUL DUFY: **Fabric design in black and white.** For Maison Bianchini-Ferier, Lyons, *c.* 1919. *Raoul Dufy, 1877–1953.* An exhibition organized by the Arts Council of Great Britain, 1983.

This design seems to bear a resemblance to the Op Art paintings of Victor Vasarely or Bridget Reilly of the 1960s. But such a resemblance is entirely superficial. When hung in folds the design looks comparatively conventional.

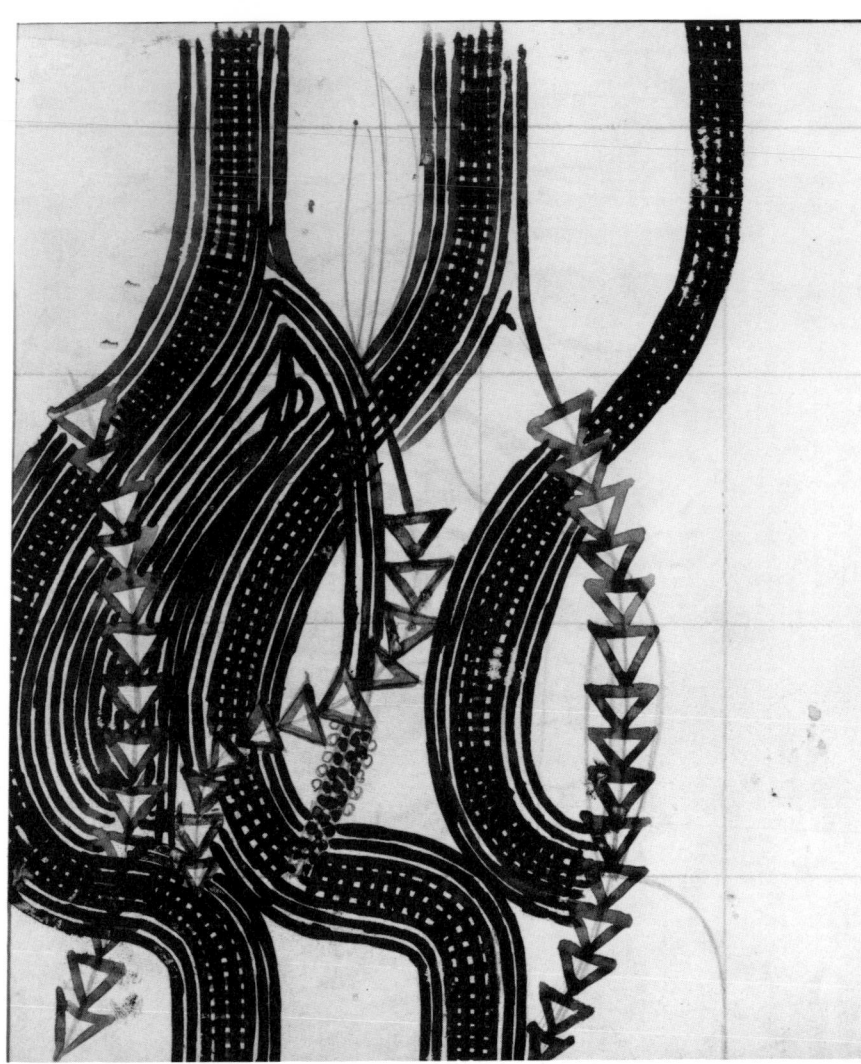

10.16 *Above* PAUL DOLEZEL EZEL: **Arrangements of simple elements.** *Elementare Entwicklung des Ornaments,* n.d. (*c.* 1920).

Ezel, like Gauthier (Plate 10.17), was a lecturer in ornament. Similarly, he was concerned with the manipulation of simple, apparently arbitrary, decorative elements. Here he illustrates the application of such elements to 'all-over' designs.

10.15 *Left* CHARLES RENNIE MACKINTOSH: **Preliminary sketch for a textile.** After 1916. The Print Room, Victoria and Albert Museum, London.

This design dates from Mackintosh's Chelsea period—from 1916 to 1923. By this date his architectural practice had dwindled.

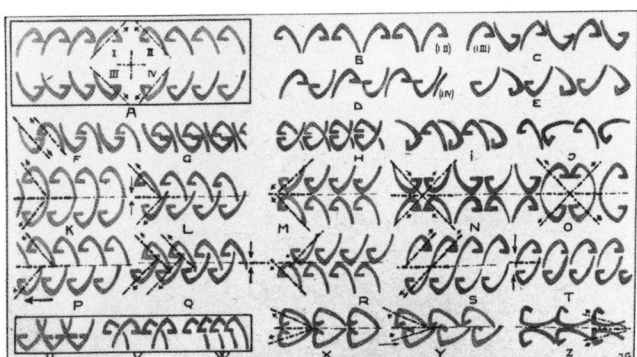

10.17 *Above* JOSEPH GAUTHIER: **Various arrangements of a single decorative element. For borders.** *Douze Leçons de Composition Décorative* (1920).

Gauthier was a professor at the Ecole Regionale des Beaux Arts at Nantes, where he taught decorative composition. His somewhat mechanical approach to teaching ornament had its origins in the nineteenth century. Almost infinite variations of simple borders could be produced by the method illustrated here.

10.18 *Right* CHARLES RENNIE MACKINTOSH: **Preliminary sketch for a textile.** After 1916. The Print Room, Victoria and Albert Museum, London.

This grid-like design suggests the influence of Hoffmann.

10.19 *Above* CONSTANCE IRVING: **Machine-printed cretonne.** For W. Foxton, *c.* 1922. *Design in Modern Industry. The Year-Book of the Design in Industries Association*, 1922.

A simple, unaffected design which is characteristic of the modest style encouraged by the Design in Industries Association which had been founded in 1915. The early ideals of the DIA were those of the Arts and Crafts Movement.

10.20 *Above right* JOSEF HOFFMANN: **Carpet design.** Manufactured by Max Schmidt, *c.* 1914. *Österreichische Werkkultur*, 1916.

This design was exhibited in the Austrian pavilion of the Werkbund Exhibition at Cologne in 1914. Hoffmann was a most versatile decorative designer and his influence was widely felt outside Austria. Paul Poiret, a patron of Dufy, was a great admirer of his early work. The affinities between this design and Dufy's floral designs of the same date are very apparent.

10.21 DAGOBERT PECHE: **Carpet design.** Manufactured by Max Schmidt, *c.* 1914. *Österreichische Werkkultur*, 1916.

Peche was even more susceptible to historicist influences than Hoffman—his senior by some seventeen years. This design has a distinctly eighteenth-century quality about it. Peche was to become one of the leading designers for the Wiener Werkstätte in the post-war period. *Österreichische Werkkultur* commemorates the Austrian contribution to the Werkbund exhibition, Cologne, 1914.

10.22 *Top* EMANUEL JOSEF MARGOLD: **Vignette,** *c.* 1910. *Das Interieur*, XI, 1910.

Margold, an architect, contributed a number of designs to the Viennese periodical *Das Interieur*. He studied under Hoffmann, whose influence is evident.

10.23 *Above* JOSEF ZOTTI: **Design for a painted wooden box,** *c.* 1910. *Das Interieur*, XI, 1910.

A typical Viennese design.

10.24 *Right* RAOUL DUFY: **Fabric design.** For Maison Bianchini-Ferier, Lyons, *c.* 1914–21. *Raoul Dufy, 1877–1953*. An exhibition organized by the Arts Council of Great Britain, 1983.

Like a skilled nineteenth-century designer, Dufy achieved serene, balanced compositions. His design, though highly fashionable in its day, has the timeless quality of the best decorative art.

10.26 *Above* RAOUL DUFY: **Silk damask.** For Bianchini-Ferier, Lyons, *c.* 1921. Victoria and Albert Museum, London.

10.25 *Above left* RAOUL DUFY: **Fabric design.** For Maison Bianchini-Ferier, Lyons, *c.* 1914. *Raoul Dufy, 1877–1953.* An exhibition organized by the Arts Council of Great Britain, 1983.

Dufy was able to arrange floral forms with enviable economy.

10.27 RAOUL DUFY: **Woven silk in green and silver.** From the Margaret Bulley Collection, 1920s. Victoria and Albert Museum, London.

An accomplished, but fairly conventional, Art Déco design.

10.28 *Left* MAX LAUGER: **Design for textile.** For the Deutschen Werkstätten, Hellerau, *c.* 1912. *Jahrbuch des Deutschen Werkbundes*, 1912.

Max Lauger, an architect, was a member of the Deutsche Werkbund. In many ways this design is the ideal exemplar of Proto-Art Déco design which is discussed in the main text.

10.30 *Below* Claud Lovat Fraser: **Design for hand-printed double-warp cotton.** For W. Foxton, *c.* 1921. *Design in Modern Industry. The Year-Book of the Design in Industries Association*, 1922.

Lovat Fraser is now best known for his costume and set designs. Like many contemporaries, he was greatly influenced by folk and traditional design.

10.29 *Above* Charles Rennie Mackintosh: **Preliminary design for textile.** After 1916. The Print Room, Victoria and Albert Museum, London.

This design dates from Mackintosh's Chelsea period. Mackintosh was an able botanical draughtsman, although in this design he treats flowers and leaves in an abstract way.

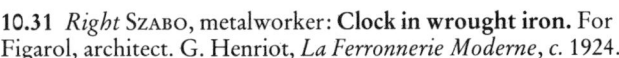

10.31 *Right* Szabo, metalworker: **Clock in wrought iron.** For Figarol, architect. G. Henriot, *La Ferronnerie Moderne, c.* 1924.

During the 1920s and early 1930s art metalwork underwent an extraordinary renaissance in France. The achievements of such virtuoso craftsmen as Edgar Brandt, Szabo, Schenk, Raymond Subes etc., were widely publicized and emulated. Szabo's clock has strong affinities with the graphic style found in Parisian journals of the early 1920s.

10.32 *Far left* MADAME DE ANDRADA: **Furnishing fabric in resist printed cotton,** *c.* 1925. Victoria and Albert Museum, London.

Madame de Andrada was a very successful French textile designer in the 1920s. Her style evidently owes much to Dufy.

10.33 *Left* CONSTANCE IRVING: **Hand-printed double-warp cotton.** For W. Foxton, *c.* 1922. *Design in Modern Industry. The Year-Book of the Design in Industries Association,* 1922.

Although in many ways not unlike a Dufy floral pattern, Constance Irving's design has a pronounced folksiness about it. A textile such as this would seem appropriate in a garden-suburb 'cottage'.

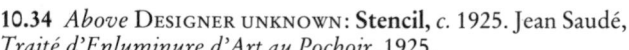

10.35 *Above* EILEEN GRAY: **Lacquered screen in brown and silver,** *c.* 1924. *Wendigen,* June 1924.

Eileen Gray learned the art of lacquering in the early 1900s under the Japanese craftsman Sugawara. The Dutch architect J. J. P. Oud, one of the leading figures in the De Stijl movement, was especially impressed with her work, which he first saw at the Salon des Artistes Décorateurs in Paris in 1923. As a result of this encounter Eileen Gray's work made its first major international appearance in the influential Dutch architectural journal *Wendigen.*

10.34 *Above* DESIGNER UNKNOWN: **Stencil,** *c.* 1925. Jean Saudé, *Traité d'Enluminure d'Art au Pochoir,* 1925.

'*Pochoirs*', or stencils, were widely used in Paris for producing books in colour. This hand-process was extremely labour-intensive and hence expensive. Many of the portfolios of decoration which were published in Paris in the 1920s and early 1930s were produced by the *pochoir* process. The stencil illustrated is typical of Parisian floral decoration of the early 1920s.

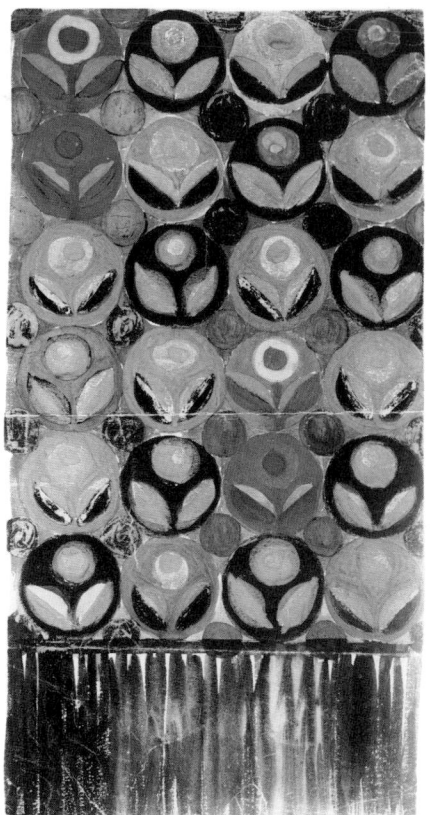

10.36 *Left* René Gabriel: **Textile designs.** Gaston Quenioux, *Les Arts Décoratifs Modernes (France)*, mid-1920s.

Typical French floral and fruit-based designs of the mid-1920s.

10.37 *Right* Minnie Macleish: **Colour sketch for textile.** For Morton Sundour, late 1920s. Victoria and Albert Museum, London.

Minnie Macleish was a prolific designer who was particularly active during the 1920s and 1930s. These simple floral motifs bear a slight resemblance to Mackintosh's early decorative work.

10.38 *Below left* Raoul Dufy: **'La Peche'. Textile.** For Bianchini-Ferier, Lyons, 1911. Gaston Quenioux, *Les Arts Décoratifs Modernes (France)*, mid-1920s.

10.39 *Below right* Raoul Dufy: **'Le Tennis'. Scarf.** For Bianchini-Ferier, Lyons (1918–24). Now in the Musée d'Art Moderne, Paris. Gaston Quenioux, *Les Arts Décoratifs Modernes (France)*, mid-1920s.

Dufy shows considerable ingenuity in using a contemporary theme for a textile design.

10.40 *Right* RAOUL DUFY: **'La Jungle'. Textile.** For Lampas, *c.* 1920. Gaston Quenioux, *Les Arts Décoratifs Modernes (France)*, mid-1920s.

The hallmark of traditional all-over pattern design is the balanced organization of elements. Here Dufy demonstrates a mastery of this art which equals that of William Morris. 'Exotic' themes were popular throughout the 1920s.

10.41 *Far right* EDGAR BRANDT: **Fire-screen in wrought iron.** H. Clouzot, *La Ferronnerie Moderne à l'Exposition des Arts Décoratifs* (1925).

This fire-screen was exhibited at the Pavillon du Collectionneur at the Paris Exhibition of 1925. Here, with extraordinary virtuosity, Brandt transforms an essentially graphic design into metal. The similarities between this design and Dufy's textiles are very clear.

10.42 *Above* F. V. CARPENTER: **'Metropolis'.** For the Stehli Silk Corporation, *c.* 1929. *The Studio*, Vol. 97, 1929.

An American design based on the street life of crowded, downtown New York.

10.43 *Above* MADAME DE ANDRADA: **'Marché Breton'. Printed cotton.** For Galeries Lafayette, Paris, 1925. *Reports on the Present Position and Tendencies of the Industrial Arts, as indicated at the International Exhibition of Modern Decorative and Industrial Arts, Paris, 1925,* n.d.

Madame de Andrada, as did Dufy in his design 'Tennis' (see Plate 10.39), takes a theme from contemporary life, but peasant life instead of bourgeois life.

10.44 *Above* RECO CAPEY: **'Storm'. Design for cotton print,** *c.* 1926. *The Studio*, Vol. 91, 1926.

A storm at sea is here transformed into a light-hearted event for decorative effect. It seems likely that Capey was aware of the 'Pictorial' designs of Raoul Dufy. He taught for a time at the Royal College of Art, South Kensington.

10.45 *Above* M. RODIER: **Furnishing fabric. Jacquard woven silk and cotton,** *c.* 1925. Victoria and Albert Museum, London.

The chevron motif was widely used in urban vernacular design until the late 1930s. It could be produced in an almost infinite number of variations.

10.46 *Left* PAUL NASH: **Patterned paper for the Curwen Press,** 1928.

Nash is now most admired for his restrained Surrealist paintings. Nevertheless, decorative design formed a regular, if minor, part of his output. This design is derived from a single woodblock put into repeat.

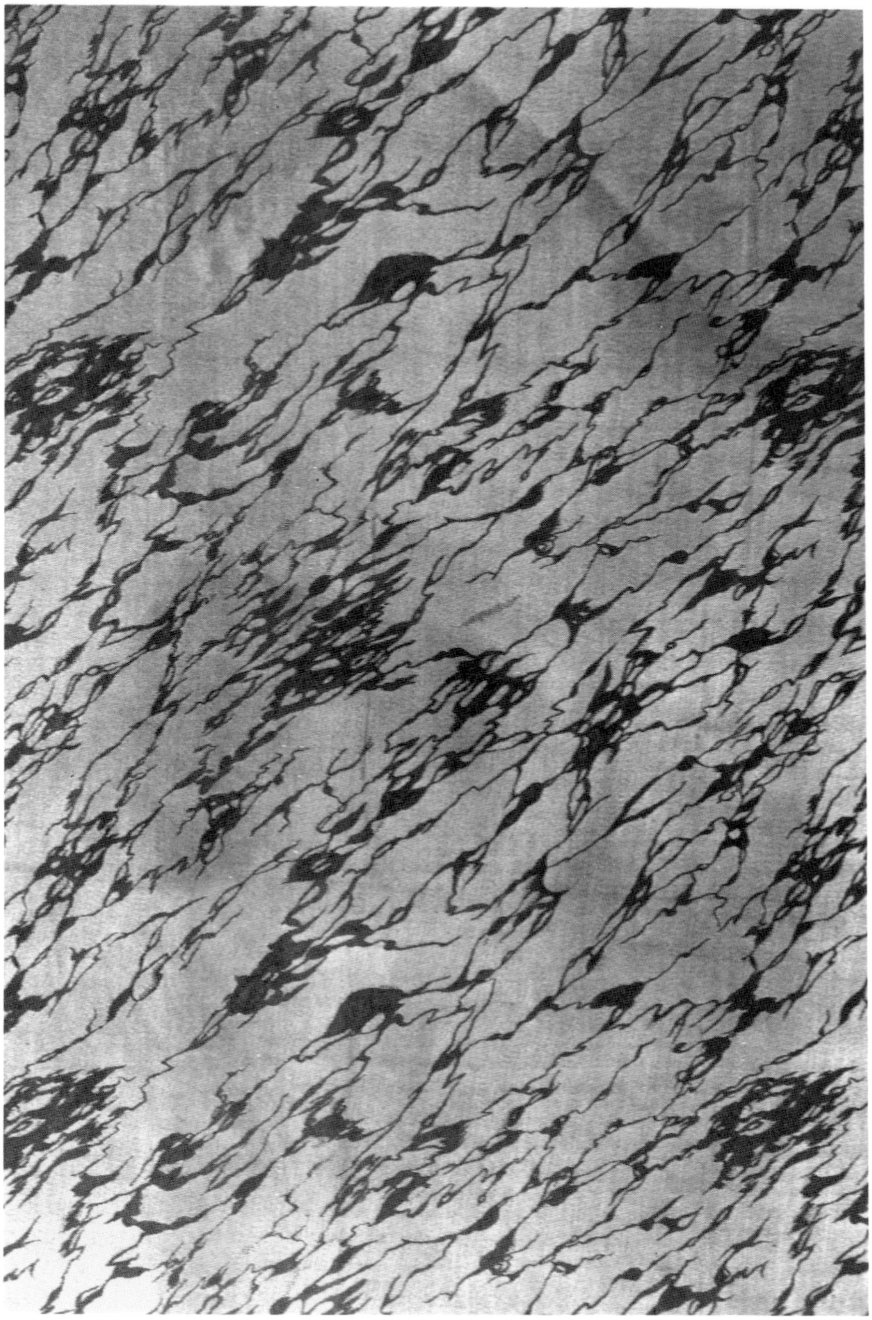

10.48 *Above* PAUL NASH: **'Alperton'.** Moquette used by the London Passenger Transport Board, *c.* 1928. Victoria and Albert Museum, London.

Out of the simplest elements, Nash produces a fairly complex and arresting design. He appears here to be anticipating the starker designs of the following decade. .

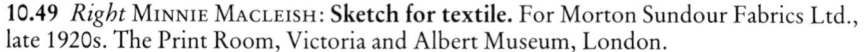

10.47 *Above* BERTRAND WHITTAKER: **'Marble'. Textile in woven cotton and rayon.** For Warner and Sons Ltd., 1925. Victoria and Albert Museum, London.

The idea of imitating in fabric the texture of an unlikely material like marble was comparatively daring in the 1920s. This textile was shown at the Paris Exhibition of 1925.

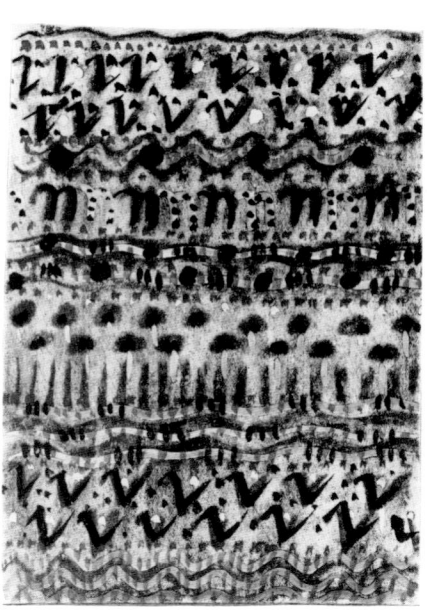

10.49 *Right* MINNIE MACLEISH: **Sketch for textile.** For Morton Sundour Fabrics Ltd., late 1920s. The Print Room, Victoria and Albert Museum, London.

This sketch comes from a small staple-bound book with a note by Minnie Macleish pencilled on the cover: 'A set of small close patterns designed to give a rich . . . effect without being obtrusively patterny.' Seen out of its true context this design bears a passing resemblance to a miniature by Paul Klee.

10.50 *Above* EDWARD STEICHEN: **'Matches and Match Boxes'.
'Americana' print design from a photograph by Steichen.**
For the Stehli Silk Corporation, *c.* 1929. *The Studio*, Vol. 97,
1929.

Although decorative designers had begun to use photographs of
plants as sources of inspiration in the nineteenth century, the use
of an actual photograph for imprinting on a fabric seems to have
been an innovation.

10.51 WALTER FÜRST: **Linoleum.**
Manufactured by the Deutschen
Linoleum-Werke, Delmenhorst, Bremen.
Jahrbuch des Deutschen Werkbundes,
1913.

10.52 PAUL DOLEZEL EZEL: **Bands of
decoration.** *Elementare Entwicklung des
Ornaments,* n.d. (*c.* 1920).

10.53 ANONYMOUS: **Design for printed crêpe de Chine.** Manufactured by Albert Godde, Bedin & Cie, Lyon and Mulhouse. *Art, Goût, Beauté*, 1923.

10.54 ALBERT RUTHERSTON: **Illustration from *A Box of Paints.*** The Curwen Press, dated 1923. *Reports . . . at the International Exhibition of Modern Decorative and Industrial Arts, Paris, 1925.* (n.d.).

10.55 L. Chapuis: **Decoration.** Jean
Saudé, *Traité d'Enluminure d'Art au
Pochoir*, 1925.

10.56 Henri Gillet: **Decoration.**
Nouvelles Fantasies Décoratives (c. 1920).

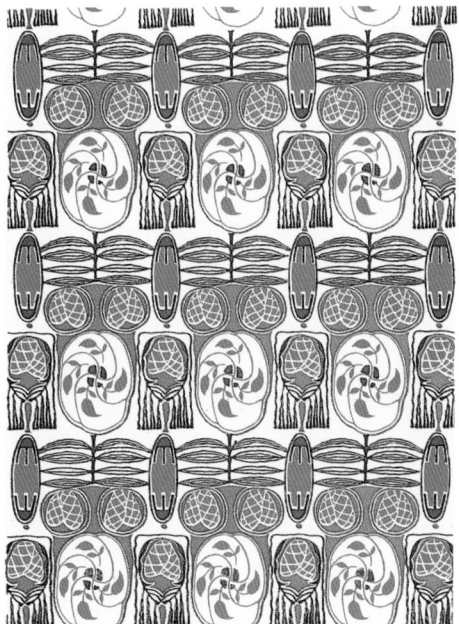

10.57 A. GARCELON: **Wallpaper.** Henri Clouzot, *Papiers Peints et Tentures Modernes* (c. 1925).

10.59 *Opposite* RAYMOND SUBES: **Interior grille in wrought iron,** *c.* 1930. *La Ferronnerie*, 4eme Série, 1930?

Subes was a leading French craftsman in metal. This grille, perhaps for the entrance to a Parisian apartment block, has the severity of the graphic style of such artists as A. J. Cassandre (1901–68).

10.58 EDOUARD BÉNÉDICTUS: **Decoration.** Jean Saudé, *Traité d'Enluminure d'art au Pochoir, 1925.*

CHAPTER ELEVEN

Modernism

Of Modernist polemics, and there were many, by far the most influential was Le Corbusier's *Vers une Architecture* (1923). Although Le Corbusier's ideas, in their wonderful simplicity, were very widely disseminated, it was not until Frederick Etchells' translation of the book as *Towards a New Architecture* in 1927 that they became entirely accessible to the English-speaking world. Le Corbusier's thinking was to become part of the studio folklore of an international generation of architects, artists and designers. His style has the brusque authority of earlier Futurist or Vorticist manifestos. Above all, however, Le Corbusier viewed the future with an infectious optimism:

A great epoch has begun.
There exists a new spirit.
There exists a mass of work conceived in the new spirit; it is to be met particularly in industrial production. Architecture is stifled by custom.
The 'styles' are a lie. Style is a unity of principle animating all the work of an epoch, the result of a state of mind which has its own special character.
Our epoch is determining, day by day, its own style.
Our eyes, unhappily, are unable yet to discern it.

The styles of the past would have no place in the sane and healthy world of the future. The case against ornament seemed unanswerable in the 1920s and 1930s. Its loss seemed a trifling price to pay for a progress which extended beyond aesthetics—or technology itself—and which, it was claimed by its apostles, had an ethical and moral basis. It is only recently that these claims have been questioned and the work of those, such as Lutyens and Raymond Erith, who held fast to the traditional values of academic or classical architecture, is being re-appraised.

In 1932, Henry Russell Hitchcock and Philip Johnson published *The International Style*, which gave the new architecture its most familiar name. They proclaimed that one of its essential constituents was the 'avoidance of applied decoration'. Hitchcock and Johnson saw that there were two salient problems for ornament in both the nineteenth and the twentieth centuries: 'The failure of revivalism lay quite as much in the inability to recreate the conditions of craftsmanship which once applied ornament aesthetically valid, as in the impossibility of adapting the spirit of old styles to new methods of construction.' Ruskin, or Lethaby for that matter, could well have said the same thing.

Surprisingly for a book which was written when the Modern Movement was approaching its zenith and its exponents were confidently sweeping all counter-arguments aside, Hitchcock and Johnson added a rider: 'It would be ridiculous to state categorically that there will never be successful applied ornament in architecture again.' It is only with hindsight—at a time when the Post-Modern revisionists appear to have triumphed—that this remark seems significant. When it was made it was prompted by no more than prudent academic caution, so complete seemed the victory of Modernism in the early 1930s.

11.1 *Opposite* GUNDA STADLER STÖLZL: **Working design for a carpet,** *c.* 1927. The Print Room, Victoria and Albert Museum, London.

A design based upon a simple grid. Modernist designers went to considerable pains to ensure that no configurations within such a format resembled recognizable objects.

The Modern Movement was essentially a movement of architects,[1] and it was the propaganda of architects, above all, which made ornament the object of ridicule. The ideals of the Modern Movement, however, were by no means entirely incompatible with the ornamenting of buildings. Even a building as allegedly influential as Gropius and Meyer's Model Factory at the Werkbund Exhibition of 1914, in Cologne, was not entirely without ornament—although historians have sometimes chosen to suppress this fact.

In 1892, Louis Sullivan, a prolific designer of sensual, plant-based, architectural ornament and a pioneer of skyscraper architecture, stated: 'It would be greatly for our aesthetic good if we should refrain entirely from the use of ornament for a period of years, in order that our thought might concentrate acutely upon the production of buildings well formed and comely in the nude.'[2] Sullivan himself never abjured ornament, but his call for abstinence was a healthy questioning of the often unthinking decoration of structures which was so prevalent at the end of the nineteenth century.

Whether to use ornament was never a great issue for Arts and Crafts designers—but ornament was to be used with discretion, it was to have meaning, and it was to proclaim joy in labour. Architects such as Peter Behrens, Josef Hoffmann, Josef Maria Olbrich, Charles Rennie Mackintosh and Eliel Saarinen were all accomplished and prolific designers of ornament. And all, at some stage in their careers, inhabited the hinterland of ideals that lay between the nineteenth century—with its preoccupation with an architecture laden with meaning—and the twentieth century—with its search for an architecture expressive of rationality. Even Le Corbusier's early houses at La Chaux-sur-Fonds are ornamented.

Adolf Loos' attack on ornament in 'Ornament and Crime' has frequently been cited as the most important of the early assaults upon ornament. But like Sullivan, Loos was not averse to using ornament in his architecture—although his ornament was wholly of Classical derivation. 'Ornament and Crime' was written in 1908 when the Vienna Secession had just begun to lose the first bloom of youth. Not only Vienna, but the whole of that part of Europe which was dominated by German ideas, was surfeited with Jugendstil ornament. Loos' response to such excess was to ridicule it. 'The evolution of civilization', he declared, 'is measured by the removal of ornament from objects of use.' Ornament had become superfluous—almost as if by the process of natural selection. 'We have overcome ornament, we have struggled free of ornament', he triumphantly announced. 'Ornament and Crime' caused little stir when it was published and it languished in obscurity until it was gleefully rediscovered in the 1920s by the leaders of the new movement in architecture.

The occasion of the Exposition Internationale des Art Décoratifs in Paris in 1925 prompted Le Corbusier to publish *L'Art Décoratif d'Aujourd'hui* ('The Decorative Arts of To-day'). Here, as in no other of his writings, he poured scorn on the decorated object. Earlier, in *Towards a New Architecture*, he had declared: 'The "decorative arts" are going strong! After thirty years of underground work they are at their height ... All we need remember of this adventure—which will finish badly—is that something more is being born than a rebirth of decoration.'

It was true that at the time of the birth of Modernism the decorative arts were buoyant. The 1925 Paris Exhibition demonstrated this with its ornate and ingenious pavilions, French and foreign, and the elaborate decorative metalwork of designers such as Edgar Brandt and Ruhlmann, whose more chastely decorated 'furniture de luxe' was greatly admired. However, the 1925 Exhibition was not the last great sortie of the decorative tradition.

The gospel of Modernism was most effectively taught by the Bauhaus, which had been founded in 1919. Walter Gropius, its director, described the

ARCHITECTURE
□AVANT-1914□

institution in *The New Architecture and the Bauhaus* (1935). Inevitably, 'the liberation of architecture from a welter of ornament' was high in the list of priorities. But the greatest Bauhaus achievement was its development of a comprehensive teaching method, which was still in vogue in the 1950s and 1960s. The first task, wrote Gropius, was 'to liberate the pupil's individuality from the dead weight of conventions and allow him to acquire that personal experience and self-taught knowledge which are the only means for realizing the natural limitations of our creative powers.' The mind of the Bauhaus pupil was to be purged of traditions and transformed into a *tabula rasa*.

This part of Bauhaus teaching—the idea that personal experience is more important than received knowledge—was particularly influential. This, more than anti-ornament invective, helped to undermine the programme of teaching the design of ornament which had been developed in the nineteenth century. Once the teaching of the historical and national styles of ornament—or the grammar and syntax of ornament—was omitted from the curricula of art-teaching institutions, the ornamental tradition itself began to wither.

Paradoxically, certain elements of the teaching of ornament were absorbed into the Bauhaus system. It is possible to detect, for example, in Paul Klee's *Pädagogisches Skizzenbuch*,[3] the second of the Bauhaus books—published in 1925—the influence of earlier methods of teaching the design of ornament, or repeat pattern (see Plate 11.6). Klee's approach—at first glance a wholly empirical one—bears a distinct relationship to the drawing exercises used as a prelude to the designing of ornament in design institutions since the 1840s.[4]

Herbert Read, in *Art Now. An Introduction to the theory of modern painting and sculpture* (1933) produced the first British account of contemporary—mainly continental—developments in art. It is not a work of naïve polemic like so much inspired by Modernism. Read chose, rather, to concentrate upon the psychological potentiality of modern art: 'The more mechanical the world becomes ... the less spiritual satisfaction there is to be found in the appearances of this world. The inner world of the imagination becomes more and more significant, as if to compensate for the poverty and the drabness of every-day life.'[5]

Read's views on ornament are to be found in *Art and Industry. The principles of industrial design* (1934). He does not write as a designer, of course, but as an aesthetician. His thinking on the problem of ornament was as undoctrinaire as were his ideas on modern painting. Here he is on 'The Function of Decoration':

> The necessity of ornament is psychological. There exists in man a certain feeling which has been called *horror vacui*, an incapacity to tolerate an empty space ... It may be an ineradicable feeling: it is probably the same instinct that causes certain people to scribble on lavatory walls, or others to scribble on their blotting-pads ... Whilst I think that a little discipline would be a very good thing, I by no means wish to urge the total suppression of the instinct to fill blank spaces.

But Read asserted: 'The only real justification for ornament is that it should in some way emphasise form ... Legitimate ornament I conceive as something like mascara and lipstick—something applied with discretion to make more precise the outlines of an already existing beauty.' Read's view is a detached and reasonable one—and remarkable for the fact that it was expressed at a time when the champions of Modernism were all too vociferous in their condemnation of ornament. And not a little bigoted.

For all the anathemas of the founding fathers of the Modern Movement, the era of Modernism produced ornament. The language of ornament is

ARCHITECTURE
▫APRÈS-1918▫

11.2, 11.3 *Left and above* Antoine Pompe: **Satirical drawings.** *Left*, architecture before 1914; *right*, architecture after 1918. Archives d'Architecture Moderne, Brussels. (Reproduced in *Images et Imaginaires d'Architecture*, 1984.)

Pompe was a Belgian architect. While the Modernist views of McGrath are clear in his drawing (see Plate 11.4) Pompe's intentions are more ambiguous.

adaptable and is perfectly able to convey the ideals of an age which put its faith in a mechanized and rationalized world. That great popular apologist of streamlining, Norman Bel Geddes (1893–1958), wrote about the future in *Horizons* in 1932:

> We are entering an era which ... shall be characterized by design ... Design in social structure to insure the organization of people, work, wealth, leisure. Design in machines that shall improve working conditions by eliminating drudgery. Design in all objects of daily use that shall make them economical, durable, convenient, congenial to everyone. Design in the arts, painting, sculpture, music, literature and architecture, that shall inspire the new era.

The great weakness of the Modern Movement was the failure of its leaders to recognize the value of continuity and familiarity in design. Modernism and ornament were not necessarily inimical. As Herbert Read understood, ornament is a kind of psychological necessity. This thought poses us few problems today. Had Gropius or Mies van der Rohe or Le Corbusier recognized the importance of ornament in 'explaining' the significance of a building to the lay person, their work would be better popularly understood than it is. Yet, in a sense, forms of ornament were happily able to exist within the framework of Modernism—as Bauhaus textiles or the few ornamental designs of such artists as Paul Nash (Plate 10.46), Henry Moore, Eileen Gray (Plate 11.7) and Marion Dorn (Plates 11.28, 54) establish. Ornament is a sturdy plant. Modernism did little to diminish its grass-roots vitality. Some fine ornament was produced during its ascendancy. But propaganda weakened the teaching of ornament. (Although a major Russian constructivist architect—Yacov Chernikov—made use of ornamental exercises as an introduction to the invention of form.[6]) The greatest damage to the ornamental tradition inflicted by Modernism was to have discredited the teaching of ornament.

11.4 Raymond McGrath: **Satirical vignette.** *Twentieth Century Houses*, 1934.

A clean-cut modern couple confront their curvilinear, ostentatious, Victorian counterparts. McGrath's book gives an excellent account of the impact of the International Style on domestic architecture.

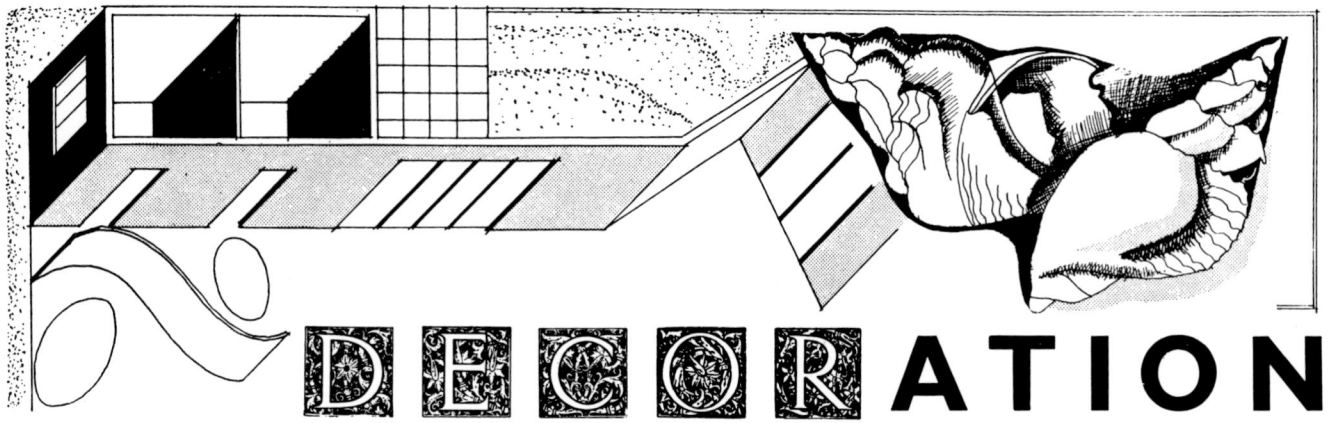

DECORATION

11.5 *Above* ANONYMOUS GRAPHIC DESIGNER: **Headpiece.** For an article by Geoffrey Boumphrey. *The Architectural Review*, Vol. LXXVII, 1935.

An amusing design which perfectly conveys the mood of the Modern Movement in Britain in the mid-1930s. The message of the metamorphosis of the decorated letters into sensible sans-serif ones is plain. Boumphrey toed the strict Modernist line.

11.6 *Right* PAUL KLEE: **A page from** *Pedagogical Sketchbook*, 1925.

Klee's *Pedagogical Sketchbook* is one of the earliest primers of abstract design. (Although Denman Ross's *Theory of Pure Design* should not be forgotten—see Chapter Three, Plates 3.31–2.) Klee's method of encouraging visual invention is not altogether unlike that of Christopher Dresser or W. R. Lethaby, who both advocated 'designing games'.

11.7 *Below right* EILEEN GRAY: **Hand-woven rug in dark brown, grey-brown and black,** *c.* 1924. *Wendigen*, June 1924.

Eileen Gray was one of the earliest designers to use abstract forms decoratively. There are clear affinities between this design and the Purist paintings of Le Corbusier and Ozenfant.

11.8 *Below* VILMOS HUSZHAR: **Vignette.** From *De Stijl. Images et Imaginaires d'Architecture*, 1984.

De Stijl, the journal founded in 1917 by Theo von Doesburg, expressed the ideas of a group which included Mondrian, Oud and Rietveld. It stood for the most austere form of abstract art. This vignette, however, can be perceived as either an abstract or a decorative composition.

Fig. 18: Both dimensions combined, seen diagonally.

Fig. 18:

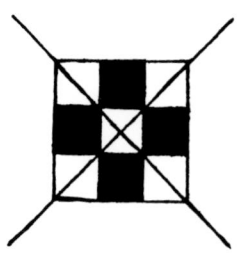

Fig. 19: Linear variation.

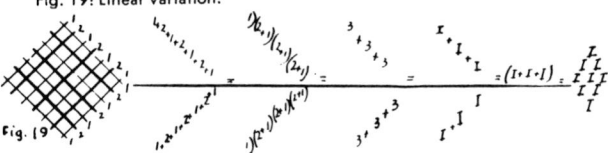

Since these figure arrangements rest on the principle of repetition, any number of parts can be added or taken away without changing their rhythmic character.

Fig 20 | **Therefore the structural character is divisional.**

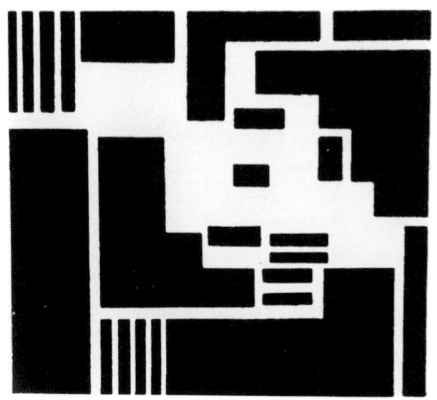

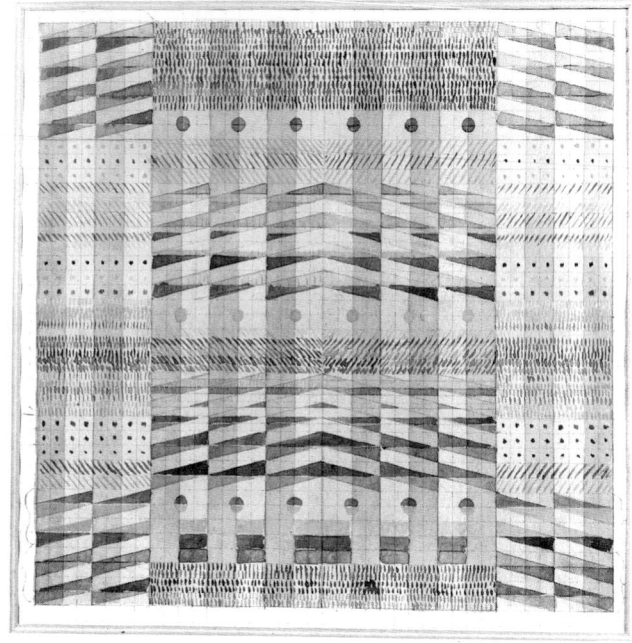

11.9 *Above left* GUNDA STADLER STÖLZL: **Working design for a wall-hanging, to be Jacquard-woven,** 1928–9. The Print Room, Victoria and Albert Museum, London.

Gunda Stadler Stölzl was the leading weaver at the Bauhaus. Here she exploits the essential qualities of the Jacquard process. The deliberate asymmetry of this design should be noted.

11.10 *Top* GUNDA STADLER STÖLZL: **Working design for a wall-hanging, to be Jacquard-woven,** 1928–9. The Print Room, Victoria and Albert Museum, London.

Although this design is at first glance very similar to that in Plate 11.9 examination will show that it is different in a number of respects. It is possible, of course, to produce an infinite number of variations using a grid. (Truchet, see Chapter Three Plates 3.6, 9, established this theoretically as early as 1704.) Modern Movement designers were frequently obsessed with the idea of designing within a grid.

11.11 *Left* PABLO PICASSO: **Harlequin with a guitar.** *The Architectural Review*, December 1930 (Supplement on Decoration and Craftsmanship).

Picasso's painting is suggested as a model for the design of a carpet. At about the same time, the Parisian designer Bénédictus published a *pochoir* portfolio of his designs, many of which derive their inspiration from Picasso's work.

11.12 *Above* KARNA ASKER: **Knotted carpet,** *c.* 1930. Dr Nils G. Wollin, *Modern Swedish Decorative Art* (1931).

This design should be compared with the examples by Atelier Kunis, Berlin. Karna Asker, however, shows a far greater sympathy for the ideals of modern painting.

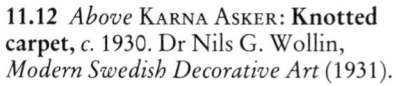

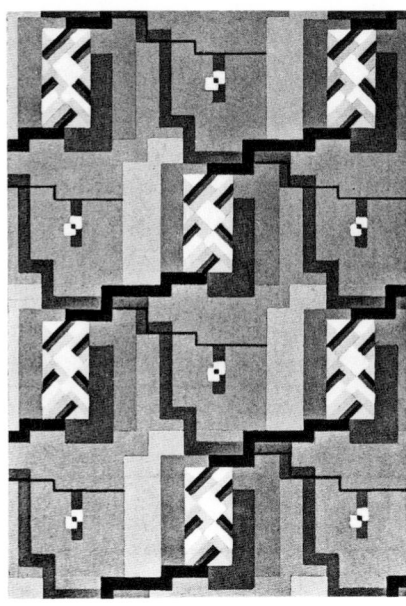

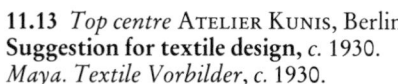

11.13 *Top centre* ATELIER KUNIS, Berlin: **Suggestion for textile design,** *c.* 1930. *Maya. Textile Vorbilder,* *c.* 1930.

The mannerisms of modern painting were quickly adopted by designers and manufacturers of textiles, carpets and wallpapers. Paul Nash in *Room and Book* attacked what he considered to be such a debasing of Modern Movement ideals.

11.15 *Above left* ATELIER KUNIS, Berlin: **Suggestion for textile design,** *c.* 1930. *Maya. Textile Vorbilder,* *c.* 1930.

An all-over pattern in a style which could be described as 'Modern Movement vernacular'.

11.14 *Top right* ATELIER KUNIS, Berlin: **Suggestion for textile design,** *c.* 1930. *Maya. Textile Vorbilder,* *c.* 1930.

This design incorporates elements which were too naturalistic to accord with the tenets of the Modern Movement.

11.16 *Above right* ATELIER KUNIS, Berlin: **Suggestion for textile design,** *c.* 1930. *Maya. Textile Vorbilder,* *c.* 1930.

A design which hints at Kandinsky's abstract paintings.

11.17 *Left* SOFIA WIDEN: **'Stockholm'. Tapestry,** 1930. Dr Nils G. Wollin, *Modern Swedish Decorative Art* (1931).

A view of modern Stockholm. Sofia Widen's pictorial composition is reminiscent of Arts and Crafts work, in which strenuous efforts were made to make design 'meaningful'.

11.18 *Above* Rebecca Crompton: **'Diana'. Decorative panel embroidered in organdie,** 1930. Victoria and Albert Museum, London.

The theme of Diana the Huntress had been popular since the time of the Renaissance. Here, however, Diana has been demoted from a goddess to a devotee of physical fitness.

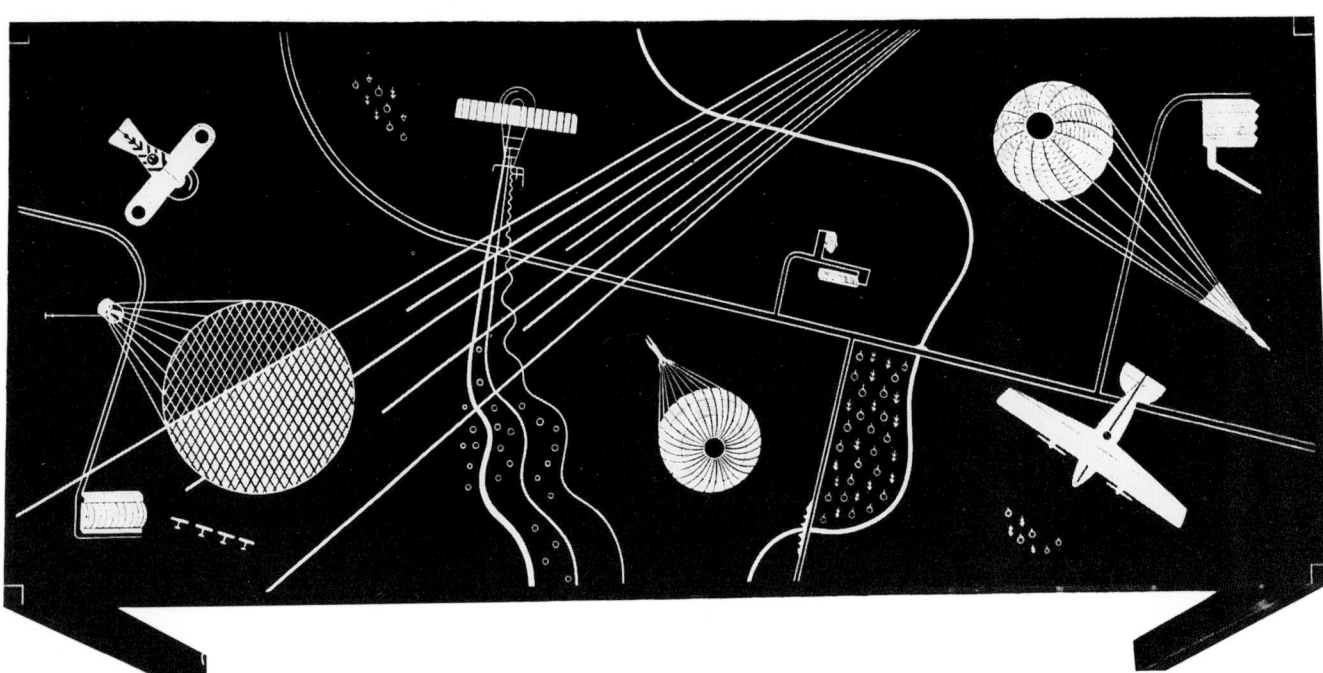

11.20 *Above* T. Ryberg: **Ebony table-top, inlaid with ivory.** *The Architectural Review*, August 1930.

This was used as a headpiece to an article by D. H. Lawrence, 'Mining-Camp Civilization. The English contribution to civilization'. The aeroplane was a powerful symbol for the exponents of the Modern Movement—Le Corbusier was to publish a book on the subject in 1936.

11.19 *Top right* Rebecca Crompton: **'The Magic Garden'. Worked in appliqué in patterned and coloured silks,** *c.* 1930. Victoria and Albert Museum, London.

The juxtapositioning of energetic patterns suggests the influence of Picasso.

11.21 *Above* RAYMOND McGRATH: **Design for wallpaper,** *c.* 1933. Victoria and Albert Museum, London.

Raymond McGrath had a very great enthusiasm for modern progress. He advocated the use of pictorial symbols for annotating architectural drawings and even went as far as to propose the use of a simplified English vocabulary.

11.22 *Below* UNKNOWN DESIGNER: **'The Tunnel'. Cotton print,** late 1920s. *Art into Production. Soviet Textiles, Fashion and Ceramics, 1917–1935*, 1984.

Seen at a distance this textile appears to be a typical 'scale' design. When seen in close proximity the tunnel—a symbol of Soviet industrial progress—is very clear.

11.23 C. BURYLIN: **'Tractor'. Cotton print,** 1930. *Art into Production. Soviet Textiles, Fashion and Ceramics, 1917–1935,* 1984.

The tractor is seen as a symbol of Soviet agricultural progress. The way it is represented here is probably based on the stencil technique used widely in Japan. This technique was publicized in the West in the early years of the century.

11.24 *Far left* BETTY JOEL: **Damask, woven in blue cotton and yellow silk.** French, mid-1930s. Victoria and Albert Museum, London.

Betty Joel did much to further the ideals of the Modern Movement through her shop in Sloane Street.

11.25 *Left* DESIGNER UNKNOWN: **'Araby'. Woven cotton and artificial silk.** French, *c.* 1931. Victoria and Albert Museum, London.

With its abstract design and its simple, bold geometry, this textile has Modern Movement characteristics. Nevertheless, it has a certain fussiness which establishes it as belonging to the genre of popular Modernism which was so widespread in the 1930s.

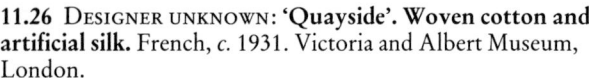

11.26 DESIGNER UNKNOWN: **'Quayside'. Woven cotton and artificial silk.** French, *c.* 1931. Victoria and Albert Museum, London.

A design based upon child-like illustrations of ships and dockside equipment. An evocation of bustling modern life.

11.27 DESIGNER UNKNOWN: **Damask. In shades of grey.** French, mid-1930s. Victoria and Albert Museum, London.

A design based upon simplified leaves or petals.

11.30 *Opposite* ALEX HUNTER: **Woven cotton,** 1933. Victoria and Albert Museum, London.

The wave motif conjures up romantic thoughts of the sea and voyages to distant places. Travel imagery was particularly popular during the 1930s.

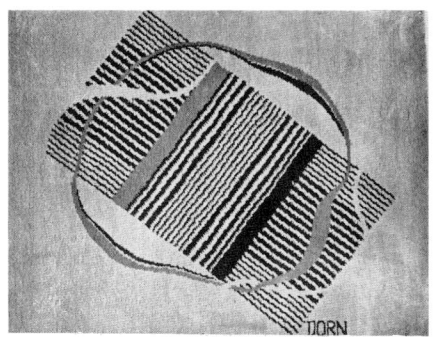

11.28 *Above* Marion Dorn: **Hand-made rug. Cream ground with dark brown lines and ribbons of grey-blue and Chartreuse green,** *c.* 1932. *The Architectural Review*, September 1932.

Marion Dorn was born in the United States and is best known for her Modernist rug designs.

11.29 *Right* Designer unknown: **Woven cotton and artificial silk.** French, *c.* 1931. Victoria and Albert Museum, London.

11.31 *Below right* Norman Webbe: **'Sperrin'. Jacquard-woven linen.** For the Old Bleach Linen Co. Ltd., *c.* 1933. Victoria and Albert Museum, London.

An effective design of extreme graphic simplicity. This fabric would perfectly complement an austere Modernist interior.

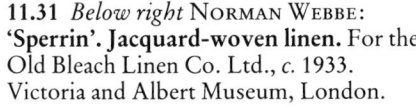

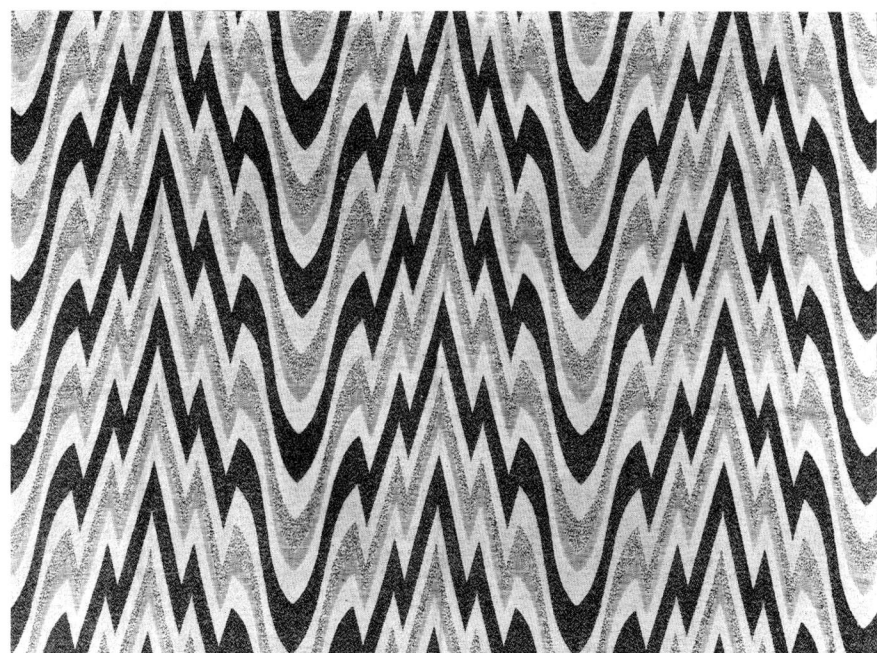

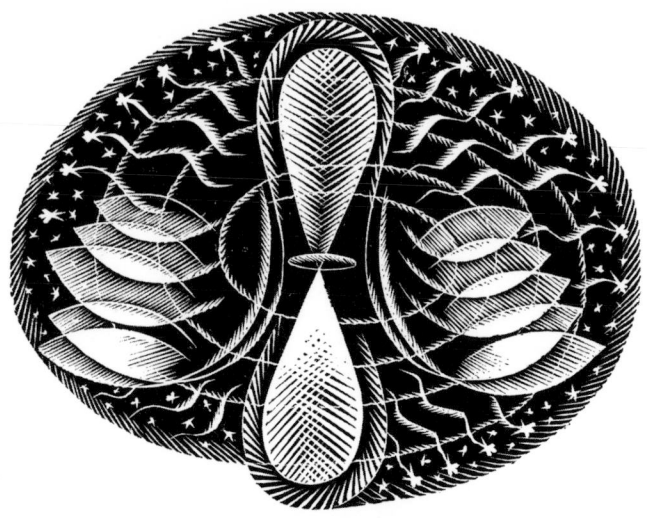

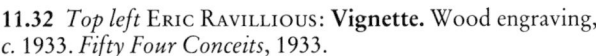

SCARF BORDER   SKETCH   SQUARE SCARF

ALL OVER PATTERN

HOW TO USE ARCHITECTURAL FORM IN VARIOUS WAYS

11.32 *Top left* ERIC RAVILLIOUS: **Vignette.** Wood engraving, *c.* 1933. *Fifty Four Conceits*, 1933.

Ravillious did much to revive the technique of wood engraving in the 1930s. His sense of design is typical of the 1930s—and in particular those designers who had been influenced by Paul Nash.

11.33 *Above* ERIC RAVILLIOUS: **Vignette.** Wood engraving, *c.* 1933. *Fifty Four Conceits*, 1933.

Ravillious' decorative devices were widely used by fine printers such as the Curwen, Golden Cockerell and Nonesuch Presses. He designed numerous advertisements and book jackets.

11.34 *Top right* THOMAS J. CORBIN: **'How to use architectural form in various ways'.** *Handblock Printing on Fabrics*, 1934.

From a book intended for schools or amateurs. The designs evoke a secure, pastoral world. Such imagery is reminiscent of the thinking of the Arts and Crafts Movement. The terse stylization of the farmhouse, however, is characteristic of the graphic style of the 1930s.

11.36 *Right* BETTY JOEL: **Damask, woven in red wool and buff cotton, with grey silk weft.** French, mid-1930s. Victoria and Albert Museum, London.

An essentially abstract design which, nevertheless, suggests leaves or petals.

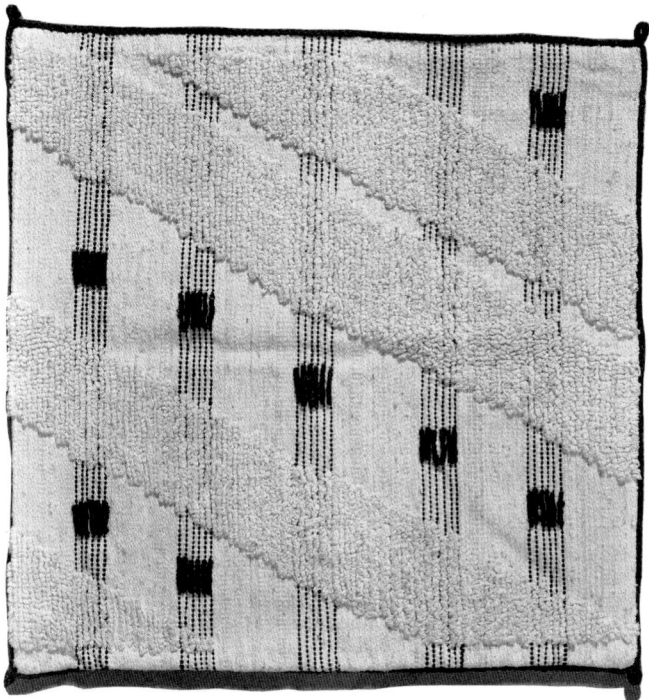

11.37 ETHEL MAIRET: **Woven cushion cover in cotton.** Victoria and Albert Museum, London.

Ethel Mairet began weaving when the Arts and Crafts Movement was in its heyday. However, she was successful in coming to terms with the teachings of the Modern Movement.

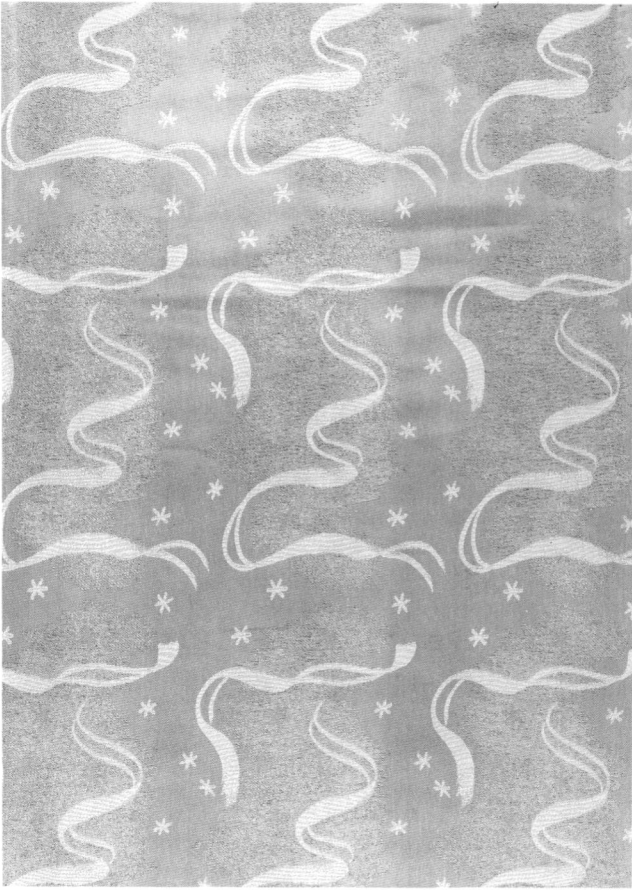

11.38 ASHLEY HAVINDEN: **'Milky Way'. Jacquard-woven cotton.** For Edinburgh Weavers, 1936. Victoria and Albert Museum, London.

An early example of Alexander Morton's enlightened patronage of modern designers for his family firm. Havinden was a most versatile designer. He is now best known for his elegant posters for the W. S. Crawford advertising agency.

11.35 *Opposite* DESIGNER UNKNOWN: **Uncut moquette,** 1935. Victoria and Albert Museum, London.

A design which is somewhat suggestive of the architectural style of Erich Mendelsohn—or, more likely, those architects of cinemas and garages who borrowed his ideas. This is a good example of 'Moderne' design.

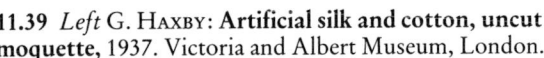

11.39 *Left* G. HAXBY: **Artificial silk and cotton, uncut moquette,** 1937. Victoria and Albert Museum, London.

The somewhat three-dimensional representation of the spheres conflicts with the pure Modernist aesthetic.

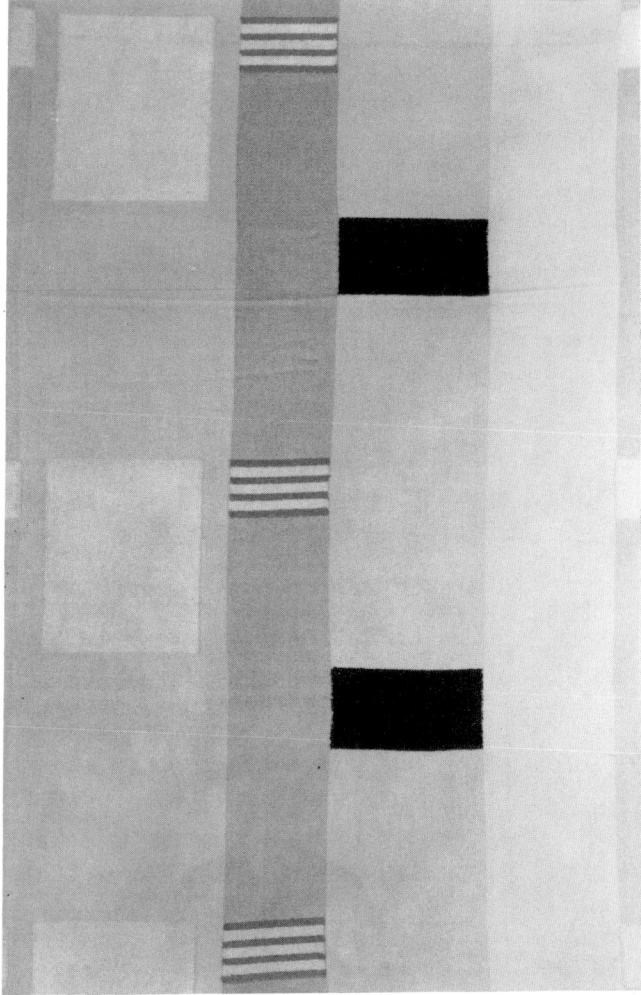

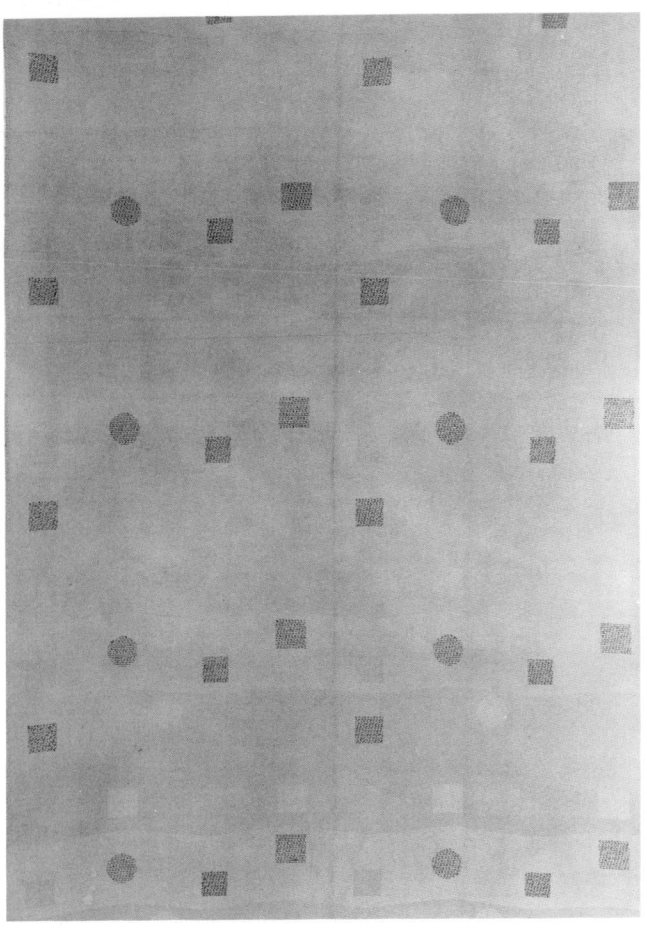

11.40 *Above* BARBARA HEPWORTH: **'Pillar'. Jacquard-woven cotton and rayon.** For Edinburgh Weavers, 1937. Victoria and Albert Museum, London.

Barbara Hepworth was among the leading exponents of Abstractionism in Britain in the 1930s. The extreme restraint of this textile is reminiscent of the artist's sculpture.

11.41 *Left* BEN NICHOLSON: **'Counterpoint'. Jacquard-woven cotton.** For Edinburgh Weavers, 1937. Victoria and Albert Museum, London.

Of all British artists of the 1930s, Nicholson was the most admired by the new generation of Modern Movement architects. He was a member of Unit One, a propagandizing Modernist group founded in 1933 which included Hepworth, Moore, Paul Nash, Wadsworth, and the architects Colin Lucas and Wells Coates.

11.42 GEORGES VALMIER: **Suggestions for decorations.** Album No. 1 (late 1920s).

Some of these designs suggest the influence of Georges Braque, one of the founders of Cubism.

11.43 ANONYMOUS: **Decoration.** Karl Luth, manufacturer. From a stencil catalogue *Moderne Wand und Decken Dekoration* (1932).

The swastika may be intentional—or purely accidental.

11.45 EDOUARD BÉNÉDICTUS: **Decoration.** *Relais 1930* (1930).

11.44 *Opposite* E. A. SÉGUN: **Decoration.** *Prismes* (after 1931).

11.46 Edouard Bénédictus: **Decoration.** *Relais 1930* (1930).

11.47 Raymond McGrath: **Design for a rubber floor.** For the foyer of a cinema.
The Architectural Review, Vol. LXVIII, 1930.

This design is based upon film spools.

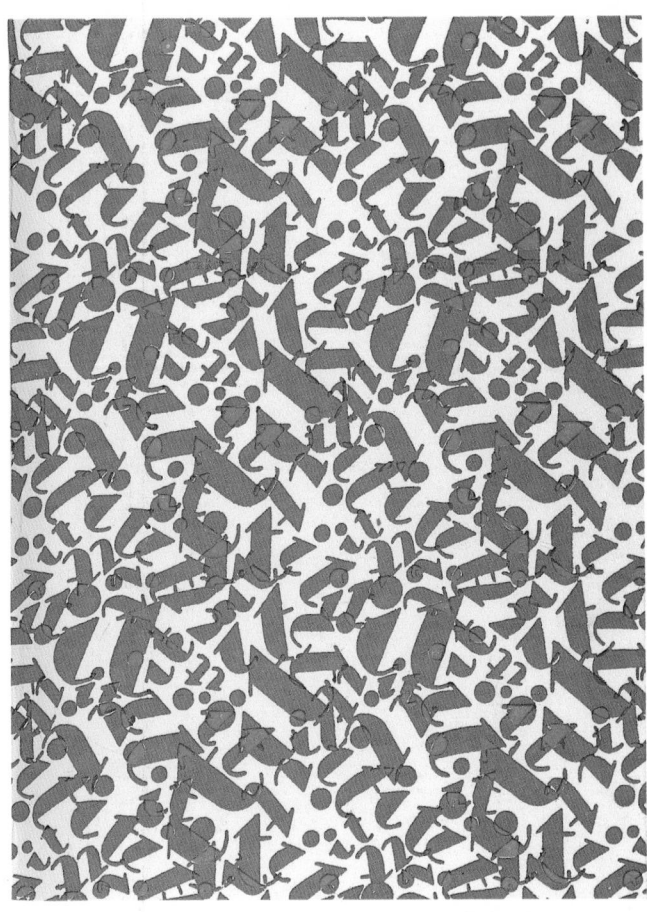

11.48 Ruzzie Green: **'It'. Fabric.** For the Stehli Silk
Corporation. *The Studio*, Vol. 97, 1929.

11.49 Gunda Stadler Stölzl: **Design for a wall-hanging,**
c. 1927. The Print Room, Victoria and Albert Museum, London.

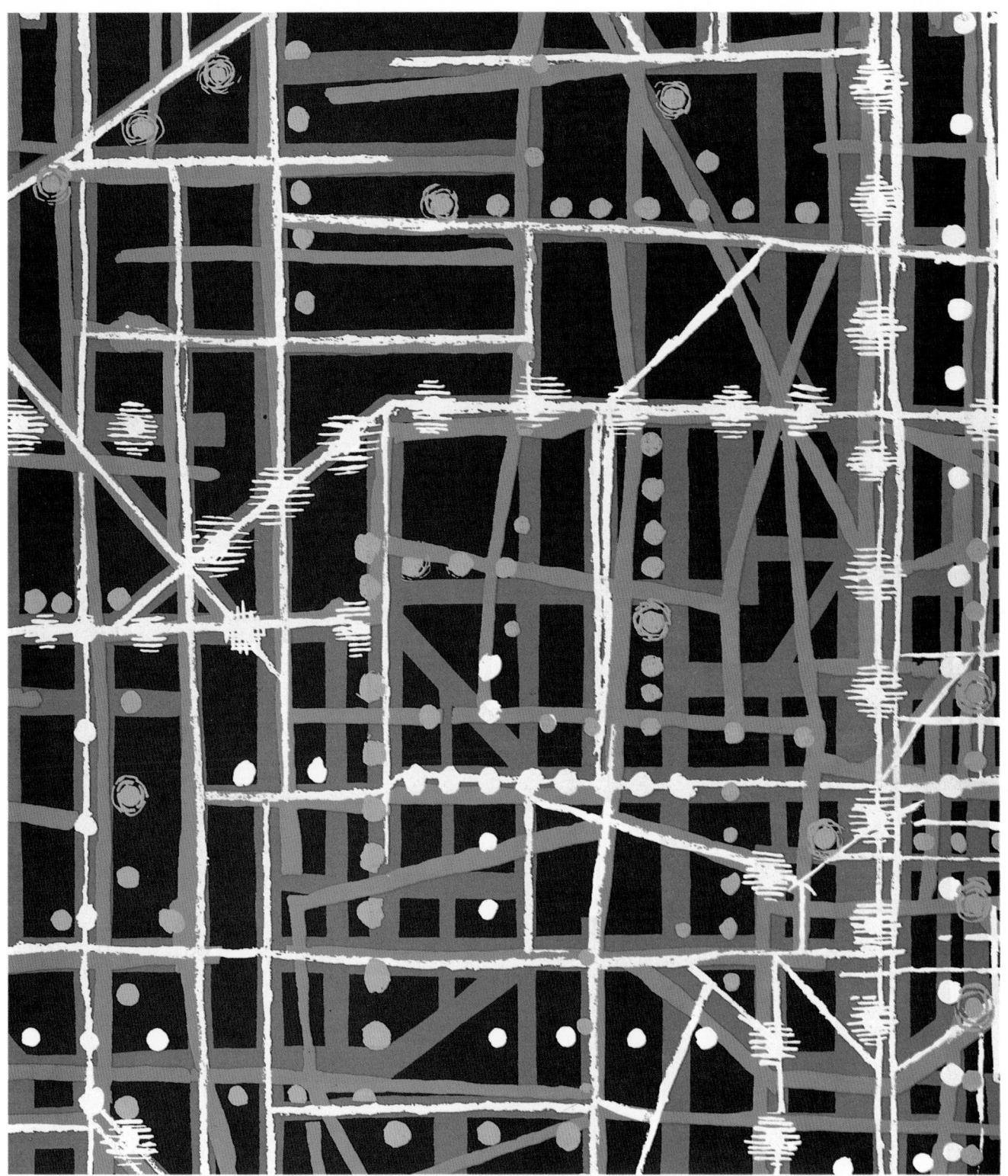

12.1 ROGER NICHOLSON: **Wallpaper. 'Aerial'.** From Palladio
Collection No. 5, 1961. Manufactured by Arthur Sanderson &
Sons Ltd. From the Sanderson Archive.

11.50 *Opposite* GUNDA STADLER STÖLZL:
Design for a wall-hanging, *c.* 1927. The
Print Room, Victoria and Albert Museum,
London.

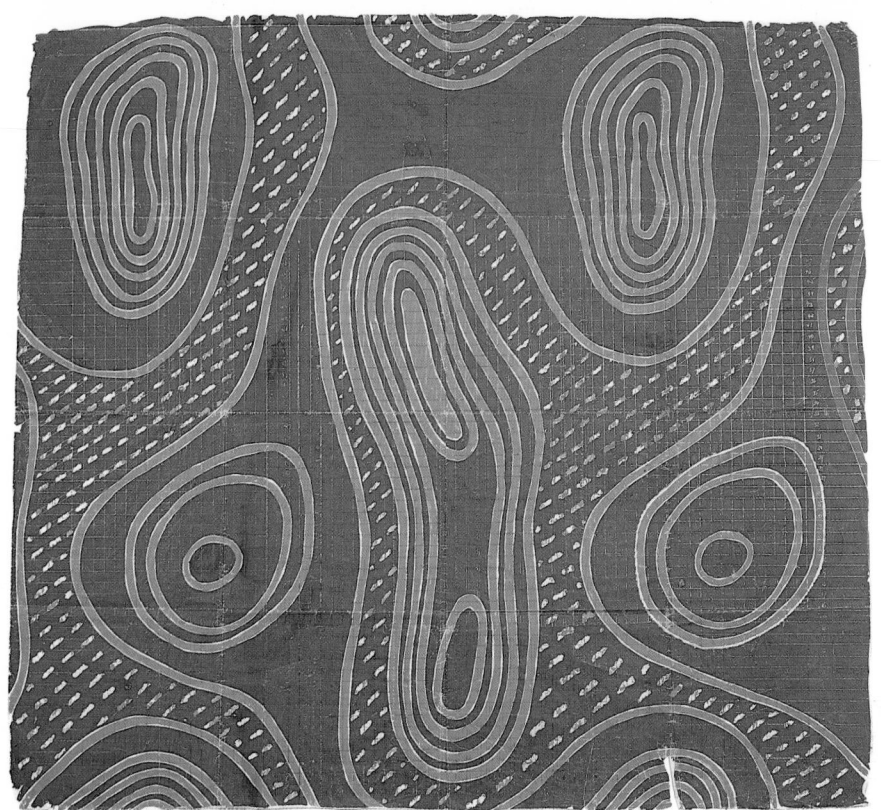

12.2 MARIANNE STRAUB: **Design for furnishing fabric 'Surrey'.** Manufactured by Warner and Sons Ltd., 1951. The Print Room, Victoria and Albert Museum, London.

This design is based upon a crystalline structure.

12.3 RAYMOND LOEWY: **Wallpaper. 'Kyoto Petals'.** From Sanderson's Centenary Collection, 1960. From the Sanderson Archive.

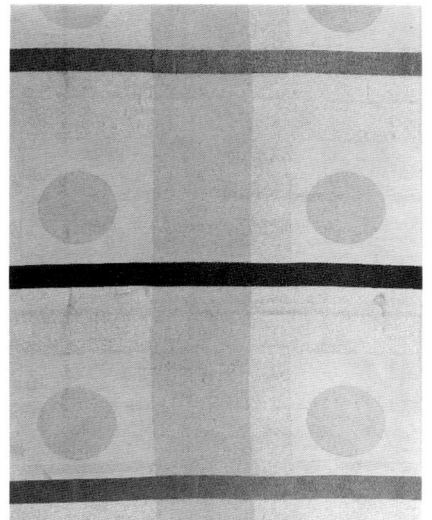

11.51 Ben Nicholson: **Fabric in woven cotton and rayon.** For Edinburgh Weavers, 1938. Victoria and Albert Museum, London.

Nicholson's few textile designs are closer in style to his reliefs than his painting. Had he not been such an extreme devotee of the Modernist aesthetic there is no doubt that his decorative sensibility—latent in his painting—would have enabled him to design fine textiles.

11.52 Ben Nicholson: **Relief,** *c.* 1935. *The Architectural Review*, Vol. LXXVIII, 1935.

An illustration to 'Ben Nicholson. Carved Reliefs', by Paul Nash, an account of Nicholson's exhibition at the Lefevre Galleries in September and October 1935.

11.53 *Above* ASHLEY HAVINDEN:
**'Uccello'. Jacquard-woven mercerized
cotton and rayon.** For Edinburgh
Weavers, 1937–8. Victoria and Albert
Museum, London.

This design has a particular poignancy
about it, for the bird undoubtedly
represents the dove of peace. The fabric
was designed at a time when it seemed
possible that a European war could be
avoided.

11.54 *Right* MARION DORN: **Woven
cotton.** For Edinburgh Weavers, *c.* 1939.
Victoria and Albert Museum, London.

Another design which uses the silhouette
of a dove. The Ionic columns and capitals
are perhaps intended to symbolize the
'permanent' values of European
civilization.

11.55 *Far right* J. L. LINDSAY: **Jacquard-
woven linen.** For the Old Bleach Linen
Co. Ltd., 1938. Victoria and Albert
Museum, London.

A modest, unaffected design. Its
simplicity suggests the restraint counselled
by the Modern Movement.

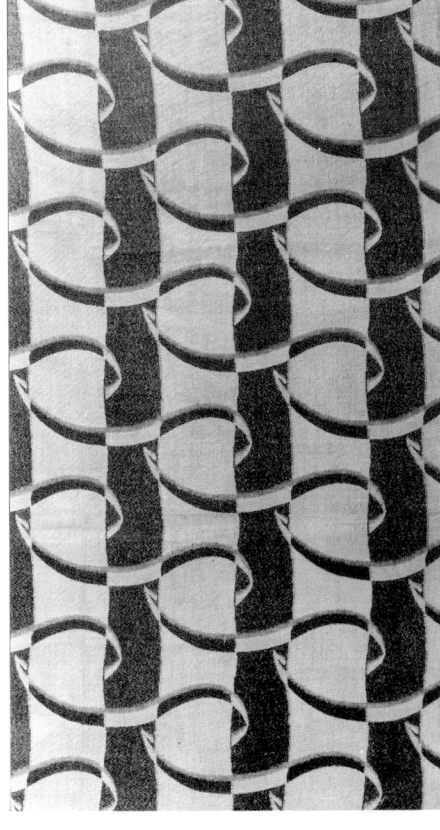

11.56 *Right* KATHLEEN MANN: **'Design for hand-printed textile based on the lily motif'.** *Design from Peasant Art*, 1939.

European peasant art was a popular source of inspiration for patterns in the 1930s. This was an extension of the Arts and Crafts enthusiasm for British vernacular design. Kathleen Mann's interpretation of a traditional design captures the light-hearted spirit of the Modernism of the late 1930s.

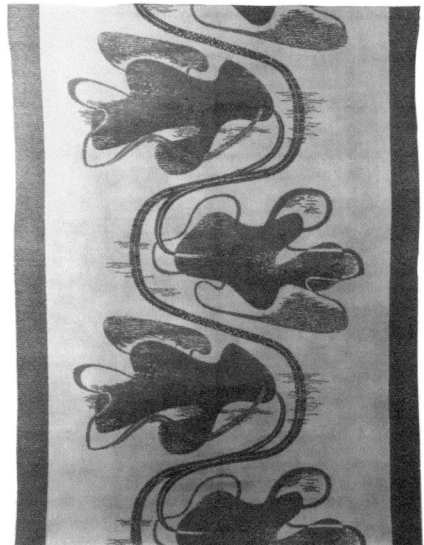

11.57 *Far left* DESIGNER UNKNOWN: **Artificial silk and cotton damask.** For F. O. R. Plaistow. English, 1930s. Victoria and Albert Museum, London.

A competent updating of the decorative style of the late 1920s. Simplification of forms and a certain casualness reveal the influence of the Modern Movement.

11.58 *Left* HANS AUFSEESER (TISDALL): **Woven textile.** For Edinburgh Weavers, 1938–9. Victoria and Albert Museum, London.

With Ashley Havinden, Barbara Hepworth and Ben Nicholson, Hans Tisdall was among the avant-garde designers who were invited to design textiles by Alistair Morton. This design is obviously based on a painting.

1940 to the Present—Revival

The decorative tradition has survived the massive assault of the Modern Movement in the 1920s and 1930s. But by no means unscathed. Ornament was to form a decreasingly important part of art and design teaching. The great encyclopedias of ornament were taken off the library shelves. Plaster casts of approved classical ornament began to gather dust in basements. 'Basic design', a kind of terse grammar of abstract design, which was intended to foster 'creativity' was now in vogue. The teaching of ornament had come to represent, for the rising generation of Moderns, the monotonous, unadventurous past.

How could generations of students have meekly tolerated the tedious ritual of drawing the orders of architecture—Greek Doric, Tuscan, Roman Doric, Ionic, Corinthian and Composite? Or learning the significance of guilloches, palmettes, fleurons, diapers, half-drops, scrolls, trophies and the like? A whole vocabulary was to be almost forgotten. Within a decade, knowledge of the syntax of ornament—like knowledge of the Classics—had become superfluous. Clean-cut, positive, Modernism had prevailed. So it seemed.

Many decorative designers of the 1930s borrowed the mannerisms of the Modern Movement[1]. In Britain this practice was rather successful and the muted Modern Movement textiles, wallpapers and carpets of many British artists have weathered the passage of time well (see Plates 11.21, 51). Alastair Morton (1910–63) of Edinburgh Weavers, Carlisle, was a particularly enlightened patron of the British avant-garde, and manufactured textiles designed by a number of Modern Movement artists (see Plates 11.38, 40–1).

In France in the 1930s Jean Lurçat (1892–1966) tried to revive tapestry weaving as an art. But his work, though undoubtedly possessing decorative qualities, manifests the mannerisms of the painting of the time—in particular the bold simplifications of Picasso and Braque—and is only incidentally decorative, unlike that of Alastair Morton's protégés, and for this reason it lies beyond the confines of this book.

But, for all the minor triumphs of decorative art in the 1930s, by the end of the decade the general consensus among the artistically sophisticated was that the designing of decoration was no longer important. It was unlikely ever again to emerge as anything other than the most trivial of the activities associated with architecture and the applied arts. To claim that a design was possessed of decorative—rather than formal—qualities was to dismiss it. Of course a vigorous vernacular or demotic decorative tradition existed. But Modernists, who could often acknowledge the excellent qualities of primitive or folk design, could not recognize merit in the decorated machine-manufactured productions consumed by the proletariat and the bourgeoisie. Modern urban folk art was not to become influential until the 1960s.

In 1939, with the outbreak of the Second World War, the advance of the Modern Movement was halted in Europe. A few years earlier, Germany, under Adolf Hitler's baleful influence, had rejected what it saw as its internationalist, leftist teachings. Walter Gropius and Mies van der Rohe, the two principal practitioners of Bauhaus Modernism, had already fled to the United States. Erich Mendelsohn, another important, though less dogmatic

12.4 LUCIENNE DAY: **Wallpaper. 'Serif'.** From the Modus First Collection. Manufactured by Wallpaper Manufacturers Ltd. (Architects' Department). Late 1950s or early 1960s. Courtesy Arthur Sanderson & Sons Ltd. Archive.

The Modus collection was clearly intended for architects or interior designers with avant-garde taste.

Modernist, after a few successful years in Palestine, settled in the United States in 1941. America was to become the centre of Modern Movement activity.

Sheltered from the European storm, the Modern Movement in exile flourished. Gropius and Mies gathered American disciples around them; the two were apotheosized. The transfusion of major European talent encouraged America to contemplate artistic self-sufficiency. Abstract Expressionism, the first American art movement to exert any international influence, was born in the 1950s.[2]

Abstract Expressionism can be seen as the late and unhappy child of Modernism. Its adherents were opposed to the formal, geometric approach of artists of the 1930s and 1940s. The movement was in its essence romantic. Its exponents—like alchemists seeking to transmute base metal into gold—tried to express the inexpressible with sensuous, capricious paint. But because of its private language and remoteness from ordinary experience, it lacked popular appeal. Its ascendancy as a movement did not endure for long.

Another largely American art movement—Pop Art—took its imagery from sources with which everyone in industrialized nations was familiar—advertising and strip cartoons. As Roy Lichtenstein put it: 'Pop Art looks out into the world.' It is 'anti-contemplative, anti-nuance . . . anti-movement-and light, anti-paint-quality, anti-Zen . . .'[3]

The discovery of a vigorous twentieth-century urban folk culture had an immensely vitalizing effect upon the arts. It was avidly devoured by Pop artists and its influence is still very much with us. Many Pop art painters have become household names.[4] At much the same time that Pop Art came to the fore—the 1960s—Marshall McCluhan popularized the idea that the seemingly ephemeral mass-consumption culture of industrialized society was as worthy of serious analysis as high culture.[5] Commercial art has henceforward been treated with respect.

But by celebrating the demotic culture of industrialized society, Pop artists placed themselves in a position of opposition to orthodox Modernists. They revelled in the decorative qualities of popular art, while Modernists abhorred irrelevant frippery. (Had not Walter Gropius, in 1935, talked of 'liberating' architecture from ornament?) Pop Art helped to modify the intellectual climate. Ornament became again a subject of conversation.

Pop Art, however, was not the only factor involved in the tempering of attitudes towards ornament. In 1936, Nikolaus Pevsner in his *Pioneers of the Modern Movement* (later to be republished as *Pioneers of Modern Design*) had shown that the Gothic Revival, the Arts and Crafts Movement, Art Nouveau, and Jugendstil could all be seen as evolutionary stages in the development of Modernism. Pevsner's arguments are impressively marshalled and meticulously detailed. Fifty years after its publication, his book justly remains a standard work. At the time of its first publication it served as potent Modernist propaganda. As time went on, however, the book was seen as giving a new status to the movements which had preceded the Modern Movement itself. Perverse, laughable Art Nouveau was worth re-examining. The Gothic Revival could be seen as being in the apostolic line of succession which led—via the Arts and Crafts—to the Modern Movement; it was now more than a mere historical aberration which had interrupted the march towards Modernism.

In 1952 came two important exhibitions. One attempted to encapsulate Art Nouveau, while the other provided an as yet unsurpassed documentation of Victorian and Edwardian design. The first of these exhibitions was held at the Zurich Kunstgewerbemuseum; the second at the Victoria and Albert Museum, London—both are commemorated by invaluable catalogues.[6] The new interest in Art Nouveau resulted in four well-documented studies of the subject: Henry F. Lenning's *The Art Nouveau* (1951), Stephan Tschudi

12.5 ANONYMOUS: **Wallpaper. 'Malaga'.** Manufactured by Lightbown Aspinall for Wallpaper Manufacturers Ltd. *c.* 1956. Courtesy Arthur Sanderson & Sons Ltd. Archive.

This comes from the first 'Palladio' sample book described as 'a special range of screen-printed wallpapers for the architect and interior designer . . . for the new architecture of today'. The Palladio range of wallpapers was successfully commercially and artistically. Leading designers were to design for it.

Madsen's *Sources of Art Nouveau* (1956); Peter Selz's and Mildred Constantine's *Art Nouveau. Art and Design at the turn of the century* (1959); and Robert Schmutzler's influential *Art Nouveau*, first published in German in 1962.

The 1950s also saw the publication of a book which, perhaps at an unconscious level, pointed out the inability of orthodox Modernism to satisfy popular aspirations. This was Barbara Jones' *The Unsophisticated Arts*. (Much of her material had appeared earlier in *The Architectural Review*, which often took a somewhat neutral line on Modernism.) Barbara Jones was an accomplished and scholarly illustrator, rather in the Eric Ravillious or Edward Bawden mould. She felt that such naïve arts as canal boat decoration, fairground roundabout painting, tattooing, or weekend riverside bungalow ornament were soon likely to vanish. 'One factor', Barbara Jones observed, 'is constant through all the vernaculars: energy.' Always, there was 'vitality to replace a lack of selection, technique or taste'. Such energy 'lurks in the most vitiated of us, displaying itself in elaborate hair-styles, well-polished shoes, or model-making; some of it only appears on suburban Sundays, diverted from creation to cleaning the car.' *The Unsophisticated Arts* should not, however, be interpreted as being anti-Modernist in tone. Primarily it drew attention—as had George Orwell in his memorable essay on Donald McGill,[7] the designer of risqué seaside postcards—to the protean dynamism of popular art.

In late 1960, the Council of Europe mounted a large exhibition at the Musée d'Art Moderne in Paris called Les Sources du XXᵉ Siècle, les Arts en Europe de 1884 à 1914. The exhibition was commemorated by a splendidly illustrated book written jointly by Jean Casson, Emile Langui and Nikolaus Pevsner which was published in an English edition as *The Sources of Modern Art* in 1962. In his introduction Jean Casson concluded:

> The years of the last quarter of the nineteenth century and the beginning of the twentieth, with their variety of events, their wonderful mixture of ideas, feelings and themes, were assuredly some of the richest and most fruitful in the whole history of the human spirit.

The prelude to the Modern Movement was to be seen with increasing frequency as a heroic age. In the 1960s scholarly studies of Victorian and proto-Modern design proliferated. Alf Bøe, a young Norwegian historian, published his *From Gothic Revival to Functional Form. A Study in Victorian Theories of Design* in 1957. It was a work which was essentially Pevsnerian in its approach and brought to light yet more evidence to confirm the vitality of Victorian design. Inevitably, the Modern Movement's assumption of its superiority over historical tradition was beginning to be questioned. Soon Parnassus would no longer be located at Weimar, or Dessau. Despite its insistent propagandizing—and its intellectual brilliance—the Modern Movement had not succeeded in endearing itself to the public at large. Enthusiasm for it was confined to an informed élite, comprised for the most part of professional architects.

In 1966, the American architect Robert Venturi published *Complexity and Contradiction in Architecture*. In 'Nonstraightforward Architecture: A Gentle Manifesto' he declared his intentions:

> Architects can no longer be intimidated by the puritanically moral language of orthodox Modern architecture. I like elements which are hybrid rather than 'pure', compromising rather than 'clean', distorted rather than 'straightforward', ambiguous rather than 'articulated', perverse as well as impersonal, boring as well as 'interesting', conventional rather than 'designed', accommodating rather than excluding, redundant rather than simple, vestigial as well as innovating,

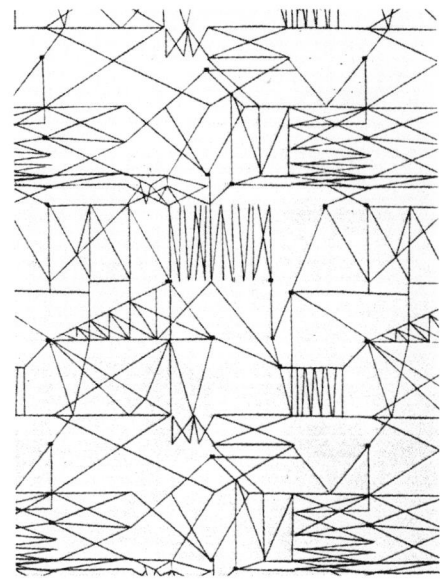

12.6 LUCIENNE DAY: **Furnishing fabric. 'Graphica'.** For Heal & Son. Early 1950s. From Terence Conran, *Printed Textile Design*, 1957.

This design has certain affinities with the work of Paul Klee.

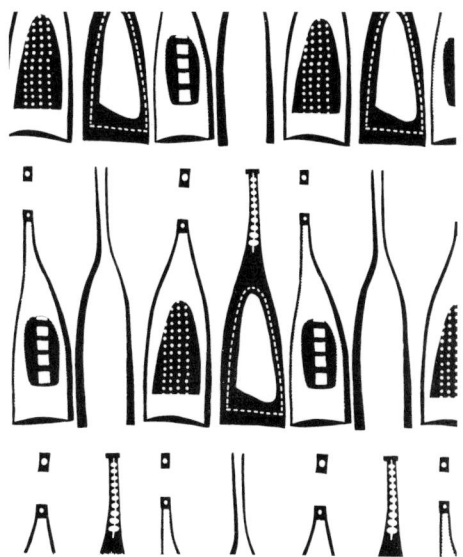

12.7 DAVID BARTLE: **Wallpaper. 'Gandalf'.** From Palladio Collection 9. Manufactured by Arthur Sanderson & Sons Ltd. 1971. Courtesy Arthur Sanderson & Sons Ltd. Archive.

A design which suggests turn-of-the-century ornament by such designers as Henry Van de Velde.

inconsistent and equivocal rather than direct and clear. I am for messy vitality over obvious unity. I include the non sequitur and proclaim the duality.

Complexity and Contradiction in Architecture was, looking back on it, the Ur-text of Post-Modernism. The critic Vincent Scully described the book as 'probably the most important writing on architecture since Le Corbusier's *Vers une Architecture* of 1923'. This may well be the case.

Venturi cites a very wide range of buildings to make his point. He is especially fond of the Mannerist, Baroque and Rococo styles. He comments on the work of many architects—Michelangelo, Hawksmoor, Soane, William Butterfield, Frank Furness, H. H. Richardson, Louis Sullivan, Gaudí, Luytens—not one of whom produced bland buildings. And Hawksmoor, Butterfield, Gaudí and Furness were inclined towards excess, if not vulgarity. Venturi takes ornament in his stride. It is no longer a moral issue.

In *Learning from Las Vegas: the forgotten symbolism of architectural form* (1972), Venturi, in collaboration with Denise Scott Brown and Steven Izenour, assisted on occasions by their Yale students, produced a detailed and percipient study of popular architecture in a brash city. Their ideas are eclectic, partly inspired by Pop Art, and partly derived from semiotics, the study of visual signals and signs, which had blossomed in the 1960s. Historical parallels are drawn: the Arch of Constantine, Rome, is compared with a hoarding advertising Tanya sun-tan oil; the decoration of the Amalienburg Pavilion, Nymphenburg, with the strip-lit Golden Nugget Casino in Las Vegas. Appropriate symbolism—to which ornament may contribute—is seen as an important element in successful architecture.

Classic Modernism, at all events, was now ailing, if not moribund. The era of Post-Modernism had dawned.

Charles Jencks, the architect and critic, discussed the 'death of Modern Architecture' in *The Language of Post-Modern Architecture* (1977). He was not entirely satisfied with the portmanteau term Post-Modern. 'All it admits is ... that certain architects and buildings have moved beyond or counter to modern architecture.' Nevertheless, it was 'precisely this vagueness and implied pluralism' which his title was intended to suggest. The key word is 'pluralism'. Post-Modernism is not, like Purism or Brutalism, a single style. It is generally eclectic and consequently appropriate to our pluralist age. For the foreseeable future, I think, our visual culture will continue to be pluralist. The Modern Movement was essentially anti-pluralist. The time had come for it to be killed off intellectually. Tom Wolfe's *From Bauhas to Our House* (1981), an amusing, vituperative, if not scurrilous, account of the Modern Movement in America, captures the mood. No doubt, one of Pluralism's 'many mansions' will be able to accommodate Modernism as a style. But not, of course, in the manner to which it had become accustomed.

Robert Jensen and Patricia Conway—both architects—supply us with a survey of contemporary developments in the ornamental revival in *Ornamentalism: the new decorativeness in architecture and design* (1982): 'At the heart of the Ornamental movement is an awakening of the long-suppressed decorative impulse and a desire to reassert the legitimate pleasures that flow from that impulse.'

The direction is set firmly. There is no doubt now that ornament will come into its own again. But a kind of stylistic anarchy prevails. Architects make pastiches of the decorated styles, revive vernaculars, and experiment with Classicism—and even advocate pattern-book architecture. The decorative crafts flourish. If diversity is a sign of health, then the applied arts are indeed healthier now than they have been for two generations. Who can predict what will come of this?

12.8 JACK LENOR LARSEN: **Textile. 'Oberon'.** 1969. From *Stil, Trend, Produkt, 10. Stuttgarter Forum Textil-Design*. See Dr Bernd Rau: 'Das Textil-Design in Spannungsfeld der bildenden Künste'.

This is seen by Dr Rau as relating to the work of Gustav Klimt, in particular his Die Erwartung of 1905–9, the mosaic frieze in Josef Hoffmann's Palais Stoclet, Brussels.

12.9 GRAHAM SUTHERLAND: **Printed furnishing fabric.** For Helios Ltd. *c. 1946. From Design '46. Survey of design as displayed at the 'Britain Can Make It' Exhibition*, 1946.

Several of Sutherland's original designs are to be found in the Print Room of the Victoria and Albert Museum.

12.10 *Below* ROBERT SEVANT: **Wallpaper.** For John Line & Sons. For the Festival of Britain, 1951. Victoria and Albert Museum.

This design is based upon the crystalline structure of insulin. Several other designs based on diagrams of crystal structures were exhibited in the Festival of Britain. Dr Helen Megaw, of Girton College, Cambridge, had earlier suggested that crystal structures could be applied to textile design. (See Susan Lambert (editor) *Pattern and Design. Design for the Decorative Arts, 1480–1980*, 1983—catalogue of V and A exhibition.)

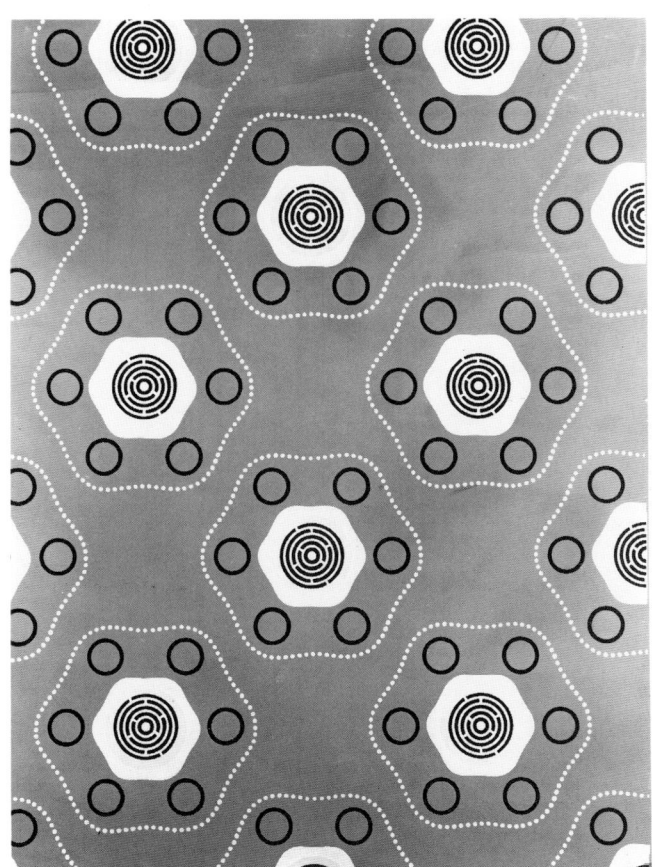

12.11 JOHN MINTON: **Wallpaper. 'Tuscany'.** John Line & Sons, 1951. The Victoria and Albert Museum.

John Minton, the painter and illustrator, was particularly interested in classical themes. Picasso had earlier shown a similar enthusiasm.

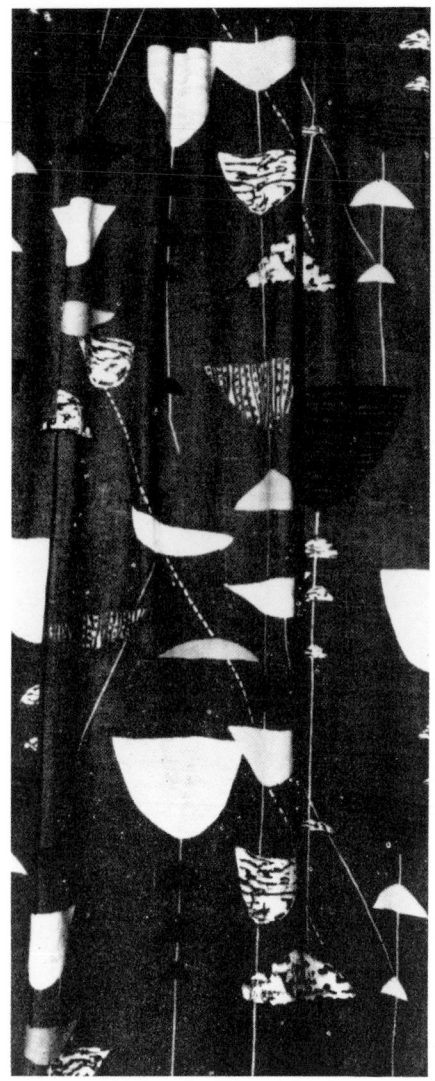

12.12 *Above* LUCIENNE DAY: **Linen. 'Calyx'.** For Heal & Son Ltd. Designed for Robin Day's section of the Festival of Britain, 1951. From Terence Conran, *Printed Textile Design*, 1957.

An 'abstract' design, based presumably upon the calyx—the leaves covering the flower before it opens.

12.13 *Above right* MARGARET HILDEBRAND: **Cotton curtain fabric. 'Atlanta'.** 1955. From *Textildesign 1934–1984 am Beispiel Stuttgarter Gardinen 1984*. (Catalogue of an exhibition held at the Design Center, Stuttgart.)

A design which is seemingly based upon an enlarged photograph of woven cotton.

12.14 FRANK LLOYD WRIGHT: **Wallpaper. 'Design 706'.** Hand printed for the 'Taliesin Line'. Schumacher & Co., New York, 1956. The Victoria and Albert Museum.

In his earliest buildings Wright exhibited a liking for geometrical decoration, particularly in stained-glass windows. His late wallpaper designs were not successful commercially.

12.15 *Right* Lucienne Day: **Linen. 'Spectators'.** For Heal & Son Ltd. Early 1950s. From Terence Conran, *Printed Textile Design*, 1957.

Simple representation of people watching, probably, a sporting event. The figures are reminiscent of those of the sculptor Barbara Hepworth.

12.16 *Right* Alexander Girard: **Screen-printed linen.** For the Herman Miller Furniture Co. Ltd. *c.* 1957. From Terence Conran, *Printed Textile Design*, 1957.

Girard, an architect, was particularly interested in native American design. 'Fabric design is not easel painting or illustrating . . . realistic centralized motifs. . . .' declared Girard, 'should be avoided.'

12.17 *Below* Dorothy Smith: **Experimental print on paper.** 1950s. From Terence Conran, *Printed Textile Design*, 1957.

Dorothy Smith was a second-year student in the Textile Department of the Central School of Art and Design, London, when this design was executed.

12.18 *Below right* Eduardo Paolozzi: **Screen print.** 1950s. From Terence Conran, *Printed Textile Design*, 1957.

This design is reminiscent of Paolozzi's collages of the early 1950s. Paolozzi taught textile design at the Central School of Art and Design from 1949 to 1955.

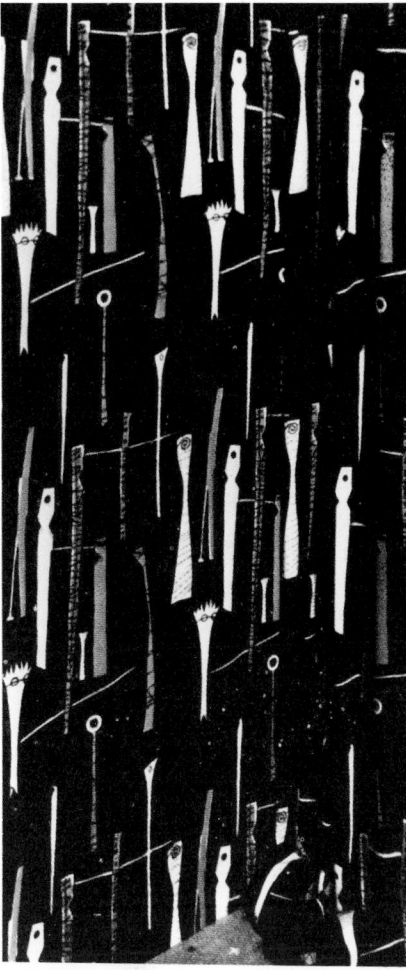

12.19 DAVID GENTLEMAN: **Wallpaper. 'Andalucia'.** From Palladio Collection 3. Manufactured by Lightbown Aspinall, for Wallpaper Manufacturers Ltd. 1958. Courtesy Arthur Sanderson & Sons Ltd. Archive.

David Gentleman is a well-known graphic designer and illustrator. There has long been a demand for pictorial wallpapers—in the nineteenth century Walter Crane was a leading exponent of this genre. Raoul Dufy also designed pictorial wallpapers.

12.21 ERIC THOMAS: **Wallpaper. 'Harbour'.** From Palladio Collection 3. Manufactured by Lightbown Aspinall, for Wallpaper Manufacturers Ltd. 1958. Courtesy Arthur Sanderson & Sons Ltd. Archive.

This design is reminiscent of the work of painters of the St Ives School, in particular Christopher Wood and Alfred Wallis.

12.20 *Left* ROGER NICHOLSON: **Wallpaper. 'Montacute'.** From Palladio Collection 3. Manufactured by Lightbown Aspinall, for Wallpaper Manufacturers Ltd. 1958. Courtesy Arthur Sanderson & Sons Ltd. Archive.

Palladian architecture and Renaissance statuary. This design makes an interesting contrast with Terence Conran's less formal architecture in Plate 12.23.

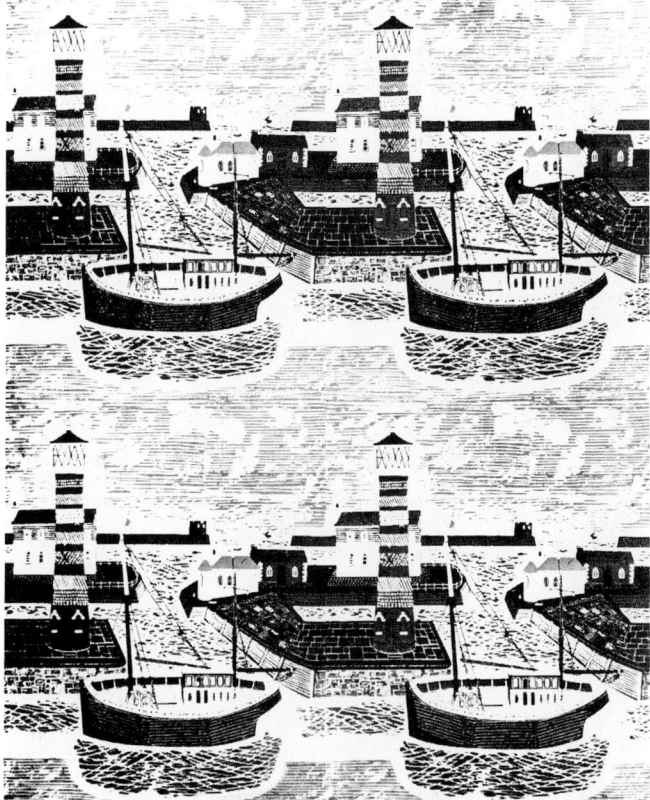

12.22 WILLIAM SCOTT: **Furnishing fabric. 'Nearing Circles'.** Woven wool and rayon. Manufactured by Edinburgh Weavers, Carlisle. 1962. The Victoria and Albert Museum.

12.23 *Above* TERENCE CONRAN: **Wallpaper. 'Portal'.** From the Modus First Collection. Manufactured by Wallpaper Manufacturers Ltd. (Architects' Department). Late 1950s or early 1960s. Courtesy Arthur Sanderson & Sons Ltd. Archive.

Conran's light-hearted architecture is mildly reminiscent of the drawing style of Paul Klee.

12.24 ALISTAIR MORTON: After a painting by Victor Vasarely. **Furnishing fabric. 'Osta'.** Woven. Manufactured by Morton Sundour Ltd. 1962. The Victoria and Albert Museum.

Vasarely is one of the principal painters associated with the Op Art movement. His work attracted particular attention during the 1960s.

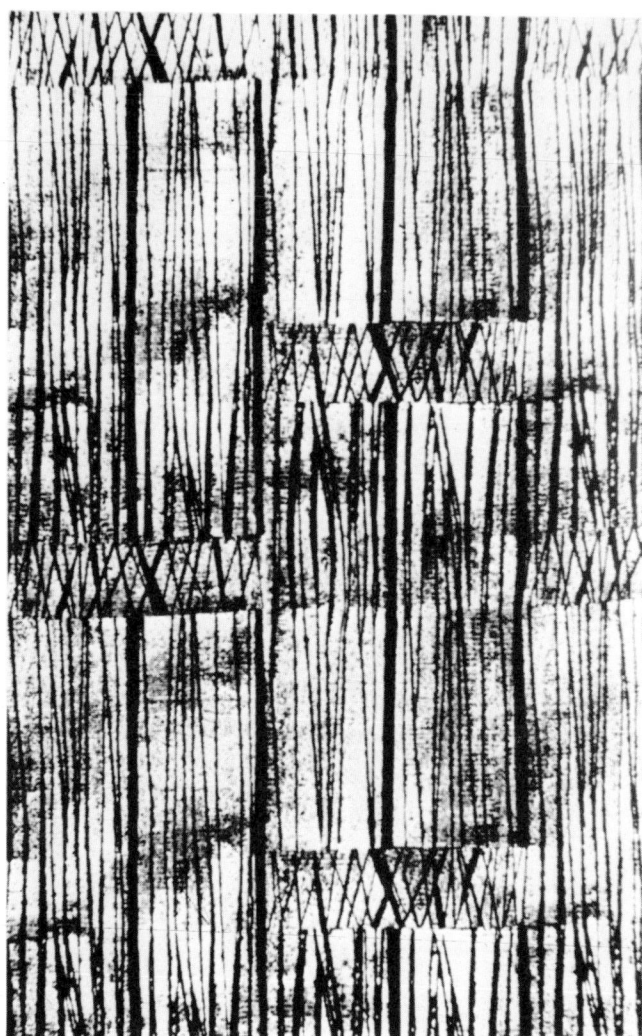

12.25 *Above left* WOLF BAUER: **Textile. 'Katja'.** 1971. From *Stil, Trend, Produkt, 10. Stuttgarter Forum Textil-Design*. See Dr Bernd Rau: 'Das Textil-Design in Spannungsfeld der bildenden Künste'.

This design is seen by Dr Rau as relating to the work of the painter Jean Dubuffet.

12.26 *Above* KUNO FISCHER: **Textile. 'Utrecht'.** 1966. From *Stil, Trend, Produkt, 10. Stuttgarter Forum Textil-Design*. See Dr Bernd Rau: 'Das Textil-Design in Spannungsfeld der bildenden Künste'.

This is seen by Dr Rau as relating to Paul Klee's painting *Air-tsu-dni* of 1927.

12.28 JEREMY TALBOT: **Wallpaper. 'Boulevard'.** From Palladio Collection 8. Manufactured by Wallpaper Manufacturers Ltd. 1968. Courtesy Arthur Sanderson & Sons Ltd. Archive.

12.27 EDWARD POND: **Wallpaper. 'Berkley'.** From Palladio Collection 8. Manufactured by Wallpaper Manufacturers Ltd. 1968. Courtesy Arthur Sanderson & Sons Ltd. Archive.

12.29 JOHN WILKINSON: **Wallpaper. 'Main Street'.** From Palladio Collection 9. Manufactured by Arthur Sanderson & Sons Ltd. 1971. Courtesy Arthur Sanderson & Sons Ltd. Archive.

This design ingeniously combines two painting styles—Op Art and Pop Art. The five-pointed star was particularly popular with Pop artists.

12.30 *Below* PETER JONES: **Wallpaper. 'Solaria'.** From Palladio Collection 9. Manufactured by Arthur Sanderson & Sons Ltd. 1971. Courtesy Arthur Sanderson & Sons Ltd. Archive.

This design is slightly reminiscent of the compositions composed of Art Déco architectural motifs painted by Roy Lichtenstein.

12.31 *Below right* ANN BERWICK: **Wallpaper. 'Calyx'.** From Palladio Collection 9. Manufactured by Arthur Sanderson & Sons Ltd. 1971. Courtesy Arthur Sanderson & Sons Ltd. Archive.

In its organization this design recalls late nineteenth-century floral ornament, although the designer is more concerned with overall effect than botanical accuracy.

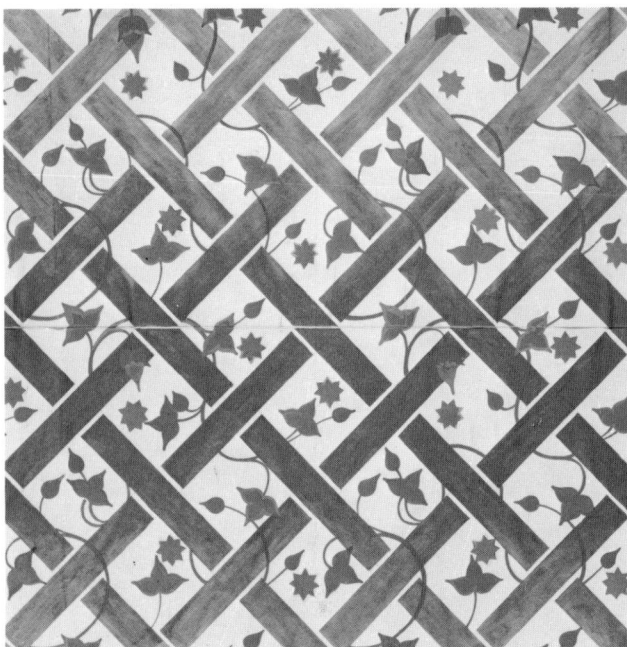

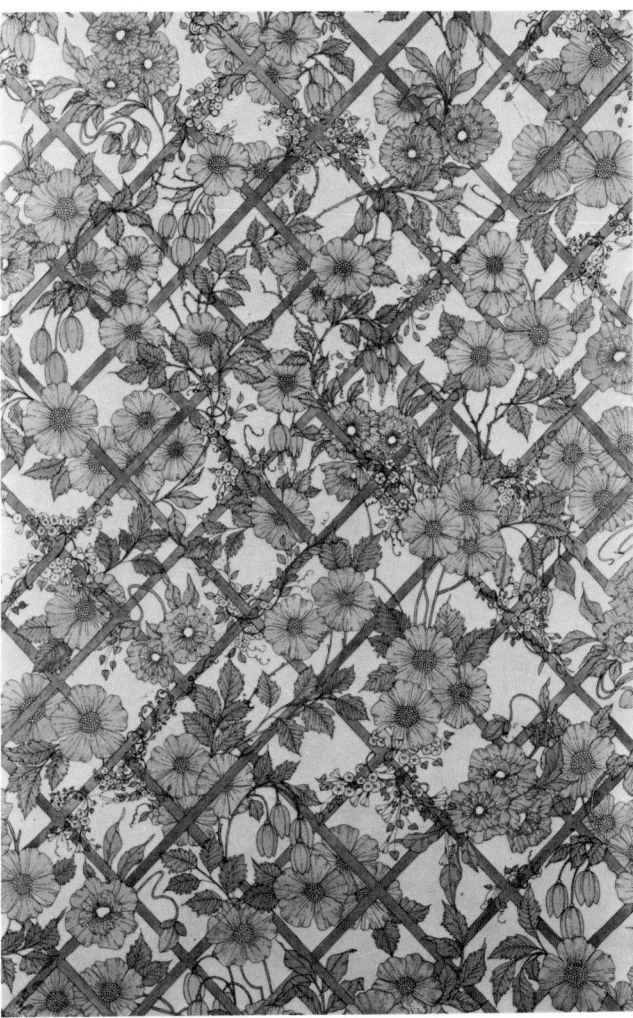

12.32 *Top left* JOHN WILKINSON: **Wallpaper. 'Apollo'.** From Palladio Collection 9. Manufactured by Arthur Sanderson & Sons Ltd. 1971. Courtesy Arthur Sanderson & Sons Ltd. Archive.

12.33 *Top right* PETER JONES: **Wallpaper. 'Sikhara'.** From Palladio Collection 9. Manufactured by Arthur Sanderson & Sons Ltd. 1971. Courtesy Arthur Sanderson & Sons Ltd. Archive.

12.34 *Above* ANTHONY LITTLE: Design for wallpaper, gold paint and gouache. Produced by Osborne & Little Ltd., London. 1975. The Victoria and Albert Museum.

12.35 JENNIE RHODES: **Wallpaper.
'Sugar and Spice'.** For Shand Kydd.
c. 1976. The Victoria and Albert Museum.

12.36 *Right* AUDREY LEVY: **Wallpaper.
'Pebble'.** From Palladio Collection No. 3,
c. 1959. Manufactured by Lightbown
Aspinall for Wallpaper Manufacturers
Ltd. From the Sanderson Archive.

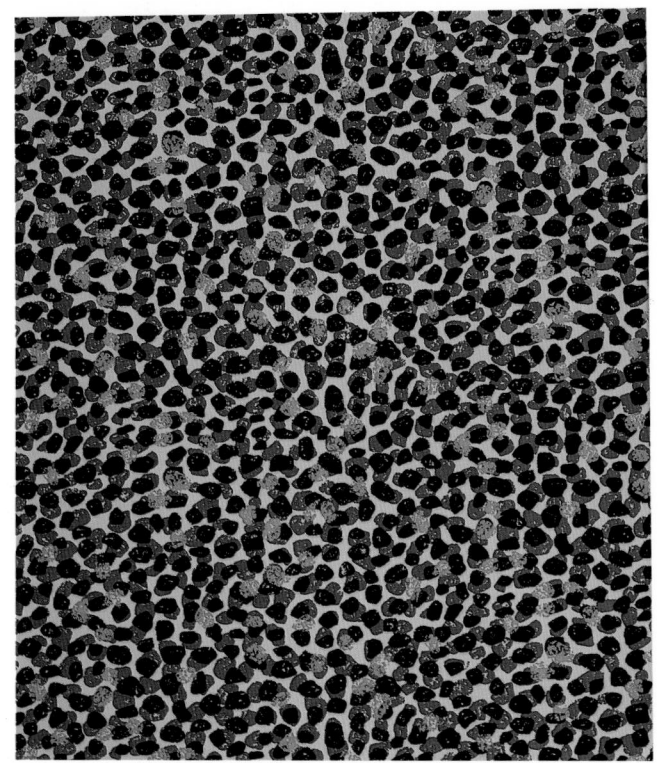

12.37 ANONYMOUS: **Wallpaper. 'Synchro'.** From Palladio
Collection No. 7, 1964/5. Wallpaper Manufacturers Ltd. From
the Sanderson Archive.

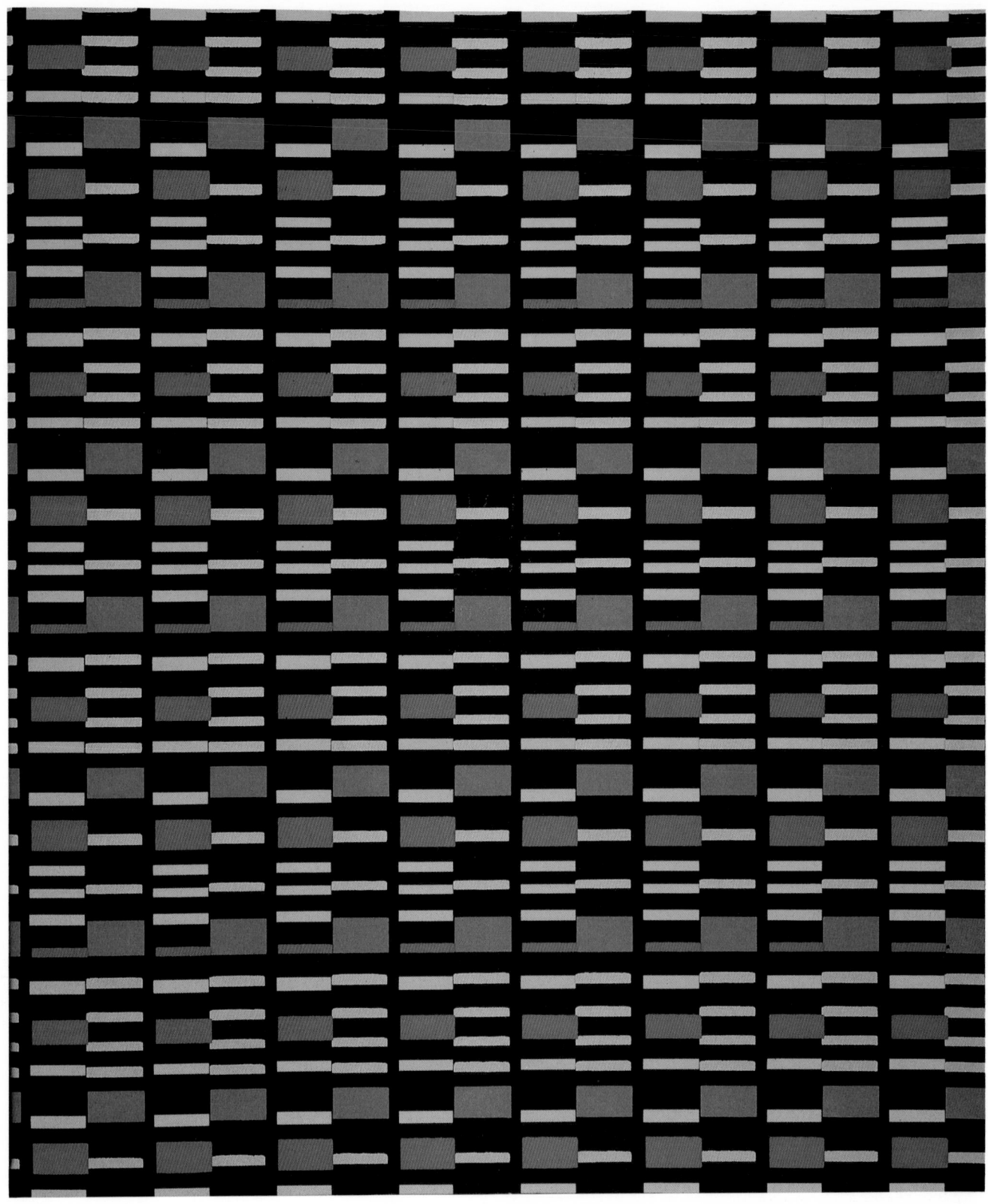

12.38 Humphrey Spender: **Wallpaper. 'Pannus'.** From the
Palladio Magnus Collection, early 1960s. Manufactured by
Lightbown Aspinall for Wallpaper Manufacturers Ltd. From the
Sanderson Archive.

12.39 NATALIE GIBSON: **Wallpaper. 'Venessa'.** From Palladio Collection No. 9, 1971. Manufactured by Arthur Sanderson & Sons Ltd. From the Sanderson Archive.

12.40 KIM MACCONNEL: **Decorative painting—The Loop.** Acrylic and glitter epoxy on canvas. 243.8 cm × 233.7 cm. *Dekor.* An Exhibition curated by Raman Schlemmer, 1980.

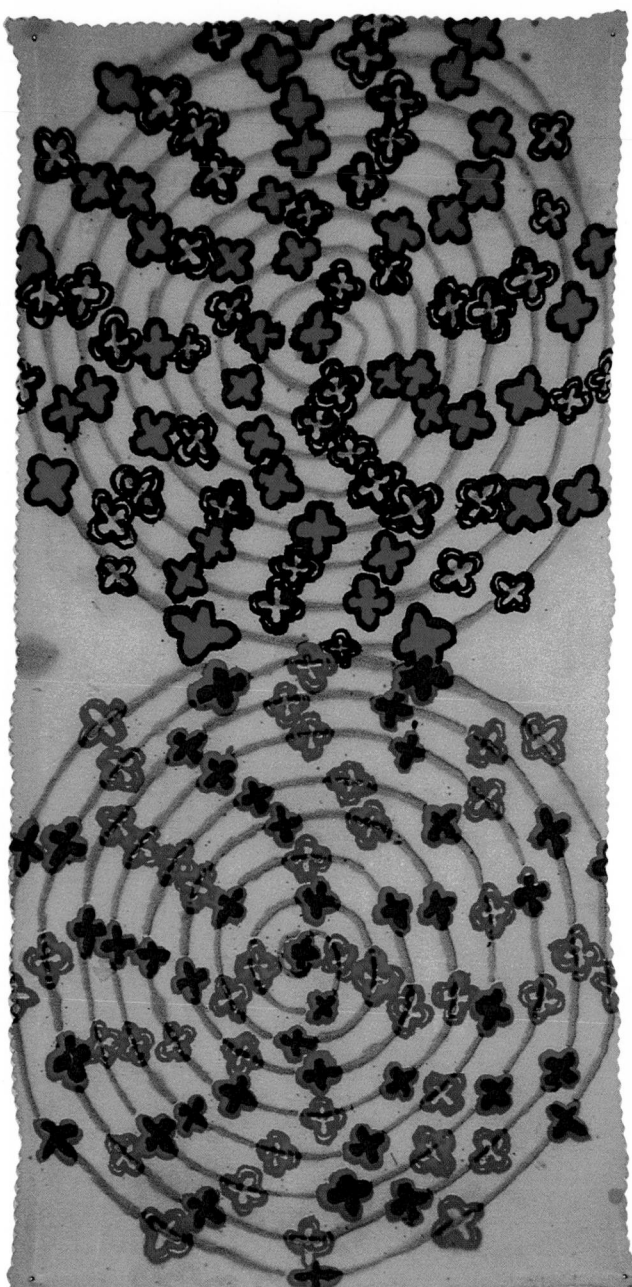

12.41 ZANDRA RHODES: **'Spiral Flowers'.** Print on crepe, 1962. Courtesy of Zandra Rhodes.

Designed while a student at the Royal College of Art.

12.42 ZANDRA RHODES: **'Cactus Volcano'.** Print on silk chiffon, 1945. Courtesy of Zandra Rhodes.

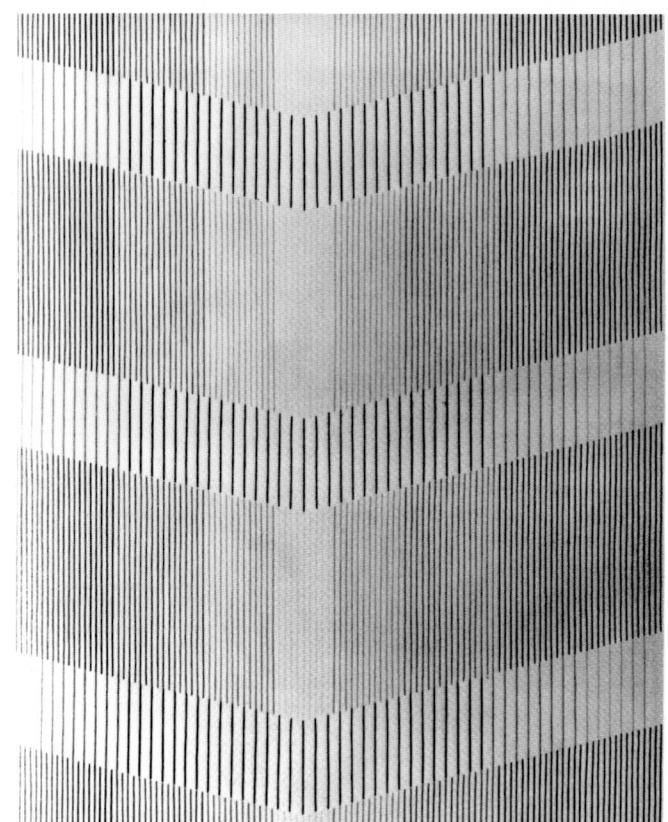

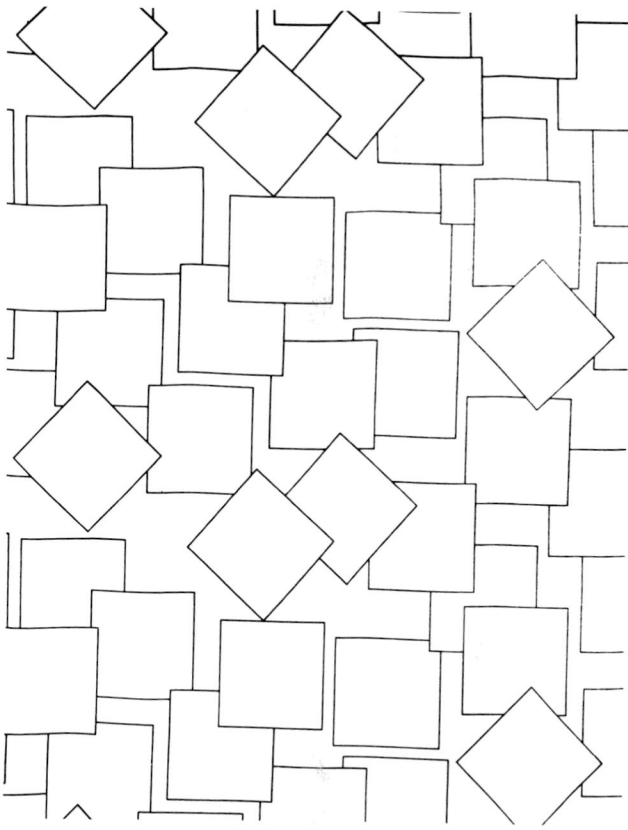

12.43 *Above* Antoinette de Boer:
Cotton curtain fabric. 'Quibble'. 1980.
From *Textildesign 1934–1984, am Beispiel Stuttgarter Gardinen 1984*. (Catalogue of an exhibition held at the Design Center, Stuttgart.)

Antoinette de Boer, with her austere, cerebral designs has held fast to the visual ideals of the Modern Movement.

12.44 *Above right* Antoinette de Boer:
Printed polyester and cotton curtain fabric. 'Tirana'. 1983. From *Textildesign 1934–1984, am Beispiel Stuttgarter Gardinen 1984*. (Catalogue of an exhibition held at the Design Center, Stuttgart.)

12.45 Eduardo Paolozzi: **Design for tapestry for Cleish Castle.** 1972–3. From *Eduardo Paolozzi. Private Vision—Public Art*, 1984. (Catalogue of an exhibition held at the Architectural Association, London.)

This and two other similar tapestries, together with fibre glass ceiling panels, were commissioned by the architect, Michael Spens, for his restoration of Cleish Castle. In 1975 Paolozzi was awarded the Saltire Society Award—a biennial prize for art and architecture in Scotland—for his work for Cleish.

Notes

Encyclopedias of Ornament

1. The majority of Jombert's suites of ornament had been issued much earlier by the publishers Nicolas Langlois and Jean Mariette, whose stocks of copper plates Jombert had acquired.

2. When giving evidence before the Parliamentary Select Committee of Arts and Manufactures in 1835, J. B. Papworth, first Director of the Government School of Design, praised Percier and Fontaine's work, adding: 'Europe is greatly indebted to these artists.'

3. Senefelder succeeded in producing coloured lithographs in 1818. (Electrina Stuntz, Baroness von Freyburg, had produced a two-coloured lithograph in 1810.) See *Homage to Senefelder. Artists' Lithographs from the Felix H. Man Collection*. Catalogue of an exhibition held at the Victoria & Albert Museum, 1971.

4. Among those involved in the museum venture were Matthew Digby Wyatt, J. B. Waring, James Fergusson, A. H. Layard and C. J. Richardson.

5. E. H. Gombrich, *The Sense of Order*, 1979.

Nature and Ornament

1. Sir James Hall in his *Essay on the Origin, History and Principles of Gothic Architecture* (1797) had put forward the seductive idea that medieval builders had simply copied the forms of crude huts made from willow branches and the like.

2. Originally published in German as *Kunstformen der Natur* (1899–1904) this work had a considerable influence on Jugendstil design.

3. See Stefan Tschudi Madsen, *Sources of Art Nouveau*, 1956, and *Art Nouveau*, 1967; Robert Schmutzler, *Art Nouveau*, 1964. The other main works on Art Nouveau are listed in the bibliography.

Geometrical Ornament

1. See *The Letters of Sir William Jones*. Edited by Garland Cannon, 1970.

2. See K. A. C. Cresswell, *Early Muslim Architecture. Umayyads, AD 622–750 . . . 1932–40*, this edition 1969. See also Cresswell, *A Short Account of Early Muslim Architecture*, 1958.

3. See Samuel Lysons, *An Account of Roman Antiquities discovered at Woodchester in the County of Gloucester*, 1797.

4. See Jurgis Baltrušaitis, *Le moyen âge fantastique. Antiquités et exotismes dans l'art gothique*, 1955.

5. See Jean Bony, *The English Decorated Style. Gothic architecture transformed, 1250–1350*, 1979.

6. See Peter Ward-Jackson, *Some Main Streams and Tributaries in European Ornament from 1500 to 1750*, Victoria and Albert Museum Bulletin, Vol. III, Nos. 2–4, April, July and October 1967.

7. Father Dominique Douat published Truchet's ideas in his *Methode pour faire une infinité de desseins differens, avec des carreaux mi-parties de deux couleurs par une ligne diagonale: ou Observations du Pere Dominique Douat . . . présenté par le Reverend Pere Sebastien Truchet . . .*, 1722. E. H. Gombrich also discusses this book in *The Sense of Order. A Study in the psychology of decorative art*, 1979.

8. Identical copies of this work sometimes bear the title *An Essay on Ornamental Design . . .*, 1844.

9. J. M. Schleiden's *Principles of Scientific Botany*, 1849, which first appeared in German in 1846, gives a comprehensive and well-illustrated account of cellular structures. This work was very widely known. Schleiden was co-originator—with Theodor Schwann—of the cell theory. Bourgoin was also known to be a keen admirer of the mathematician Augustin Cournot (1810–77).

10. Laura L. Plaisted's important *Handwork and its place in Early Education* first appeared in 1913.

11. Other similar devices for producing mechanical designs mentioned by Alabone include the 'harmonograph', the 'cycloidotrope' for magic lantern display, and the 'elliptic pendulum'.

12. Dynamic symmetry has a certain affinity with Le Corbusier's proportional system as expounded in his *Le Modulor* of 1951 (first English edition, 1954).

13. Namely Richard Allen, John Ernest, Malcolm Hughes, Colin Jones, Michael Kidner, Peter Lowe, James Moyes, David Saunders, Geoffrey Smedley, Jean Spencer, Jeffrey Steele and Gillian Wise Ciobataru.

14. This was jointly produced by a group of designers—Keith Albarn, Jenny Miall Smith, Stanford Steele and Dinah Walker.

Eclecticism

1. Goethe's *Farbenlehre* ('Theory of Colour') of 1810, which is concerned not merely with colour but with the wider phenomenon of perception, did not appear in English until 1840. There is no evidence in Phillips' book that he knew it.

2. This passage also appears in Jones' *An Attempt to Define the Principles which should regulate the Employment of Colour in Architecture, with a few words on the present necessity of an Architectural Education on the part of the public*, 1852.

3. *The Chromolithograph* began life as *Nature and Art*, which was first published in June 1866. It became *The Chromolithograph* in November 1867 and ceased publication in 1869.

4. Among the principal exponents of Queen Anne domestic architecture were Maurice B. Adams, Basil Champneys, Owen W. Davis, W. Edis, Ernest George, E. W. Godwin, Ernest Newton, George Gilbert Scott, J. J. Stephenson and T. H. Wyatt. Philip Webb also fell under the spell of Queen Anne.

5. See 'Ornamentation considered as High Art' in *Journal of the Royal Society of Arts*, Vol. XIX, 1871. The paper was read on 23 December 1870.

6. In this connection the names of Jacques Ignace Hitorff (1792–1867), Henri Labrouste (1801–75), César Daly (1811–93) and Jules Saulnier (1828–1900) should be mentioned. Viollet-le-Duc also frequently designed in an eclectic manner.

Orientalism

1. I have mentioned only the most important books. Probably the earliest British scholar who had any serious interest in Oriental art was Archbishop Laud (1573–1635), Fellow of St John's College, Oxford. Laud founded the Chair of Arabic in Oxford and in 1640 gave his magnificent collection of some 1300 manuscripts to the Bodleian Library. Among Laud's gifts were Mughal miniatures and a collection of Indian ragamala paintings from the Deccan.

Ragamala paintings depicted the personifications and conventional associations of the modes (ragas) of North Indian music. But though vigorous and colourful, they were probably thought of as no more than curiosities. See Herbert J. Stooke and Karl Khandalawala, *The Laud Ragamala Miniatures. A study in Indian painting and music*, 1953.

2. See Nicholas Cooper, 'Indian Architecture in England 1780–1830', *Apollo*, August 1970.

3. Earlier Spanish works which deal with the Alhambra include those of Bermúdez de Pedraga (1608), Juan Alvarez de Colemar (1741) and Juan de Echeverría (1764). Eighteenth-century British writers who discuss Moorish architecture include Richard Twiss, author of *Travels through Portugal and Spain*, 1775, and Henry Swinbourne, author of *Travels through Spain*, 1779.

4. Curiously, Murphy gave the book, besides the ordinary date, its Hegira date of 1228, perhaps in deference to long-dead Moorish builders. Publication was completed in 1816, two years after Murphy's death.

5. See the account of Owen Jones' 'Alhambra Court' in M. Digby Wyatt, *Views of the Crystal Palace and Park, Sydenham*, 1854.

6. Jones' *Alhambra* is surpassed only by F. Ongania's massive and partially photographic documentation of the Basilica of San Marco in Venice, which was completed in the 1880s.

7. There was already a group of brilliant scholars at work there, studying ancient remains. The group included Bonomi, James Burton, Haliburton, Fox Strangways, Hay, Humphreys, Linant and Wilkinson.

8. This is the criticism of Max von Berchem, the early twentieth-century authority on Islamic architecture. It is reproduced in K. A. C. Cresswell's monumental *Bibliography of the Architecture, Arts and Crafts of Islam*, 1961.

9. Bourgoin's *Les Elements de l'Art Arabe* has been re-issued by Dover Publications of New York, and is still the most complete study of geometrical decoration. Unfortunately the text was not considered worthy of inclusion.

'The Cult of Japan'

1. See Richard Storry, *A History of Modern Japan*, 1960.

2. See 'The Japanese Court', *The Gentleman's Magazine*, ccxii, 1862. Quoted by J. Mordaunt Crook, *William Burges and the High Victorian Dream*, 1981.

3. The title is the late Charles Handley-Read's. It is taken from an exhibition which he and his wife Lavinia conceived of early in 1969 entitled 'The Aesthetic Movement and the Cult of Japan'. The exhibition was mounted by the Fine Art Society, Bond Street, London, in October 1972, after the Handley-Reads' deaths. J. Mordaunt Crook, op. cit., supplies a sympathetic memoir of Handley-Read.

4. See Rutherford Alcock, *Catalogue of Works of Industry and Art, sent from Japan*, 1862.

5. The British collection which Dresser took to Japan also seems to have been lost. Were it to be found it would provide an incomparable record of British art manufactures of the 1870s.

6. See *Time and Tide . . . twenty-five letters to a working man of Sunderland*, 1867, letter VI, 'The Corruption of Modern Pleasure—The Japanese Jugglers'.

7. One of two contributions to *Lectures on Art, delivered in*

support of the Society for the Protection of Ancient Buildings (1882). Morris may well have been echoing the ideas of G. G. Zerffi, whose *Manual of the Historical Development of Art* (1876) contained a chapter called 'Ethnology in its Bearing on Art', which is discussed in Chapter Eight.

8. See Elizabeth Aslin, 'The Furniture Designs of E. W. Godwin', *Victoria and Albert Museum Bulletin*, October 1967, Vol. III, No. 4.

9. For an account of this piece see: *The Aesthetic Movement and the Cult of Japan*, The Fine Art Society, 1972, cat. no. 298. (The anonymous account is by Simon Jervis.)

10. See Mark Girouard, *The Victorian Country House*, 1971, and *The Aesthetic Movement and the Cult of Japan*, op. cit.

11. See *The Aesthetic Movement and the Cult of Japan*, op. cit., cat. no. 324.

12. George Ashdown Audsley and his brother William James Audsley appear to have practised as architects from about 1860 to 1883. They designed numerous Liverpool churches, including the Presbyterian Church of Wales, Princes Avenue, 1865, and the Synagogue, Princes Road, 1875. They also designed the Church of Edward the Confessor, Philadelphia. See J. Quentin Hughes, *Liverpool*, 1969.

13. In his *The Art of Chromolithography* (1883) Audsley demonstrates the way in which a chromolithographic image is built up in progressive stages.

'Primitivism'

1. See Jean-Jacques Rousseau, 'Discourse on Inequality'. This is discussed by Claude Lévi-Strauss in 'Jean-Jacques Rousseau. Founder of the Science of Man', which is reproduced in *Structural Anthropology*, Vol. II, 1976.

2. The Société d'Anthropologie was founded in Paris in 1859. The earliest British university lecturer in anthropology was Edward Burnett Tylor, author of *Researches into the Early History of Mankind and the Development of Civilization*, 1865, and *Primitive Cultures*, 1871.

3. W. G. Collingwood, the father of the philosopher R. G. Collingwood, was Ruskin's secretary for many years.

4. Charles Wiener, *Pérou et Bolivie, récit de voyage suivi d'études archéologiques et ethnographiques et de notes sur l'écriture et les langues des populations indiennes* (1880).

5. See F. G. Dumas and L. De Fourcaud, *Revue de L'Exposition Universelle* (n.d.).

6. See Frank Cundall, editor, *Reminiscences at the Colonial and Indian Exhibition*, 1886.

7. See Pierron, 'Le Village Pahouin (Gabon-Congo)' in *Revue de L'Exposition Universelle* (n.d.).

8. Pol-Neveux, 'Le Village Sénégalais' in *Revue de L'Exposition Universelle* (n.d.).

9. The dates of publication are October 1900, February 1901, March 1902, October 1903 and March 1905.

10. General Pitt-Rivers (1827–1900) had given his extensive collection of primitive artefacts and examples of technology—including a large number of weapons—to Oxford University in 1883.

11. Claude Lévi-Strauss sees evidence of split representation in the early art of Asia and of the Americas. Haddon was interested in the same phenomenon.

12. See in particular Laura L. Plaisted, *Handwork and its Place in Early Education* (1913).

Notes

The Arts and Crafts Movement

1. It is worth pointing out that *Wood Carving* comes from John Hogg's *The Artistic Crafts*, a series of 'technical handbooks' which were edited by W. R. Lethaby. The series furnishes a comprehensive record of Arts and Crafts practice and theory. Other handbooks in the series include: Mrs Archibald H. Christie on embroidery and tapestry; Douglas Cockerell on bookbinding; Edward Johnston on writing and illumination; Talbert Hughes on dress design; Henry Wilson on silverwork etc.

2. 'William Morris and His Art' in *Art Journal* Easter Annual. I have also quoted this passage in my essay 'William Morris and Victorian Decorative Art' which appeared in *William Morris and Kelmscott*, The Design Council, 1981.

Art Déco—The Evolution of a Style

1. The interior of Olbrich's studio in the Ernst Ludwigs Haus, the building which he designed for the artists' colony in Darmstadt, is illustrated in the publisher Wasmuth's *Architektur von Olbrich*, I–III, 1901–14, Vol. I. It can also be seen in Ian Latham, *Joseph Maria Olbrich* (1980), although the reproduction is small.

2. See E. F. Steckler, *Josef Hoffmann. Das Architektonische Werk*, 1982. The relief bears a passing resemblance to stage settings by Edward Gordon Craig and Adolph Appia, though it probably antedates their experiments with abstract scenery.

3. The Wiener Werkstätte was a craft studio founded in 1903 by the banker Fritz Wärndorfer, with Hoffmann and Moser as artistic directors. It went into liquidation in 1932. Wärndorfer had visited England and had been particularly impressed by C. R. Ashbee's Guild of Handicraft.

4. See *Reports on the Present Position and Tendencies of the Industrial Arts, as indicated at the International Exhibition of Modern Decorative and Industrial Arts, Paris, 1925* (n.d.).

5. Just as Robert Schmutzler in his *Art Nouveau* writes of 'proto-Art Nouveau', one could equally well speak of 'proto-Art Déco'. Some of Olbrich's work might fall into this category, particularly his Hochzeitsturm (Wedding Tower), built in Darmstadt in 1905–6 by the Grand Duke Ernst Ludwig to celebrate his marriage to his second wife. Hoffmann and Olbrich were by no means the only exponents of the Viennese proto-Art Déco style as a list of the principal Viennese designers of the 1900s will demonstrate. These include: G. O. Czeschka (1878–1960); Rudolf Kalvach (b. 1883); Berthold Löffler (1874–1960); Emanuel Joself Margold (b. 1889); Koloman Moser (1868–1918); Emil Orlik (1870–1932); Dagobert Peche (1887–1923); Michael Powolny (1871–1954); Otto Prutscher (1880–1949); Alfred Roller (1864–1935); Oskar Strnad (1879–1935); and Eduard Wimmer (1882–1961). Less well known, but nevertheless accomplished, designers working in the same idiom include: Max Benirschke, Lotte Frömel-Fochler, Josef Frank, Philipp Häusler, Adolf Holub, Heinrich Kathrein, Arnold Nechansky, Otakar Novotny, Robert Oerley, Cesar Popovits, Carl Witzmann, and Emmy Zweybrück-Prochaska. In the 1920s the architect Josef Urban exported the Viennese style to the United States and made rather a success of it there.

Modernism

1. Its leaders were: Henry van der Velde, Peter Behrens, Hans Poelzig, Tony Garnier, Frank Lloyd Wright, Adolf Loos and Josef Hoffmann. Among the younger generation were: Walter Gropius (1883–1969), Ludwig Mies van der Rohe (1886–1969), Erich Mendelsohn (1887–1953), Le Corbusier (1887–1966) and Hans Scharoun (1893–1972). Holland produced Willem Marinus Dudok (1884–1974) and Gerrit Rietveld (1888–1964). Brazil's Oscar Niemeyer (b. 1907), who once worked with Le Corbusier, partially abandoned the ideals of the Modern Movement in the 1950s. Of British exponents of the style one should include: Wells Coates (1895–1958), E. Maxwell Fry (b. 1899), Raymond McGrath (1903–77) and F. R. S. Yorke (1906–62). The firms of Connell, Ward and Lucas, as well as Tecton, should also be mentioned.

2. See 'Ornament in Architecture', *Engineering Magazine*, III, August 1892. Reprinted in *Kindergarten Chats and Other Writings*, 1947.

3. See Paul Klee, *Pedagogical Sketchbooks*. Introduction and translation by Sibyl Moholy-Nagy (n.d.).

4. Early works dealing with the rudiments of ornament include: William Dyce, *The Drawing Book of Government School of Design* (1842–3); Gaetano Ferri, *Corso Elementare di Ornato* (1854); Christopher Dresser, *The Art of Decorative Design* (1862); Jules Bourgoin, *Théorie de l'Ornement* (1873). Of the many late nineteenth-century writers dealing with the subject are Walter Crane, Lewis F. Day, Frank Jackson, H. Mayeux. Eugène Grasset's *Méthode de Composition Ornementale* is possibly the most comprehensive of all the works.

5. It is worth pointing out the extraordinary similarity between Read's statement and a remark of Edward Burne-Jones: 'The more materialistic science becomes the more angels shall I paint.'

6. Chernikov was a lecturer at the Leningrad Institute for Highway Engineering. See his *Ornament kompozutzionno-klassicheskiye postroyenya*, 1930.

1940 to the Present—Revival?

1. These artists include: Edward Bawden (b. 1903); F. Gregory Brown (1887–1948); Marion Dorn (1889–1964); Duncan Grant (1885–1978); Ronald Grierson (b. 1901); Ashley Havinden (1903–73); Eileen Hunter; Betty Joel (b. 1896); Ethel Mairet (1872–1952); Enid Marx (b. 1902); Brian O'Rorke (1901–74); Marian Pepler; Marianne Straub (b. 1909); Riette Sturge Moore; and Hans Tisdall (formerly Aufseeser) (b. 1910). Major figures in the Modern Movement in Britain also tried their hand at decorative design. These include Serge Chermayeff (b. 1900); Barbara Hepworth (1903–75); Raymond McGrath (1903–77); E. McKnight Kauffer (1890–1954); Paul Nash (1889–1946); and Ben Nicholson (b. 1894). Another artist who experimented with decorative design in the early 1930s was Francis Bacon (b. 1909), who besides designing entire interior schemes, also designed a number of rugs. Other designers who should be mentioned include: Bernard Adeney, John Aldridge, T. Bradley, H. J. Bull, T. Cockerill, E. Dean, Nancy Ellis and Sheila Walsh. See *Thirties. British art and design before the war*. Catalogue of an exhibition at the Hayward Gallery, 1979.

2. The principal painters who were associated with Abstract Expressionism in the United States are: William Baziotes (b. 1912); James Brooks (b. 1906); Sam Francis (b. 1923); Arshile Gorky (1905–48); Adolph Gottlieb (1903–73); Philip Guston (b. 1913); Grace Hartigan (b. 1922); Franz Kline (1910–62); Willem de Kooning (b. 1904); Robert Motherwell (b. 1915); Barnett Newman (1905–70); Jackson Pollock (1912–56); Mark Rothko (1903–70); Theodoros Stamos (b. 1922); Clifford Still (b. 1904); Bradley Walter Tomlin (1899–1953), and Jack Tworkov (b. 1900). See *The*

New American Painting, a catalogue of an exhibition held at the Tate Gallery in 1959.

3. See 'What is Pop Art?', *Art News*, Vol. 62, No. 7, November 1963. Reproduced also in *Roy Lichtenstein*, catalogue of an exhibition at the Tate Gallery, London, 1968.

4. American artists who can be associated with the Pop movement include: Jasper Johns (b. 1930); Roy Lichtenstein (b. 1923); Claes Oldenburg (b. 1929); Robert Rauschenberg (b. 1925); Andy Warhol (b. 1930?); among British artists are Peter Blake (b. 1932); Derek Boshier (b. 1939); Patrick Caulfield (b. 1936); David Hockney (b. 1937); Allen Jones (b. 1937); Peter Phillips (b. 1939); Max Shepherd (b. 1936); Norman Toynton (b. 1939); Brian Wright (b. 1937). Italian artists include: Valerio Adami (b. 1935); Enrico Baj (b. 1924); Dino Buzzati; Lucio del Pezzo (b. 1933); Piero Dorazio (b. 1927); Giosetta Fioroni and Silvio Pasotti.

5. It is interesting to note that even in the early 1950s Eduardo Paolozzi (b. 1924) had begun collecting strip cartoons and commercial illustrations.

6. See *Um 1900. Art Nouveau und Jugendstil*, Zurich, Kunstgewerbemuseum, June–September 1952; and *Victorian and Edwardian Decorative Arts*, The Victoria and Albert Museum, October 1952.

7. See *Horizon*, February 1942.

Bibliography

Encyclopedias and General Works

Ackerman, Phyllis: *Wallpaper, its History, Design and Use*, London 1926.

The Age of Neoclassicism. The Royal Academy and the Victoria and Albert Museum, London. The Arts Council of Great Britain, 1972, London 1972.

Amaya, Mario: *Art Nouveau*, London 1966.

Art Nouveau from Germany, London 1972.

Audsley, George Ashdown: *The Art of Chromolithography*, London 1883.

Audsley, W. & G.: *Outlines of Ornament in the Leading Styles*, London 1881.

Baldry, A. Lys: *Modern Mural Decoration*, London 1902.

Ballantine, James: *Essay on Ornamental Art as Applicable to Trade and Manufactures*, London 1847.

Batchelder, E. A.: *The Principles of Design*, Chicago 1904.

Batchelder, E. A.: *Design in Theory and Practice*, New York 1914 (3rd ed.).

Bayley, Stephen (ed.): *Taste. An exhibition about values in design*, London 1983. A book accompanying the Boilerhouse Project exhibition.

Benton, Tim and Charlotte, and Sharp, Dennis: *Form and Function. A sourcebook for the history of architecture and design, 1890–1939*, London 1975.

Beuth, Peter: *Forbilder für Fabrikazten und Handwerker*, Berlin 1830.

Bind, L.: *Münchener Muster-Sammlung für Kunstler, Gewerbtreibende und Laien*, Munich 1862.

Blanc, C.: *Art in Ornament and Dress*. Tr. from the French, London 1877.

Blanc, Charles: *Grammaire des Arts du Dessin, Architecture, Sculpture, Peinture*, Paris 1867.

Blashfield, J. M.: *A Selection of Vases, Statues, Busts, etc. from Terra Cottas*, London 1857.

Boase, T. S. R.: *English Art, 1800–1870*, Oxford 1959.

Bøe, Alf: *From Gothic Revival to Functional Form. A study in Victorian theories of design*, Oslo 1957.

Boetticher, C.: *Ornamenten-Buch*, Berlin 1856.

Boetticher, C. E. Von: *Ornamenten-Buch*, Berlin 1834–44.

Bossert, H. Th.: *Das Ornamentwerk*, Berlin 1924.

Bossert, H. Th.: *Ornament in Applied Art*, New York 1924.

Bossert, H. Th.: *Peasant Art in Europe*, Berlin 1926.

British Association for the Advancement of Science: *Portfolio of lithographic drawings of the principal articles of manufacture exhibited at the Birmingham Exposition 1849*, Birmingham 1849.

British Parliamentary Papers. Industrial Revolution—Design. Shannon, Ireland, 1968–70. 4 vols. (Contains material relating to the Schools of Design, from 1837 to 1852.)

Brown, F. P.: *South Kensington and its Art Training*. With a foreword by Walter Crane, London 1912.

Brown, W. N.: *A History of Decorative Art*, London 1903.

Burty, Philippe: *Chefs d'Oeuvre of the Industrial Arts*, London 1869.

Cassou, Jean, Langui, Emile, and Pevsner, Nikolaus: *The Sources of Modern Art*, London 1962.

Charvet, L.: *Enseignement de l'Art Décoratif*, Paris (1889).

Chevreul, M. E.: *De la loi du contraste simultané des couleurs et de l'assortiment des objets colorés considérés d'après cette loi*, Paris 1889.

Choisy, Auguste: *Histoire de l'Architecture*, Paris 1899.

Christie, A. H.: *Traditional Methods of Pattern Designing. An introduction to the study of decorative art*, Oxford 1910.

Clouzot, Henri: *Le Papier Peint en France de XVIIe au XIXe siècle*, Paris 1931.

Clouzot, H., and Follot, Ch.: *Histoire du Papier Peint en France*, Paris 1935.

Collins, Peter: *Changing Ideals in Modern Architecture, 1750–1950*, London 1965.

Conner, Patrick (ed.): *The Inspiration of Egypt. Its influence on British artists, travellers and designers, 1700–1900*, Brighton 1983. Exhibition catalogue.

Constantine, Mildred (ed.), and Selz, Peter: *Art Nouveau. Art and design at the turn of the century*, New York 1959.

Coulson, Anthony J.: *A Bibliography of Design in Britain, 1851–1970*, London 1979.

Cremona, Italo: *Il Tempo dell' Art Nouveau*, Florence 1964.

Curl, James Stevens: *The Egyptian Revival, an introductory study of a recurring theme in the history of taste*, London 1982.

Debes, Dietmar: *Das Ornament, Wesen und Geschichte. Ein Schriftenverzeichnis.* A classified bibliography listing some 2026 books and articles. Leipzig 1956.

Dickson, T. Elder: *The Elements of Design*, London 1933.

Dolmetsch, H.: *The Historic Styles of Ornament*, London 1898.

Dolmetsch, H.: *Der Ornamenten Schatz*, Stuttgart *c.* 1910 (4th ed.).

Dresser, Christopher: *Development of Ornamental Art*, London 1862.

Dupont-Auberville, M.: *L'Ornement des Tissus*, Paris 1877.

Ehresmann, Donald L.: *Applied and Decorative Arts. A bibliographic Guide to basic reference works, histories and handbooks*, Littleton, Colorado 1977.

Encyclopédie d'Architecture. Revue mensuelle des travaux publics et particuliers, Paris 1872–7.

Entwistle, E. A.: *The Book of Wallpaper*, London 1954.

Entwistle, E. A.: *The Literary History of Wallpaper*, London 1960.

Entwistle, E. A.: *Wallpapers of the Victorian Era*, Leigh-on-Sea 1964.

Evans, Joan: *Pattern. A Study of Ornament in Western Europe from 1180 to 1900*, Oxford 1931 (reissued New York 1975).

Evans, Joan: *Style in Ornament*, Oxford 1950.

Exhibition of Victorian and Edwardian Decorative Arts, Catalogue, London 1952.

Exhibition catalogue, Victoria and Albert Museum.

Fantastic & Ornamental Drawings. A selection of drawings from the Kaufman Collection, Portsmouth 1969.

Farr, Dennis: *English Art, 1870–1940*, Oxford 1978.

Fischer, Marianne: *Katalog der Architektur und Ornament-stichsammlung. Teil 1 Baukunst England*, Berlin 1977.

Gedde, Wa(lter): *A Booke of Sundry Draughtes, principaly serving for glaziers and not impertinent for plasterers, and Gardiners*, London 1615 (facsimile London *c.* 1900).

Gelis-Didot, P., and Laffillée, H.: *La Peinture Décorative en France du XI au XVI Siècle*, Paris *c.* 1875.

Glazier, R.: *Historic Textile Fabrics*, London 1923.

Glazier, R.: *A Manual of Historic Ornament*, London 1899.

Goblet d'Alviella: *The Migration of Symbols*, with an Introduction by George Birdwood, London 1894 (1st ed. in French 1891).

Gombrich, E. H.: *The Sense of Order. A study in the psychology of decorative art*, London 1979.

Gonse, Louis: *L'Art Ancien à l'Exposition de 1878*, Paris 1879.

(The Great Exhibition, 1851): *Royal Commission for the Great Exhibition of the Works of Industry of All Nations, 1851*, London 1851–3.

(The Great Exhibition, 1851) Wyatt, M. Digby: *The Industrial Arts of the Nineteenth Century*, London 1851–3.

Greysmith, Brenda: *Wallpaper*, London 1976.

Griesbach, C. B.: *Historic Ornament: A Pictorial Archive*, New York 1975.

Gruner, L.: *The Decorations of the Garden-Pavilion in the Grounds of Buckingham Palace*, London 1846.

Gruner, L.: *Fresco Decorations and Stuccoes of Churches and Palaces in Italy, during the fifteenth and sixteenth centuries*, London 1854 (2nd ed.).

Gruner, L.: '*Lo Scaffale*'; or, presses in the sacristy of the church of Sta Maria delle Grazie at Milan, London 1859–60.

Gruner, L.: *Specimens of Ornamental Art*, London 1850.

Gruner, L.: *The Terra-Cotta Architecture of North Italy (XIIth-XVth centuries)*, London 1867.

Guadet, J.: *Eléments et Théorie de l'Architecture. Cours professé à l'Ecole Nationale et Spéciale des Beaux Arts*, Paris n.d.

Guilmard, D.: *Les Maîtres Ornemantistes. Dessinateurs, peintres, architectes, sculpteurs et graveurs*, Paris 1880. Facsimile reprint Amsterdam 1968.

(Gustav Klimt) Nebehay, Christian M.: *Gustav Klimt. Dokumentation*, Vienna 1969.

Habert-Dys, J.: *Fantaisies Décoratives*, Paris n.d. (*c.* 1900).

Hamlin, A. D. F.: *A History of Ornament, Ancient and Medieval*, London 1916.

Hamlin, A. D. F.: *A History of Ornament, Renaissance and Modern*, London 1923.

(Handley-Read, Charles): *Design, 1860–1960*, London 1968. Includes Handley-Read on High Victorian Design.

(Handley-Read, Charles, and Handley-Read, Lavinia): *Victorian and Edwardian Decorative Art. The Handley-Read Collection*, London 1972. Exhibition catalogue, The Royal Academy of Arts, ed. Simon Jervis.

Hargreaves, B.: *A First Book of Pattern Design with some Examples of Historic Craft Work*, London 1924.

Hatton, R. G.: *Design*, London 1925 (3rd ed.).

Hatton, R. G.: *A Text-Book of Elementary Design*, London n.d. (*c.* 1900) (3rd ed.).

Hatton, R. G.: *Principles of Decoration*, London 1925.

Hay, D. R.: *The Laws of Harmonious Colouring*, Edinburgh 1836 (3rd ed.).

Henry, Françoise: *The Book of Kells, with a study of the Manuscript*, London 1974.

Higgins, W. Mullingar: *The House Painter; or Decorator's Companion*, London 1841.

Hittorff, J. I.: *Restitution de Temple d'Empedocle à Selinonte ou l'architecture polychrome chez les Grecs*, Paris 1851.

Hoffmann, Julius, Jr.: *Bilderschatz für das Kunstgewerbe. Eine internationale Rundschau*, Stuttgart 1892.

Honour, Hugh: *Neo Classicism*, Harmondsworth 1968.

Hulme, F. Edward: *The Birth and Development of Ornament*, London 1893.

Hulme, F. Edward: *Principles of Ornamental Art*, London 1875.

(Humbert, Claude): *Ornamental Design. Europe, Africa, Asia, The Americas, Oceania*, London 1970.

Images et Imaginaires d'Architecture. Dessin, peinture, photographie, arts graphiques, théâtre, cinéma en Europe aux XIXe et XXe Siècles, Paris 1984.

Exhibition catalogue.

(The International Exhibition, London 1862) Waring, J. B.: *Masterpieces of Industrial art and Sculpture at the International Exhibition, 1862*, London 1863.

Jackson, Frank G.: *Decorative design*, London 1888.

Jackson, Frank G.: *Theory and Practice of Design*, London 1893 (new ed.).

Jervis, Simon: *The Penguin Dictionary of Design and Designers*, Harmondsworth 1984.

Jessen, P.: *Katalog der Ornamentstichsammlung der staatlichen Kunstbibliothek*, Berlin 1939.

Jessen, P.: *Ornamentstich*, Berlin 1920.

Jombert, Charles Antoine: *Repertoire des Artistes, ou Recueil de Compositions d'Architecture et d'Ornemens Antiques ct Modernes de Toute Espece. . . .* Paris 1765.

Jones, O.: *The Grammar of Ornament*, London 1856.

Jones, O.: *The Leading Principles in Composition of Ornament of every period*, London n.d.

Jones, Owen, and Humphrey, Henry Noel: *Illuminated Books of the Middle Ages*, London 1844.

Justema, William: *Pattern. A Historical Panorama*, London 1976.

Lacroix, Paul, and Sere, Ferdinand: *Le Moyen Age et la Renaissance, Histoire et Description des Moeurs et Usages, du Commerce et de l'Industrie, des Sciences, des Arts, des Littératures et des Beaux Arts en Europe*, Paris 1848–51 (5 vols).

La Décoration Intérieure Allemande et les Métiers d'Art à l'Exposition de Bruxelles, 1910, Stuttgart n.d.

Lambert, Susan (ed.): *Pattern and Design. Designs for the decorative arts 1480–1980. With an index to designers' drawings in the Victoria and Albert Museum*, London 1983.

Leith, Samuel (ed.): *The Tradesman's Book of Ornamental Designs*, London 1847.

Lewis, Philippa, and Darley, Gillian: *Dictionary of Ornament*, London 1985.

MacClelland, Nancy: *Historic Wallpapers*, Philadelphia 1924.

Macdonald, Stuart: *The History and Philosophy of Art Education*, London 1970.

Mackie, T. C. Campbell: *Pattern*, London 1928.

Martel, C.: *The Principles of Form in Ornamental Art*, London *c.* 1870.

(Maskell, Rev. W.): *The Industrial Arts*, London 1876.

Mayers, Frederick J.: *Carpets, Designs & Designing*. Benfleet 1934.

Meurer, M.: *Italienische Majolica-fliesen aus dem Ende des fünfzehnten und Anfang des sechszehnten Jahrhunderts*, Berlin 1881.

Meyer, F. S.: *A Handbook of Ornament*.

Revised by Hugh Stannus, London 1896 (3rd ed.).

Miles, Walter: *Designs for Craftsmen*, New York 1962.

Minton, 1798–1910, London 1976. Exhibition catalogue.

Mirow, Gregory: *A Treasury of Design for Artists and Craftsmen*, New York 1969.

Nichols, George Ward: *Art Education Applied to Industry*, New York 1877.

Nicol, J. W.: *Brush-Drawing*, London 1900.

Oman, C. C.: *Catalogue of Wall-Papers*, London 1929. Catalogue of the Victoria and Albert Museum collection.

Oman, C. C., and Hamilton, J.: *Wallpapers*, London 1982.

(Paris Exhibition 1844): *Exposition des Produits de l'Industrie Française en 1844. Rapport du Jury Central*, Paris 1844.

(Paris Universal Exhibition 1889): *Revue de l'Exposition Universelle de 1889*, Paris n.d.

Percier, C., and Fontaine, P. F. L.: *Recueil de Décorations Intérieures, comprenant tout ce qui a rapport à l'ameublement*, Paris 1812.

Petrie, W. M. Flinders: *Decorative Patterns of the Ancient World*, London 1930.

Petrie, W. M. Flinders: *Egyptian Decorative Art*, London 1895.

Pevsner, Sir Nikolaus: *Studies in Art, Architecture and Design. Vol. II, Victorian and after*, London 1968.

Pfnor, Rodolphe: *Motifs d'Ornements pour Roses-Rosaces, Médaillons, Fonds, et Panneaux circulaires des XVI, XVII, XVIII siècles*, Paris 1876.

Pfnor, Rodolphe: *Ornementation Usuelle de toutes les époques dans les arts industriels et en architecture*, Paris 1866–8.

Phillips, George: *Rudiments of Curvilinear Design*, London 1839.

Physick, John, and Darby, Michael: *'Marble Halls'. Drawings and Models for Victorian Secular Buildings*, London 1973. Exhibition catalogue, Victoria and Albert Museum.

Pollen, J. H.: *Ancient and Modern Gold and Silver Smith's Work in the South Kensington Museum*, London 1878.

Polygraphica Curiosa. The book of initial letters and ancient alphabets for ornamental purposes, London 1844.

The Practical Teacher's Art Monthly, London 1898–1904.

Racinet, M. A.: *L'Ornement Polychrome*, Paris 1869–83 (2 vols).

Raoul-Rochette, M.: *Choix de Peintures de Pompei*, Paris 1867.

Redgrave, Gilbert E. (ed.): *Outlines of Historic Ornament*, London 1884.

Redgrave, Richard: *Manual of Design*, London n.d. (1876).

Redgrave, Richard: *Reports of the Juries*.

Exhibition of the works of industry of all nations 1851, London 1852 (contains Redgrave's *Supplementary Report on Design*).

Rhead, G. Woolliscroft: *The Principle of Design*, London 1905.

Rheims, Maurice: *L'Art 1900, ou le style Jules Verne*, Paris 1965.

Richardson, C. J.: *Studies of Ornamental Design*, London 1851.

Riegl, A.: *Spätromische Kunstindustrie*, this edition Vienna 1927.

Riegl, A.: *Stilfragen*, Vienna 1893.

Robinson, J. C.: *Studies of Ornamental Design*, London 1851.

Robinson, J. C.: *Catalogue of the Various Works of Art forming the Collection of Matthew Uzielli*, London 1860.

Robinson, J. C.: *The Treasury of Ornamental Art*, London c. 1856.

Rock, Daniel, Rev.: *Textile Fabrics*, London 1876. A South Kensington Museum Art Handbook.

Rock, Daniel, Rev.: *Textile Fabrics; a descriptive catalogue*, South Kensington Museum, London 1870.

Roger-Marx: *La Décoration et les Industries d'Art à l'Exposition Universelle de 1900*, Paris 1901.

Russell Taylor, John: *The Art Nouveau Book in Britain*, London 1966.

Sano, Masao: *Printed Textiles of the 20th Century*, Osaka 1980 (3 vols).

Sano, Takahiko (ed.): *British Textile Design in the Victoria and Albert Museum*, London 1980 (3 vols).

Sano, Takahiko (ed.): *Wallpaper Design in the Deutsches Tapetenmuseum, Kassel*, Tokyo 1980.

Schinkel, Karl Friedrich: *Sammlung von Möbel-Entwurfen*, Berlin 1862.

Schmutzler, Robert: *Art Nouveau*, London 1964.

Schwartz, P. R., and de Micheaux, R.: *A Century of French Fabrics, 1850–1950*, Leigh-on-Sea 1964.

Scott, W. Bell: *The Ornamentist*, London 1845.

Selz, Peter, and Constantine, Mildred (eds): *Art Nouveau. Art and design at the turn of the century*, New York 1959.

Semper, G.: *Der Stil in den technischen und tektonischen Kunsten, oder praktische Aesthetik*, Frankfurt/Munich 1860–3 (2 vols).

Serra, J. (ed.): *El Consultor del Ornamentista tratado teorico y practico de pintura decorativa*, Barcelona n.d. (1888).

Shaw, Henry: *The Encyclopedia of Ornament*, London 1842.

(Silver Studio): *A London Design Studio 1880–1963. The Silver Studio Collection*, London 1980. Exhibition catalogue.

Sims, Reed & Fogg Ltd (booksellers): *Ornament. Catalogue 41. A collection of books and original designs*, London 1982. Compiled by Stuart Durant.

Smith, Allan: *Fabric Printing*, London 1953.

(Soden-Smith, R. H.): *A List of Works on Ornament in the National Art Library*, London 1883 (2nd ed.).

Sparrow, Walter Shaw (ed.): *The Modern Home. A book of British domestic architecture for moderate incomes*, London n.d. (1906, or after).

Speltz, Alexander: *The Coloured Ornament of all Historical Styles*, Leipzig n.d.

Stafford, Maureen, and Ware, Dora: *An Illustrated Dictionary of Ornament*, New York 1974.

Stephenson, C., and Suddards, F.: *A Text Book dealing with Ornamental Design for Woven Fabrics*, London 1897.

Sugden, Alan Victor, and Edmondson, John Ludlam: *A History of English Wallpaper, 1509–1914*, London (1925).

Taylor, E. R.: *Elementary Art Teaching*, London 1893.

Tschudi Madsen, S.: *Art Nouveau*. Tr. R. I. Christopherson, London 1967.

The Turn of a Century, 1885–1910. Art Nouveau-Jugendstil Books, Harvard 1970. Exhibition catalogue.

Turnor, Reginald: *Nineteenth Century Architecture in Britain*, London 1950.

Victorian Architectural Source Books, London 1973.

Victorian Church Art, London 1971. Exhibition catalogue, Victoria and Albert Museum.

Victorian and Edwardian Decorative Arts, London 1952.

Viollet-le-Duc, E.: *L'Art Russe*, Paris 1877.

Ward, James: *Colour Harmony and Contrast for the use of art students, designers, and decorators*, London 1910 (3rd ed.).

Ward, James: *Elementary Principles of Ornament*, London 1890.

Ward, James: *Historic Ornament*, London 1897 (2 vols).

Ward, James: *The Principles of Ornament* (ed. George Aitchison), London 1892 (4th ed. 1899).

Ward, James: *Progressive Design for Students*, London 1902.

Waring, J. B.: *A Record of my Artistic Life*, London 1873.

Weinreb, Ben (bookseller): *Various catalogues*, London 1961 to the present.

Weitbrecht, C.: *Ornamenten Zeichnungs-Schule*, Stuttgart 1852.

Whittick, Arnold: *Symbols for Designers*, London 1935.

Wilde, Oscar: *Essays and Lectures*, London 1908.

Wilkinson, Sir J. Gardner: *On Colour and on the Necessity for a General Diffusion of Taste among all Classes*, London 1858.

Woods, Christie (ed.): *Sanderson 1860–1985*, London 1985. Exhibition catalogue.

Wornum, Ralph N.: *Analysis of Ornament*, London 1856. Contains extensive bibliographies.

Wornum, Ralph N.: *Catalogue of Ornamental Casts in the Possession of the Department; Third Division, The Renaissance Styles*, London 1854.

Wyatt, Matthew Digby: *Notices of Sculpture in Ivory*, London 1856.

Yapp, G. W.: *Art Industry. Furniture, Upholstery, and House-Decoration*, London n.d. (c. 1875).

Zahn, Wilhelm: *Ornamente aller klassischen Kunstepochen*, Berlin 1831–43.

Nature and Ornament

Art Studies from Nature, as Applied to Design: for the use of architects, designers and manufacturers. Reprinted from the *Art Journal*, London 1872.

Baker, R. T.: *The Australian Flora in Applied Art*, Part I, Sydney 1915.

Baldwin, Muriel F.: *Plant Forms in Ornament. A selective list of references in the libraries of New York City. (Bulletin of the New York Public Library)*, New York 1933.

Barrett, W. A.: *Flowers and Festivals for the Floral Decoration of Churches*, London 1868.

Bentley, W. A., and Humphreys, W. J.: *Snow Crystals*, New York 1931.

Binet, R.: *Esquisses Décoratives*, Paris c. 1905.

(Blossfeldt, Karl): *Karl Blossfeldt, photographs*, Oxford 1978.

Blossfeldt, K.: *Urformen der Kunst*, Berlin 1928.

Blossfeldt, K.: *Wundergarten der Natur*, Berlin 1932.

Butterfield, L. P.: *Floral Forms in Historic Design mainly from objects in the Victoria & Albert Museum but including examples from designs by William Morris and C. F. A. Voysey*, London 1922.

Clark, Ernest E.: *A Handbook of Plant-Form*, London 1904.

Day, Lewis Foreman: *Nature and Ornament*, London 1908–9 (2 vols).

Day, Lewis Foreman: *Nature in Ornament*, London 1902 (3rd ed.).

Dresser, Christopher: *The Art of Decorative Design*, London 1862.

Dresser, Christopher: 'On the Relation of Science and Ornamental Art', London 1857. (Abstract of a paper.)

Dresser, Christopher: *The Rudiments of Botany*, London 1859.

Dresser, Christopher: *Unity in Variety, as deduced from the vegetable kingdom*, London 1859.

Durant, Stuart: *Aspects of the Work of Dr Christopher Dresser, 1834–1904, Botanist, Designer and Writer*, 1973. An unpublished thesis for the Royal College of Art, London.

(Dyce, W.): *The Drawing book of the Government School of Design*, London 1842–3.

Eckmann, Otto: *Neue Formen. Dekorative Entwürfe für die Praxis*, Berlin 1897.

Escofet, Y. C.: *Pavimentos Artisticos*, Barcelona n.d. (*c.* 1900). Tile designs by leading Barcelona 'modernists'.

Favart, Emile: *Flowers and Plants from Nature*, Nottingham n.d.

Ferri, G.: *Corso Elementare di Ornato tratto dal Naturale*, Macerata 1854.

(Finsterlin, Hermann): *Hermann Finsterlin*, Munich 1968. Exhibition catalogue.

Foord, J.: *Decorative Flower Studies. For the use of Artists, Designers, Students and Others*, London 1901.

Fraipont, G.: *Application de la Forme à l'Espace à Décorer*, Paris *c.* 1905.

Fraipont, G.: *Décorations Florales*, Paris n.d. (1904).

Grasset, Eugène: *Méthode de Composition Ornementale*, Paris 1896. 2 vols.

Grönwoldt, Ruth: *Art Nouveau Textil-Dekor um 1900*, Stuttgart 1980. Exhibition catalogue.

Guimard, H.: *Le Castel Béranger*, Paris 1898.

(Haeckel, Ernst) Bölsche, Wilhelm: *Haeckel, his Life and Work*, London 1906.

Haeckel, Ernst: *Kunstformen der Natur*, Leipzig 1899–1904.

Haité, G. C.: *Plant Studies for Artists, Designers, and Art Students*, London 1886.

How to Draw Floral and Vegetable Forms. 96 studies from nature, London n.d. (*c.* 1870).

Hulme, F. Edward: *Plants. Their natural growth and ornamental treatment*, London 1874.

Hulme, F. Edward: *A Series of Sixty Outline Examples of Freehand Ornament*, London n.d. (1870s).

Hulme, F. Edward: *A Series of Sketches from Nature of Plant Form*, London 1868.

Hulme, F. Edward: *Suggestions in Floral Design*, London 1878.

Irving, Henry: *Flowers and Plants for Designers and Schools*, London 1907.

Janus, H.: *Baumeister Natur*, Stuttgart 1953.

Kirkwood, Esther J. G.: *Plant and Flower Forms*, London 1922.

Klickmann, Flora: *Fruit and Flower Studies. A book for amateur artists*, London 1914.

Klinger, J., and Anker, H.: *La Ligne Grotesque et ses Variations dans la Décoration Moderne*, Paris *c.* 1900.

Kuijper, J.: *De plant in de historische stijlen en decoratieve kunst*, The Hague 1910.

Lilley, A. E. V., and Midgley, W.: *A Book of Studies in Plant Form*, London 1898.

Lindley, John: *The Symmetry of Vegetation*, London 1854.

Lyongrun, Arnold: *Der moderne Stil*, Leipzig 1899.

Lyongrun, Arnold: *Neue freie Dekorationsmotive entwickelt aus dem Tier- und Pflanzenreich*, Leipzig 1899.

Meheut, M.: *Etude de la Mer. Faune et flore de la manche et de l'océan.* Texte par M.-P. Verneuil, Paris 1924 (new ed.).

Meheut, M.: *Etudes d'Animaux*, Paris n.d. (*c.* 1905).

Meurer, M.: *Vergleichende Formenlehre des Ornamentes und der Pflanze*, Dresden 1909.

Mucha, Alphonse Marie: *Documents Décoratifs*, Paris 1902.

(Obrist, Hermann): *Hermann Obrist. Wegbereiter der Moderne*, Munich 1968. Exhibition catalogue.

Page, I.: *Guide for Drawing the Acanthus, and every description of ornamental foliage*, London 1840.

Pettigrew, J. Bell: *Design in Nature*, London 1908 (3 vols).

Plauszewski, P.: *Herbier ornemental*, Paris 1885. (Photographs of plants intended as a pattern book.)

Pugin, A. Welby: *Floriated Ornament*, London 1849 (2nd ed. 1875).

Quénioux, G.: *Eléments de Composition Décorative*, Paris 1912.

Richter, H. Davis: *Floral Art, Decoration and Design.* Foreword by Frank Brangwyn, London 1932.

Rowe, William: *Flora and Fauna Design Fantasies*, New York 1976.

Ruprich-Robert, V.-M.-C.: *Flore Ornementale*, Paris 1866.

Ruskin, John: *The Laws of Fesole. A familiar treatise on the elementary principles and practice of drawing and painting*, Orpington 1877.

Ruskin, John: *Proserpina. Studies of wayside flowers*, Orpington 1875–86.

Ruskin, John: *The Two Baths: being lectures on art, and its application to decoration and manufacture*, London 1859.

(Sauvage, Henri): *Henri Sauvage, 1873–1932*, Brussels 1976; Paris 1977. Exhibition catalogue.

Séguy, E. A.: *Insectes*, Paris n.d. (1920s).

Séguy, E. A.: *Papillons*, Paris n.d. (1920s).

Stannus, Hugh: *The Decorative Treatment of Natural Foliage*, London 1891.

Stephenson, T. A.: *Seashore Life and Pattern*, Harmondsworth 1944.

Stoll, Christian: *Moderne Blumen – Ornamentik*, Leipzig (?) n.d. (1907).

Strange, Edward F.: *Flowers and Plants for Designers and Schools.* Photographed from nature by Henry Irving, London 1907.

Sturm, G.: *Tierleben in Ornament*, Stuttgart 1895.

Sullivan, Louis H.: *The Autobiography of an Idea.* Foreword by Claude Bragdon, New York 1956 (1st ed. 1924).

Sullivan, Louis H.: *A System of Architectural Ornament*, New York 1924.

(Sullivan, Louis H.) Sprague, Paul E.: *The Drawings of Louis Henry Sullivan*, Princeton 1977.

(Sullivan, Louis H.) Wright, Frank Lloyd: *Genius and the Mobocracy*, London 1972. (On Sullivan's ornament.)

Thompson, D'Arcy Wentworth: *On Growth and Form*, ed. J. T. Bonner, Cambridge 1961 (1st ed. 1917).

Townsend, W. G. Paulson: *Plant and Floral Studies for Designers, Art Students, and Craftsmen*, London 1901.

Van de Velde, H.: *Die Renaissance in modernen Kunstgewerbe*, Berlin 1901.

Van de Velde, H.: *La Mia Vita*, Milan 1966. Tr. from the German.

(Van de Velde): *Henry van de Velde zum 100 Geburtstag*, Stuttgart 1963. Exhibition catalogue.

Verneuil, M. P.: *Etude de la Plante. Son application aux industries d'art*, Paris *c.* 1900.

Viollet-le-Duc, E. E.: *Histoire d'un Dessinateur*, Paris 1879.

Wadsworth, J.: *Designing from Plant Forms*, London 1910.

Waring, J. B.: *Illustrations of Architecture and Ornament*, London 1865.

Watson-Baker, W.: *World beneath the Microscope*, London 1935.

Weller, Herbert J.: *Nature and Design*, London n.d. (*c.* 1895).

Weltausstellung St Louis, 1904, Oesterreich. K. K. Ministerium für Kultur und Unterricht. Ausstellung K. K. Kunstgewerblicher Lehranstalten, Vienna 1904. Contains an account of official Austrian art instruction.

Geometrical Ornament

Alabone, Edwin W.: *Multi-Epicycloidal and other Geometric Curves*, London n.d. (1910).

Albarn, Keith; Miall Smith, Jenny; Steele, Stanford; Walker, Dinah: *The Language of Pattern. An inquiry inspired by Islamic decoration*, London 1974.

Bain, G.: *Celtic Art. The method of construction*, Glasgow 1944.

Barratt, Krome: *Logic and Design, in Art, Science and Mathematics*, London 1980.

Billings, R. W.: *The Power of Form Applied to Geometric Tracery*, London 1851.

Bourgoin, J.: *Grammaire Elémentaire de l'Ornement*, Paris 1880.

Bourgoin, J.: *Les Elements de l'Art Arabe. Le trait des entrelacs*, Paris 1879.

Bourgoin, J.: *Théorie de l'Ornement*, Paris 1873.

Bragdon, C.: *Projective Ornament*, New York 1915.

Chernikov, Ya(cov): *Ornament. Kompozutzionno-klassicheshiye postroyenya*, Leningrad 1930.

Critchlow, Keith: *Islamic Patterns*, London 1976.

Day, Lewis Foreman: *Ornamental Design*, London 1897 (4th ed. rev.).

Day, Lewis Foreman: *Pattern Design*, London 1923 (3rd ed.).

Day, Lewis Foreman: *The Planning of Ornament*, London 1887.

Diefenbach, Leonhard: *Geometrische Ornamentik*, Berlin n.d. (1892).

Dürer, Albrecht: *Underweysung de messung mit dem zirckel und richt scheyt in linien ebnen und gantzen corporen*, Nüremberg 1533 and 1538.

Edwards, Edward B.: *Dynamarhythmic Design. A book of structural pattern*, New York 1932.

El-Said, Issam, and Parman, Ayse: *Geometric Concepts in Islamic Art*, London 1976.

Ezel, P. D.: *Elementarische Entwicklung des Ornaments*, Berlin n.d. (*c.* 1920).

Fenn, Amor: *Abstract Design*, London 1930.

Forichon, F.: *L'Ornement Géometrique*, Paris 1902.

Gauthier, Joseph: *12 Leçons de Composition Décorative*, Paris 1920.

Gauthier, J., and Capelle, L.: *Traité de Composition Décorative*, Paris n.d.

Hankin, E. H.: *The Drawing of Geometric Patterns in Saracenic Art*, Calcutta 1925.

Hay, D. R.: *An Essay on Ornamental Design*, London 1844.

Hay, D. R.: *The Science of Beauty, as Developed in Nature and Applied in Art*, Edinburgh 1856.

Horemis, Spyros: *Optical and Geometrical Patterns and Designs*, New York 1970.

Hornung, C. P.: *Handbook of Designs and Devices*, New York 1932.

Hyman, Anthony: *The Computer in Design*, London 1973.

Jones, O.: *Designs for Mosaic and Tessellated Pavements*, London 1842.

Lorch, Alfred: *Modern Geometric Design*, London 1971.

(Martin, Kenneth): *Kenneth Martin. Drawings and Prints*, London 1977. Exhibition catalogue.

Montú, Aldo (ed.): *La Scoperta del Pentagono*, Bologna 1981.

(Morellet, François): *François Morellet*, Birmingham 1974. Exhibition catalogue.

(Morellet, François): *Morellet*, Paris 1967. Exhibition catalogue.

Morris, I. H.: *Geometrical Drawing for Art Students*, London 1901 (8th ed.).

Munari, Bruno (ed.): *La Scoperta del Quadrato*, Bologna 1978.

Munari, Bruno (ed.): *La Scoperta del Triangolo*, Bologna 1976.

Phillips, Dave: *Graphic and Op-Art Mazes*, New York 1976.

Ricks, G.: *Hand-and-Eye Training*, London 1889 (2nd ed.).

Ross, Denman W.: *A Theory of Pure Design, Harmony, Balance, Rhythm*, Boston 1907.

Schauermann, F. L.: *Theory and Analysis of Ornament Applied to the Work of*

Elementary and Technical Schools, London 1892. (Derived entirely from J. Bourgoin's *Théorie de l'Ornement*.)

Somervell, E. L.: *A Rhythmic Approach to Mathematics*, London 1906.

Stevens, Peter S.: *Handbook of Regular Patterns. An introduction to symmetry in two dimensions*, Cambridge, Mass., 1980.

Symonds, J. A.: *The Principles of Beauty*, London 1857.

Systems. Arts Council 1972–3, London 1972. Exhibition catalogue.

(Truchet, Sébastien): *Méthode pour faire une infinité de desseins differents avec des Carreaux mi-partis de deux couleurs par une ligne diagonale*, Paris 1722.

ULM 12/13 Zeitschrift der Hochschüle für Gestaltung, Ulm 1965.

von Wersin, Wolfgang: *Das elementare Ornament und seine Gesetzlichkeit*, Ravensburg 1953 (3rd ed.).

Wade, David: *Pattern in Islamic Art*, London 1976.

Wong, Wucius: *Principles of Two-Dimensional Design*, New York 1972.

Wyatt, Matthew Digby: *Specimens of the Geometrical Mosaic of the Middle Ages*, London 1848.

The Gothic Revival

Adams: *Recueil de Sculptures Gothiques*, Paris 1856–66.

Audsley, W. and G.: *Polychromatic Decoration as Applied to Buildings in the Mediaeval Styles*, London 1882.

Blackburne, E. L.: *Sketches Graphic and Descriptive of the Decorative Painting applied to English architecture during the Middle Ages*, London 1847.

Brandon, R. and J. A.: *An Analysis of Gothic Architecture*, London 1847.

Burges, William: *Architectural Drawings*, London 1870.

(Burges, William): *The Architectural Designs of William Burges, ARA*, ed. R. P. Pullan. London 1883.

(Burges, William): *The Strange Genius of William Burges 'Art Architect', 1827–1881*, Cardiff 1981.

(Burges, William) Crook, Joseph Mordaunt: *William Burges and the High Victorian Dream*, London 1981.

(Butterfield, William): *Instrumenta Ecclesiastica*, London 1847–56.

(Butterfield, William): *Specimens of Ancient Church Plate; Sepulchral Crosses; etc.*, Oxford 1845.

(Butterfield, William) Thompson, Paul: *William Butterfield*, London 1971.

Carter, John: *Specimens of the Ancient Sculpture and Painting now remaining in this Kingdom from the earliest period to the reign of Henry VIII*, London 1780–94.

Clarke, Basil F. L.: *Church Builders of the Nineteenth Century. A study of the Gothic Revival in England*, London 1938.

Clark, Sir Kenneth: *The Gothic Revival*, London 1950 (1st ed. 1928).

Cutts, Rev. E. L.: *An Essay on Church Furniture and Decoration*, London 1854.

De la Motte, Philip: *Choice Examples of Art Workmanship*, London 1851.

Dolby, Anastasia: *Church Embroidery; Ancient and Modern*, London 1867.

Eastlake, Charles L.: *A History of the Gothic Revival*, London 1872.

Eastlake, Charles L.: *Hints on Household Taste in Furniture, Upholstery and other Details*, London 1878 (4th ed. rev.).

Freeman, Edward A.: *An Essay on the Origin and Development of Window Tracery in England*, Oxford and London 1851.

Gailhabaud, J.: *L'Architecture du Ve au XVIe Siècle, et les Arts qui en Dépendent*, Paris 1851.

Germann, Georg: *The Gothic Revival in Europe and Britain: sources, influences and ideas*, London 1972.

Halfpenny, Joseph: *Gothic Ornaments in the Cathedral Church of York*, York 1795.

Hall, Sir James: *Essay on the Origin, History and Principles, of Gothic Architecture*, London 1813.

(Hardy, Thomas): *The Architectural Notebook of Thomas Hardy*, Dorchester 1966.

Heideloff, C.: *Collection of Architectural Ornaments of the Middle-Ages*, London 1844.

Hull, E.: *A Treatise on the Building and Ornamental Stones of Great Britain and Foreign Countries*, London 1872.

Jewitt, E.: *Manual of Illuminated and Missal Painting*, Oxford n.d. (*c.* 1850).

Kellen, D. van der: *Muurschilderingen in de groote op St Bavo's-kerk to Haarlem*, 's-Gravenhage 1861. (A study of early polychromy in the manner of Merimée, Viollet-le-Duc etc.)

King, T. H.: *Orfèvrerie et Ouvrages en Metal du Moyen-Age*, Bruges 1852–4 (2 vols).

Langley, Batty and Thomas: *Gothic Architecture, Improved by Rules and Proportions*, London 1747.

Macaulay, James: *The Gothic Revival, 1745–1845*, Glasgow 1975.

Merimée, P.: *Notices sur les Peintures de l'Eglise de Saint-Savin*, Paris 1845.

Milner, John: *A Treatise on the Ecclesiastical Architecture of England during the Middle Ages*, London 1811.

Minton & Co.: *Examples of old English tiles manufactured by Minton & Co.*, London 1842.

Moyr Smith, J.: *Studies for Pictures*, London 1868.

Murphy, James Cavanah: *Plans, Elevations, Sections and Views of the Church of Batalha*, London 1795.

Nesfield, W. Eden: *Specimens of Mediaeval Architecture*, London 1862.

Pugin, A. W. N.: *Contrasts*, London 1841 (1st ed. 1836).

Pugin, A. W. N.: *Designs for Iron and Brass Work in the Style of the XV and XVI centuries*, London 1836.
Pugin, A. W. N.: *Fifteenth and Sixteenth Century Ornaments*, Edinburgh 1904.
Pugin, A. W. N.: *Glossary of Ecclesiastical Ornament and Costume*, London 1844.
Pugin, A. W. N.: *Gothic Ornaments*. Drawn on stone by J. D. Harding, London 1854.
Pugin, A. W. N.: *A Treatise on Chancel Screens and Rood Lofts*, London 1851.
Pugin, A. W. N.: *The True Principles of Pointed or Christian Architecture*, London 1841.
(Pugin, A. W. N.) Stanton, Phoebe: *Pugin*, Preface by Nikolaus Pevsner, London 1971.
Rickman, Thomas: *An Attempt to Discriminate the Styles of Architecture in England*, London (1825) (1st ed. 1817).
Robson-Scott, W. D.: *The Literary Background of the Gothic Revival in Germany*, Oxford 1965.
(Ruskin, John): *John Ruskin*, London 1983. Exhibition catalogue.
(Ruskin, John): *Ruskin and his Circle*, London 1964. Exhibition catalogue.
Ruskin, J.: *The Seven Lamps of Architecture*, London 1849.
Ruskin, J.: *The Stones of Venice*, London 1852–3.
Ruskin, J., and Acland, Henry W.: *The Oxford Museum*, London 1859.
Scott, G.: *Lectures on the Rise and Development of Mediaeval Architecture*, London 1879 (2 vols).
(Scott, Sir Gilbert): *Sir Gilbert Scott (1811–1878). Architect of the Gothic Revival*, London 1978. Exhibition catalogue, Victoria and Albert Museum.
Shaw, Henry: *Dresses and Decorations of the Middle Ages*, London 1843 (2 vols).
Shaw, Richard Norman: *Architectural Sketches from the Continent*, London 1858.
Street, George Edmund: *Brick and Marble in the Middle Ages: notes of tours in the North of Italy*, London 1874.
Street, George Edmund: *Some Account of Gothic Architecture in Spain*, London 1865.
Talbert, Bruce J.: *Gothic Forms applied to Furniture, Metal Work and Decoration for Domestic Purposes*, Birmingham 1867.
(Viollet-le-Duc, E. E.): *Compositions et Dessins de Viollet-le-Duc*, Paris 1884.
Viollet-le-Duc, E. E.: *De la Décoration Appliquée aux Edifices*, Paris 1880.
Viollet-le-Duc, E. E.: *Dictionnaire Raisonné de l'Architecture Française de XIe au XVI siècle*, Paris 1854–68.
Viollet-le-Duc, E. E.: *Dictionnaire Raisonné du Mobilier Français de l'Epoque Carolingienne à la Renaissance*, Paris 1858.
Viollet-le-Duc, E. E.: *Entretiens sur l'Architecture*, Paris 1863–72. Atlas 1864.
Viollet-le-Duc, E. E.: *How to Build a*

House: an architectural novelette, Tr. by Benjamin Bucknall, London 1874.
(Viollet-le-Duc, E. E.): *Eugène Emmanuel Viollet-le-Duc, 1814–1879. Architectural Design Profile*, London 1980.
Viollet-le-Duc, E. E.: *Peintures Murales des Chapelles de Notre Dame de Paris*, Paris 1870.
Waring, J. B.: *Architectural, Sculptural and Picturesque Studies; in Burgos and its Neighbourhood*, London 1852.
Watkinson, Raymond: *Pre-Raphaelite Art and Design*, London 1970.
Wyatt, Matthew Digby: *Specimens of Ornamental Art Workmanship*, London 1852.

Eclecticism

Arrowsmith, H. W. and A.: *The House Decorator and Painter's Guide*, London 1840.
Audsley, G. A. and M. A.: *The Practical Decorator and Ornamentist*, Glasgow 1892.
Batley, H. W.: *A Series of Studies for Domestic Furniture and Decoration*, London 1883.
Capel, H.: *Art Furniture*, London c. 1880. A catalogue of furniture by Brightwen Binyon.
Carrier-Belleuse, A.: *Application de la Figure Humaine à la Décoration et à l'Ornementation Industrielle*, Paris c. 1890.
Chenavard, Aimé: *Album de l'Ornementiste*, Paris 1845.
Chenavard, Aimé: *Recueil des Dessins*, Paris n.d. (c. 1830).
Clerget, Charles Ernest: *Mélanges d'Ornemens Divers*, Paris 1838.
Clerget, Charles Ernest and Martel: *Encyclopédie Universelle d'Ornements*, Paris n.d. (1840?).
Conway, M. D.: *Travels in South Kensington with notes on Decorative Arts and Architecture in England*, London 1882.
Daly, César: *L'Architecture Privée au XIXe siècle*, Paris 1870, 1872, 1877.
Daly, C.: *Décorations Intérieures Peintes*, Paris 1877. (2 vols).
Davis, Owen W.: *Art and Work*, London 1885.
Day, Lewis Foreman: *Every-Day Art: short essays on the arts not fine*, London 1882.
Day, Lewis Foreman: *Instances of Necessary Art*, London 1880.
Day, Lewis Foreman: *Ornament and its Application*, London 1904.
Dresser, Christopher: *Modern Ornamentation*, London 1886.
Dresser, Christopher: *Principles of Decorative Design*, London 1874.
Dresser, Christopher: *Studies in Design*, London 1874–6.

Durand, J. N. L.: *Recueil et Parallèle des Edifices de Tout Genre*, Paris n.d. (1813).
Edis, Robert W.: *Decoration and Furniture of Town Houses*, London 1881.
The Evergreen. A northern seasonal, Edinburgh 1895–7. In 4 parts.
Examples of the Works of Art in the Museum and of the decoration of the Building with Brief Descriptions (South Kensington Museum), London 1881–2.
Garrett, Rhoda and Agnes: *House Decoration*, London 1876.
Garrett, Rhoda and Agnes: *Suggestions for House Decoration*, London 1876.
Girouard, Mark: *Sweetness and Light. The 'Queen Anne' Movement, 1860–1900*, Oxford 1977.
(Godwin, E. W.): *Art Furniture from designs by E. W. Godwin, FSA and others*, London 1877.
(Godwin, E. W.) Harbron, Dudley: *The Conscious Stone: The life of Edward William Godwin*, London 1949.
Hamilton, Walter: *The Aesthetic Movement in England*, London 1882.
Haweis, Mrs H. R.: *The Art of Decoration*, London 1881.
Haweis, Mrs H. R.: *Beautiful Houses*, London 1882.
Heaton, A.: *Beauty and Art*, London 1897.
Isabey, L., and Leblan, E.: *Villas, Maisons de Ville et de Campagne*, Paris 1864.
Javet: *Dessin Industriel*, Paris n.d.
Jones, O.: *Scenes from The Winter's Tale*, London 1866. (Illustrations in the neo-Greek style.)
Jones, O., and Warren, H.: *The History of Joseph and his Brethren*, London 1865. (Illustrations in the Egyptian style.)
Leighton, J.: *Suggestions in Design being a Comprehensive Series of Original Sketches in Various Styles of Ornament*, London 1880.
Leith, Samuel, and Ballantine, James: *The Tradesman's Book of Ornamental Designs*, Manchester (1847).
Lienard: *Specimens de la Décoration et de l'Ornementation au XIX siècle*, Liege 1866.
Limmer, Luke (Leighton, John): *Suggestions in Design*, London 1853.
Lockwood, M. S., and Claister, E.: *Art Embroidery*, London 1878. The designs are by Thomas Crane.
Mayeux, H.: *A Manual of Decorative Composition*, Tr. by J. Conino. Revised by Walter Millard, London 1898 (3rd ed.).
Moody, F. W.: *Lectures and Lessons on Art*, London 1873 (3rd ed.).
Moyr Smith, J.: *Ornamental Interiors*, London 1887. Illustrates work by Owen Davis, G. C. Haité, Bruce Talbert, C. F. A. Voysey.
Spofford, Harriet Prescott: *Art Decoration Applied to Furniture*, New York 1878.
Talbert, Bruce J.: *Examples of Ancient and Modern Furniture, Metal Work, Tapestries, Decorations, etc*, London 1876.

Bibliography

The Universal Decorator. Ed. F. B. Thompson. A complete guide to ornamental design. London 1858–9.

Wagner, Ludwig: *Moderne Decorations-Malereien in farbiger Ausführung,* Düsseldorf n.d. (*c.* 1900).

Watson, R. M.: *The Art of the House,* London 1897.

Wyatt, Matthew Digby: *Views of the Crystal Palace and Park,* London 1854. (Views of the Egyptian, Nineveh, Medieval and Alhambra Courts, etc.)

Orientalism

Birdwood, G. C. M.: *Handbook to the British Indian Section,* London/Paris 1878.

Birdwood, G. C. M.: *The Industrial Arts of India,* London 1884.

Bourgoin, J.: *Les Arts Arabes,* Paris 1873.

Bourgoin, J.: *Précis de l'Art Arabe,* Paris 1892.

Carmona, S., and Lozano, Don Pablo: *Antiguedades Arabes de España,* Madrid 1804.

Carre, Jean-Marie: *Voyageurs et Ecrivains Français en Egypte,* Cairo 1932. (Contains an account of Prisse d'Avennes etc.)

Castellazzi, G.: *Ricordi di Architettura Orientale presi dal vero,* Venice 1871.

Collin, J.: *Etude pratique de la Décoration Polygonale Arabe,* Paris n.d. (1911).

Collinot, E., and de Beaumont, A.: *Encyclopédie des Arts Décoratifs de l'Orient. Ornements de la Perse,* Paris 1880. *Ornements Arabes,* Paris 1883. *Ornements Turcs,* Paris 1883. *Ornements Vénitiens, Hindous, Russes, etc,* Paris 1883.

Cresswell, K. A. C.: *A Bibliography of the Architecture, Arts and Crafts of Islam to 1st Jan 1960,* Cairo 1961.

Diez, Ernst: *Die Kunst der Islamischen Völker,* Berlin 1917.

Fergusson, James: *History of Indian and Eastern architecture,* London (this ed. 1891).

Gabriel-Rousseau: *L'Art Décoratif Musulman,* Paris 1934.

Girault de Prangey: *Choix d'Ornements Moresques de l'Alhambra,* Paris n.d. (1842).

Hessemer, F. M.: *Arabische und alt-Italienische Bau-verzierungen,* Berlin 1842.

Honour, Hugh: *Chinoiserie. The Vision of Cathay,* London 1961.

Irwin, John: *The Kashmir Shawl,* London 1973.

Irwin, John, and Murphy, Veronica: *Batiks,* London 1969.

Jones, O.: *The Alhambra Court of the Crystal Palace,* London 1854.

Jones, O.: *Examples of Chinese Ornament selected from objects in the South Kensington Museum and other collections,* London 1867.

Jones, O., and Goury, J.: *Plans, Elevations, Sections and Details of the Alhambra: from drawings taken on the spot in 1834 and 1837,* London 1842–5.

Landau, Roth: *The Arabesque: the abstract art of Islam,* San Francisco 1955.

Lane, Edward William: *An Account of the Manners and Customs of the Modern Egyptians,* ed. Edward Stanley Poole, London 1860.

Lane, Edward William: *The Thousand and One Nights,* London 1841.

Langdon, William B. (Curator): *A Descriptive Catalogue of the Chinese Collection, at St George's Place, Hyde Park Corner,* London 1843 (19th ed.).

Mitter, Partha: *Much Maligned Monsters. History of European reactions to Indian art,* Oxford 1977.

Murphy, James Cavanah: *The Arabian Antiquities of Spain,* London 1813.

Parvillée, Léon: *Architecture et Décoration Turques au XVe siècle.* Preface de E. Viollet-le-Duc, Paris 1874.

Priestman, Mabel Tuke: *Handicrafts in the Home,* London 1910. See: 'Batik: an Ancient Javanese Handicraft'.

Prisse d'Avennes, E.: *L'Art Arabe d'après les Monuments du Kaire depuis le VIIe siècle jusqu'à la fin du XVIIe,* Paris 1877.

Prisse d'Avennes, E.: *La Décoration Arabe,* Paris 1885.

Rám Ráz: *Essay on the Architecture of the Hindus,* London 1834.

Ridley, Michael: *Style, Motif and Design in Chinese Art,* Poole, Dorset, 1977.

Riegl, Alois: *Altorientalische Teppiche,* Vienna 1891.

Simakoff, N.: *L'Art de l'Asie Centrale,* St Petersburg 1883 (text in Russian and French).

Stassoff, Wladimir: *L'Ornement Slave et Oriental,* St Petersburg 1887 (text in Russian and French).

Stevens, Mary Anne (ed.): *The Orientalists: Delacroix to Matisse,* London 1984. Exhibition catalogue.

Texier, Charles: *Description de l'Arménie, la Perse et la Mésopotamie,* Paris 1842.

Weltkulturen und moderne Kunst, Munich 1972. Exhibition catalogue. (Eng. tr. published as *World Cultures and Modern Art,* Munich 1972.)

Wijdeveld-Schotman, J. W.: *Der geesten gemoeting,* Amsterdam 1927 (5 vols).

'The Cult of Japan'

The Aesthetic Movement and the Cult of Japan, London 1972. Exhibition catalogue.

Alcock, Sir Rutherford: *Art and Art Industries of Japan,* London 1878.

Alcock, Sir Rutherford: *The Capital of the Tycoon: a narrative of three year's residence in Japan,* London 1863.

Alcock, Sir Rutherford: *Catalogue of Works of Industry and Art sent from Japan, International Exhibition,* London 1862.

Anderson, William: *The Pictorial Arts of Japan,* London 1886.

Audsley, George Ashdown: *The Ornamental Arts of Japan,* London 1882–4.

Audsley, G. A., and Bowes, J. L.: *Keramic Art of Japan,* Liverpool 1875.

Bing, S.: *Artistic Japan,* London 1888–1891.

Bowes, James Lord: *Japanese Enamels,* London 1886.

Brinkley, Capt F. (ed.): *Japan, Described and Illustrated by the Japanese,* Boston 1897–8.

(Burges, William): *An Album Catalogued by Burges as 'Polychromy'. Dated October 18, 1858.* The Print Room, Victoria and Albert Museum, London.

Burty, Philippe: *Les Emaux Cloisonnés Anciens et Modernes,* Paris 1868.

Catalogue de l'Exposition Retrospective de l'Art Japonais, Paris 1883.

Chesneau, Ernest: *L'Art Japonais,* Paris 1868.

Cutler, T. W.: *A Grammar of Japanese Ornament and Design,* London 1880.

Dresser, Christopher: *Japan. Its architecture, art and art manufactures,* London 1882.

Franks, Augustus: *Japanese Pottery, being a Native Report,* London 1880. (South Kensington Museum Art Handbook.)

Gonse, Louis: *L'Art Japonais,* Paris 1883.

Hart, E.: *Stencils of Old Japan from Originals in the Collection of Ernest Hart,* London 1895.

Hirase, Koichiro: *Shell Section Drawings,* Kyoto 1909. (Text in Japanese.)

Humbert, Aimé: *Le Japon Illustré,* Paris 1870.

Japonisme. Japanese influence on French art, 1854–1910, Cleveland, Ohio 1975. Exhibition catalogue. (Contains an extensive bibliography.)

(The Japan Textile Colour Design Centre): *Textile Designs of Japan,* Tokyo and London 1980 (3 vols).

Leighton, John: *On Japanese Art,* London 1863, privately printed.

Le Japon à l'Exposition Universelle de 1878, Paris 1878.

Macfarlane, Charles: *Japan; an account, geographical and historical,* London 1852.

Morse, Edward S.: *Japanese Homes and their Surroundings,* London 1888.

Moser, D. H.: *A Book of Japanese Ornamentation,* London 1880.

Mutual Influences between Japanese and Western Arts, Tokyo 1968. Exhibition catalogue.

Osborn, Capt Sherard, R. N.: *Japanese Fragments,* London 1861.

Perry, Commodore M. C.: *Narrative of the Expedition of an American Squadron to the China Seas and Japan,* compiled by Francis L. Hawks, New York 1856.

Reed, Sir Edward: *Japan: its History, Traditions and Religions,* London 1880.

Rein, J. J.: *The Industries of Japan*, London 1889.

Rein, J. J.: *Japan*, London 1889.

Silver, J. M. W.: *Sketches of Japanese Manners and Customs*, London 1867.

Strange, Edward F.: *Japanese Illustration, a history of the arts of wood-cutting and colour printing in Japan*, London 1897.

Tanaka, Yoshio: *San-moko dzu setsu. Flore du Japon arrangée selon le système de Linné; par Inuma Yokusai*, Tokyo 1874. Illustrated with Japanese wood-cuts.

Titsingh, M.: *Illustrations of Japan*, London 1821.

Tuer, A. W.: *The Book of Delightful and Strange Designs being one hundred facsimile illustrations of the art of the Japanese stencil-cutter*, London c. 1895.

'Primitivism'

Balfour, H.: *The Evolution of Decorative Art*, London 1893.

Boas, F.: *Primitive Art*, Oslo 1917 (this edition New York 1955).

Duerdon, D.: *African Art*, London 1968.

Haddon, Alfred Cort: *The Decorative Art of New Guinea. A study in Papuan ethnography*, Dublin 1894.

Haddon, A. C.: *Evolution in Art: as illustrated by the life-histories of designs*, London 1895.

Hildebrand, Hans: *The Industrial Arts of Scandinavia in the Pagan time*, London 1883. A South Kensington Museum Handbook.

Holm, Bill: *Northwest Coast Indian Art, an Analysis of Form*, Seattle 1965.

Lévi-Strauss, Claude: *Structural Anthropology*, Harmondsworth 1977 (2 vols).

Robley, H. G.: *Moko; or Maori Tattooing*, London 1896.

Start, Laure E.: *The McDougall Collection of Indian textiles from Guatemala and Mexico*, Occasional papers on technology 2. Ed. by T. K. Penniman and B. M. Blackwood, Oxford 1948.

Stolpe, Hjalmar: *Studier Amerikansk Ornamentik ett bidrag till Ornamentens Biologi*, Stockholm 1896.

Waring, J. B.: *Ceramic Art in Remote Ages*, London 1874.

Weltfish, Gene: *The Origins of Art*, Indianapolis 1953.

Wenzel, Marian: *House Decoration in Nubia*, London 1972.

Wiener, Charles: *Pérou et Bolivie*, Paris 1880.

Worsaae, J. J. A.: *The Industrial Arts of Denmark*, London 1882. A South Kensington Museum Handbook.

The Arts and Crafts Movement

Art and Life, London 1897.

Arts & Crafts. A review of the work executed by students in the leading art schools of Great Britain and Ireland. Ed. Charles Holme, London 1916.

Arts Décoratifs de Grande-Bretagne et d'Irlande, London 1914. Exhibition catalogue.

Ashbee, C. R.: *A Few Chapters in Workshop Reconstruction and Citizenship*, London 1894.

Ashbee, C. R.: *Craftsmanship in Competitive Industry*, Chipping Campden 1908.

Ashbee, C. R.: *Modern English Silverwork*, Broad Campden 1908 (new ed. London 1974).

Baillie Scott, M. H.: *Houses and Gardens*, London 1906.

(Baillie Scott, M. H.) Kornwolf, James D.: *M H Baillie Scott and the Arts and Crafts Movement*, Baltimore and London 1972.

Benson, W. A. S.: *Elements of Handicraft & Design*, London 1893.

Blount, G.: *Arbor Vitae. A book on the nature and development of imaginative design for the use of teachers, handicraftsmen and others*, London 1899.

Catalogue of the works exhibited by members of the Northern Art Workers' Guild, City Gallery, Manchester 1898. See Walter Crane: 'Notes on needlework in the present century'; Lewis F. Day: 'Cotton Printing'; Richard Glazier: 'The influence of material upon design'; Edgar Wood: 'From nature to design'.

Clark, Fiona: *William Morris, Wallpapers and Chintzes*, London 1974.

Clark, Robert Judson (ed.): *The Arts and Crafts Movement in America 1876–1916*, Princeton, New Jersey 1972. (Contains an extensive bibliography.)

Clutton Brock, A.: *Socialism and the Arts of Use*, London 1915.

Coatts, Margot: *A Weaver's Life. Ethel Mairet, 1872–1952*, London 1984.

Cobden-Sanderson, T. J.: *The Arts and Crafts Movement*, 1905.

(Crane, Walter) Konody, P. G.: *The Art of Walter Crane*, London 1902.

Crane, Walter: *The Claims of Decorative Art*, London 1892.

Crane, Walter: *The Bases of Design*, London 1898.

Crane, Walter: *Ideals in Art*, London 1905.

Crane, Walter: *Line and Form*, London 1904 (3rd ed.).

Crane, Walter: *William Morris to Whistler*, London 1911.

Crow, Gerald H.: *William Morris, Designer*, London 1934.

(Gaskin, Arthur, and Gaskin, Georgie—née France, Georgie Evelyn Cave): *Arthur and Georgie Gaskin*, Birmingham 1981. Exhibition catalogue.

(Gimson, Ernest): *Ernest Gimson, his Life and Work*, Stratford 1924.

Jack, George: *Wood Carving: Design and Workmanship*, London 1903.

Johnston, Edward: *Writing & Illuminating, & Lettering*, London 1906.

Leland, C. G., Lambert, F. C., and Bolas, T.: *A selection of 6 pamphlets from the Useful Arts Series: Artificial wood and shavings in decoration; Fret-cutting; Tools and their uses; Soldering, brazing, and the joining of metals; Adornment of the home; Glue, gum, paste, and other adhesives*, n.p. c. 1895.

Lethaby, W. R.: *Architecture, Mysticism and Myth*, London 1891.

Lethaby, W. R.: *Designing Games*, Leicester 1929.

Lethaby, W. R.: *Leadwork, Old and Ornamental and for the most part English*, London 1893.

(Lethaby, W. R.) Backemeyer, Sylvia, and Gronber, Theresa (eds): *W. R. Lethaby, 1857–1931. Architecture, design and education*, London 1984.

(Lethaby, W. R.): *William Richard Lethaby, 1857–1931, by A. R. N. Roberts et al*, London 1957.

(Mackmurdo, A. H.): *Catalogue of A. H. Mackmurdo and the Century Guild Collection*, William Morris Gallery, Walthamstow 1967.

Miller, F.: *Art Crafts for Amateurs*, London 1901.

Miller, F.: *The Training of a Craftsman*, London 1898.

Morris, William: *An address delivered at the distribution of prizes to students of the Birmingham Municipal School of Art on 21 Feb 1894*, London 1898.

Morris, William: *Art and its Producers*, London 1901.

Morris, William: *Art and the Beauty of the Earth*, London 1898.

Morris, William: *Gothic Architecture*, London 1893.

Morris, William: *Hopes and Fears for Art*, London 1883 (3rd ed.).

Morris, William: *A Note by William Morris on his Aims in Founding the Kelmscott Press*, Hammersmith 1898. (Reprinted 1969.)

Morris, William: *Some Hints on Pattern-Designing*, London 1899.

(Morris, William): *William Morris and Kelmscott*, London 1981. Exhibition catalogue.

(Morris, William): *William Morris Today*, London 1984. Exhibition catalogue.

(Morris, William) Thompson, Paul: *The Work of William Morris*, London 1967.

(Morris, William) Vallance, A.: *The Art of William Morris*, London 1897. (Includes a bibliography.)

(Morris, William) Watkinson, Raymond: *William Morris as Designer*, London 1967.

(Morris, William, and his circle): *Catalogue of the Morris Collection*, William Morris Gallery, Walthamstow 1969.

Morris, William, and others: *Arts and Crafts Essays by members of the Arts and Crafts Exhibition Society*, London 1893.

Morris, William, Poole, R. S., Richmond,

Bibliography

W. B., Poynter, E. J., Micklethwaite, J. T.: *Lectures on Art*, London 1882.
Morris & Co.: *A Brief Sketch of the Morris Movement and of the firm founded by William Morris*, London 1911.
(Morris & Co.): *Morris and Company*, London 1979. Exhibition catalogue.
(Morris & Co.): *Morris & Company in Cambridge*, Cambridge 1980.
(Morris & Co.): *Morris & Co.*, Exhibition catalogue. Stanford University 1975. (Contains a bibliography and list of catalogues of previous Morris exhibitions.)
(Morris & Co.) Fairclough, O., and Leary, E.: *Textiles by Morris & Co, 1861–1940*. Intro. by Barbara Morris, London 1981.
Naylor, Gillian: *The Arts and Crafts Movement*, London 1971 (2nd ed. 1980).
Ruskin, John: *The Elements of Drawing*, Orpington 1892 (1st ed. 1857).
Sedding, John D.: *Art and Handicraft*, London 1893.
Sedding, Wilson H.: *A Memorial of the late J. D. Sedding*, London 1892.
Sleigh, B.: *A Handbook of Elementary Design*, London 1934.
Transactions of the National Association for the Advancement of Art and its Application to Industry, 1889, London 1890. (Contains addresses by William Morris, Walter Crane, C. R. Ashbee, J. D. Sedding, Cobden Sanderson, Patrick Geddes, among others.)
Triggs, Oscar Lovell: *Chapters in the History of the Arts and Crafts Movement*, New York 1979 (Facsimile of early edition).
Vallance, Aymer: *The Decorative Art of Sir Edward Burne-Jones, Baronet*, London 1900. A special number of the *Art-Journal*.
(Voysey, C. F. A.) Floud, Peter: *The Wallpaper Designs of C. F. A. Voysey*. (Reprinted from *The Penrose Annual*, Vol. 52, 1958.)
(Voysey, C. F. A.) Jones, John Brandon: *C. F. A. Voysey. A Memoir*, London n.d. (1957).
(Webb, Philip) Lethaby, W. R.: *Philip Webb and his Work*, London 1935.
Whall, C. W.: *A Text-Book for Students and Workers in Glass*, London 1905.
White, Gleeson (ed.): *Practical Designing*, London 1899 (4th printing).
(Wragge, George, and Wood, Edgar): *George Wragge, Wardry Metal Works, Salford, Manchester*, Manchester n.d. (c. 1898). (A trade catalogue.)

Art Déco—The Evolution of a Style

Art & Design in Vienna: 1900–1930, New York 1972. Exhibition catalogue.
Battersby, Martin: *The Decorative Twenties*, London 1971.
(Behrens, Peter): *Peter Behrens (1868–1940)*, Kaiserslautern 1966. Exhibition catalogue. (Includes an extensive bibliography.)
Benirschke, M.: *Buchschmuck und Flachenmuster*, Vienna c. 1900.
Bertet, Gabriel: *La Tenture Moderne et son Application Technique*, Paris 1928.
Best-Maugard, A.: *A Method of Creative Design*, London 1926.
Billcliffe, Roger: *Mackintosh Textile Designs*, London 1982.
Carmo, Charles de, and Winslow, Leon Loyal: *Essentials of Design*, New York 1924.
Clouzot, Henri: *Le Décor Moderne dans la Teinture et le Tissu*, Paris 1929.
Clouzot, Henri: *Papiers Peints et Teintures Modernes*, Paris 1928.
Clouzot, H.: *Tentures Murales de Papiers Modernes*, Paris n.d. (1920s).
Delaunay, Sonia: *Ses Peintures, ses Objets, ses Tissus simultanés, ses Modes*, Paris 1924.
(Dufy, Raoul): *Raoul Dufy, 1877–1953*, London 1983. Exhibition catalogue.
Eisler, Max: *Osterreichische Werkkultur. Herausgegeben vom Osterreichischen Werkbund*, Vienna 1916.
(Erté—Romain de Tirtoff) Barthes, Roland: *Erté (Romain de Tirtoff) . . . with an extract from Erté's memoirs*. Tr. by William Weaver, Parma 1972.
Exposition internationale des Arts Décoratifs et Industriels Modernes. Rapport general, Paris 1929 (12 vols).
Frühes Industrie Design Wien 1900–1908. Wagner, Kolo Moser, Loos, Hoffmann, Olbrich, Ofner, Vienna 1977. Exhibition catalogue.
Gladky, Serge: *Nouvelles Compositions Décoratives. 1ère série*, Paris n.d.
Hevesi, Ludwig: *The Art Revival in Austria*. Studio Special Number. London, 1906.
Hillier, Bevis: *Art Déco of the 20s and 30s*, London 1968.
Hillier, Bevis: *The World of Art Deco*, London 1971. Exhibition catalogue.
(Hoffmann, Josef) Sekler, Eduard F.: *Josef Hoffmann. Das architektonische Werk. Monographie und Werkverzeichnis*, Salzburg 1982.
Howard, C. H.: *Design*, London 1926.
Howarth, Thomas: *Charles Rennie Mackintosh and the Modern Movement*, London 1952.
Les Années '25' Art Deco, Bauhaus, Stijl, Esprit Nouveau, Paris 1966. Exhibition catalogue.
(Lissim, Simon) Cogniat, R., Lechevallier-Chevignard, G., Reau, L. (eds.): *Simon Lissim*, Paris n.d.
(Mackintosh, Charles Rennie): *A Centenary Exhibition. Charles Rennie Mackintosh (1868–1928)*, London 1968. Exhibition catalogue, Victoria and Albert Museum.
(Mallet-Stevens, Robert): *Rob. Mallet-Stevens, Architecte*, Brussels 1980.

Matet, M. M.: *Tapis Modernes*, Paris n.d.
Menten, Theodore: *The Art Déco Style*, New York 1972.
(Moser, Koloman): *Koloman Moser*, Vienna 1964.
Moussinac, Léon: *Etoffes d'Ameublement tisées et brochées*, Paris 1925.
Moussinac, Léon: *Tapis*, Paris 1925.
(Olbrich, Joseph M.): *Architektur von Olbrich, I–III*, Berlin 1901–14.
(Olbrich, Joseph M.): *Joseph M. Olbrich, 1867–1908. Das Werk des Architekten*, Darmstadt 1967. Exhibition catalogue.
(Olbrich, Joseph M.) Latham, Ian: *Joseph Maria Olbrich*, London 1980.
The Omega Workshops 1913–19. Decorative arts of Bloomsbury, London 1984. Exhibition catalogue.
(Peche, Dagobert) Eisler, Max: *Dagobert Peche*, Vienna 1925.
Reports on the Present Position and Tendencies of the Industrial Arts as indicated at the International Exhibition of Modern Decorative and Industrial Arts, Paris, 1925. With an introductory survey, London, HMSO, n.d.
(Rowe, William): *Original Art Deco Designs. 80 plates by William Rowe*, New York 1973 (Art Déco pastiches).
(Süe, Louis, and Mare, André): *1921 Architectures. Recueil publié sous la direction de Louis Süe & André Mare*, Paris n.d. (1921).
Veronesi, Giulia: *Josef Hoffmann*, Milan 1956.
Veronesi, Giulia: *Stile 1925. Ascesa e caduta delle 'Arts Deco'*, Rome 1966.
Verneuil, M. P.: *Etoffes et Tapis Etrangers*, Paris 1926.
Vienna 1888–1938, Cambridge, Mass. 1967. Exhibition catalogue.
Vienna Moderne 1898–1918. An early encounter between taste and utility, New York 1979. Exhibition catalogue.
Vienna Secession. Art Nouveau to 1970, Vienna 1971. Exhibition catalogue.
(Wagner, Otto): *Otto Wagner. Das Werk des Wiener Architekten, 1914–1918*, Darmstadt 1963. Exhibition catalogue.
Wegert, Friederich: *Die Farbe als Stimmungselement. Flächen und Raumlösen in Malerei und Spritztechnik*, Munich n.d. (1929).
Wettergren, Erik: *L'Art Décoratif Moderne en Suède*, Malmo (1925). English tr. 1927.
Wien um 1900, Vienna 1964. Exhibition catalogue.
Die Wiener Werkstätte. Modernes Kunsthandwerk von 1903–1932, Vienna 1967.
The Yearbooks of the Design in Industries Association, London 1922 and later.

Modernism

'Art into Production.' Soviet Textiles, Fashion and Ceramics, 1917–1935, Oxford 1935. Exhibition catalogue.

Banham, Reyner: *Theory and Design in the First Machine Age*, London 1960. See: 'Adolf Loos and the problem of ornament'.

Battersby, Martin: *The Decorative Thirties*, London 1971.

Bel Geddes, Norman: *Horizons*, Boston, USA 1932.

Bénédictus (Edouard): *Relais 1930. Quinze planches donnant quarante-deux motifs décoratifs*, Paris n.d. (1930).

Bertram, Anthony: *Design*, Harmondsworth 1938.

Capey, Reco: *The Printing of Textiles*, London 1930.

Corbin, Thomas J.: *Handblock Printing on Fabrics*, London 1934.

Defries, A.: *Purpose in Design*, London 1938.

(Delaunay, S.): *Tapis et Tissus Presentés par Sonia Delaunay*, Paris n.d. Designs by Albers, Delaunay, Eileen Gray, Joseph Hoffmann, Jourdain, Léger, Lurçat, etc.

De la Valette, John (ed.): *The Conquest of Ugliness. A collection of contemporary views on the place of art in industry*, London 1935. (See: Goodhart-Rendel, H. S.: 'The future of ornament'.)

(Deutscher Werkbund): *Die Form ohne Ornament. Werkbundaustellung 1924*, Stuttgart 1925.

'Everyday Things' 1936, London 1936. Exhibition catalogue.

Exhibition of British Art in Industry, London 1935. Exhibition catalogue.

Exposition 1937: Pavillons Français. Régionalisme. Sections Etrangères. Décoration Intérieure. All Paris 1937.

Frankl, Paul T.: *Form and Re-Form*, New York 1930.

Gross, P., and Hildebrand, F.: *Geschmackbildende Werkstättübungen*, Leipzig 1912. (An account of an educational experiment which foreshadows the Bauhaus.)

Hitchcock, Henry Russell, and Johnson, Philip: *The International Style*, New York 1966. (Originally published as *The International Style. Architecture since 1922*.)

Holme, Geoffrey: *Industrial Design and the Future*, London 1934.

Jahrbuch des Deutschen Werkbundes 1912. Die Durchgeistigung der Deutschen Arbeit, Jena 1912. (See: K. Gross, 'Das Ornament'.)

Jahrbuch des Deutschen Werkbundes 1913. Die Kunst in Industrie und Handel, Jena 1913.

Jahrbuch des Deutschen Werkbundes 1914. Der Verkehr, Jena 1914.

Jahrbuch des Deutschen Werkbundes 1915. Deutsche Form im Kriegsjahr. Die Ausstellung Köln, 1914, Munich 1915.

Klee, Paul: *Pedagogical Sketchbook*. Intro. and tr. by Sibyl Moholy-Nagy, London n.d. (First published as *Pädagogisches Skizzenbuch*, 1925.)

Kuns (Atelier): *Maya. Textile Vorbilder*, Berlin n.d. (1930s).

Lambert, Susan: *Paul Nash as a Designer*, London 1975. Exhibition catalogue, Victoria and Albert Museum.

Luth, Karl (manufacturer): *Moderne Wand und Decken Dekoration*, Kiel n.d. (1932). Catalogue of stencil decorations.

Marshall, H. G. Hayes: *British Textile Designers Today*, Benfleet, Essex, 1939.

McGrath, Raymond: *Twentieth Century Houses*, London 1934.

Alastair Morton and Edinburgh Weavers. Abstract art and textile design, Edinburgh 1978. Exhibition catalogue.

Morton, Jocelyn: *Three Generations in a Family Textile Firm*, London 1971.

The Mortons. Three Generations of Textile Creation . . . Alexander Morton & Co., Morton Sundour Fabrics, Edinburgh Weavers, London 1973. Exhibition catalogue.

Münz, Ludwig and Künstler, Gustav: *Der Architekt Adolf Loos*, Vienna 1964.

Nash, Paul: *Room and Book*, London 1932. (Illustrates work by Duncan Grant, E. McKnight Kauffer, Wadsworth, Mackintosh etc.)

Papini, Roberto: *Le Arti d'Oggi*, Milan 1930.

Pevsner, Nikolaus: *Industrial Art in England*, Cambridge 1937.

Pevsner, Nikolaus: *Pioneers of Modern Design. From William Morris to Walter Gropius*, Harmondsworth 1960. (First published as *Pioneers of the Modern Movement*, London 1936.)

Read, Herbert: *Art and Industry*, London 1934.

Read, Herbert: *Art Now*, London 1933.

Read, Herbert (ed.): *Unit 1. The Modern Movement in English Architecture, Painting and Sculpture*, London 1934.

Thirties. British Art and design before the war, London 1980. Exhibition catalogue.

(Thorn Prikker, Johan): *Johan Thorn Prikker (1868–1932)*, Amsterdam 1968. Exhibition catalogue.

Wingler, Hans M.: *The Bauhaus, Weimar, Dessau, Berlin, Chicago*, Cambridge, Mass., 1969.

Woller, H.: *Teaching Fabric Printing in Schools*, London n.d. (c. 1938).

1940 to the Present—Revival

Annual Catalogues of the Design Center Stuttgart des Landesgewerbeamts, Baden–Württemberg. (For examples of German textiles.)

Auger, Boyd: *A Return to Ornament. Communication No 5 at the XII World Congress of the UIA Madrid 1975*. Unpublished typescript.

Conran, Terence: *Printed Textile Design*, London 1957.

Council of Industrial Design. Design '46, London 1946. (Includes: Thomas Marchetti: Carpets; T. A. Fennemore: Wallpapers; Enid Marx: Furnishing Fabrics.)

Davern, Jeanne M.: *Architecture 1970–1980. A decade of change*, New York 1978.

Farr, Michael: *Design in British Industry*, Cambridge 1955.

(Festival of Britain, 1951): *Design at the Festival*, London 1951.

Jencks, Charles A.: *The Language of Post-Modern Architecture*, London 1977.

Jensen, Robert, and Conway, Patricia: *Ornamentalism. The new decorativeness in architecture and design*, New York 1982.

Krier, Rob: *Rob Krier on Architecture*, London 1982.

(Paolozzi, Eduardo): *Eduardo Paolozzi. Private Vision–Public Art*, London 1984. Exhibition catalogue.

(Paolozzi, Eduardo) Kirkpatrick, Diane: *Eduardo Paolozzi*, London 1970.

(Schlemmer, Raman): *Dekor*, Oxford 1980. Exhibition catalogue.

Stil, Trend, Produkt, 10. Stuttgarter Forum Textil-Design, Stuttgart 1980. (See Bernd Rau, 'Das Textil-Design . . .'.)

Venturi, Robert: *Complexity and Contradiction in Architecture*, New York 1966.

Wolfe, Tom: *From Bauhaus to Our House*, New York 1981.

Periodicals

Architectural Design, London 1930.

Architectural Review, London 1896–

L'Art Décoratif, Paris 1898–1914.

The Art-Journal, London 1839–1911 (published as *The Art Union* until 1847).

Decoration, London 1881–9.

Dekorative Kunst, Munich 1897–1929.

Design, London 1949.

Innen-Dekoration, Darmstadt 1889–1939.

Das Interieur, Vienna 1900–12.

The Journal of Decorative Art, London 1881–1937.

The Journal of Design and Manufactures, London 1849–52.

Kunst und Handwerk, Munich 1898–1932.

The Magazine of Art, London 1878–1904.

Pan, Berlin 1895–1900.

The Studio, London 1893–   .

Ver Sacrum, Vienna 1898–1903.

Biographies

Aitchison, George, 1825–1910: architect. After studying at the Royal Academy Schools and at University College, London, travelled to the Continent with William Burges (*q.v.*). Among his early commissions were warehouses along the Thames. Leighton House, for the painter Sir Frederick, later Lord Leighton, 1830–96, was his most important domestic commission. Aitchison was a particularly accomplished decorative designer.

Alabone, Edwin W., fl. 1910: doctor of medicine. Author of several works on the treatment of consumption. His experiments with the harmonograph were entirely for his own amusement.

Alcock, Sir Rutherford, 1809–97: diplomat. Began his career as a surgeon, but was interested in foreign travel and joined the Diplomatic Service. In 1844 he was appointed Consul in Fuchow, China. After distinguishing himself in China he was appointed first British Consul General in Japan. He was knighted in 1862. Alcock returned to China in 1865 and retired in 1871. He published several works on Japan, including two books on the Japanese language.

Allan, Richard, b. 1933: artist in residence at the University of Sussex, 1967. One of the leading systems artists.

Angus, Christine, fl. 1900: artist. A student of Herbert McNair, who was a close friend of Charles Rennie Mackintosh.

Anning Bell, Robert, 1863–1933: painter, illustrator and sculptor. Trained in Paris and later with Frampton (*q.v.*) in London. Taught at Liverpool University and at the Glasgow School of Art. Was Professor of Design at the Royal College of Art, London, 1914–18.

Ashbee, Charles Robert, 1863–1942: architect, writer and theorist. Educated at Cambridge. In 1883 he was articled to the Gothic Revival architect G. F. Bodley. Conducted evening classes for young artisans in London's East End and in 1888 founded the Guild of Handicraft, which principally produced furniture and metalwork. In 1902 Ashbee moved the Guild and its members to Chipping Campden. Despite international success the Guild went into voluntary liquidation in 1908. Ashbee returned to architectural practice but, in 1915, accepted an appointment as lecturer in English at Cairo University. In 1919 he became Civic Adviser to Palestine under the British Mandate.

Aubert, Félix, b. 1866: decorative designer. Born in Normandy. A member of the group Les Cinq, which included Selmersheim (*q.v.*) and Charpentier.

Audsley, George Ashdown, 1838–1925: architect and author. Born in Elgin, Scotland. Moved to Liverpool in 1856, where he set up an architectural partnership with his brother William. The two published chromolithographic books in the manner of Owen Jones—their first venture was *The Sermon on the Mount*, 1861. The Audsleys' studies of Japanese art are amongst the most ambitious of chromolithographic books.

Batley, Henry W., fl. 1872–1908: designer. Articled to Bruce Talbert (*q.v.*). Founder of the Guild of Decorators Syndicate Ltd in 1908.

Beardsley, Aubrey Vincent, 1872–98: illustrator and graphic designer. Largely self-taught, Beardsley was given early encouragement by E. Burne-Jones. His first major project was his *Morte d'Arthur*, 1891–2, which was publicized in the first issue of *The Studio*. He was highly eclectic in his approach and his influences range from the Pre-Raphaelites and French seventeenth-century engraving through to the Japanese woodblock. He will always be associated with *The Yellow Book*, first published in 1894.

Beckford, William, 1759–1844: the builder of Fonthill Abbey, Salisbury Plain. The son of a millionaire who had made his fortune in the West Indies. James Wyatt, 1746–1816, was Beckford's architect for Fonthill, which was begun in 1796. Beckford was the author of *Vathek*, 1781, an early 'Gothic' novel.

Behrens, Peter, 1868–1940: architect and designer. Began his career as a painter but, like Van de Velde, was drawn to design after reading the works of Morris. His first building (1901) was his own house in the Darmstadt artists' colony, which was widely publicized. In 1907 he was appointed design director of A.E.G.—he designed factory buildings, electrical goods and catalogues. This was the most important phase in his career. Le Corbusier worked in his Berlin office during this time. Behrens' post-1918 work was less distinguished and, for the most part, conventionally Modernist.

Bel Geddes, Norman, 1893–1958: designer. Studied briefly at the Art Institute of Chicago. Besides his industrial design, Bel Geddes also designed successfully for the theatre.

Bell, Vanessa, 1879–1961: artist. The sister of Virginia Woolf. Married Clive Bell in 1907. Exhibited in the second Post-Impressionist Exhibition of 1910. Co-director of the Omega Workshops from 1913–19. Later designed sets for the ballet.

Bénédictus, Edouard, 1878–1930: decorative designer and painter. Born in Paris. A prolific designer of textiles. Was also a scientist and was involved in research during the 1914–18 war.

Berlage, H. P., 1856–1934: architect. Trained at the Zurich Polytechnic, where he was influenced by Gottfried Semper (*q.v.*). His Amsterdam Exchange (begun 1897) perhaps best expresses his architectural style. He also designed its furniture, ironwork and lighting. He was responsive to the ideas of Louis Sullivan (*q.v.*) and Frank Lloyd Wright (*q.v.*). Berlage had a considerable international following.

Berain, Jean, 1640–1711: engraver and designer. The son of a gunsmith. In 1659 he published designs for the decoration of gun barrels and stocks etc. Among the most prominent of seventeenth-century French decorative designers.

Beuth, Peter Christian Wilhelm, 1781–1853: civil servant. Began his career as a lawyer. With K. F. Schinkel (*q.v.*) he was involved in the Prussian government's attempts to raise national standards of design.

Binet, René, 1866–1911: architect. Studied for a time at the Ecole des Beaux Arts in Paris. Designed silverware and jewellery in the late 1890s. His best-known architectural work was the elaborate entrance to the Paris Exhibition of 1900.

Bing, Samuel, 1838–1905: entrepreneur and collector. Born in Hamburg. Opened his first shop in Paris in the early 1870s. Travelled in the Far East in 1875 and in 1877 opened a new shop selling Chinese and Japanese wares. His shop L'Art Nouveau—which gave its name to the style—was opened in 1895. Bing had his own pavilion at the Paris Exhibition of 1900. Henry Van de Velde (*q.v.*) wrote about Bing in his autobiography.

Blossfeldt, Karl, 1865–1932: artist and photographer. Began training as a modeller for a cast-iron manufacturer. Later, he was awarded a scholarship in Berlin where he received an academic training in art. In 1891 he was awarded a scholarship to Rome; there he studied under M. Meurer, from whom he learned how to model plants. In 1899 he was appointed assistant professor at the Royal Museum of Arts and Crafts in Berlin. In the same year he began taking photographs of plants.

Blount, Godfrey, 1859–1937: artist and craftsman. After Cambridge he studied at the Slade School. In 1896 he founded the Haslemere Peasant Industries which produced woven textiles, embroideries and simple furniture. He also founded the Peasant Arts Society. His writings include: *For Our Country's Sake. An Essay on the return to the land and the revival of Country Life and Crafts* and *The Rustic Renaissance*. Also wrote on religious matters.

Boas, Franz, 1858–1942: anthropologist. Boas' writings on North American Indian cultures are of very great importance. He was a leading pioneer in the development of modern anthropology.

Bötticher, Karl von, 1806–99: architect. His publications reflect the influence of Schinkel (*q.v.*). He was interested in architectural polychromy, indicating that he was fully aware of the work of the architect J. I. Hittorff, 1792–1867, whose studies of the colouring of Greek architecture caused a sensation in the 1830s.

Bradley, Will, 1868–1962: graphic designer. Worked as a wood-engraver in Chicago. Later turned to design; he was particularly influenced by the work of Aubrey Beardsley (*q.v.*) and to a lesser extent by the Parisian designer Eugène Grasset (*q.v.*). His work, though not original, is of outstanding technical quality. He was also a distinguished typographer.

Bragdon, Claude, 1866–1946: architect. After working for several architects as a draughtsman, Bragdon set up his own architectural practice in Rochester, New York. In 1923 he retired from architectural practice and designed theatre sets. He was deeply interested in mysticism.

Brandt, Edgar, 1880–1960: metalworker. The leading exponent of decorative wrought-iron work at the Paris 1925 Exhibition.

Braquemond, Joseph Auguste (Félix), 1833–1914): artist and designer. Discovered coloured wood-block prints by Hokusai in Delâtre's shop in Paris in 1856. Thus began the Parisian enthusiasm for Japan. Also known for his etchings.

Burges, William, 1827–81: architect. The son of a civil engineer. Began his training in the office of Edward Blore; later worked for Matthew Digby Wyatt (*q.v.*). In 1851 Burges joined Henry Clutton, another graduate of Blore's office. Burges and Clutton won the international competition for Lille Cathedral but their design was not executed. After quarrelling with Clutton, Burges set up on his own. His principal works are Cork Cathedral, 1862–76, additions to Cardiff Castle, 1865, the re-modelling of Castell Coch, near Cardiff, 1875, and his own house in Melbury Road, Kensington, 1875. Burges had an extensive knowledge of Christian iconography.

Burne-Jones, Sir Edward Coley, 1833–98: painter. A lifelong friend of William Morris who was a fellow student at Exeter College, Oxford. Like Morris, he was greatly influenced by D. G. Rossetti. His paintings seem to epitomize the widespread nineteenth-century desire to escape from reality.

Butterfield, Lindsay Philip, 1869–1948: decorative designer. Began selling designs commercially in the early 1890s.

Butterfield, William, 1814–1900: architect. Among the most innovative of Gothic Revival architects (certainly he was less concerned with archaeological exactitude than Scott or Street), Butterfield made great play with patterned brickwork—Keble College, Oxford, 1867–75, being the most notable example.

Capey, Reco, 1895–1961: designer. Trained at the Royal College of Art where he taught from 1924–35. President of the Arts and Crafts Exhibition Society, 1938–42. Designed textiles, pottery, glass, metalwork, etc.

Carrier-Belleuse, Albert Ernest, 1824–87: designer and modeller. Studied in Paris. Worked for some years for Minton's, the ceramic manufacturers, in Stoke-on-Trent. His work was seen at many international exhibitions during his lifetime.

Carter, John, 1748–1817: architect and antiquarian. The son of a London marble carver. He was trained by his father and later by a surveyor and mason. In 1786 he was employed by the Society of Antiquaries to prepare drawings and etchings—he was elected a Fellow in 1795. Among his patrons were Sir John Soane and Horace Walpole.

Cellini, Benvenuto, 1500–71: goldsmith. Born in Florence and worked there and in Bologna before moving to Rome. Designed a number of vases in the Mannerist style and enjoyed great success in France (from 1540 to 1545) and Florence. His celebrated autobiography gives a highly coloured account of his life.

Chernikhov, Ya'cov Georgievich, 1889–1957: architect. Born in the Ukraine. He first worked in a photographic studio, and attended Odessa College of Art, 1907–14. He began freelance teaching in 1912. He moved to Petrograd in 1914, where he taught technical drawing. He started to study architecture in 1916, but because of the interruption of war service did not qualify until 1925. Later he became a Professor in the Leningrad Institute of Communication Engineers. Chernikhov designed many chemical plants throughout the USSR.

Chorlton, H. C. D., printer and graphic designer. A close friend of the Manchester Arts and Crafts architect Edgar Wood (*q.v.*). He was Master of the Northern Art Workers Guild in 1901–2.

Clerget, Charles Ernest, b. 1812: designer. Designed porcelain for the Sèvres factory and tapestry for the Gobelins factory. Produced a number of books of ornament and published designs for wallpapers and goldsmith's work, as well as collections of sixteenth-century ornament.

Cole, Henry, 1808–82: civil servant. The first Director of the South Kensington Museum—later the Victoria and Albert Museum. His *Journal of Design and Manufactures*, 1849–52, was the first British publication to consider seriously the problem of design for industrial production. Prince Albert's adviser and confidant during the Great Exhibition period.

Colling, James Kellaway, 1816–1905: architect. First practised in Norfolk. Was one of the founders of the Architectural Association in 1846. His publications were widely used as pattern-books by Gothic Revival architects.

Collingwood, William Gershom, 1854–1932: secretary to John Ruskin (*q.v.*). Like Ruskin, he was deeply interested in geology and was the author of *Limestone Alps of Savoy*. He accompanied Ruskin on some of his later continental journeys. He makes frequent appearances in Ruskin's diaries, where he is called 'Collie'.

Conran, Sir Terence Orby, b. 1931: designer and founder of the chain of Habitat furniture stores. Born in Esher, Surrey. Trained as a textile designer at the Central School of Art. Opened first Habitat shop in May 1964.

Coste, Pascal Xavier, 1787–1879: architect and civil engineer. Born in Marseilles. Studied at the Ecole des Beaux-Arts, Paris. Went to Egypt in 1818, where he became architect to Mehemet Ali. On his return to France in 1828 designed several churches in Marseilles.

Crane, Walter, 1845–1915: illustrator and designer. Apprenticed to a wood-engraver. He first came to prominence with his novel and partly Japanese-influenced children's books in the late 1860s. A founding member of the Art Workers' Guild in 1884, Crane became an important Arts and Crafts propagandist. His approach to design, however, was invariably that of an eclectic.

Cutler, Thomas William, 1842?–1909: architect. Designed the Hotel Metropole, Folkstone, and the Italian Hospital, Queen

Biographies

Square, London. He was particularly interested in health and sanitation. Author of *Cottages and Country Buildings*, 1896.

Davis, Owen William, 1838–1913: architect and designer. Trained under J. K. Colling (*q.v.*). Assisted Sir Matthew Digby Wyatt (*q.v.*) for a number of years. Designed furniture, metalwork and carpets for major manufacturers.

Day, Lewis Foreman, 1845–1910: designer. Worked intitially as a stained-glass designer. A founding member of the Art Workers' Guild in 1884 and of the Arts and Crafts Exhibition Society in 1888. His first pattern-book *Instances of Accessory Art*, 1880, shows him to have been an eclectic with a particular penchant for Japan. His inexpensive manuals on ornamental design are still of practical value to designers.

Day, Lucienne: textile designer. One of the leaders in her field in Britain. She was especially influential during the 1950s. She is married to the well-known designer Robin Day, b. 1915.

De Boer, Antoinette: designer. Studied in Hamburg under Professor Marget Hildebrand. Presently head of the design studio of the Stuttgarter Gardinenfabrik. She has received several awards for her work.

Denon, Dominique Vivant, 1747–1825: connoisseur and collector. Principally remembered for his *Voyage dans la Basse et la Haute Egypte* (1802), which he wrote after his travels to Egypt with Napoleon. The book immediately attracted enormous interest and undoubtedly influenced the English furniture designer Thomas Hope. His *Description de l'Egypte* followed, 1809–22. Denon also acted as art adviser to Napoleon and built up his own collection of drawings.

Dorn, Marion, 1899–1964: designer. Born in San Francisco and educated at Stanford University. Was particularly successful during the 1930s and designed for all the leading British textile and carpet manufacturers. Her one attempt at illustration—William Beckford's *Vathek*, 1929—is particularly impressive.

Dresser, Christopher, 1834–1904: designer, botanist and writer. The son of a Yorkshire customs officer, Dresser was born in Glasgow. He received his earliest education in Bandon, County Cork, Eire. Entered the School of Design, Somerset House, when he was thirteen, where he won scholarships and prizes. Exhibited considerable skill as a botanical draughtsman and turned towards scientific botany. His failure to obtain the Chair of Botany at University College, London, in 1860 may well have prompted him to return to design. However, he continued to hold professorships of botany at several important London institutions until the late 1860s. Dresser ran a large design office with many assistants. He supplied designs for wallpapers, carpets, fabrics, lace, linoleum, ceramics, furniture, cast iron, silver and silver plate. He died in Mulhouse at the age of seventy while selling designs produced by his studio.

Du Cerceau, Jacques Androuet, c. 1515–c. 85: architect, engraver and publisher. Strongly influenced by Italian Mannerist design. Du Cerceau's principal achievements were his patterny books for architects and craftsmen, rather than his buildings.

Dufrêne, Maurice, 1876–1955: designer of furniture, fabrics, wallpapers, carpets, metalwork, glass and ceramics. Studied at the Ecole des Arts Décoratifs, Paris. He was particularly interested in industrial techniques.

Dufy, Raoul, 1877–1953: painter and decorative designer. Born in Le Havre. Was for some time associated with the Fauves. Began designing textiles in 1911 for Paul Poiret, the fashion designer. From 1912 until the late 1920s Dufy designed numerous textiles for the Lyonnais silk manufacturer Bianchini Férier. In the 1930s he designed a series of textiles for a New York firm.

Dyce, William, 1806–64: painter and educationalist. Although gifted in the sciences—he was winner of a prize for an essay on *The Relations between Electricity and Magnetism*—Dyce determined early in his youth to become a painter. Richard Redgrave was later to write of his works as 'learned more than original' and 'calling forth our approval in a greater degree than our love'. He brought his keen intellect to bear on the new subject of design education in the late 1830s and early 1840s and made it academically respectable.

Edwards, Edward B., 1873–1948: designer and illustrator. Trained at the Art Students' League, New York, and in Paris. Director of the American Institute of Graphic Art. Designed handbooks for the Metropolitan Museum of Art and other institutions.

Ehmke, Fritz Hellmuth, b. 1878: lecturer and graphic designer. Taught in Düsseldorf and Munich. One of the leading German poster designers of the pre-1914 period.

Endell, August, 1871–1925: architect, sculptor and designer. First studied philosophy. He was strongly influenced by the work of Hermann Obrist (*q.v.*). His first important architectural work was the façade of the Elvira Photographic Studio, Munich, 1897–8, which is particularly reminiscent of Obrist. His later work was more restrained and included department stores in Berlin and Breslau.

Erith, Raymond, 1904–73: architect. Designed neo-Georgian buildings. Quinlan Terry (b. 1937) is his successor.

Etchells, Frederick, 1886–1973: painter and architect. Studied painting at the Royal College of Art. Exhibited in the second Post-Impressionist Exhibition, 1912. Designed for the Omega Workshops in 1913, but left when Wyndham Lewis resigned. Took up architecture in about 1920.

Fairfax-Muckley, Louis, fl. 1895: artist. Student of the Birmingham School of Art. Exhibited at the New Gallery, London, 1889, and at the Royal Academy, 1890.

Ferri, Gaetano, fl. 1854: Italian professor of drawing. Ferri's method of teaching ornament was very similar to the one in vogue in contemporary France.

Fischer von Erlach, Johann Bernhard, 1656–1723: architect. Visited Italy in 1674 where he is said to have studied under Carlo Fontana. Settled in Vienna in 1685. He was appointed court architect in 1704. He designed several important churches: the Karlskirche in Vienna, begun in 1716, is his best-known building.

Fisher, Alexander, 1864–1936: sculptor and enameller. Studied at the National Training Schools, South Kensington (later the Royal College of Art). Also studied in Rome and Paris. In the late 1880s he was greatly influenced by the ideas of the Arts and Crafts Movement and he began experimenting in enamelling. From 1893 he lectured on this technique at the City Guilds of London Institute.

Fontaine, Pierre François Léonard, 1762–1853: architect. Studied at the Ecole des Beaux-Arts, where he first met Charles Percier (*q.v.*). The two began working on the Château of Malmaison for Napoleon in 1799. Fontaine and Percier developed a decorative eclectic Neo-Classical and architectural style which particularly suited Napoleon's flamboyant taste.

Foord, Miss J.: botanical artist. Miss Foord is known solely through her book *Decorative Flower Studies*, 1901, some of the plates in which are dated 1899. She may have been a gifted amateur. Her book was praised by Verneuil in *Art et Décoration*.

Forbes, Edward, 1815–54: naturalist. One of the leading naturalists of his generation. Forbes was able to present his ideas to non-specialist audiences. Like Ernst Haeckel (*q.v.*) he viewed nature as a totality.

Foxton, William, d. 1945: textile manufacturer. One of the founding members of the Design in Industries Association, 1915. An enlightened patron of avant-garde design in the 1920s.

Frampton, George, 1860–1928: sculptor and teacher. Trained in London, under W. S. Frith, and in Paris, under Antonin Mercié. Was very closely associated with the Arts and Crafts Movement and in 1894 was appointed joint head of the Central School of Arts and Crafts with W. R. Lethaby (*q.v.*). His most famous sculpture is Peter Pan, Kensington Gardens, 1911.

France, Georgie (Georgiana) Evelyn Cave, 1866–1934: designer and jeweller. Trained at the Birmingham School of Art. Married Arthur Gaskin (1862–1928), a fellow student, in 1894. Collaborated with her husband in the making of jewellery from 1899.

Fraser, Claud Lovat, 1890–1921: designer. Designed textiles, theatre sets and costumes. He was also successful as an illustrator. His designs for *The Beggar's Opera*, revived in 1920, were a sensation.

Freeman, Edward A., fl. 1850s. Student of medieval architecture. Freeman was a one-time Fellow of Trinity College, Oxford. He was author of *The History of Architecture* and *The Architecture of Llandaff Cathedral*. His *Window Tracery*, 1851, was based upon papers read before the Oxford Architectural Society between 1846 and 1848.

Froment-Meurice, François Désiré, 1802–55: designer. Principal of large design firm in Paris. Winner of prizes at the Great Exhibition of 1851 and the Paris Exhibition of 1855.

Fry, Roger, 1866–1934: writer and artist. Studied natural science at Cambridge. Wrote on art for the *Burlington Magazine* and the *Athenaeum*. Curator of paintings at the Metropolitan Museum of Art from 1906–10. Organizer of the Post-Impressionist Exhibitions of 1910 and 1912 in London. Founded the Omega Workshops in 1913.

Furness, Frank, 1839–1912: architect. Practised in Philadelphia, where he designed many buildings in an aggressive Gothic style. Louis Sullivan (*q.v.*) worked briefly in his office. Christopher Dresser (*q.v.*) praised Furness' ornament.

Gaudí, Antoni, 1852–1926: architect. Studied at Barcelona University, and most of his buildings are in that city. His Casa Vicens (1883–5) incorporates Moorish elements. His Cathedral of the Sagrada Familia is one of the most capricious and inventive buildings of the nineteenth century. It is still unfinished.

Gauthier, Joseph, fl. 1920: educator. Professor of L'Ecole Regionale des Beaux-Arts at Nantes, where he taught ornament.

Gentleman, David, b. 1930: designer, painter and muralist. Trained at the Royal College of Art, 1950–3. Has designed book illustrations, murals, postage stamps, wallpapers, etc. His *London*, published in 1985, was widely acclaimed.

Gibson, Nathalie: textile designer. Studied at Chelsea School of Art, 1956–8, and the Royal College of Art, 1958–61. She has designed for many major manufacturers in Britain and elsewhere.

Godwin, Edward William, 1833–86: architect and designer. Born in Bristol. His architectural works include the town halls of Northampton (1861–4) and Congleton (1864). Both are in a bold Gothic Revival style. Later Godwin became one of the leading exponents of the Queen Anne style. Lived for several years with the actress Ellen Terry. Edward Gordon Craig was the offspring of this liaison. Godwin was a close friend of William Burges (*q.v.*) and designed J. M. Whistler's White House in Tite Street, Chelsea. He produced many designs for the theatre towards the end of his life.

Goodhart-Rendel, H. S., 1887–1959: architect and writer. Studied music at Cambridge, but took up architecture later. Started his own practice in 1910. Director of the Architectural Association School of Architecture, 1937–9. President of the RIBA.

Grant, Duncan, 1885–1978: painter. Studied at Westminster School of Art and in Paris. Exhibited at the second Post-Impressionist Exhibition. Met Roger Fry (*q.v.*) in 1910. Co-director of the Omega Workshops from 1913–19. Two retrospective exhibitions, 1929 and Tate Gallery 1959.

Grasset, Eugène, 1841–1917: designer. Born in Lausanne. Studied architecture in Zurich. Moved to Paris in 1871, where he began to design textiles. Later Grasset was to design books and typefaces. He was one of the founders of the Société des Artistes Décorateurs. His books on decorative design are amongst the most comprehensive to have been published.

Gray, Eileen, 1878–1976: designer and architect. Born in Ireland. Trained at the Slade School of Art. In 1902 she moved to Paris, where she lived for most of her life. In Paris she learned the art of lacquering under the Japanese master Sugawara. Her work was admired by the pioneers of the Modern Movement. She again became fashionable right at the end of her life.

Gropius, Walter, 1883–1969: architect. Assistant to Peter Behrens (*q.v.*), 1908–10. Set up in practice with Adolf Meyer, 1910. Director of the Bauhaus, Weimar and Dessau, 1919–34. Worked in Britain with E. Maxwell Fry, 1934–37. Moved to the United States in 1937, where he became the leading champion of the Modern Movement.

Gruner, Ludwig (sometimes Lewis), 1801–82: artist. Originally trained as a scene-painter and engraver in Dresden. After spending several years in Rome he moved to England in the early 1840s. He was appointed Prince Albert's art adviser in 1843. He was to exert a considerable influence upon Albert's taste and was responsible for some of the decoration of Buckingham Palace.

Guimard, Hector, 1867–1942: architect and designer. Entered the Ecole des Beaux-Arts in 1885. Here he became interested in the novel ideas contained in Viollet-le-Duc's published *Discourses (Entretiens)*. Unlike Viollet-le-Duc (*q.v.*), however, Guimard had an ability to design picturesque buildings which made an appeal to a wide public. Guimard's best-known building is the Castel Béranger, 1894–8, a large and complex bourgeois apartment block with virtuoso external and internal decorative detailing. His Humbert de Romans Concert Hall, 1897–1901, now demolished, while exhibiting similar characteristics, was architecturally more cohesive. His famous cast-iron details for the Paris Métro serve as a reminder of Guimard's decorative inventiveness.

Haddon, Arthur C., 1855–1940: anthropologist and zoologist. Leader of the important Cambridge expedition to the Torres Straits. The Haddon Library in Cambridge is named after him.

Haeckel, Ernst Heinrich Philipp August, 1834–1919: marine biologist, zoologist, draughtsman and writer. Received some of his early training under the great botanist M. J. Schleiden. A chair in zoology was created for him in the University of Jena in 1865. After accepting Darwinism, Haeckel abandoned the Christian concept of a personal God. Several of his books were translated into English including his *Freedom in Science and Teaching*, 1879.

Haité, George Charles, 1855–1924: designer. The son of a Paisley textile designer. One of the most successful of late Victorian textile designers.

Halfpenny, Joseph, 1748–1811: draughtsman and engraver. The son of the gardener of the Archbishop of York. Apprenticed to a house-painter. Later became a topographical artist. Halfpenny drew the ornaments in York Minster from the scaffolding erected during its restoration.

Hall, Sir James, 1761–1832: geologist. One of the leading British geologists of his day. He presented his paper on the origins of Gothic architecture before the Royal Society of Edinburgh, of which he was later to become president. .

Hambidge, Jay, b. 1867: theorist and lecturer. Hambidge, who taught at Yale University, believed that good proportion was not a matter of instinct, but was governed by law. Both the Egyptians and the Greeks, he believed, understood such laws. (Islamic, Chinese, Hindu and Gothic designers also knew them.) Hambidge taught that the laws of proportion had been distilled from nature and he made use of the writings of A. H. Church, the British botanist, on the growth of plants.

Hildebrand, Marget: professor of textile design. A leading contemporary German designer.

Harvey, William, 1796–1866: wood-engraver and draughtsman. Born in Newcastle-on-Tyne. Was articled to the engraver Thomas Bewick, with whom he became a great favourite.

Havinden, Ashley (Eldrid), 1903–1973: designer. Studied at the Central School of Arts and Crafts. Joined the W. S. Crawford advertising agency in 1923 as a trainee. In 1929 he was elected to the board as Director of Art and Design. He became Vice-Chairman in 1960. President of the Society of Industrial Artists, 1956. Although he is best remembered for his advertisements, Havinden was active in many fields of design. He was also an abstract painter.

Hay, David Ramsay, 1796–1866: interior decorator and amateur scientist. Born in Edinburgh. After being apprenticed to a decorative painter, Hay set up his own business in Edinburgh in 1828. He ultimately employed as many as fifty workers. Hay wrote a number of works on the theory of colouring and proportion, several of which ran into more than one edition. He assisted J. Clerk Maxwell (1831–79) who is best known for his researches into the characteristics of electromagnetic waves and the phenomena of colour.

Hepworth, Barbara, 1903–75: sculptor. Trained at Leeds College of Art and the Royal College of Art. Married to Ben Nicholson. Important in British and Continental Modernist circles in the 1930s.

Hessemer, Friedrich Maximilian, 1800–60: architect and draughtsman. Born in Darmstadt. Studied natural science and philosophy in Geissen. Was trained in architecture by his uncle, Georg Muller, Chief Surveyor of Darmstadt. Travelled widely in Italy and Egypt. His second book, *Neue Arabesken*, was published in 1854.

Hildebrand, Hans, 1842–1913: archaeologist. Custodian of National Monuments in Sweden, 1879–1907. Member of the Swedish Academy from 1895.

Hoffmann, Josef, 1870–1956: architect and designer. For a short time a pupil of Otto Wagner (*q.v.*). After extensive travels Hoffmann joined Wagner's office, where he worked until 1899. Hoffmann was appointed Professor of Architecture at the Vienna School of Applied Arts (Kunstgewerbeschule) in 1899, a position which he held until 1941. Hoffmann's Puckersdorf Sanatorium (1903–6), a plain symmetrical structure, sometimes seen as a harbinger of the International Style, is generally considered to have been his most important building.

Hope, Thomas, c. 1770–1831: connoisseur. Travelled widely in Europe, Asia and Africa as a young man. His collection of antique sculpture and works by leading Neo-Classical sculptors was displayed in his house in Duchess Street, London, to which he at one time actually issued tickets for admission. His *Household Furniture and Interior Decoration* of 1792 helped to spread the Neo-Classical style.

Hornung, Charles Pearson, fl. 1932: designer. Studied architectural history at Columbia University under Professor A. D. F. Hamlin. His work on trademarks was greatly admired.

Horta, Victor, 1861–1947: architect. Studied in Paris and Brussels. He was particularly interested in the structural and expressive possibilities of ironwork, and the exposed ironwork of his Hôtel Tassel in Brussels (1892) is an excellent example of his predilection for organic form. The lavish Hôtel Solvay, also in Brussels, with its splendidly decorated dining-room, places him in the forefront of Art Nouveau designers.

Housman, Laurence, 1865–1959: writer and illustrator. Brother of A. E. Housman, the poet and classicist. See his autobiography *The Unexpected Years*.

Huff, William S., teacher. Educated at Yale and New Haven. 1956–7 Fulbright Scholarship. Taught basic design at the Ulm Hochschule für Gestaltung under Tomas Maldonado, 1958–60.

Hulme, Frederick Edward, 1841–1909: botanical draughtsman, botanist, designer and teacher. In 1858 began studying at the South Kensington Schools, where Dresser was lecturing on 'artistic botany'. He wrote on a wide variety of subjects ranging from popular botany, heraldry, ornament and entomology to symbolism in Christian art.

Hunter, Alec, 1899–1958: designer and weaver. His father was the owner of the St Edmondsbury Weaving Works at Haslemere, which was taken over by Morton Sundour Fabrics in 1928. He was responsible for some of the earliest Edinburgh Weavers productions.

Image, Selwyn, 1849–1930: artist and designer. Destined originally for the church but left it to devote himself to art. Was associated with A. M. Mackmurdo (*q.v.*) in founding the Century Guild. Master of the Art Workers' Guild, 1900. Slade Professor of Fine Art, Oxford, 1910–16.

Jack, George, 1855–1932: architect. Born in Long Island, NY. Entered Philip Webb's office in 1880 and took over his practice in 1900. Was chief furniture designer for Morris & Co after about 1890.

Jackson, Frank G.: educationalist. Taught at the Birmingham School of Art, a leading centre of Arts and Crafts teaching, at the turn of the century.

Jaudon, Valerie, b. 1945: painter and designer. Educated at the Memphis Academy of Art, Memphis, Tennessee, the University of the Americas, Mexico City, Mexico, and St Martin's School of Art, London. Has exhibited at the Holly Solomon Gallery, New York, and at Zurich, Düsseldorf, etc.

Jeckyll, Thomas, 1827–81: architect and designer. Worked in Norfolk and London. First came to prominence with a large set of cast-iron gates manufactured by Barnard, Bishop and Barnard, which were shown at the 1862 Exhibition. In 1876 designed a room for R. Leyland which was subsequently transformed by Whistler into the famous Peacock Room.

Jencks, Charles, b. 1939: critic and architect. Born in Baltimore, USA. Jencks' writings have helped to give form to the current movement in architecture and design which can be seen as a reaction to the vaunting intellectual assumptions of the Modern Movement.

Joel, Betty, b. 1896: designer. With her husband, David Joel, founded the firm of Betty Joel Ltd with premises in Sloane Street, London, shortly after the 1914–18 war. Was very influential in disseminating non-extreme Modernism in Britain during the 1930s. She retired at the peak of her success in 1937.

Jones, Owen, 1809–74: architect, designer and theorist. The son of Owen Jones (Owain Myfyr), 1741–1814, a successful furrier and authority on early Welsh literature. He was articled to a London architect, Lewis Vulliamy. After completing his articles he travelled extensively. Between 1832 and 1834 he visited Greece, Constantinople, the Holy Land, Egypt and Spain. In Athens Jones encountered Jules Goury, a young French architect and archaeologist, with whom he published *Views on the Nile*, 1843. In *The Alhambra*, 1836–45, Jones also collaborated with Goury, who died in the very early stages of the project. His first 'illuminated book', Lockhart's *Ancient Spanish Ballads*, was published in 1841; his second was *The Sermon on the Mount* of 1845. Many others were to follow, the last being *Scenes from a Winter's Tale*, 1866. His most important project was the great *Grammar of Ornament*, 1856, a bible for many later designers. Jones designed fabrics, carpets, book-covers, packaging, playing-cards etc. He designed comparatively few buildings, but he cannot be considered unsuccessful. His project for an exhibition building at St-Cloud, Paris, had it been built, would have been one of the greatest glass buildings of the century. Jones was a close friend of George Eliot and her consort G. H. Lewes.

Kawashima, Jimbe, fl. 1910: manufacturer. Head of the firm of Kawashima & Co, Kyoto, an important textile manufactory.

Kay, John Illingworth, 1870–1950: designer. Born in Kirkcaldy, Scotland. Began working in the Silver Studio (*q.v.*) in the early 1890s. Left the studio in 1900 to work for the Essex Wallpaper Company, where he remained for 22 years. Also taught at the Central School of Arts and Crafts.

King, Jessie Marion, 1876–1949: designer and illustrator. Trained at the Glasgow School of Art. Best remembered for her delicate and original book illustrations.

Klee, Paul, 1879–1940: painter. Studied at Munich under Franz von Stuck. Taught at the Bauhaus between 1920 and 1931, where he was director of the stained-glass workshop, the weaving and the painting courses. His *Pädagogisches Skizzenbuch* (Pedagogical Sketchbook), which sets out his teaching method, was translated into English in 1953.

Klimt, Gustav, 1862–1918: painter. Trained in Vienna. Klimt's earliest work is in a conventional academic style. In 1898 he was one of the founders of the Vienna Secession. His paintings, particularly his portraits, often incorporate decorative elements laden with symbolic meaning.

Korin, Ogata, 1658–1716: artist. Foremost decorative artist of the Edo period.

Kristian, Roald, b. 1893: artist. Born in Norway. Trained in Paris. Executed woodcuts for the first two of Roger Fry's Omega books. Deported from Britain in 1917 as an enemy alien.

Lalique, René, 1860–1945: jeweller and artist in glass. Founded his manufactory for glass in Paris in 1885. His early work was based upon floral forms. He collaborated briefly with Samuel Bing (*q.v.*) of L'Art Nouveau fame. He had his own pavilion, with a luminous fountain, at the Paris Exhibition of 1925.

Lane, Edward William, 1801–76: Arabic scholar and artist. The son of a clergyman. After abandoning a plan to enter the church, he was articled to an engraver in London. Bad health, however, forced him to seek a warmer climate. He had long had an interest in the East and left for Egypt in 1825 in the hope of obtaining a diplomatic post. He was soon fluent in Arabic and became one of the foremost Arabists of his day. He died while working on his Arabic dictionary.

Le Blond, Jean-Baptiste Alexandre, 1679–1719: architect. Born in Paris. Worked in Russia on the Peterhof Palace (begun 1716) in St Petersburg, where he introduced the French Rococo style. In interior decoration he believed in a more intimate arrangement of rooms, where display was subservient to comfort.

Le Corbusier, Charles Edouard (Jeanneret), 1887–1966: architect. Born in La Chaux-de-Fonds, Switzerland. Worked for a while with Peter Behrens in Berlin. One of the most influential architects of the twentieth century, whose ideas on the mass production of housing and town planning have transformed architectural practice. His villa at Garches (1927) and Villa Savoye at Poissy (1929–31) are of particular interest. In Chandigarh in the Punjab he laid out a whole town, as well as building the Law Courts and Secretariat.

Leighton, John, 1822–1912: designer. Designed the title-page of *The Art-Journal Catalogue of the Great Exhibition*, 1851. A founder member of the Photographers' Society of London. His stained-glass designs were exhibited at the Royal Academy in 1854. Elected a member of the Society of Antiquaries in 1855. He was the designer of numerous book decorations; he also designed bank-notes.

Lemmen, George, 1865–1916: painter. Born in Brussels. Painted initially in a French Impressionist manner. Van de Velde described him as a 'pessimistic' man and compared his ornament to that of Otto Eckmann and Hermann Obrist (*q.v.*).

Le Pautre, Jean, 1618–82: engraver and designer. His engravings of chimney-pieces, published in 1665, introduced a simpler, lighter design. He also published engravings of designs by Le Brun, which were widely circulated and helped spread Le Brun's fame beyond France.

Lethaby, William Richard, 1857–1931: architect and theorist. The most important exponent of the Arts and Crafts philosophy. After working in the offices of provincial architects, he became Richard Norman Shaw's principal assistant in 1881. In 1893 he was appointed joint principal—with George Frampton—at the new Central School of Arts and Crafts. In 1900 he was made first Professor of Design at the Royal College of Art. Although he was among the most accomplished of the architects associated with the Arts and Crafts Movement, Lethaby's executed works are few. He was a champion of Philip Webb. An able writer, he was editor of Hogg's influential *Artistic Crafts* Series and the author of several major theoretical studies.

Levy, Audrey, b. 1928: designer. Trained at the Royal College of Art. Winner of several awards. Is keenly interested in design education. Now a design consultant.

Lindley, John, 1799–1866: botanist and teacher. At the age of 16 he was sent to Belgium as the agent for a London seed merchant. His first original contribution to botanical science was a history of roses which was published in 1820. In 1829 Lindley was appointed first Professor of Botany at London University. He was the author of several standard textbooks on botany.

Ling Roth, H., 1855–1925: anthropologist. One of the first students of Benin art.

Loewy, Raymond, b. 1893: designer. Born in Paris. Settled in New York in 1919, where he worked as a window-dresser and later as a fashion illustrator. His first important essay in industrial design was a duplicator for the Gestetner Company of 1929. Loewy has established one of the largest industrial design practices, with several offices in America and Europe. During the 1930s he was among the leading exponents of the streamlined style. His steam and electric locomotives were among the most impressive of the decade.

Loos, Adolf, 1870–1933: architect. Born in Brno, Moravia. Worked in Vienna, where he came under the influence of Otto

Wagner. His restrained use of ornament arose from his dislike of Secessionist and Jugendstil decoration. His famous article 'Ornament and Crime' first came out in 1908, but was not greatly heeded at the time. Some of its ideas, such as those on the barbarity of tattooing, seem to derive from the Italian criminologist Cesare Lombroso (1836–1909).

Lutyens, Sir Edwin, 1869–1944: architect. His earliest works are in the Arts and Crafts manner. He later embraced Classicism. Lutyens had many imitators but none possessed his ability to orchestrate the elements of Classical architecture.

Macbeth, Ann, 1875–1948: designer and embroiderer. Lost the sight of one eye in childhood, which prevented stereoscopic vision. She claimed her interest in design and flat pattern stemmed from this event. Was on the teaching staff of the Glasgow School of Art for many years. She was the author of several textbooks on needlework, etc.

MacConnel, Kim, b. 1946: painter and designer. Educated at the University of California at San Diego. 1970 California State Scholar. Exhibitions at Holly Solomon Gallery, New York, Zurich and London, etc.

Mackintosh, Charles Rennie, 1868–1928: architect, designer and painter. The son of a Glasgow police superintendent. Was originally trained in the office of John Hutchison. In 1889 he entered the office of Honeyman and Keppie, a major Glasgow partnership. He won a number of architectural students' competitions, including the Alexander Thomson travelling scholarship which enabled him to visit Italy, France and Belgium in 1892. In 1896, while still working for Honeyman and Keppie, Mackintosh won the competition for the new Glasgow School of Art, a building of great originality. His work was widely admired in Europe, but he gained no major commissions in Britain.

Mackintosh, Margaret Macdonald, 1865–1933: designer. Wife of Charles Rennie Mackintosh, she collaborated with him on a number of decorative schemes.

Mackmurdo, Arthur Heygate, 1851–1942: architect. Articled to James Brooks, an important Gothic Revival architect. He set up his own practice in 1875. His earliest design–a house for his mother—reveals the influence of Norman Shaw (*q.v.*). In 1882 Mackmurdo, under the influence of William Morris, founded the Century Guild of Artists. This aimed 'to render all branches of art the sphere no longer of the tradesman but the artist'. The Century Guild, after some initial success, was disbanded in 1888. Mackmurdo's few buildings show him to have been an architect of real originality.

Macleish, Minnie, b. 1876: graphic and textile designer. Designed for Morton Sundour Fabrics Ltd, Carlisle, and advertisements.

Mairet, Ethel, 1872–1952: weaver and teacher. Was for a time married to Amanda K. Coomaraswamy, the renowned authority on Indian art. During visits to Ceylon (Sri Lanka) and India learned traditional weaving techniques. Her weaving workshop at Ditchling, Sussex, was greatly admired.

Mallet-Stevens, Robert, 1886–1945: architect. Born in Paris. His early designs reflect the influence of Josef Hoffmann (*q.v.*). Although he was to become a leading exponent of the International Modern Style, he was not wholly opposed to ornament. Designed some film sets.

Margold, Emanuel Josef, b. 1889: architect and designer. Studied under Josef Hoffmann (*q.v.*) in the Vienna Kunstgewerbeschule. Was associated with the Wiener Werkstätte. Later taught in Darmstadt. Settled in Berlin in 1929.

Marot, Jean, c. 1619–79: architect and engraver. Born in Paris. Designed for Louis XIV.

Martin, Kenneth, b. 1905: artist. Studied at the Royal College of Art, 1929–32. Produced his first abstract paintings 1948–9. Married to Mary Martin, the artist (d. 1969).

Marx, Enid, b. 1902: designer and printmaker. Trained at the Central School of Arts and Crafts and the Royal College of Art. Has designed textiles, wallpapers, ceramics, postage stamps, book jackets. Has also illustrated children's books.

McGrath, Raymond, 1903–77: architect, designer and writer. Studied architecture at Sydney University, Australia. After three years as a research student at Cambridge University set up his own architectural practice in London. Became co-ordinator of a team of avant-garde designers responsible for the interior of the BBC's headquarters—Broadcasting House. Settled in Ireland 1940. From 1948–68 was Principal Architect to the Office of Public Works, Republic of Ireland.

Meheut, Mathurin, b. 1882: painter and designer. Published *Etude de la Plante, Etude d'Animal, Etude de la Mer* etc.

Meurer, Moritz, 1839–1916: painter. Studied under Schnorr von Carolsfeld (1794–1872), the Nazarene, at the Academy of Dresden. From 1871–83 he taught in Berlin, and lived in Rome from 1884 to 1915. Meurer was the teacher of Karl Blossfeldt (*q.v.*).

Mies van der Rohe, Ludwig, 1886–1969: architect. Worked for Peter Behrens (*q.v.*) 1908–11. His pavilion for the Barcelona Exhibition, 1929, which is exquisitely detailed, exemplifies his austere philosophy. He was director of the Bauhaus from 1930 to 1933. He later emigrated to the United States, where he acquired an immense reputation.

Minton, Francis John, 1917–57: painter. Trained at St John's Wood School of Art. Minton was much in demand as a teacher and taught at all the leading London art colleges. His art was eclectic, but it nevertheless belonged essentially to the English topographical tradition. He was an accomplished portrait painter. He also designed for the theatre.

Moody, Francis Wollaston, 1824–86: artist and teacher. Instructor in Decorative Art at the South Kensington Museum in the 1870s. He was much influenced by the sculptor Alfred Stevens (*q.v.*). He was evidently a popular teacher and his *Lectures and Lessons on Art*, 1873, ran into five editions. He was vociferously opposed to Christopher Dresser's approach to ornamental design.

Moore, Henry, b. 1898: sculptor. Trained at Leeds School of Art and the Royal College of Art. Retrospective exhibitions at the Museum of Modern Art, New York, 1946; the Tate Gallery, 1978. His present immense reputation began gathering momentum in the 1930s.

Morellet, François, b. 1926: artist. A founder member of the Groupe de Recherche d'Art Visuel. He is probably best known for his constructions composed of lattices of metal rods, which create surprising optical effects.

Morris, May J., 1860–1947: designer, embroiderer and lecturer. The second daughter of William Morris, by whom she was trained. An accomplished designer, she designed textiles, wallpapers and embroideries for Morris & Co. She was among the founders of the Women's Guild of Arts, 1907. May Morris was the author of *William Morris, Artist, Writer, Socialist*, 1936.

Morris, Talwin, 1865–1911: graphic designer. Art director of Blackie's, the publishers, Glasgow, from 1893. Moved in the Glasgow School of Art circles.

Morris, William, 1834–96: designer, craftsman, writer and political activist. Born into a wealthy middle-class family. Originally intended to take up a career in the church, but while a student at Oxford became interested in the arts. Articled himself to G. E. Street, a leading Gothic Revival ecclesiastical architect. He soon abandoned architecture in order to become a painter, but quickly realized that this was not his vocation. He married Jane Burden, a girl from a poor family, and in 1859 commissioned Philip Webb, whom he had met in Street's office, to design their house, the Red House at Upton in Kent. The experience gained in furnishing and decorating the Red House prompted Morris to set up a co-operative of designers which included Webb, Burne-Jones, Rossetti and Ford Madox Brown. The 'Firm', Morris, Marshall, Faulkner & Co—after 1875 Morris & Co—was to exert a wide influence on British taste. Morris was a tireless worker and attained a high degree of perfection in several crafts. His views on the alienation of workers in industrialized society were particularly advanced.

Morton, Alistair, 1910–63: textile manufacturer. The son of Sir James Morton, Chairman of Morton Sundour Fabrics Ltd. Appointed Artistic Director of Edinburgh Weavers, subsidiary of Morton Sundour, in 1932–3. He was also a painter and designer.

Moser, Koloman (Kolo), 1868–1918: painter and designer. Studied at the Vienna Academy between 1886–92 and the Kunstgewerbeschule until 1895. Was one of the founders of the Secession (1897) and the Wiener Werkstätte (1903). He also played an important part in the founding of the Secessionist Journal *Ver Sacrum* (1898). From 1899 taught with Josef Hoffmann at the Kunstgewerbeschule. Moser was particularly influential as a graphic designer. He designed books, posters, postage stamps and bank-notes.

Mucha, Alphonse, 1860–1939: graphic designer. Born in Ivancice, now Czechoslovakia. Began his career in Vienna as a set-painter for the theatre. Went to Paris in 1888. He came to popular notice in 1892 with his poster for Sarah Bernhardt's *Gismonda*. In the 1960s Mucha was rediscovered and, as was the case with Aubrey Beardsley (*q.v.*), ideas borrowed from him became visual clichés.

Munthe, Gerhard Peter Frantz Vilhelm, 1849–1929: painter. Born in Norway. In the 1890s Munthe attempted to re-create a specifically Norse art. He drew on Norwegian folk traditions and Viking art. His work was well known outside Norway. *The Studio*, VIII, 1896, contains an interesting article on his work.

Murphy, James Cavanah, 1760–1814: architect and antiquarian. Born in Cork, Ireland, the son of poor parents. Although apprenticed as a bricklayer his drawing talents were noticed and he was allowed to enter the drawing school of the Dublin Society when he was about fifteen. He practised as an architect in Dublin and assisted with James Gandon's projects. In 1788 he was commissioned to prepare drawings of the Dominican church at Batalha by William Burton Conyngham. He began his study of Moorish architecture in Spain in 1802.

Nash, Paul, 1889–1946: painter and designer. Trained at the Slade School. As an official war artist in the 1914–18 war Nash painted the devastated landscape of the Northern French battlegrounds. In the 1930s he adopted a restrained Surrealist manner in his paintings. He designed many textiles, books, posters and some interiors. He published *Room and Book*, 1932, in which he set out his views on book production and interior design.

Nesfield, William Eden, 1835–88: architect. Partner of Richard Norman Shaw (*q.v.*) for a period. With Shaw, Nesfield was one of the pioneers of the eclectic Queen Anne style, which came to prominence in the 1870s. Although less prolific than Shaw, his country houses show him to have been an architect of great inventiveness.

Newbery, Jessie R., b. 1864: embroiderer. The daughter of a Paisley shawl-maker, she trained at the Glasgow School of Art. She married Francis H. Newbery, the principal, in 1889. Taught embroidery at the school between 1894 and 1908.

Newill, Mary J., 1860–1947: designer and embroiderer. Trained at the Birmingham School of Art and, with the aid of a scholarship, in Paris. Taught design and embroidery at the Birmingham School of Art from about 1882 until 1919. She was a member of the Arts and Crafts Exhibition Society.

Nicholson, Ben, 1894–1982: painter. Trained at the Slade School. Retrospective exhibition at the Tate Gallery, 1969. Married to Barbara Hepworth (*q.v.*). Of British abstract painters Nicholson has the widest international reputation.

Nicholson, Roger, b. 1922: painter, muralist and designer. Taught graphic design at St Martin's School of Art. Professor of Textile Design, the Royal College of Art, 1958–84. Consultant to several major manufacturers.

Obrist, Hermann, 1862–1927: sculptor, painter, designer and ceramicist. The son of a Swiss doctor and a Scottish mother. Began studying medicine and the natural sciences. However, in 1886, a vision of a radiant city directed his ambitions towards art. In 1888 he began to study ceramics; he later moved to Paris to study sculpture. In 1892 he moved to Florence, where he studied marble techniques. He founded his atelier for embroidery in Munich in 1895. One of the most important designers of the Jugendstil period.

Olbrich, Josef Maria, 1867–1908: architect. Born in Silesia. Studied architecture in Vienna. Winner of the Rome Prize, 1893. Worked under Otto Wagner for a number of years. Designed the Secession House in Vienna, 1897–8, which owes something to Klimt's preliminary sketch. Designed a number of important buildings for the Artists' Colony at Darmstadt, founded by Ernst Ludwig of Hesse. Died of leukemia while he was at the very height of his powers.

Ospovat, H., b. 1877: artist. Born in Russia. Apprenticed to a lithographer. Subsequently studied design in the National Art Training Schools—later the Royal College of Art, London. Painted some portraits.

Page, I., fl. 1840: designer and engraver. Page is an interesting figure, despite his obscurity. He taught ornament and design at the School for Promoting Practical Design, Leicester Square. This idealistic institution, however, declined in influence as Government Schools of Design were set up throughout the country.

Paley, William, 1743–1805: archdeacon of Carlisle. Educated at Cambridge. He was appointed rector of Musgrave, Cumberland, in 1775. In 1785 his *Principles of Moral and Political Philosophy* was adopted as a textbook in Cambridge. Paley was the author of numerous religious works.

Paolozzi, Eduardo, b. 1924: sculptor, printmaker and designer. Born in Leith, Scotland. Studied in Edinburgh and London. Worked in Paris, 1947–50. Taught textile design at Central School of Art and Design, 1949–55. Lecturer in Ceramics, Royal College of Art, 1968. Professor of Ceramics, Fachhochschule, Cologne, 1981. Professor of Sculpture, Akademie de Bildenden Künste, Munich, 1981. Winner of numerous awards.

Peche, Dagobert, 1887–1923: designer. Studied architecture in Vienna. Visited England and Paris. Designed a room in the Austrian pavilion in the important Werkbund Exhibition at Cologne, 1914. Began to design for the Wiener Werkstätte in 1915. Peche admired Rococo and brought a certain frivolity to Werkstätte design.

Percier, Charles, 1764–1838: architect and designer. Born in Paris. Studied under A. F. Peyre, in whose office he was to meet

Fontaine (*q.v.*), his future partner. With Fontaine he was to dominate French architecture during the time of Napoleon.

Phillips, George, fl. 1838–40: possibly an architect. No biographical data concerning Phillips appears to have come to light so far. His ornamental compositions, which abound with architectural detail, suggest the hand of a trained architect. The fact that he was very well versed in aesthetic theory indicates that he was a man of some education.

Pompe, Antoine, 1873–1980: architect. The son of a Dutch jeweller, he studied in Germany. Worked in Belgium, where he was prominent in the 1920s. His first important building was the Van Neck private orthopaedic clinic, 1910. He was essentially a traditionalist.

Pond, Edward, b. 1929: designer. Born in London. Studied textiles and lithography at the South East Essex Technical College. Also studied at the Royal College of Art, where he was awarded a silver medal for a thesis on A. H. Mackmurdo (*q.v.*), the early Arts and Crafts architect. 'Designer of the year', 1959. Founded the shop Paperchase, 1969.

Praetorius, C. J., draughtsman and writer. Artist to the Society of Antiquaries, London, for many years. Died at a great age in the 1950s.

Prisse d'Avennes, Achille-Constant-Théodore-Emile, 1807–79: Egyptologist and Arabist. Born in Avesnes-sur-Helpe, Nord, the son of an inspector of forests. Claimed to have been descended from an old Welsh family (Price or Preece). Fought in the Greek War of Independence. Was greatly attracted by ancient as well as modern Egypt. Was for a time tutor to the children of Ibraham Pasha. From 1836 onwards devoted himself mainly to archaeology. Visited India, Nubia and Ethiopia.

Prutscher, Otto, 1880–1949: architect and designer. Born in Vienna. Studied under Josef Hoffmann (*q.v.*) in the Vienna Kunstgewerbeschule, where he subsequently became a professor. Designed for the Wiener Werkstätte.

Pugin, Augustus Welby Northmore, 1812–52: architect, designer and writer. The son of Augustus Charles Pugin, 1769–1832, a French émigré, architect and draughtsman. Pugin was trained by his father and began designing while still in his teens. He was converted to Roman Catholicism in 1835. Pugin was responsible for the Gothic detailing of Barry's Houses of Parliament. He designed many Catholic churches for extremely modest budgets. Was a member of the committee charged with selecting objects from the Great Exhibition for the purpose of setting up the Museum of Ornamental Art, which was later to become the Victoria and Albert Museum.

Racinet, Albert Charles August, 1825–93: draughtsman and chromolithographer. Born in Paris. His *L'Ornement Polychrome,* 1869 (second series 1885), modelled upon Owen Jones' *Grammar of Ornament,* 1856, actually surpasses the latter in the perfection of its coloured lithographs. Racinet was also the author of a magnificent work on costume.

Rám Ráz, c. 1790–c. 1830: judge, antiquarian and linguist. He was said to have been a collateral descendant of the last King of Vijayanagar. He spent 23 years in the service of the East India Company and began his career as a clerk in the office of the Military Auditor General. He knew Sanskrit, Telugu, Tamil, Marathi and English. He was a corresponding member of the Royal Asiatic Society.

Ravilious, Eric, 1903–42: painter and wood-engraver. Studied at Eastbourne School of Art and the Royal College of Art, where Paul Nash (*q.v.*) was among his teachers. Illustrated numerous books and designed ornaments for the Curwen Press. Was appointed an official war artist in 1940 and was lost during a flight from Iceland.

Read, Sir Herbert, 1893–1968: critic and poet. After distinguished service in the 1914–18 war, Read joined the ceramics department of the Victoria and Albert Museum. From 1929–30 he was Professor of Fine Arts at Edinburgh University. He became friends with Henry Moore (*q.v.*), Barbara Hepworth (*q.v.*) and Ben Nicholson (*q.v.*) and publicized their work. Read was the leading champion of avant-garde art in Britain during the 1930s.

Redgrave, Richard, 1808–88: subject and landscape painter and educationalist. (Of his paintings Redgrave was to say that his 'best efforts' had been 'aimed at calling attention to the trials of the poor and oppressed'.) He began his association with the School of Design, Somerset House, in 1847. He was appointed Art Superintendent of the Department of Practical Art in 1852. In 1857 he became Inspector for the Department of Science and Art. He held the post of Surveyor of Crown Pictures from 1857 to 1880, of which he compiled a detailed catalogue.

Rhodes, Zandra, b. 1940: designer and couturier. Born in Chatham, Kent. Trained at the Medway College of Art and at the Royal College of Art. First printed dresses produced in 1967/8. Zandra Rhodes UK founded in 1974.

Riegl, Alois, b. 1858: art historian. Joined the staff of the Oesterreichische Museum für Kunst und Industrie—an institution comparable with the Victoria and Albert Museum—in 1886. Here he became a keeper in the Department of Textiles. His first book *Altorientalische Teppiche,* 1891, was based on his knowledge of the museum's fine collection of oriental carpets. Riegl concluded that several of the motifs used in such carpets had been adapted from classical Greek decoration. (E. H. Gombrich in *The Sense of Order,* 1979, devotes a considerable amount of space to discussing Riegl's theories.)

Ricketts, Charles, 1866–1931: painter, engraver, book-designer, typographer, sculptor, designer of theatrical sets and costumes. Served his apprenticeship as a wood-engraver. A lifelong friend of the artist and collector Charles Shannon (1863–1937).

Rickman, Thomas, 1776–1841: architect and antiquarian. The son of a Quaker apothecary. Studied medicine briefly and entered commerce before developing his antiquarian interests. Rickman designed numerous churches—mostly in the North of England. He designed St John's College, New Court, Cambridge, 1827–31.

Ricks, George, fl. 1888: Inspector of Schools for the School Board of London. One of the first education officials to introduce design training to elementary schools. He was an advocate of the Froebel method.

Robinson, Charles, 1870–1937: illustrator. Brother of W. Heath Robinson. One of the most accomplished of the Edwardian book illustrators. Some of his designs for nursery books anticipate the style of Walt Disney.

Ross, Denman Waldo, 1853–1935: educator and connoisseur. Lecturer in the theory of design at Harvard University from 1899. Fellow of the American Academy of Arts and Sciences and Trustee of the Museum of Fine Arts, Boston. Author of *Drawing and Painting,* 1912, and *Painter's Palette,* 1919. He described his book *Theory of Pure Design,* 1907, as a contribution to science rather than art.

Roupert, Louis, seventeenth-century goldsmith and designer. Born in Metz. Known primarily for his suite of designs *Dessins de Feuillage,* 1668.

Ruhlmann, Jacques Emile, 1879–1933: designer and craftsman. Began exhibiting furniture at the Salon d'Automne in 1915. His work was particularly prominent at the Paris Exhibition of 1925. He used a wide variety of materials, often in sensuous combinations. He also designed carpets and textiles.

Ruskin, John, 1819–1900: writer and artist. The son of a wealthy Scottish sherry merchant, he was educated privately and at Christ Church, Oxford, where he won the Newdigate prize for poetry. His numerous writings were to exert an influence upon such diverse figures as William Morris and Proust. His autobiography *Praeterita*, 1889, tells of those things which 'brought him joy'. His diaries are only partly revealing.

Sauvage, Henri, 1873–1932: architect. Made his first public appearance with the Villa Majorelle, Nancy, 1898, for the furniture designer Louis Majorelle. His major works include the Pavilion for Loie Fuller at the Paris Exhibition of 1900, additions to the Samaritaine department store, Paris, 1926, and numerous apartment blocks.

Schinkel, Karl Friedrich, 1781–1841: architect, also a painter, stage designer and interior designer. His earliest buildings are Grecian, such as the Theatre (1818–21) and Museum (1823–30) in Berlin. He worked almost exclusively in Prussia, although he did travel to England in 1826, where he seems to have been impressed by industrial developments. He was the leading force in nineteenth-century German architecture.

Schwabe, Carlos, 1866–1926: illustrator. Born in Altona, Germany; studied in Paris. He illustrated Baudelaire's *Fleurs du Mal*.

Scott, George Gilbert, 1811–78: architect. The son of a clergyman, he began by designing workhouses. He restored a number of churches and cathedrals and became one of the most prolific and successful of Gothic Revival architects. Among his buildings are the chapel of Exeter College, Oxford (1856), St Pancras Station, London (1865), and the Albert Memorial (1872).

Scott, Mackay Hugh Baillie, 1865–1945: architect. One of the most influential and successful of the Arts and Crafts domestic architects. Designed many medium-sized and small country houses. His work was very well-known in Europe and America. His *Houses and Gardens*, 1906, was translated into German in 1912. Until comparatively recently Scott's work was considered cloyingly picturesque by historians. Now it is being reappraised. Scott was a particularly accomplished decorator.

Scott, William, b. 1913: painter. Born in Scotland. Trained at the Belfast College of Art, 1928–31, and at the Royal Academy Schools, 1931–5. There have been numerous international exhibitions of his work.

Scott, William Bell, 1811–90: educationalist and artist. Master at the School of Design in Newcastle from 1844–64. He achieved some success as a muralist.

Seddon, John Pollard, 1827–1906: architect. Much of his major work was in Wales. His most important was the University College of Wales, 1869–72, Aberystwyth. He was also the restorer of Llandaff Cathedral, 1852–62. Designed furniture for Morris, Marshall, Faulkner & Co.

Selmersheim, Tony, b. 1871: architect and furniture designer, particularly important during the Art Nouveau period. He was associated with the group Les Cinq, founded in 1892 (Charpentier, Dampt, Aubert and Moreau-Nelaton). With the arrival of Charles Plumet (1861–1928), the group became known as Les Six.

Semper, Gottfried, 1803–79: architect and theorist. Studied architecture in Munich. Lived and worked in Dresden. Took part in the Revolution of 1849 and fled to Paris and subsequently London, where he taught metalwork at the Department of Practical Art. In 1855 he left London for Zurich, but settled finally in Vienna. Of his numerous buildings his two identical Viennese museums of 1873 and 1881 are probably the most admired. In *Der Stil* Semper expounded his belief that all styles have their origin in craft processes.

Senefelder, Aloys, 1771–1834: the inventor of lithography. After a good education Senefelder began his career as a strolling player. He also wrote plays, one of which met with considerable success. His 'chemical printing' was perfected in 1798. It was first used for printing music. Senefelder patented his lithographic process in Britain in 1801.

Shaw, Henry, 1800–73: writer, antiquarian and draughtsman. His scholarly publications on medieval art were particularly influential. His *Dreams and Decorations of the Middle Ages*, 1843, presents a romantic picture of medieval life that matches that of Sir Walter Scott.

Shaw, Richard Norman, 1831–1912: architect. Born in Edinburgh. He worked for a time for George Edmund Street, taking Philip Webb's place. With his friend W. Eden Nesfield (*q.v.*) Shaw developed the 'Queen Anne' style which is, in actuality, an eclectic style—an amalgam of authentic Queen Anne, vernacular, Elizabethan and Dutch elements. The most influential British architect from the 1870s until the 1890s.

Silver Studio, The, 1884?–1963. Arthur Silver, 1853–96, founder of the studio, was born at Reading and was apprenticed to H. W. Batley (*q.v.*). After his premature death his brothers Rex, 1879–1965, and Harry, b. 1881, took over the studio with Harry Napper, d. 1930, as design manager. The studio supplied decorative designs to many leading manufacturers and also to Liberty and Co. Its work, often of a high technical standard, reflected changes in taste. The contents of the Silver Studio are now held by Middlesex Polytechnic. This collection is an excellent record of middle-of-the-road taste.

Sleigh, Bernard, 1872–1954: designer and educator. Trained at the Birmingham School of Art. Began his career as an illustrator in William Morris' Kelmscott tradition. Some of his work is illustrated in Vol. XIV of *The Studio*, 1898.

Smith, J. Moyr, fl. 1868–94: decorative designer. Moyr Smith dedicated his *Studies for Pictures*, 1868, to Christopher Dresser 'in memory of his kindness on my coming to London'. On this basis, as well as the appearance of designs obviously by Moyr Smith in Dresser's *Studies in Design*, 1874–6, it can be assumed that he worked for Dresser some time during the 1860s. Ruskin had a great contempt for Moyr Smith and inscribed on the flyleaf of his own copy of *Studies for Pictures*: 'Keep this as an example of distortion in modern mind'.

Solon, Léon Victor, 1872–1957: designer. The son of Marc Solon, 1835–1913, who distinguished himself at the Sèvres porcelain factory and later with Minton's of Stoke-on-Trent. Léon also worked for Minton's as a designer from 1900 until 1909. He emigrated to the United States, where he decorated the Philadelphia Museum of Fine Arts.

Spender, Humphrey, b. 1910: photographer and designer. Began his training at the Architectural Association School of Architecture, but decided to abandon architecture in favour of photography. An important photo journalist, particularly during the late 1930s.

Stadler-Stölzl, Gunta, b. 1897: weaver. Born in Munich. Began studies at the Bauhaus in 1919. From 1926 taught at the Bauhaus. Settled in Zurich in 1931.

Stannus, Hugh Hatton, 1840–1908: sculptor. Alfred Stevens' (*q.v.*) favourite assistant. He became an important member of the Art Workers' Guild.

Steichen, Edward (Jean), 1879–1973: photographer. Began his career in fine art. Self-taught as a photographer. Founder member of the Photo-Secession, New York, 1902. Commander of photographic division, US Expeditionary Forces, during the 1914–18 war. Steichen was an extremely versatile photographer.

Stephenson, T. A., zoologist. Professor of Zoology at the University of Wales. He was an accomplished watercolourist and monochrome artist. Writing in his *Seashore Life and Pattern*, 1944, he declared that he had been painting 'seashore subjects' for 35 years. Looking at the black and white designs in his book it seems plausible that he knew the work of such French designers as Verneuil or Habert Dys, whose decorative designs based on sea creatures were featured in *Art et Décoration* in 1905.

Stevens, Alfred, 1817–75: sculptor, painter and designer. Spent nine years in Italy. He was for some time employed in the studio of the Danish sculptor Bertel Thorvaldsen, 1770–1844, in Rome. Stevens' sculpture is in a confident Renaissance manner. He had many disciples—among them were Godfrey Sykes, 1824–66, and F. W. Moody (*q.v.*).

Stolpe, Hjalmar, 1841–1905: ethnographer and archaeologist. Lectured at Lund University, Sweden. Undertook world voyage in 1883–5. Was also distinguished as a student of Viking archaeology.

Straub, Marianne, b. 1909: designer and weaver. Born in Switzerland and trained at the Kunstgewerbeschule, Zurich. Has taught at many leading colleges, including the Central School of Art and Design and the Royal College of Art.

Street, George Edmund, 1824–81: architect. Largely trained in the office of George Gilbert Scott. In 1850 he was appointed diocesan architect of Oxford. He moved to London in 1856, where he built up a very large practice as a designer and restorer of churches. His ideas are generally seen to presage those of Arts and Crafts designers.

Sullivan, Louis Henry, 1856–1924: architect. Born in Boston. Studied architecture briefly at the Massachusetts Institute of Technology and later in the atelier of Vaudremer in Paris. Joined the office of Dankmar Adler in 1879. With Adler, Sullivan was to design a number of important buildings including the Auditorium, Chicago, 1886–90, the Wainwright Building, Buffalo, 1890–1, etc. After Adler's death in 1900 Sullivan failed to attract major clients. He attached an almost mystical significance to ornament, as his *New System of Architectural Ornament*, 1924, reveals.

Sumner, George Heywood Maunoir, 1853–1940: designer, artist and archaeologist. Originally intended to study law, but while lodging with W. A. S. Benson, 1854–1924, an Arts and Crafts architect, resolved to devote his life to art. A member of the Art Workers' Guild, of which he became Master in 1894. Was associated with A. A. Mackmurdo's Century Guild—a co-operative of designers run on Morrisian lines.

Sutherland, Graham Vivian, 1903–80: painter, born in London. Originally destined for a career in engineering, but studied painting at Goldsmiths' School of Art 1921–6. His early work was influenced by Samuel Palmer, and later by Paul Nash. He worked as an official war artist 1941–4. Besides his expressive landscapes he is well known for his portraits.

Talbert, Bruce J., 1838–81: architect and designer. Born in Dundee, Scotland. Trained as an architect in Glasgow and was awarded a medal for drawing by the Edinburgh Architectural Association in 1862. Moved to London in 1865 where he quickly established himself as a fashionable furniture designer. His designs were shown in the international exhibitions of the 1860s and 1870s. Occasionally supplied drawings to the *Illustrated London News*.

Texier, Charles Félix Marie, 1802–71: architect and archaeologist. Began his career as an inspector of buildings in Algeria. Later lectured in archaeology at the Collège de France. His publications include *L'Architecture Byzantine*, 1864, and *The Principal Ruins of Asia Minor*, 1865. In these two works he collaborated with R. Popplewell Pullan.

Thorn Prikker, Johan, 1868–1932: painter, mural painter, graphic designer, stained-glass artist and mosaicist. In 1881 began studying at the Academy of Fine Art in The Hague. In 1893 exhibited at the exhibition of Les Vingt in Brussels and at the Libre Esthètique, also in Brussels, in 1896. Began teaching at the Kunstgewerbeschule in Krefeld in 1904. Worked subsequently in The Hague (1910–23), Düsseldorf (1923–6), and Cologne (1925–32). Thorn Prikker's early stained glass has affinities with the work of the German Expressionists, his later work with that of the De Stijl designers.

Tisdall, Hans (formerly Aufseeser), b. 1910: painter and designer. Born in Germany. Studied in Munich. Settled in London in 1930. Awarded Medal of Honour at the Paris International Exhibition, 1939. Taught for many years at the Central School of Art and Design.

Toorop, Jan, 1858–1928: artist. Born in Java where he spent his childhood. Studied at the Academy of Fine Art in Amsterdam. One of the most innovative Dutch artists of the 1890s.

Townsend, Charles Harrison, 1851–1928: architect. Among the most successful of the architects to be associated with the Arts and Crafts Movement. Designed a wide variety of buildings—domestic, ecclesiastical and institutional. Best known for his Horniman Museum, Forest Hill, South London, 1899–1901, and for the Whitechapel Art Gallery, 1900. His less-renowned buildings, however, exhibit a comparable degree of innovation.

Valmier, Georges, b. 1885: painter and designer. Exhibited in the Salon des Indépendants, 1913–14. Also designed for the theatre.

Van de Velde, Henry Clemens, 1863–1957: architect, designer, painter and theorist. Born in Antwerp into a prosperous middle-class family. Began his career as a painter—he was influenced, in particular by Gauguin and Seurat. After reading Morris and Ruskin he became increasingly interested in design. Designed his own house at Uccle in 1895, in a neo-vernacular or Arts and Crafts style. From 1899–1917 worked in Germany. He was director of the Weimar School of Arts and Crafts, the precursor of the Bauhaus. His later architecture resembles that of the school of Oud. Van de Velde's autobiography *Geschichte meines Lebens* was published in 1962.

Vasarély, Victor, b. 1908: painter. Born in Hungary, Moholy-Nagy was among his teachers. Known primarily for his Op Art paintings. Lives and works in France.

Venturi, Robert, b. 1925: architect. Born in Philadelphia. Educated at the Episcopal Academy and at Princeton. Rome Prize Fellowship, 1954–6. His first influential building was his Guild House, 1965, in Philadelphia. This demonstrated his rejection of the conventions of the Modern Movement. Venturi is married to the architect Denise Scott-Brown.

Verneuil, Maurice Pillard, 1869–1942: designer and writer. Born in Saint-Quentin. A pupil of Eugène Grasset (*q.v.*)—he was responsible for several plates in Grasset's *La Plante et ses Applications Ornamentales*, 1897. Contributed frequently to *Art et Décoration*. Verneuil was a very versatile designer, who worked in a variety of media.

Viegers, Allen F., fl. 1900: textile and wallpaper designer. Also an illuminator.

Viollet-le-Duc, Eugène Emanuel, 1814–79: architect, restorer, historian and theorist. Viollet-le-Duc's first teaching appointment was that of Professor of Ornamental Composition in Paris at the age of twenty. His energies were subsequently mainly directed towards restoration and his historical and theoretical writings. His principal restorations include Notre-Dame (1845–65), Carcassonne (1852–79), and the Château of

Pierrefonds (1858–70). His executed architectural works include the large church at Saint-Denis, Paris (1864–7), and a number of Parisian apartment buildings. His theoretical writings were widely influential and their impact can be seen in the work of such architects as Gaudí (*q.v.*) and Guimard (*q.v.*).

Voysey, Charles Francis Annesley, 1857–1941: architect and designer. The son of an unorthodox Anglican clergyman who was dismissed from the church for his unconventional beliefs. (He founded a new Church—The Theistic Church—'the religion of common sense'.) Voysey was articled to John Seddon (*q.v.*) in 1874. Later he worked for Saxton Snell and George Devey. Set up in practice in 1882. Designed numerous small and medium-sized houses, including H. G. Wells' Spade House, Sandgate, Kent, 1899. Designed textiles and wallpapers throughout his career.

Wagner, Otto, 1841–1918: architect. Became Professor of Architecture at the Academy in Vienna in 1894. His earlier buildings are in an elegant, profusely decorated, Schinkleresque style. With the founding of the Vienna Secession in 1898 Wagner allied himself with younger architects, including Josef Hoffmann (*q.v.*) and Olbrich (*q.v.*)—both of whom had worked under him. Wagner was the dominant figure in Viennese architecture until his death.

Walpole, Horace, Fourth Earl of Orford, 1717–97: writer and connoisseur. The son of Sir Robert Walpole. Walpole, who possessed a very considerable income began Gothicizing Strawberry Hill, originally a modest and nondescript house, in about 1750. Walpole published the first edition of *The Castle of Otranto*, 1765, under a pseudonym.

Waring, John Burley, 1823–75: architect. An accomplished draughtsman, Waring published a detailed study of the cathedral of Burgos in 1852. He collaborated with M. D. Wyatt (*q.v.*) in the guide books of the Crystal Palace, Sydenham, and supplied Owen Jones (*q.v.*) with some of the text of his *Grammar of Ornament*, 1856.

Watts, Mrs G. F. (Mary Fraser-Tytler), 1849?–1938: painter and sculptor. Met G. F. Watts, 1817–1904, the painter, while teaching at a boys' club in Whitechapel. They were married in 1887. They moved to Compton, near Guildford, Surrey, in 1891. After her marriage Mary Watts devoted most of her time to her husband. She was an avid collector of details of ornament.

Webb, Philip, 1831–1915: architect. Became chief assistant to George Edward Street (*q.v.*), a leading Gothic Revivalist, in 1852. Met William Morris (*q.v.*) during the latter's brief sojourn in Street's office. Designed the Red House for Morris and his wife Jane, which was completed in 1860. Designed furniture, embroidery, glass and metalwork for Morris & Co, and a number of important country houses including Clouds, East Knoyle, 1881–6, and Standen, East Grinstead, 1891. Webb was greatly revered by the generation of Arts and Crafts architects.

Whall, Christopher Whitworth, 1849–1924: stained-glass artist. First trained as a painter at the Royal Academy Schools. Exhibited stained-glass designs at the first Arts and Crafts Exhibition in 1888. Began teaching stained glass at the Central School of Arts and Crafts in 1896 and the Royal College of Art in 1898. Whall collaborated with several of the leading Arts and Crafts architects.

White, Gleeson, 1852–98: editor, writer and designer. As editor of the influential monthly *The Studio* Gleeson White was in a unique position to further the cause of the Arts and Crafts Movement. He publicized, in particular, the work of Voysey, Baillie Scott and the members of the Glasgow School, including Mackintosh and the Macdonald sisters.

Wiener, Charles, nineteenth century anthropologist and archaeologist. He was responsible for three expeditions to South America in 1875, 1876, 1877, sponsored by the Ministère de l'Instruction Publique. His brief was to establish the routes of pre-historic migrations and to retrace the route of the Spanish Conquistadores. He organized the large collection of objects at the newly founded ethnographical museum in Paris.

Wijdeveld, H., b. 1885: architect. Editor of the influential Dutch architectural magazine *Wendigen*. He was particularly interested in typography.

Wilson, Henry, 1864–1934: architect and teacher. Took over the practice of J. D. Sedding, a leading Gothic Revivalist and early champion of the Arts and Crafts. He was closely associated with W. R. Lethaby (*q.v.*) and was editor of *The Architectural Review* between 1896 and 1901. Wilson's architectural commissions were principally ecclesiastical and his church plate in particular typifies the Arts and Crafts approach. He was author of *Silverwork and Jewellery*, 1903, the standard contemporary work on the subject.

Wood, Edgar, 1860–1935: architect. Practised in Manchester, in partnership with Henry Sellers. He was the leading provincial Arts and Crafts architect and the founder of the Northern Art Workers' Guild.

Wornum, Ralph Nicholson, 1812–77: painter and art critic. Abandoned legal studies in order to take up painting. Practised as a portrait painter for a time. In 1848 began lecturing on the history of ornament at the Government School of Design. Was for many years keeper of the National Gallery, London.

Worsaae, Jens Jacob Asmussen, 1821–85: archaeologist. In 1847 he was appointed Inspector of the Danish Department of Antiquities. From 1855–66 he was Reader in Archaeology at Copenhagen University. In 1867 he was appointed Director of the Museum for Nordic Antiquities. He became Minister for Culture in 1874. Author of *Records of Danes and Norwegians in England, Scotland and Ireland*, 1851, etc.

Wragge, George, fl. 1898–1903: metalworker. Wragge had a factory in Salford and showrooms off the Strand in London. His 1898 catalogue contains decorative metalwork and furniture which was designed by Edgar Wood (*q.v.*). (It is on this basis that the designs illustrated in Chapter Nine are attributed to Wood.)

Wright, Frank Lloyd, 1869–1959: architect. Worked for some time for Louis Sullivan (*q.v.*). Wright is one of the most inventive of twentieth-century architects. His theoretical writings, laden with the idealism of the nineteenth century, lay stress on an 'organic' architecture. In his early years, particularly, he was an accomplished designer of decoration.

Wyatt, Matthew Digby, 1820–77: architect. A member of the Wyatt family, which had produced several notable architects, Wyatt played an important role in the organization of the Great Exhibition of 1851. With I. K. Brunel, he was the designer of Paddington Station, 1854–5, the courtyard of the former India Office, Whitehall, 1867, etc.

Zahn, Johann Karl Wilhelm, 1800–71: painter, architect, lithographer and archaeologist. Educated at the Academy in Kassel. After two years in Paris he visited Rome, Naples and Pompeii. On his return to Kassel he was commissioned to design the new palace. He returned to Italy in 1830 and began collecting material for his *Ornamente aller Klassischen Kunstepochen*.

Zerffi, G. G., fl. 1876: lecturer. Taught at the National Art Training School, London (now the Royal College of Art). Read extensively in mythology—a subject which was attracting increasing attention in the late nineteenth century.

Zovetti, Ugo, b. 1879: designer. Born in Curzola, Dalmatia, now Yugoslavia. Studied in the Vienna Kunstgewerbeschule. Was an assistant to Koloman Moser (*q.v.*). Worked for the Wiener Werkstätte.

Index